THE RISE OF THE
PEKING OPERA
1770–1870

A Chinese theatre. Painting by George Chinnery (c. 1846)

The Rise of the Peking Opera

1770-1870

SOCIAL ASPECTS OF THE THEATRE IN MANCHU CHINA

COLIN P. MACKERRAS

CLARENDON PRESS · OXFORD

1972

Oxford University Press, Ely House, London W.1

GLASGOW NEW YORK TORONTO MELBOURNE WELLINGTON
CAPE TOWN IBADAN NAIROBI DAR ES SALAAM LUSAKA ADDIS ABABA
DELHI BOMBAY CALCUTTA MADRAS KARACHI LAHORE DACCA
KUALA LUMPUR SINGAPORE HONG KONG TOKYO

PRINTED IN GREAT BRITAIN
BY WILLIAM CLOWES & SONS, LIMITED
LONDON, BECCLES AND COLCHESTER

PREFACE

IN CHINA there are some 300 forms of regional theatre. The core of this book is concerned with the development of one of them, the Peking Opera (*Ching-chü*).

The phrase 'Peking Opera' has become a part of the English language, but in fact the term 'opera' here carries connotations quite different from those we normally associate with the English word. Peking Opera, like its Western counterpart, includes both singing and acting, and indeed there has been in China until quite recently no such thing as an entirely spoken theatrical piece. However, whereas the aural element is paramount in Western opera, the conventions of the *Ching-chü* require that an actor should master highly stylized acting techniques just as much as singing. Costumes and facial make-up, too, are more stylized and symbolic than in the West. Furthermore, the orchestra which accompanies the singing is quite different in form from a Western orchestra. Throughout this work I have normally used the vaguer term 'drama' to refer to the pieces performed on the Chinese stage.

Unlike European operas, items of the Chinese popular theatre cannot normally be ascribed to individual composers or librettists. A Chinese enthusiast of the theatre will identify a particular piece not by the men who created it but by its region of origin. The various local types of the Chinese theatre differ principally in their tunes and orchestral accompaniment, as well as in the dialect used in their libretti. They are based on several different musical systems, each of which proliferated and developed into many different forms of music. These are in fact subdivisions of a 'system' or 'systems' and are usually called 'styles' of drama. The importance of these terms will become clear during the course of this book.

The references to the Western opera in the preceding paragraphs raise the fascinating problem of cross-cultural comparisons in the theatre. The reader will notice many points of contact and contrast with other civilizations. However, to deal with this subject thoroughly would require several further volumes, and I have decided not to embark upon it here.

No characters have been written in the text or notes unless they are absolutely necessary to explain a point. All characters are found in the glossary at the conclusion of the book or in the List of Works Cited. Dates and ages of people are given according to Western reckoning unless otherwise stated. The system of romanization used throughout is the Wade-Giles. However, following current practice, I have omitted the circumflex over the *e* and breve over the *u*.

I have referred to the Chinese provinces by the postal names normally used in English-speaking countries. In the case of cities, however, I have transcribed the names according to the Wade-Giles romanization, but made exceptions for a few, like Peking, Canton, and Tientsin, to conform to generally accepted practice.

A problem which arises in any work where Chinese actors are discussed is how to refer to them. They carried several names apart from their surname—a *ming*, a *tzu* and also a name by which they were known on the stage. In most cases I have called them by their stage-names since that is the practice usually followed in the primary sources. Otherwise, I have made it clear which of their names is being used.

In the translation of the names of streets, city-gates, temples, and other places I have made no attempt at rigid consistency, but given an English rendering only when the sense demands it. Thus, 'Pei-men' is translated as 'North Gate' but the name of a gate like 'Te-sheng' is left in the original Chinese. In the charts and maps, however, all streets, gates and temples are called by their Chinese names. The titles of dramas and *ch'uan-ch'i* are translated in the text the first time they occur unless they are treated separately in appendix C. In that case a translation of the title is given there together with the heading under which the piece is discussed. Novels are named by their English translated titles when mentioned in the text.

It is my pleasure to thank all those who have helped me during the preparation of this work, which is based on my doctoral thesis. They are too numerous to be listed in detail. However, I should like to acknowledge my debt in particular to the Australian National University which enabled me to undertake this research; and to Dr. Igor de Rachewiltz of the Department of Far Eastern History, A.N.U., and Professor Liu Ts'un-yan, head of the Department of Chinese, A.N.U. They were very generous with their time and rendered me invaluable assistance in methodology, in deciding how to present my material and in understanding the sometimes very difficult primary sources. Professor Liu also went to enormous trouble to check my material and translations. I should like also to thank my wife, Alyce, who went through the entire manuscript and made many helpful suggestions, and Mrs. Jill Hardy, who typed it for publication.

January 1971   COLIN MACKERRAS

CONTENTS

LIST OF ILLUSTRATIONS

ABBREVIATIONS

CAKHC	*Ch'ang-an k'an-hua chi*
CKKT	*Chung-kuo ku-tien hsi-ch'ü lun-chu chi-ch'eng*
CPCY	*Chü-pu ch'ün-ying*
CTTLC	*Chin-t'ai ts'an-lei chi*
CTYT	*Ch'ing-tai Yen-tu li-yüan shih-liao*
CYHYHP	*Ch'in-yün hsieh-ying hsiao-p'u*
HCHY	*Hua-chien hsiao-yü*
HFHC	*Hsiao-fang hu-chai yü-ti ts'ung-ch'ao*
HJKCL	*Hsin-jen kuei-chia lu*
HTTL	*Hsiao-t'ing tsa-lu*
JHKHC	*Jih-hsia k'an-hua chi*
LYCH	*Li-yüan chiu-hua*
MHSP	*Meng-hua so-pu*
PCLYCK	*Pei-ching li-yüan chang-ku ch'ang-pien*
PCLYCS	*Pei-ching li-yüan chin-shih wen-tzu lu*
PPLYCC	*Pei-p'ing li-yüan chu-chih tz'u hui-pien*
TCHT	*Ta-Ch'ing hui-tien shih-li*
TCHY	*T'ing-ch'un hsin-yung*
YCHFL	*Yang-chou hua-fang lu*
YLHP	*Yen-lan hsiao-p'u*

In the notes the full title is given the first time it occurs in each chapter, the abbreviation in all subsequent references. However, I have not used abbreviations in the main body of the text.

Shortened titles are used for Western-language and post-1911 Chinese and Japanese works in the second and subsequent references in the footnotes of each chapter. However, the identification of the shortened titles is obvious in every case, and it is unnecessary to include them in this list.

I

INTRODUCTION

IN THE West the history of Chinese drama remains a comparatively uninvestigated field of research. This is, in particular, true of Peking Opera, the development of which no Western scholar has so far explored in detail. It is an important lacuna, for possibly no form of art has played a greater part in the life of the ordinary Chinese since the early years of the nineteenth century than Peking Opera. The purpose of the present study is to help fill this gap.

Very little space is devoted here to the literary aspects of the Peking Opera and I have treated the dramas themselves only to a limited extent. Little attention has been given to dramaturgy, acting techniques, stagecraft, make-up, or costumes, since these have been described fairly extensively by other scholars writing in European languages.[1] I have concentrated, instead, on three other aspects of the Peking Opera. Firstly, I have tried to analyze the historical development of the major musical styles which form the basis of Peking Opera, showing how these various kinds of music became part of the Peking Opera and the circumstances under which they did so. Secondly, I have presented the biographies of certain famous actors who contributed directly to the development of the *Ching-chü*. Thirdly, I have drawn attention to the social implications of the growth of the popular regional theatre (*ti-fang hsi*) in general and the Peking Opera in particular. It will become clear during the course of this book that there were a number of important aspects of social behaviour which were intimately connected with the theatre. By placing the history of Peking Opera in a wider social framework, I hope to be able to point out some of the major reasons for the growth and success of the Chinese regional drama, and especially of the Peking Opera.

[1] Some good examples of such works are discussed by Daniel Shih-p'êng Yang in *An Annotated Bibliography of Materials for the Study of the Peking Theatre*, pp. 1–9.

It is necessary to introduce this subject with a brief sketch of the growth of the regional theatre, especially in the Ming (1368–1644) and early Ch'ing, and an outline summary of Chinese history during the period when the Peking Opera developed to maturity —roughly the century 1770 to 1870.

The theatrical arts have been popular in China since the most ancient times, and they are mentioned in the classical works of the pre-Christian era. But it is from the *nan-hsi* (southern drama) of the Sung (960–1279) that the development of the regional opera can most readily be traced. The *nan-hsi* was the most completely formed of the pre-Yüan types of theatre and contained elements which remained basically unchanged in the regional theatre, and were taken over by China's most widely loved operatic form, the Peking Opera.

The *nan-hsi* took its origin in Wen-chou, southern Chekiang province, at about the time when the Sung was driven from north China (1127). It was called 'the *tsa-chü* of Wen-chou' and was based partly on the folk-songs of the local villages and cities. Each piece began with an explanatory prologue, and the number of scenes was not fixed. There were seven types of actors in the *nan-hsi*. They were called *sheng, tan, mo, wai, t'ieh, ching,* and *ch'ou*. Some of these terms can still be found, with unchanged meanings, in Peking Opera today. For example, the *sheng and tan* were—and still are—the principal male and female characters respectively. The words *wai* and *t'ieh*, designating the secondary male and female characters, were used until recently in these meanings. The *ch'ou*, today the white-faced clown, had a 'face daubed with black powder and was very ugly'.[1] The *ching* was a strong male character with a painted face. These types of actors form the basis of those of later ages.

Another form of drama popular in the Sung was the northern *tsa-chü*. It developed greatly during the following centuries and reached its apogee during the Yüan (1280–1368).[2] The *tsa-chü* of that time was accompanied by stringed instruments and, in keeping with the bolder spirit of the northern region, it was more lively and vigorous than the soft and melodious southern drama.

---

[1] *Nan-tz'u hsü-lu*, p. 245.
[2] A bibliography of Chinese and Japanese works on the *tsa-chü* may be found in Lo Chin-t'ang, *Chung-kuo hsi-ch'ü tsung-mu hui-pien*, pp. 249 ff. See also James Crump, *Materials on Yüan Drama*, pp. 1–37.

Most *tsa-chü* contained four scenes or acts, as well as introductory *hsieh-tzu* or prologues. Each act used one mode which was developed into many tunes. The scenes of a *tsa-chü* began with a spoken passage (*pai*), while the opening section of the *nan-hsi* was always sung (*ch'ang*). The types of actors in the *tsa-chü* showed a wider range than in the earlier *nan-hsi*, but were nevertheless basically similar. In the *tsa-chü* of the Yüan, the main male character was called the *mo*, not *sheng*. All *nan-hsi* actors sang, but in the Yüan *tsa-chü*, only the principal male and female characters sang. The others merely spoke, either alone or in dialogue.

The *tsa-chü*, although pre-eminent in the north, quickly spread to the south, where it was already heard towards the beginning of the Yüan period. Indeed, this style of drama seems to have become familiar to virtually every part of China during the Yüan. Evidence of this is found in the *Ch'ing-lou chi* by Hsia T'ing-chih, who lived at that time.[1] The work records details of some eighty singing-girls, thirty-three of whom are reported to have performed *tsa-chü*. By noting where some of these *tsa-chü* actresses worked, Hsia T'ing-chih confirms that there were not many provinces where the *tsa-chü* was unknown. In fact, he wrote only of actresses whose reputations were known to him. His failure to mention Kansu, Szechwan, or Yunnan does not necessarily mean that *tsa-chü* were not performed in those regions.

By the end of the Yüan we already find examples of a kind of drama called *ch'uan-ch'i*. In fact this phrase probably did not refer to a completely new form, but was rather another name for the southern drama. This had already developed somewhat since its Sung beginnings, especially under the influence of the *tsa-chü*. The first piece which specifically called itself *ch'uan-ch'i* was the *P'i-p'a chi* (*The Story of the Lute*) by Kao Ming.[2] This drama became extremely famous and set the pattern for later *ch'uan-ch'i*. It was even recommended to all noble families by the first Ming emperor. A host of *ch'uan-ch'i* were written in the Ming

[1] Arthur Waley, in his *The Secret History of the Mongols*, pp. 89 ff., discusses the *Ch'ing-lou chi* at some length and translates passages relating to some of the main actresses described therein.

[2] A collection of primary sources on the *P'i-p'a chi* and its author are given by Chiao Hsün in *Chü-shuo*, 2, 106–8. For a list of translations into English, French, and German see Lo Chin-t'ang, *Chung-kuo hsi-ch'ü*, pp. 283–5.

period, and the form was favoured especially in educated circles.

Regional distinctions in theatrical music became more and more obvious as the Ming dynasty progressed. Local folk-tunes have always been a characteristic of Chinese opera. When a new style of drama arose in any given region, it would often be performed in other areas by wandering companies. Local, stationary companies in other districts would then absorb some of its tunes and elements of style, such as a method of using the chorus, singing techniques, musical instruments, or rhythm. Performers in the district visited could either add these characteristics to, or change elements in, their own local music to form a new style of drama. Regional dialect would account for further variations, and the musicians of a particular district would alter ways of expression to suit the tastes of the local inhabitants, who developed a strong love for their own style of *ti-fang hsi*. Furthermore, the music of the popular drama was transmitted orally and was subject to alterations at the hands of individual performers. When adopted by actors and actresses in other provinces, a particular tune might be so changed that it became unrecognizable to the inhabitants of its place of origin. It is my intention in this introduction to summarize the origin and development of those kinds of regional opera of greatest relevance to the Peking Opera.[1]

The Major Systems of Regional Theatre

In the early years of the sixteenth century, we find the beginnings of an extremely important type of drama, one which was to create a tremendous impact on the Chinese regional theatre and to develop into a whole system of operas comprising numerous different regional styles. This was the *I-yang ch'iang*, which, as its name suggests, originated in I-yang, Kiangsi province.

It is likely that the style died out in I-yang not very long after its appearance, but it had spread to other places, in each of which it was altered to suit local tastes in the ways just described. *Ch'ing-yang ch'iang* of Ch'ing-yang in Anhwei was one of the earliest and best known varieties. By the middle of the sixteenth century the *I-yang ch'iang* system of drama was heard in Nanking and Peking,

---

[1] I have dealt with this subject in much greater detail in 'The Growth of the Chinese Regional Drama in the Ming and Ch'ing', *Journal of Oriental Studies*, ix, no. 1 (Jan. 1971), 58–91.

Hunan, Fukien, Kwangsi, and Kwangtung.[1] Various names came to be applied to it. In Peking it was called *Ching-ch'iang*, in Hupeh and Szechwan *ch'ing-hsi* and in Kwangtung *Kao-ch'iang*.[2] This last name became the most common term to designate the *I-yang ch'iang* system, and in many of the current forms of regional drama we find a separate style called *Kao-ch'iang*. Among the most famous are *Hsiang-chü* of Hunan province, *Kan-chü* of Kiangsi and *Ch'uan-chü* or Szechwanese Opera. The first two of these styles no doubt developed from Ming *I-yang ch'iang* variants, although other tunes and elements have since been added to them, and the third seems to be of early Ch'ing origin.

The rapid proliferation of the *Kao-ch'iang* drama can be explained partly by the style's characteristics. Unlike the *ch'uan-ch'i*, it was in no way exclusive to any one group of people. Its language was based on the dialects of the villages,[3] and its music was far from elegant. Chao-lien, a Manchu royal prince writing early in the nineteenth century and referring to the *Ching-ch'iang* of Peking, wrote: 'I do not know when the *I [-yang] ch'iang* arose, but its cymbals are very noisy and its sung sections disorderly and clamourous. It is really hard on the ears of a refined person.'[4] In point of fact, the characteristics to which Chao-lien so contemptuously refers did not prevent the *Ching-ch'iang* attaining a fairly high degree of respectability among Peking's aristocracy. Yet most *I-yang ch'iang* styles were definitely popular entertainment, and the great majority of educated men would have echoed Chao-lien's sentiments had they written of the local *Kao-ch'iang* drama of their own region.

One of the most striking general characteristics of the *I-yang ch'iang* system was the so-called *pang-ch'iang* (helping chorus). 'One person would start singing and then several would take up the tune.'[5] The helping chorus came to be considered the chief hallmark of *I-yang ch'iang* styles and all recent or current *Kao-ch'iang* forms include it among their most obvious features. It is found in *Kao-ch'iang* of Szechwanese, Hunan, and Kiangsi Opera. In *Ch'ao-chü* of Ch'ao-chou and the Swatow region in Kwangtung, the helping chorus is also much in evidence.

---

[1] *Nan-tz'u hsü-lu*, p. 242. [2] *Chü-hua*, 1, 46.

[3] *K'e-tso chui-yü*, 9, 26a. [4] *Hsiao-t'ing tsa-lu*, 8, 7a.

[5] *Hsien-ch'ing ou-chi*, 2, 33. Most of this work (not including the passage quoted) has been translated into German by Helmut Martin in *Li Li-weng über das Theater*, pp. 80–218. He deals with the life of the author Li Yü, pp. 220–66.

Another central characteristic of the *I-yang ch'iang* system was the so-called *kun-tiao*, a phrase which calls for some explanation.

Many of the themes performed in the various regional styles were the same as those of the much more aristocratic and literary *ch'uan-ch'i*, the forerunner of the *K'un-ch'ü*. It became the practice to adapt the stories and texts of the *ch'uan-ch'i* to the regional drama. Because the language of the *ch'uan-ch'i* was classical and intelligible only to the educated, it was necessary to explain the words so that the masses could understand the drama. However, it was considered undesirable to change the original text too much, so sections were added in popular language and they were termed *kun-tiao*. At the beginning, middle, or end of a passage, five- or seven-character lines were inserted in colloquial speech. These might be an expansion of the text just sung, or a repetition in simpler and more comprehensible style.

Fortunately, the movement in the music of the *I-yang ch'iang* and other popular forms based on it tended to be much faster than that of the *ch'uan-ch'i* or *K'un-ch'ü*. Unlike the *K'un-ch'ü*, in which one word of the libretto frequently extended over a long musical section, the dramatic styles of the *I-yang ch'iang* system tended to be syllabic.[1] As a result, passages could be added without making the drama last too long.

It has been stressed that the *kun-tiao* were necessary to make highly classical texts intelligible to the masses for popular drama. Let us now turn to the style of theatre which replaced the earlier *ch'uan-ch'i* in the affections of the scholarly classes, the *K'un-ch'ü* or *K'un-shan ch'iang*.

The *K'un-ch'ü* takes its name from the place where it was developed, K'un-shan in Kiangsu province, not far from Su-chou. Early in the sixteenth century it was regarded as popular drama, but was later moulded by men like Wei Liang-fu and Liang Ch'en-yü into a much more sophisticated form of opera. Following the successes of these two men, many dramatists began writing for the *K'un-ch'ü* and various schools of literature grew up, each with its own special emphasis and characteristics.[2] In the Ch'ing, *K'un-ch'ü* became known as *ya-pu* or 'elegant drama', as

---

[1] *Hsien-ch'ing ou-chi*, 2, 33. The *kun-tiao* are discussed by Wang Ku-lu in his *Ming-tai Hui-tiao hsi-ch'ü san-ch'u chi-i*, pp. 5–10.

[2] A recent study in English on the schools of *K'un-ch'ü* writing may be found in Josephine Huang Hung, *Ming Drama*, pp. 101 ff.

opposed to *hua-pu* or 'flower drama', the term used to refer to all other styles of theatre.[1]

According to Hsü Wei (1521–93), *K'un-shan ch'iang* was heard in his time only in the region in and near Su-chou, so that it had not spread far by the middle of the sixteenth century.[2] By the end of the Wan-li period (1573–1620), however, it had been introduced to a variety of regions, not only in Kiangsu and Chekiang, but also in northern China, where it was later to become a significant element of the Peking Opera. There were differences in dialect in the sung text in each region, but the music did not vary greatly from district to district. This is in striking contrast to the *I-yang ch'iang*.

After the birth of *K'un-ch'ü*, many former *ch'uan-ch'i* and *tsa-chü* were rearranged and performed in that style. As a result, the northern tunes became less and less heard or were adapted into the *K'un-ch'ü*. Even in the north the *tsa-chü* lost its following. Indeed, the famous drama-patron Ho Liang-chün (1506–73), to whom I shall be returning in chapter two, is on record as predicting that the northern opera would be lost after two or three generations.[3]

In view of its popularity with the educated classes, it is not surprising that the *K'un-ch'ü* was delicate and tuneful. The Ming author Ku Ch'i-yüan wrote: 'Now, in and near Su-chou, [there is a sort of drama] which is accompanied by the *tung-hsiao* and [stringed] *yüeh-ch'in*... It is very melancholy and moves people to tears.... It is soft and melodious.'[4] From another source we know that even in its early days the *ti-tzu*, single-reeded *kuan* and *p'i-p'a* (four-stringed lute) were included among the instruments used to accompany the *K'un-ch'ü* drama.[5] The *hsiao* and *ti-tzu* are like flutes and among the gentlest in tone of those musical instruments found in the orchestras of the Chinese drama. The *hsiao* is played straight and the *ti-tzu* horizontally like a Western flute. To this day *K'un-ch'ü* music is dominated by the flute.

There was another system of drama which came into being in the Ming and was to be of great significance for the development of the *ti-fang hsi*. This was the north-western *pang-tzu ch'iang* (Clapper Opera).

It is not known exactly where the Clapper Opera originated,

---

[1] *Yang-chou hua-fang lu* (YCHFL), 5, 107.   [2] *Nan-tz'u hsü-lu*, p. 242.
[3] *Ssu-yu chai ts'ung-shuo*, 37, 337.   [4] *K'e-tso chui-yü*, 9, 26a.
[5] *Nan-tz'u hsü-lu*, p. 242.

for early historical references to it are lacking. According to the nineteenth-century writer Chang Chi-liang, who was following an earlier work by Wu Ch'ang-yüan, the Clapper music was sometimes referred to as *Kan-su ch'iang*,[1] implying that it had come originally from Kansu. However, in the relevant passage of his book, Wu Ch'ang-yüan is quoting 'a friend'[2] and had probably not heard the name used frequently. A much commoner designation for the Clapper Opera was *Ch'in-ch'iang*, suggesting that the system had begun in Shensi, since 'Ch'in' is a normal name for that province. Li T'iao-yüan (1734–1803), whose authority on the development of the *hua-pu* drama is undoubted, confirms that Shensi was the place of origin of the Clapper Opera.[3] Probably Li's statement is correct, although the system certainly spread also to Kansu, where the Clapper music is still popular.

A more precise birth-place has been put forward for the *pang-tzu ch'iang*. Chou I-pai, probably the foremost Mainland scholar on the Chinese theatre, claims that the form of Clapper Opera heard in Hsi-an, the capital of Shensi, is often called 'T'ung-chou theatre'.[4] He infers from this that it was in T'ung-chou (present Ta-li) in eastern Shensi that *Ch'in-ch'iang* was first heard. Already in the eighteenth century one of Hsi-an's main forms of music was *T'ung-chou ch'iang*[5] and Ta-li would seem a natural focal point for the early spread of the Clapper Opera to southern Shansi, where there are several ancient *pang-tzu ch'iang* styles.

The time of origin of the Clapper Opera is also uncertain. Liu Hsien-t'ing (1648–95) writes of 'the new sounds [performed by] the actors of Ch'in which are called *luan-t'an*',[6] and this is probably a reference to the *pang-tzu ch'iang* because Li T'iao-yüan equates *Ch'in-ch'iang* with *pang-tzu ch'iang* and claims that in his native Szechwan it was called *luan-t'an*.[7] Liu Hsien-t'ing seems to have been referring specifically to Hunan and Hupeh, so that the allusion to 'the new sounds [performed by] the actors of Ch'in' need imply only that *Ch'in-ch'iang* had been recently introduced to the two central-southern provinces, and could have been

---

[1] *Chin-t'ai ts'an-lei chi (CTTLC)*, 3, 5a. Both Chang Chi-liang and Wu Ch'ang-yüan are discussed below in appendix B, pp. 240, 239.
[2] *Yen-lan hsiao-p'u (YLHP)*, 5, 5b.
[3] *Chü-hua*, 1, 47. On Li T'iao-yüan see below, appendix B, p. 235.
[4] *Chung-kuo hsi-ch'ü lun-chi*, p. 221.
[5] *Ch'in-yün hsieh-ying hsiao-p'u*, p. 12b.
[6] *Kuang-yang tsa-chi*, 3, 152.   [7] *Chü-hua*, 1, 47.

popular in the north for some time. Probably the core area of southern Shansi and eastern Shensi had been familiar with it many years before the Ming dynasty fell.

Whatever its exact time and place of origin, the Clapper Opera was certainly widespread and popular by 1770, for Clapper pieces occupy an important place in the *hua-pu* section of the famous drama collection *Chui pai-ch'iu*, prefaced in that year. The system spread to many parts of south China, and was popular not only in Hunan and Hupeh, but also in provinces further east, such as Kiangsu.[1] Nowadays, there are Clapper forms in most provinces of China Proper, especially the north. In Honan, Hopeh, Shantung, Shansi, Kansu, and Shensi, the *pang-tzu ch'iang* is found in innumerable separate styles.

The Clapper Opera was accompanied not by wind but by stringed instruments. According to Li T'iao-yüan, the *yüeh-ch'in* was one of the principal instruments.[2] As its name implies, the clapper was the most important instrument for beating out the rhythm of the *pang-tzu ch'iang* drama. The clappers of the early *Ch'in-ch'iang* were made of date wood,[3] and it was this feature that distinguished them from those employed in other styles of Chinese drama.

The fourth and last system of Chinese *ti-fang hsi* is the *p'i-huang*. This is actually a combination of two styles, *hsi-p'i* and *erh-huang* which, though separate in origin, have existed together as a single entity for at least two centuries. The first of these two tends to be livelier than the second and is more suitable for exciting or joyous occasions; *erh-huang* is more solemn and reserved for tragic or lyric situations. Yet of course neither is a single tune and the rhythmic and musical structure of both is extremely complicated. It is not my purpose here to examine them from the point of view of a musicologist,[4] but to summarize their origins and history.

Hsi-p'i appears to be closely related to the Clapper Opera. Chang Chi-liang equates *hsi-p'i* with *Kan-su ch'iang* and the latter style he claims to be the same as *Ch'in-ch'iang*.[5] I mentioned

---

[1] According to Li Tou (*YCHFL*, 5, 130), Clapper operas were known in Chü-jung and Yang-chou, both in Kiangsu, by the late eighteenth century.
[2] *Chü-hua*, 1, 47.   [3] See Chou I-pai, *Lun-chi*, pp. 219–20.
[4] The music of the Peking Opera, especially *erh-huang* and *hsi-p'i*, are treated extensively, with musical notation, in Liu Chi-tien, *Ching-chü yin-yüeh chieh-shao*.
[5] *CTTLC*, 3, 5a.

earlier that Chang had applied the name *Kan-su ch'iang* to the clapper music thus implying, wrongly, that it had first arisen in Kansu province. This writer was a Fukienese and may not have been an expert in the music of the Peking Opera. Nevertheless, there is no reason to doubt that he was right in his belief that *hsi-p'i* was descended from *Ch'in-ch'iang*. Other factors bear out his opinion. One of them is the musical similarity between present-day *hsi-p'i* and the *Ch'in-ch'iang* of the Ch'ing. Thus, the main instrument used to accompany the *Ch'in-ch'iang* was the *hu-ch'in*, a kind of fiddle played with a bow, and the secondary one the *yüeh-ch'in*.[1] This is the same as present-day *hsi-p'i*, but a little different from modern *Ch'in-ch'iang*, which is the principal regional opera of Shensi. In the *Yüeh-chü* currently popular in Kwangtung province, the tune called *hsi-p'i* in Peking Opera is named *pang-tzu* and this strongly suggests an origin in Clapper music. Authorities later than Chang Chi-liang persisted in the view that *hsi-p'i* was derived from *Ch'in-ch'iang*. One author, writing in 1876, says that 'once it had changed to *hsi-p'i*, the music of Ch'in surged high and clear',[2] and this clearly implies a relationship between the two styles.

The origin of the name *hsi-p'i* has been explained by the contemporary scholar Ou-yang Yü-ch'ien. He says, 'In Hupeh "singing" is called "skin" (*p'i*), so that a section of song is called "a stretch of skin".'[3] Thus it is reasonable to assume that *hsi-p'i* was originally the name given in Hupeh to the method of singing popular in the west (*hsi*), that is, Shensi. It had spread down the Han river through Hsiang-yang in northern Hupeh and become extremely popular in its new home by the early Ch'ing.

The origins of the other component of the *p'i-huang* system, *erh-huang*, is an extremely difficult problem, and several theories have been put forward to solve it. It is unnecessary to discuss them in this brief introduction, but the most likely explanation of its genesis is that it arose in I-huang country, Kiangsi, in the late Ming period, and took its name from its first home, dialect differences accounting for the change from I-huang to *erh-huang*.[4]

[1] *YLHP*, 5, 5b.   [2] *Huai-fang chi*, p. 13b.
[3] 'T'an erh-huang hsi', in Cheng Chen-to, ed., *Chung-kuo wen-hsüeh yen-chiu*, p. 491.
[4] See my article 'The Growth of the Chinese Regional Drama in the Ming and Ch'ing', pp. 84–90.

From I-huang it soon spread to Anhwei, and may easily have begun its long and close affiliation with the *hsi-p'i* style in that province. In the hands of great actors in towns like An-ch'ing, *erh-huang* grew extremely popular in Anhwei and was, indeed, far more highly regarded there than in its home province. Companies which performed *erh-huang* came to be known as Anhwei companies (*Hui-pan*), the origin in Kiangsi having been almost completely forgotten. Certainly it was from An-ch'ing that *erh-huang* was introduced to the cosmopolitan salt-city of Yangchou,[1] where it was enthusiastically received late in the eighteenth century. By that time it had spread also to other provinces, including Chekiang, Hupeh, Hunan, Kwangsi, and Kwangtung, in each of which it was heard together with *hsi-p'i*. Most important of all, it was taken to Peking, where it was to become part of China's most famous form of opera, the Peking Opera.

Historical Background

The period when styles of all these four systems came together in Peking and then developed into the mature Peking Opera covers roughly the century leading up to the T'ung-chih Restoration (1862–74). No artistic development takes place in a historical void, and it will therefore be useful to recall the major political trends and events that were unfolding in China concurrently with the Peking Opera's gestation, birth, infancy, and growth to maturity.

This period was, at first, a time of great prosperity in China. The Manchu dynasty was at the height of its power under Ch'ien-lung (1736–96) and Turkestan had been reconquered in 1758–9, adding an enormous area to the empire. Chinese scholarship flourished, and books were printed and collected in large numbers, even though fierce censorship caused others to be destroyed and greatly restricted the range of opinion scholars could express.

The ninth decade of the eighteenth century ushered in a period of splendour for the Peking theatre, but an era of steady decline in the political situation at court and throughout the empire. Corruption became widespread in the bureaucracy, government expenses rose and the treasury became increasingly impoverished. As usual, it was mainly the ordinary people who suffered from

[1] *YCHFL*, 5, 130.

these trends and rebellion became a problem for the central government.

Meanwhile at court, the aging Emperor Ch'ien-lung handed over most of his power to his unscrupulous minister Ho-shen. By the end of 1775, this man had won the complete confidence of the Emperor and remained in a position of virtually total power until the death of his protector in 1799. In that year, Ch'ien-lung's successor Chia-ch'ing, who had acceded to the throne in 1796 upon the abdication of his father, dismissed and arrested Ho-shen, and the minister then committed suicide.

Chia-ch'ing (d. 1820) was a capable emperor and attempted to curb government expenditure by cutting back the costs of the central administration and the personal expenses of his own household. Although his efforts met with some success, the national economy remained in a lamentable condition. Moreover, it proved to be beyond Chia-ch'ing's powers to stem the tide of disintegration he had inherited from his father. Corruption continued unabated, and the problem of rebellion burst forth with full fury upon the Emperor. In 1796 the members of an ancient religious secret society called the White Lotus Sect (Pai-lien chiao) revolted in Hupeh and Szechwan. The uprising soon spread to several other provinces and was not suppressed for nearly a decade. Shortly afterwards, another religious secret society, the T'ien-li chiao, rebelled in Shantung and Chihli. In 1813 some soldiers of this sect actually attacked and entered the Imperial Palaces in Peking.

These revolts exposed the weakness of the government armies, which had themselves been suffering from corruption and a decline in morale since the Ch'ien-lung period. They proved quite ineffective against the disturbances created by the secret societies and others, and in the end the authorities were forced to rely on local militia units to suppress the dissidents. Yet, despite the assistance given by these forces, the government remained suspicious of their intentions and took away their weapons as soon as the particular rebellion under attack was crushed. The impotence of the government standing armies was to be of great significance when the era of foreign invasions arrived.

Meanwhile the pressures had begun which were to lead to the era of China's humiliation at the hands of the Western powers. In 1793 the first British ambassador to China, Earl George

Macartney, was received by Ch'ien-lung at his summer residence in Jehol. The British wished to expand their trade in China. At the time Canton was the only Chinese port open to commerce with the outside world. Macartney requested, among other matters, that the Chinese government lift its restrictions and allow trade through other ports. The Emperor refused, and Macartney had accomplished nothing. A second British embassy, this time led by Earl Amherst, William Pitt, arrived in Peking in 1816 for similar purposes. It was entirely unsuccessful and even served to damage Sino-British relations. Macartney had refused to kowtow to the emperor, and a compromise was worked out by which he was allowed to follow the ceremony he would have used before the King of England. When officials were sent to Pitt to teach him the kowtow, he refused to accept the instructions and was never allowed into the imperial presence. Chia-ch'ing made known his feelings that the British were behaving arrogantly, while Pitt accused the court of insulting representatives of the British crown. The mission was a fiasco which did nothing but arouse bitterness on both sides.

The reign of Tao-kuang (1821–50) was, like that of his predecessor, an unhappy one for China. It is true that he was, like Chia-ch'ing, a reasonably frugal man; he cut back palace expenditure and discontinued the practice of earlier Manchu emperors of spending the summer in Jehol. Nevertheless, the general state of the economy went from bad to worse and the increased import of opium, which had in fact been banned since 1729, resulted in the outflow and shortage of silver. Prices rose and the living conditions of the masses deteriorated. The vain attempt of the Emperor to prevent the import of opium led to the Anglo-Chinese War of 1839–42, usually known as the Opium War, which resulted in the Treaty of Nanking (1842). Under this agreement the island of Hong Kong was ceded to the British, an enormous indemnity was to be paid to the victors, and five ports—Canton, Amoy, Fu-chou, Ning-po, and Shanghai—were opened to foreign trade.

Tao-kuang was the first Manchu emperor to see China humiliated by the Western powers. But worse was to follow and the reign of his son Hsien-feng (1851–61) was possibly the most disastrous any Ch'ing ruler, except perhaps the last, was called upon to face. The foreign powers kept up their pressure on the

Manchu government. In 1856 a French missionary was killed in Kwangsi. In the same year a dispute flared up between the Chinese and British when twelve Chinese seamen on board the ship Arrow, which was flying the Union Jack, were arrested by the authorities in Kwangtung. These events gave the Western powers the pretexts they needed to launch the so-called Arrow War of 1857–8, which led to the occupation of Canton and further Chinese concessions in the Sino-French and Sino-British Treaties of Tientsin (1858). Two years later the foreign forces actually occupied Peking, and the Emperor fled to Jehol.

Hsien-feng faced serious problems at home, the most pressing being, as usual, that of rebellion. The imperial government was threatened by several major uprisings, of which the most significant was the T'ai-p'ing. Beginning in 1850, this movement won quick success and in 1853 took Nanking, which was made its capital. In the following years the T'ai-p'ing were able to take most of central China and even sent a force against Peking itself. In 1860–1, the Ch'ing forces were disastrously defeated in the lower Yangtze valley, allowing the rebels to seize all the main cities of the region.

Many observers in 1860 were predicting the imminent collapse of the Manchu dynasty. However, events were to prove them wrong, and the 1860s witnessed not the fall of the Ch'ing, but the so-called T'ung-chih Restoration.[1] Prince Kung (1833–98), the sixth son of Tao-kuang, succeeded in negotiating the withdrawal of the foreign troops from Peking and China, and foreign relations were stabilized. This was especially so after the foundation in January 1861 of the Tsung-li yamen, designed to guide China's external affairs. Even as the T'ai-p'ing armies were winning important victories in the south, the Ch'ing were beginning to gain the upper hand in the north. In September 1861 the imperial forces made a decisive gain in the south with the capture of An-ch'ing, Anhwei province, and the tide turned against the rebels. By 1866 they had been completely defeated, partly through the effective actions of Tseng Kuo-fan's Hunan army. The newly revived Manchu dynasty also succeeded in putting down the various other rebellious campaigns which faced it.

[1] This period is the subject of Mary Wright's excellent monograph, *The Last Stand of Chinese Conservatism*.

The achievements of the restoration leaders extended far beyond such matters. These men reorganized civil administration, and took effective measures to reduce corruption; they refurbished the army and overhauled the nation's economy. Most important of all, they injected new life and meaning into the Confucian ideals upon which the Chinese state had been based for so long.

Considering the situation in China in 1860, the accomplishments of the T'ung-chih Restoration leaders were truly remarkable. Yet in the end they provided only a temporary antidote to the forces of disintegration; they postponed, but did not prevent, the fall of the Manchus. And although the era of major concern in this book opened and closed with short periods of reasonable success, it cannot be accounted anything but a generally unhappy century of Chinese history. It forms a sombre background to the rise of what may be considered one of China's finest forms of theatrical art.

II

DRAMA IN SOCIETY (SIXTEENTH TO EIGHTEENTH CENTURIES)

By THE early Ch'ing, drama had become an integral part of the lives of virtually all classes of Chinese society, especially in the provinces south of the Yangtze River. This we may state without fear of contradiction, though there are actually not enough references in the primary sources to document rigorously the growth of customs connected with the theatre, and thus to present a detailed sociological survey of the place of the drama in late Ming and early Ch'ing China.

The cultural life of China during the eras under consideration was heavily concentrated on the region south of the Yangtze. This culturally favoured so-called Kiangnan area, which included the provinces of Kiangsi and Chekiang and the most important parts of Kiangsu and Anhwei,[1] produced painters, dramatists, and writers out of all proportion to its population. Similarly the south-eastern region, including Fukien, made a disproportionate contribution to the government bureaucracy.[2] Su-chou could claim to be China's first city for the arts and its trends frequently set the pattern for other places.

Kiangnan was not only important culturally; it was also China's economic centre. Most of the empire's key sources of wealth, including rice, salt, tea-leaves, cotton, silk, porcelain and lacquerware, were produced in these provinces. Kiangsu was the main salt-producing region, while Kiangsi and Kiangsu, as well as

---

[1] In the Ming dynasty, Anhwei and Kiangsu formed together one province called Nanking, but this name was changed, in 1645, to Kiangnan. In 1661–2, the province of Anhwei was set apart under a governor at An-ch'ing, and the name Kiangsu came into use in 1667. See Hummel, *Eminent Chinese of the Ch'ing Period*, pp. 920–1.

[2] See van der Sprenkel, 'The Geographical Background of the Ming Civil Service', *Journal of Economic and Social History of the Orient*, iv, no. 3 (1961), 302–36. Material on the distribution of academic success by provinces can be found in Ho Ping-ti, *The Ladder of Success in Imperial China*, pp. 226 ff.

Hupeh and Hunan, were major rice-growing provinces.[1] Sung-chiang in Kiangsu was an important centre for the growth and processing of cotton, the area around Nanking also produced cloth of high quality, and Chekiang was the country's principal producer of raw silk and tea-leaves. Hui-chou in Anhwei was famous for its handicrafts and most of its lacquerware was sent abroad. Another significant centre in Kiangnan was Ching-te chen in Kiangsi, well known for its pottery industry. The city's porcelain was considered the finest in China and was used all over the empire, as well as being exported to foreign countries. Su-chou was, economically, among the leading cities of the region. It was the centre of Kiangsu's rich rice-growing area and was also a prosperous home for silk-processing and its companion industry, weaving.[2]

Like other regions, Kiangnan was hit by the civil wars of the late Ming and early Ch'ing; this is obvious from the famous ten-day massacre of Yang-chou (20 to 29 May 1645). Yet the area was much less affected than most other parts of China, which greatly enhanced its cultural and economic pre-eminence. Kiangnan did not, however, entirely monopolize the empire's economic activity. From the late sixteenth century onwards, textile centres in north China, especially Chihli (modern Hopeh), became increasingly prosperous at Sung-chiang's expense. Tobacco, introduced into China during the late Ming period, was grown in many parts of the country, notably, besides Kiangsi, Lan-chou in Kansu, Fukien, Shantung, and Chihli.[3]

The Ming and Ch'ing periods saw an expansion of inter-regional trade. In 1735 the French Jesuit, J. B. du Halde, wrote of Chinese commerce that:

The trade carried on within China is so great, that that of all Europe is not to be compared therewith; the provinces are like so many king-doms, which communicate to each other what they have peculiar to themselves, and this tends to the preservation of union, and makes plenty reign in all the cities. . . . All the merchandises, so readily trans-

---

[1] A discussion of food production in China may be found in Ho Ping-ti, *Studies on the Population of China*, pp. 169 ff., and of rice in Katō Shigeshi, *Shina keizai shi kōshō*, II, 638 ff.

[2] See Fujii Hiroshi, 'Shinan shōnin no kenkyū (1)', *Tōyō gakuhō* xxxvi, 1 (June 1953), pp. 12 ff., and Fu I-ling, *Ming-Ch'ing shih-tai shang-jen chi shang-yeh tzu-pen*, pp. 1–48.

[3] Ho Ping-ti, *Studies*, pp. 202–3.

ported along the rivers, are sold in a very short time; you may see, for instance, merchants who three or four days after their arrival at a city have sold six thousand caps proper for the season. Trade is never interrupted but on the two first days of the first moon.[1]

Mainly because of their magnificent network of rivers, canals, and lakes, the Kiangnan provinces constituted by themselves an enormous trading area. Not only did they carry on extensive trade with one another, they also exchanged products with other parts of China. Thus Sung-chiang in the seventeenth and eighteenth centuries obtained much of its raw cotton from Honan and western Shantung, and the processed cloth of that famous textile centre was sent to Peking, Shansi, Shensi, Hupeh, Hunan, Kiangsi, Kwangtung, and Kwangsi.[2] Silk and luxury goods from Kiangnan could be found in many parts of north China. In general, the northern and inland provinces were supplied with finished products by the Kiangnan coastal regions, which were technologically the most advanced in China.[3]

One result of this thriving interregional trade was that many merchants moved from their home town or county to other parts of China for the purpose of carrying on trade. Merchants from Hui-chou were found everywhere in the empire. People from the islands in the Tung-t'ing Lake in Hunan traded in almost every part of the country. Shansi and Shensi were the native provinces of many merchants throughout China. Those of the former province traded salt, silk, and grain, and were among the richest merchants in the empire. Those of the latter were particularly active in transporting and selling grain along the Great Wall, in trading salt in the Huai River area, cotton in Kiangsi, and tea along the western borders of China.[4]

By far the most important thoroughfares in the country were the Yangtze River and the Grand Canal (Yün-ho). This canal was enormously long and extended from Hang-chou in Chekiang to T'ung-chou near Peking. It was the most convenient route by

---

[1] *The General History of China*, II, 296. Du Halde's work is based on the accounts of travellers and residents in China. The French original of the section given above may be found in *Description de l'empire de la Chine*, II, 204.

[2] Ho Ping-ti, *Studies*, p. 201.

[3] See especially Fujii Hiroshi, 'Shinan shōnin no kenkyū', pp. 1–44.

[4] See Fu I-ling, *Shang-jen chi shang-yeh tzu-pen*, pp. 49 ff. (devoted to the merchants of Hui-chou), pp. 92 ff. (to those of the Tung-t'ing area) and pp. 161 ff. (to those of Shensi).

which to transport rice from Kiangnan to northern China. In provinces little endowed with waterways, products were commonly carried overland in carts or on the backs of mules,[1] but in general the principal means of transportation was the boat. China's lakes, rivers, and canals abounded in craft of all sizes. Du Halde writes that 'sometimes, for above a quarter of a league, you see them so close together, that it is impossible to get in one more amongst them'.[2] Although these boats were chiefly for official and commercial purposes, they could be used for transport by anybody, and trading vessels frequently took on passengers.

A detailed exposition of the economy and trade of the late Ming and early Ch'ing lies well outside the scope of the present work. I have mentioned these subjects because there are two major respects in which economic and trade factors influenced the spread of the various systems of drama.

Since merchants often lived away from their home province, they created a demand in their new home for styles of drama familiar to their native towns. They were sometimes extremely sensitive to criticism of their own local theatre: in 1819 a group of merchants from Kiangsi living in Hsiang-t'an, Hunan, were even prepared to fight and kill some locals who ridiculed a visiting troupe from Kiangsi.[3] Merchants are frequently mentioned in connection with drama in the Chinese sources. For instance, in Feng-ching chen in Chekiang, near the border with Kiangsu, merchants and traders used to gather, arrange the construction of a high stage, and invite actors to sing and dance all night.[4]

Because many acting companies were mobile, it was natural that they should make use of the trading vessels to move from place to place. One result of this practice was that the expansion of regional drama tended to follow the trade routes; this partly explains why the dramatic styles of the *I-yang ch'iang* system spread so quickly, since most of the regions where it became

---

[1] Du Halde, *Description de l'empire de la Chine*, II, 66–7.

[2] *The General History of China*, II, 275. See the French original in *Description de l'empire de la Chine*, II, 190.

[3] *Hsiang-t'an hsien-chih*, 8 *lieh-chuan*, 131a–2a; 11, 2a. I have discussed this incident in more detail in 'The Growth of the Chinese Regional Drama in the Ming and Ch'ing', *Journal of Oriental Studies*, ix, no. 1 (Jan. 1971), 90–1.

[4] *Ch'un-hsiang chui-pi*, 2, 60b.

popular lay in the provinces along the Yangtze. It adds a further explanation, too, of Kiangnan's pre-eminence in the field of local drama, for no other part of China was so well equipped with waterways.

If economic factors help to explain why systems of drama like *K'un-ch'ü* and *I-yang ch'iang* could spread so widely throughout China, others—mainly social—account for the great expansion of the theatre in the villages, towns, and cities during the late Ming and Ch'ing, and especially in the eighteenth century. There is much evidence in our primary sources to show that drama was tightly linked with many aspects of the life of the people. For the sake of convenience I shall treat the social implications of drama among the eminent groups and the ordinary people separately. It will be seen that there was a good deal of overlap between the two; people from the lower classes frequently attended drama patronized by the great families, and officials saw drama that was intended mainly for the peasants, artisans, and less illustrious merchants. Yet there was a distinction between the performances organized as part of the social life of the good families and those given primarily for the general populace.

The Prominent Clans: Quasi-Religious Drama

One of the most striking phenomena of the Sung dynasty was the growth of a distinct group spirit within each great clan. This resulted from the development of the landlord and tenant system, and the consequent increase in the economic importance of the wealthy clans.[1] It was closely related to the rise of certain practices which remained constant features of Chinese society until quite recently. One was the keeping of family records, which, though by no means unknown before the Sung, developed greatly from that time on. Of clan registers surviving in Japan, one dates from the Yüan, thirteen date from the Ming, and 892 from the Ch'ing.[2]

The newly strengthened cohesion within the great families was accompanied by an increased emphasis on ancestral sacrifices. Temples dedicated to clan forebears became more common.

[1] The great Japanese sinologist Niida Noboru has made a major contribution on the development of the great clans and the growth of clan spirit from the tenth century onwards. See especially *Chūgoku hōsei shi kenkyū*, III, 683 ff.
[2] See Taga Akigorō, *Sōfu no kenkyū*, pp. 58, 220–49.

Confucianism provided the religious basis for the sacrifices and, with its stress on filial piety, gave added impetus to the feeling of family pride of the clan members.

In the course of time, the practice arose whereby theatrical performances were given to accompany the ancestral sacrifices of the landlords. It is true that many of the strictest Confucian families held drama to be too frivolous to accompany their solemn sacrificial rites and sternly forbade them. There was, however, a strong ethical bias in many of the traditional dramas, and a considerable number of the most respected clans were prepared to allow the performance of drama along with the sacrifices, which were themselves influenced by non-Confucian creeds.

The clan register of the Shen clan of Ch'ang-hsiang in Hsiao-shan county, Chekiang province, reports that on the autumn sacrificial day, two dramatic performances were arranged in front of the ancestral shrine. Probably one was in the day and the other at night. In the tenth month, too, drama was performed for this clan, and a famous company was hired for the purpose.[1] On 9 March 1846 a rule was issued that drama should no longer be performed during the autumn sacrifice.[2] No mention, however, is made of the winter drama which presumably continued to flourish. Another instance of sacrificial drama is found in the records of the Wei clan of Lan-feng in Yü-yao county, Chekiang. There we are told that sacrifices to the clan ancestors were held four times a year and that drama was performed during the winter sacrifice.[3]

One is struck by the fact that the Wei clan saw fit to associate drama with its sacrifices in the winter only; even more striking is it that the Shen clan prohibited autumn, but not winter performances of drama. The leaders of these clans may have inclined to the view that theatrical performances were incompatible with ancestral sacrifices, but in the idle season of winter they relaxed their strictness. This factor carries all the more weight when we remember that the performances usually took place in front of,

[1] *Hsiao-shan Ch'ang-hsiang Shen-shih hsü-hsiu tsung-p'u*, 34 *tsung-yüeh*, 7a–b.

[2] Ibid., 34 *tsung-yüeh*, 10a–b.

[3] *Lan-feng Wei-shih tsung-p'u*, 3, 58a. The passage in question is a quotation from a stele dated 1800 (3, 58b). For further examples of winter sacrifices accompanied by drama see Tanaka Issei, 'Shindai shoki no sōzoku engeki ni tsuite', *Tōhōgaku* 32 (1966), pp. 104–5.

rather than inside, the temple, and the peasant villagers could therefore attend them.

Not only did the great families perform regular sacrifices to the spirits of their ancestors (called *nei-shen*, inner spirits), but also to gods who had no association by blood with their own family (*wai-shen*, outer spirits). Sacrifices to this latter group were also frequently an excuse for an opera. Witness the following comment from the register of the Chung clan in Chu-chi county, Chekiang. It refers to one branch only, itself subdivided into two, and refers to the late Ch'ing period.

On the 29th of the sixth month, we hold a gathering to honour the feastday of the City God (*Ch'eng-huang shen*), and drama is performed. The two branches take it in turns, year by year, to make the arrangements . . . The produce of the sacrificial fields (*ssu-t'ien*) is divided into two, part of it being used to hang lanterns in the city temple [at the Lantern Festival], the rest for the dramatic performances at the feastday gathering.[1]

Drama was performed also on occasions other than the regular and special sacrifices to the ancestors or other spirits. When clan forebears were accepted for worship in the Confucian temple, celebrations took place at which theatrical entertainment might be offered. An instance of this is found in the records of the Wei clan mentioned above: performances were given day and night to mark the occasion.[2]

During certain festivals, performances of theatrical pieces could add to the joyous atmosphere. On the Lantern Festival, the 15th of the first month, sacrifices were offered and two gatherings held at the ancestral temple of the same Wei clan and drama was put on.[3] Another, less joyous, festival at which drama would be performed was the Ch'ing-ming in honour of the dead, which fell about a fortnight after the spring equinox. The record of the Ch'en clan of Hsiao-shan remarks that on this day 'it was fitting

[1] *Chu-chi Chung-shih tsung-p'u*, 5 *Shu K'uei-kung ch'eng-hsien ssu-t'ien ch'an-chi*, 1a–b. On the various city gods see Doré, *Recherches sur les superstitions en Chine*, II*ème* *partie, Le panthéon chinois*, pp. 875–93. The Lantern Festival is discussed by Eberhard in *Chinese Festivals*, pp. 62–7.

[2] *Lan-feng Wei-shih tsung-p'u*, 3, 65a. The passage is a quotation from a stele dated 1878 (3, 65b). Further examples of drama performed to accompany festivities in honour of accepting ancestors for worship are given by Tanaka Issei in 'Sōzoku engeki', p. 105.

[3] *Lan-feng Wei-shih tsung-p'u*, 3, 57a. The passage is a quotation from a stele dated 1864.

that a company be engaged to perform theatrical pieces in the family temple. There were two sessions, one in the day, the other at night. That in the day was intended to pay respect to all the gods and . . . that at night to the various generations of ancestors . . . They were called "Ch'ing-ming dramas" (*Ch'ing-ming hsi*).'[1]

The numerous family occasions for thanksgiving, for celebration, or for grief could be accompanied by dramatic performances. One could rejoice by putting on a play if one had passed an official examination, or taken a bride, or recovered from an illness;[2] one could commemorate the birthdays of revered ancestors,[3] or mourn for a newly deceased relation with suitable dramas.[4] Family ties were certainly strengthened by this association of drama with their religion, itself so closely connected with the institution of the family, on which the whole of Chinese society rested.

When the leading clan of a district issued a prohibition or command, it was common to give it added force through celebrations which included drama. These carried a religious overtone calculated to impress those who would be affected by the edict.[5] An interesting instance of the custom is recorded in the clan records of the Huang family of Chin-li in Fukien. In the region of Chin-li, flooding and the silting up of irrigation canals had been caused by the deliberate uprooting of trees and other useful vegetation. In the year 1754 a clan leader strictly forbade such anti-social behaviour and issued a decree that his descendants should order periodic performances of drama as a reminder that the prohibition was still in force.[6]

---

[1] *Ch'en-shih tsung-p'u*, 3 *liu-fang nien-kuei chi-ssu*, 2a. On the Ch'ing-ming Festival, which marked the beginning of the spring labours in the fields, see Eberhard, *Chinese Festivals*, pp. 113–27.

[2] We know that in Su-chou a drama was sometimes performed at the local Ch'eng-huang (City God) Temple when a rich person recovered from an illness. The god was presented with a magnificent cap, robe, and boots as a sign of appreciation for his favours. See *Wu-ch'ü feng-t'u lu*, p. 4a.

[3] See Tanaka Issei, 'Sōzoku engeki', pp. 105–6.

[4] See Tanaka Issei, 'Shindai shoki no chihō geki ni tsuite', *Nippon-Chūgoku-gakkai-hō* 17 (1965), p. 149.

[5] See Tanaka Issei, 'Sōzoku engeki', pp. 108–9.

[6] *Chin-li Huang-shih chia-p'u*, 1, 35a. The custom recalls that followed in some guild-halls. After the T'ai-p'ing uprising, improved regulations were enacted in the Hsing-hua Sub-guild of Ning-po during 'a theatrical performance in honour of the Queen of Heaven'. See MacGowan, 'Chinese Guilds or Chambers of

It appears that these quasi-religious drama performances were frequently given both in the daytime and at night, and examples have already been cited. Sometimes one session was dedicated to the *nei-shen*, the other to the *wai-shen*. However, this was not always the case. After the special winter sacrifices of the Wei clan of Lan-feng, operas were performed both during the day and at night. The family records list thirty-eight particular ancestors honoured by the dramas. The day operas were dedicated to nineteen of them, those at night to the remainder.[1] It has been normal practice in Chinese ancestral temples to keep two rows of tablets, one on the right side, the other on the left, and probably the names in the two lists corresponded with those of the two tablets in the temple.

The clan records of the Shen family of Ch'ang-hsiang give some details about the practical arrangements for the dramatic performances. A tax was imposed to meet the cost of the ancestral sacrifices, and the total amount, which was fixed in advance, included the cost of the dramatic performances. One branch of the clan was allotted the task of making arrangements for the drama, and its members made the decision whether they could afford a famous or merely an ordinary company of actors. Although they were expected to provide entertainment worthy of the clan, they were only given extra money by the clan authorities for occasions demanding an especially good troupe. Failure to use up such a grant rendered the luckless members of the branch responsible liable to punishment.[2]

This example illustrates several points concerning dramatic performances in association with ancestral sacrifices. We learn from it that the task of organizing the drama was confined each year to one branch of the family only, the duty rotating among the different branches. The passage cited earlier from the register of the Chung clan of Chu-chi confirms that the Shen family was not alone in following this practice. Furthermore, it appears that drama companies were often hired (although we shall see later that many families maintained private companies) and that it was the branch in charge that decided the standard of the company it

Commerce and Trades Unions', *Journal of the China Branch of the Royal Asiatic Society*, xxi, nos. 3 and 4 (1886), 147.

[1] *Lan-feng Wei-shih tsung-p'u*, 3, 59b–60a. The passage is a quotation from a stele dated 1869 (3, 60b).

[2] See above, p. 21, note 1.

could afford. We learn especially that the money to finance the drama was raised by taxation which, as we know from other sources, could take several forms. Some clans, like the Chung of Chu-chi, set aside special 'sacrificial fields' for the use of local peasants, who were then required to pay some of what they earned to the plan. Others taxed the use of water from the rivers for irrigation.[1]

Considering the vast volume and enormous number of surviving clan records, it is striking how few references we find there to the drama. Perhaps the reluctance of Confucian *literati* to admit that the theatre was ever associated with ancestral sacrifices may partly account for the scarcity of references to practices which were widespread and well known. It is worth pointing out too that few of the records which survive are from north China;[2] consequently, most of the references we are discussing occur in the Kiangnan region, especially the towns near the coast of Chekiang, such as Yü-yao and Hsiao-shan. Up to the Ch'ien-lung period, it was in the Kiangnan provinces that the theatre was most flourishing. Moreover, the group spirit of the great clans was traditionally stronger there than in the north. Finally, the influence of Confucianism was not nearly so pervasive in the south as in the north.[3] Whereas the puritanical attitude towards the association of drama with ancestral sacrifices could usually be enforced in the northern provinces, it was much easier in Kiangnan to follow attractive popular customs. Probably it was no accident that the south preponderated in the theatrical references discussed above, and that the association between drama and the clan rites was largely confined to the Kiangnan provinces.[4]

A similar problem faces us in determining the exact period when the practices noted arose. The number of surviving clan records for the latter half of the Ch'ing is much greater than for

---

[1] See also Tanaka Issei, 'Sōzoku engeki', pp. 110–12.

[2] In his *Sōfu no kenkyū* (pp. 190–219), Taga Akigorō lists 1,231 registers according to the place of origin of the family in question. Different editions of the same register are given separately, but there is more than one edition of comparatively few records. Of the 1,231 mentioned, 434 are from Kiangsu, 377 from Chekiang and 120 from Anhwei, these three provinces accounting for just over three-quarters of the total number. In Chekiang, the county best represented is Hsiao-shan with 81 clan records.

[3] See Hisayuki Miyakawa, 'The Confucianization of South China', in Wright, ed., *The Confucian Persuasion*, pp. 21–46.

[4] See also Tanaka Issei, 'Sōzoku engeki', p. 114.

the earlier.[1] A custom described in detail in a late family record need not necessarily have been unknown at an earlier date, even if it is unreported in works of the period, and may in fact have been first practised in different places at different times. However, we can state with some certainty that the link between the drama and the religious life of the great clans already existed in the Ming,[2] and might have developed as early as the Sung.

The Secular Drama of the Literati

The importance of the drama in the lives of eminent citizens was by no means limited to the quasi-religious functions dealt with so far. In addition to the drama performed at the clan shrine, which was often public, the great families frequently enjoyed dramatic pieces in their own home, and these were intended for the exclusive entertainment of the clan and its guests. A number of families maintained private companies, which were sometimes hired out to other rich people. The custom whereby a man of good position kept his own actors was not unique to China and could at one time be found in Europe and other civilizations. In China, it reaches back much earlier than the Ming. The servants of Yang Tzu of Hai-yen, a well known musician and dramatist of the thirteenth century, were expert actors,[3] and provide good evidence of this.

Three famous patrons of private theatrical companies deserve special mention. They are Ho Liang-chün (1506–73), Chang Tai (1597–1684?) and Juan Ta-ch'eng (c. 1587–1646).

Ho Liang-chün came from Sung-chiang in Kiangsu. He did not enjoy an important official career but became famous as a

---

[1] The 892 Ch'ing examples in Taga's chronological list of clan records can be subdivided according to reign-period as follows:

Shun-chih	3	Tao-kuang	115
K'ang-hsi	18	Hsien-feng	33
Yung-cheng	4	T'ung-chih	97
Ch'ien-lung	63	Kuang-hsü	425
Chia-ch'ing	65	Hsüan-t'ung	48

See Taga Akigorō, *Sōfu no kenkyū*, pp. 58, 220–42. It can be seen that the great majority belongs to the last century of the dynasty.

[2] Ibid., pp. 684–6. Taga Akigorō quotes a long passage from the *Ming-chou Wu-shih chia-chi*, the records of a Wu clan in Hsiu-ning, Anhwei, written in 1591. We learn (p. 685) that the clan loved the drama but restricted its performance to times such as when giving thanks to the gods. Drama during birthday celebrations had been discontinued on the grounds that it was wasteful.

[3] See *Chü-shuo*, I, 88.

bibliophile and author.[1] He writes that he had been a lover of the drama from his youth. In his middle age he became incurably ill and, to amuse himself, taught his house-boys (*chia-t'ung*) to sing.[2] It appears that many of the girls in his service had also learned to act and sing under the instruction of the famous musician Tun Jen, who had earlier learned his trade in the Office of Music (*Chiao-fang ssu*) in Peking. Ho Liang-chün comments that the little slave-girls of his house could remember more than fifty dramatic pieces, mostly *tsa-chü* and *tz'u* of the Chin and Yüan.[3] Liang-chün was no rigid follower of the theatrical fashions of his time; although he lived in Kiangsu he was more interested in the northern drama than the *K'un-ch'ü*, and his private actors naturally catered for his tastes.

The second outstanding patron of private drama groups was Chang Tai of Shao-hsing. This man enjoyed only short success as an official. He refused to work for the Manchus after they took Shao-hsing in 1646 and spent the rest of his life in retirement. His most famous work is the *T'ao-an meng-i*, which deals with his experiences and late-Ming customs.[4] Chang Tai was the master of five theatrical companies, all of which had been handed down to him from his grandfather. By Chang Tai's time their composition had naturally changed, but the actors continued to be drawn from the servants of the Chang household.[5]

In the political life of his time, Juan Ta-ch'eng was more important than Ho or Chang. This, however, was not to his credit. He was noted for bribery, avarice and political intrigue and was for a time associated with the notorious Wei Chung-hsien (1568–1627), one of the most powerful eunuchs in Chinese history.[6] Juan was also a poet and dramatist of some distinction.[7]

---

[1] On Ho Liang-chün see also Liu Ts'un-yan, *Wu Ch'êng-ên: His Life and Career*, pp. 20, 29–30, 37. Ho was a friend of Wu Ch'eng-en.

[2] *Ssu-yu chai ts'ung-shuo*, 37, 336.

[3] Ibid., 37, 340. See also Liu Ts'un-yan, *Wu Ch'êng-ên*, pp. 34–6. Perhaps the best known of Ho's acting girls was Li Chieh, of whom Liang-chün was very fond.

[4] A biography of Chang Tai with notes on the *T'ao-an meng-i* can be found in Hummel, *Eminent Chinese*, pp. 53–4.

[5] *T'ao-an meng-i*, 4, 33–4. Chang Tai's grandfather had founded a sixth company, but its members later found employment with other masters.

[6] Wei Chung-hsien from Chihli became the virtual ruler of China during the T'ien-ch'i reign (1621–7) of the late Ming. However, when T'ien-ch'i died, Wei was promptly dismissed and he then hanged himself. See Hummel, *Eminent Chinese*, pp. 846–7.

[7] Ibid., pp. 398–9. See also Josephine Huang Hung, *Ming Drama*, pp. 174–7.

Juan Ta-ch'eng's fame as a patron of the drama was partly dependent on the reputation of one of the actors of his private company, a certain Li. This man later became a member of the well known Hua-lin company of Chin-ling (present Nanking) and, until his eclipse by the Moslem actor Ma Chin,[1] held a standing as high as any in the city. In fact, after Juan's death and the dispersal of the members of his company to other mansions, Li reported none too favourably on his former patron. It seems that Juan made his company perform his own dramas. He would curse and laugh at them, was never satisfied with their efforts and persisted all day in his merciless training. On one occasion, Li was invited by a later patron to perform in one of Juan's dramas. But he declined because he did not relish the memory of the behaviour of that notorious dramatist.[2] On the other hand, Chang Tai was a great admirer both of Juan Ta-ch'eng's dramas and his acting companies and wrote with great enthusiasm of the pieces he had seen acted in Juan's mansion.[3]

Despite the eminence of many of the privately patronized companies, there were periods when some educated men looked down on the practice of holding dramatic performances in their own houses. Arthur Waley had described the men of the early eighteenth century as 'on the whole stern and puritanical', and cites as an example the scholar and painter Chiang T'ing-hsi (1669–1732).[4] By the middle of the eighteenth century, the Chinese had become, according to Waley, 'pleasure-loving and tolerant',[5] and Chiang T'ing-hsi's son, Chiang P'u (1708–61),[6] did not share his father's tastes. Yüan Mei (1716–98), perhaps eighteenth-century China's most famous poet, wrote of Chiang T'ing-hsi:

He warned his sons and grandsons against ever having anything to do

---

[1] Ma Chin was known also as Ma Hui-hui (Ma the Moslem). It is said that he once competed with Li to perform the part of a wicked minister, but was considered inferior to his rival. He then took a job in the mansion of a famous corrupt minister in Peking and observed his employer's speech and actions in minute detail. This produced the desired effect on his acting, and his reputation rose at Li's expense. See *Chuang-hui t'ang wen-chi*, 5, 132–3. Before the Cultural Revolution, this story was very popular in contemporary China, where great emphasis is placed upon the notion that actors should live among those they portray on the stage.

[2] *Chü-shuo*, 6, 201–2.   [3] *T'ao-an meng-i*, 8, 69.

[4] See Chiang's biography in Hummel, *Eminent Chinese*, pp. 142–3.

[5] *Yuan Mei*, p. 131.   [6] See Hummel, *Eminent Chinese*, p. 143.

with actors, and as long as he was alive no actor or entertainer ever came near the house. When he had been dead for ten years (i.e. in 1742) Chiang P'u began occasionally to get actors from outside to give performances. But he still did not venture to keep a private troupe in the house. An old family servant called Ku Sheng, when chatting one day with Chiang P'u, got on to the subject of theatricals. 'A company of actors from outside', he pleaded, 'is never so good as a troupe trained in the house, or so handy. A lot of the servants here have children. Why don't you get hold of a teacher, make him select the likeliest and have them trained as a company?' Chiang P'u was much attracted by the idea.[1]

The suggestion was in fact never put into practice in this instance, but the custom which Ku Sheng thought his master should adopt was undoubtedly widespread at the time.

The most important occasions at which private companies performed were banquets given by men of good position for their friends. Indeed, these feasts were a major part of the social life of the *literati* and they are mentioned frequently in the sources. If necessary, a family could hire a company especially for the occasion. When Hsi-men Ch'ing, the main character in the late-Ming novel *The Golden Lotus*, holds a large banquet to celebrate the Lantern Festival and the birthday of one of his wives, he engages a company of twenty actors from an eminent neighbour.[2]

Performances did not usually interrupt the conversation of a banquet and, just as with similar customs elsewhere in the world, often served merely as a background to a pleasant social gathering. On the other hand, enthusiasts of music and drama might make the performance play a more central role. Juan Ta-ch'eng often invited friends and acquaintances to his mansion at Chin-

---

[1] *Hsin ch'i-hsieh*, 4, 10b. I have used the translation of Waley given in *Yuan Mei*, p. 131. The *Hsin ch'i-hsieh* is a collection of wonder-tales and much of its content appears incredible. According to Waley (p. 120), 'Yuan Mei's wonder-tales seem to be accounts of actual psychic experiences, as communicated to him by friends and contemporaries, and in some cases as experienced by himself or his family.' Certainly there seems no reason to reject the historical authenticity of the passage I have quoted.

[2] *Chin P'ing Mei tz'u-hua*, 42, 1a–2a, and Egerton, *The Golden Lotus*, II, 203–4. This novel contains numerous other examples of banquets accompanied by dramatic performances. In this respect it may be taken as an accurate reflection of social conditions. For a short bibliography on this famous novel see C. T. Hsia, *The Classic Chinese Novel*, pp. 394–5. The novel itself is discussed pp. 165–202.

ling to witness performances of his own dramas acted by
his own company. Chang Tai reports seeing three of Juan's
compositions at his house.[1] Juan no doubt expected his guests
to give at least most of their attention to the entertainment
provided.

It is worth pointing out in this connection that the Confucian
school held the drama to be an important vehicle for ethical
education; ideally therefore it should occupy more than a background position. Many stories survive showing the impact by the
moral content of the dramas. One of them describes a guest at a
Su-chou banquet who actually killed an actor portraying Ch'in
Kuei. This twelfth-century minister has always been regarded as
an arch-traitor, and the magistrate is said to have been sympathetic towards the guest and set him free.[2] The details of such
stories need not be taken too seriously. Yet surely there were, at
least among the *literati*, many Confucians who felt very strongly
about the moral lessons taught in dramas.

The usual banquet with drama was quite a small and insignifi-
cant occasion: there might be only one or a few visitors.[3] Sometimes, however, guests were numerous and high-ranking. This
was especially so if the banquet was held to celebrate some
particular event. The following is a case in point.

A certain Lu Tz'u-yün was given an official position in Fu-chou,
Kiangsi. After he had been in office six months, he arranged for
the reconstruction of the Yü-ming t'ang, the former house of the
famous dramatist T'ang Hsien-tsu (1550–1617). When the
building was finished, Lu held an enormous banquet. All the
local officials and eminent persons were invited to take part.
T'ang Hsien-tsu's most famous piece, *Mu-tan t'ing* (*The Peony*

---

[1] *T'ao-an meng-i*, 8, 69.

[2] This and other similar stories have been collected from older sources by
Chiao Hsün in *Chü-shuo*, 6, 203. It was once universally believed that Ch'in
Kuei brought about the death of the patriot Yüeh Fei, who opposed his plan to
cede north China to the Chin. However, the historical basis of the Yüeh Fei
legend is open to question. See Wilhelm, 'From Myth to Myth: The Case of
Yüeh Fei's Biography', in Wright and Twitchett, eds., *Confucian Personalities*,
pp. 146–61. It should be added that there was also a strong political element in
dramas about Yüeh Fei. As foreign rulers the Manchus held such pieces to be
aimed specifically at condemning their government.

[3] *K'e-tso chui-yü*, 9, 25b. Cf. also *Chin P'ing Mei tz'u-hua*, 72, 12a–15b, and
Egerton, *The Golden Lotus*, III, 314–16. In this passage Hsi-men Ch'ing was the
only guest, yet was entertained by singing boys.

Pavilion),[1] was performed. The feast lasted two days and various poems were written to commemorate it.[2]

The style of drama performed at banquets varied from period to period. Before the Wan-li era (1573–1620) there does not seem to have been any strict rule. At small parties, northern tunes or small-scale pieces might be given. At large gatherings almost any style was permitted, southern tunes or *I-yang ch'iang* and, later, *K'un-ch'ü*.[3]

However, after the *K'un-ch'ü* became established, all other styles of drama were considered too vulgar to be performed at the banquets of the educated. One incident in particular illustrates this vividly. The eminent poet, author, and official, Wang Shih-chen (1634–1711, *hao* Juan-t'ing)[4] was responsible for arranging a drama at a banquet given to him by a superior. He chose a piece of the *I-yang ch'iang* system. When his superior asked him what the drama was the Shih-chen quietly told him. The reply was: 'Who said that Wang Juan-t'ing was learned and accomplished?'[5] It was apparently considered insulting to have arranged an *I-yang ch'iang* piece. Although drama other than *K'un-ch'ü* continued to be performed in aristocratic mansions, this contempt for *hua-pu* drama persisted. One scholar is quoted as saying that when *pang-tzu ch'iang* was performed, 'it makes you hold your sides with laughter.'[6]

By the latter half of the Ch'ing, there was a growing body of opinion among the *literati* which recognized the value of the regional drama. The scholar Chiao Hsün (1763–1820) of Yang-chou was very keen on the *hua-pu*,[7] and we shall see in the next chapter that others in that city shared his tastes. In Shensi, *Ch'in-*

---

[1] The *Mu-tan t'ing* is a love-story prefaced 1598 by its author. It concerns the scholar Liu Meng-mei and the girl Tu Li-niang. She sees Meng-mei in a dream and dies of love-sickness for him. Three years later she is resurrected and, after Meng-mei has become a first palace graduate (*chuang-yüan*), obtains permission from her father to marry him. The plot is described in detail and the drama discussed in Josephine Huang Hung, *Ming Drama*, pp. 146 ff. See also *Ch'ü-hai tsung-mu t'i-yao*, 6, 265 ff. For a bibliography on the drama and its author see Lo Chin-t'ang, *Chung-kuo hsi-ch'ü tsung-mu hui-pien*, pp. 289–90, 298, and for a list of translations into English, French and German, pp. 282–3.

[2] *Chü-shuo*, 6, 197.   [3] *K'e-tso chui-yü*, 9, 25b–26a.

[4] See Hummel, *Eminent Chinese*, pp. 831–3. This man is not to be confused with the dramatist Wang Shih-chen (1527–90).

[5] *Chü-shuo*, 4, 154.   [6] *Chü-hua*, 1, 47.

[7] *Hua-pu nung-t'an*, p. 225. See the author's biography in Hummel, *Eminent Chinese*, pp. 144–5.

ch'iang was performed at banquets in the latter part of the Ch'ien-lung period. At one of them, many of the guests, who happened to have been born and brought up in Kiangsu or Chekiang, expressed their dislike of the style, but the scholar Yen Ch'ang-ming (1731–87) later wrote a passage defending it at great length and in no uncertain terms.[1] Probably the bias against *hua-pu* was never as strong in Shensi as in Kiangnan. The great decline in the prestige of the *K'un-ch'ü* in the nineteenth century will be discussed in subsequent chapters.

Even when *K'un-ch'ü* only was in fashion among the scholars, the question of which particular *ya-pu* item to perform at a banquet was fairly open. A number of pieces are mentioned in the sources as having been given at banquets and, in the absence of evidence to the contrary, we may assume that taboos on *K'un-ch'ü* dramas extended no further than was necessary to conform to the requirements of government censorship.

The selection of the piece was not decided in advance but left to the guests. The following comments by du Halde give some idea of how pieces were chosen at a Chinese banquet.

After all these ceremonies they place themselves at the table, which done, there enter the hall four or five principal comedians [*sic*] in rich garments, who make a profound reverence at the same instant, and beat their foreheads four times against the ground in the midst of the two rows of tables, with their faces towards a long side-table full of lights and perfuming-pans. They then rise up, and one of them, addressing himself to the head-guest, presents a book in which are written in letters of gold the names of fifty or sixty plays that they have by heart, and are ready to act upon the spot. The head-guest refuses to choose one, and refers him to the second, the second to the third, etc. but they all make excuses, and return him the book; at last he consents, opens the book, runs it over with his eyes in an instant, and appoints the play that he thinks will be most agreeable to the company: after this the comedian shews all the guests the name of the play that is made choice of, and every one testifies his approbation by a nod.[2]

Despite du Halde's picture, it appears that guests did not always

---

[1] *Ch'in-yün hsieh-ying hsiao-p'u* (*CYHYHP*), pp. 9b ff. Yen Ch'ang-ming's biography is given in Hummel, *Eminent Chinese*, p. 907.

[2] *The General History of China*, II, 193–4. The original French text can be found in *Description de l'empire de la Chine*, II, 132. Cf. *Chin P'ing Mei tz'u-hua*, 58, 8a–b, and Egerton, *The Golden Lotus*, III, 57, where a banquet in honour of Hsi-men Ch'ing's birthday is described.

agree among themselves on this question. Chiao Hsün goes so far as to say that 'the most difficult thing about a public banquet is to decide on the drama.' He describes a feast he attended in Shantung in 1795. The local examinations were over and the magistrate (*ling*) of the county gave a banquet with drama. Two of the guests started quarrelling over which piece should be performed and eventually the host's uncle had to make the decision.[1]

The above examples make it abundantly clear, I think, that the theatre, and particularly *K'un-ch'ü*, was an essential part of the lives of the Chinese *literati*. This in itself must have been a great stimulus to the drama. However, the educated group was relatively limited in number. An even greater impetus was given the drama by the fact that it percolated deeply into the lives of the far more numerous ordinary population: and it is to them that we must now turn our attention.

The Ordinary People

The life of village and town communities tended to revolve around certain religious celebrations, particularly the sacrifices to the gods of the harvest. These occasions served to bring the communities together and gave them a certain cohesion, for they were of concern to everybody.[2] By the Ming period, and possibly earlier, drama formed an important part of these village festivals, and hence of the lives of the peasants and artisans.[3] There was a shrine or temple in every village at which the performances could take place, often as part of the temple fairs once so popular in north China.[4] Sometimes the shrine of the local great clan was used also for drama by the common people of the neighbourhood.[5]

It was natural that such village performances should have taken place at the end of autumn, in the winter, or in early spring. This was the idle season; the autumn harvest had been collected, the ploughing for the following year not yet undertaken. It was the ideal interlude during which peasants could thank the gods for the harvest just reaped and pray for a good year to follow. This period of leisure was perfectly suited for the performance and

[1] *Chü-shuo*, 6, 208.
[2] See in particular the detailed research of Niida Noboru in *Chūgoku hōsei*, III, 710 ff.
[3] See Tanaka Issei, 'Chihō geki', pp. 153–4.
[4] See C. K. Yang, *Religion in Chinese Society*, pp. 82–5.
[5] Tanaka Issei, 'Chihō geki', p. 149.

enjoyment of theatrical entertainment, which consequently went hand in hand with the religious observances.

One typical reference to this quasi-religious drama concerns rural Honan in north China during the Yung-cheng period (1723–36). It runs: 'Every year after the autumn harvest the peasants had nothing to do until the second or third month of spring. So they held gatherings to worship the gods. They went from door to door collecting money with which they built elevated platforms.' Drama was then performed and music played to honour the gods.[1]

Identical customs were found in the south. The following quotation from a work on the customs of Su-chou is typical:

In the second and third months, village bullies and strong men of the markets would build stages in the thinly populated areas. The people would contribute money for the performance of operas and everybody, both men and women, would gather to watch. It was called 'spring stage drama' (*ch'un-t'ai hsi*) and was designed to pray for good fortune for the peasants.[2]

There were parallel practices in the towns and cities, with the important difference that the urban population was not so dependent on the seasons. We find people of the same profession forming guilds under a patron god, to whom on special occasions sacrifices were offered, with dramas, in the hope that he would send his clients good business. This custom is well illustrated in a passage to be found in the gazetteer of Shansi province. The 28th of the fourth month was celebrated as the birthday of Yao-wang (the God of Medicine), and on that day the pharmacists habitually sacrificed an animal, and offered sweet wine and dramatic performances to the god.[3]

This particular day was of special importance to one group of people, but the drama also formed part of the celebrations of the

---

[1] *Fu-Yü hsüan-hua lu*, 4, 46a.

[2] *Wu-ch'ü feng-t'u lu*, p. 3b. Another text, referring to Hunan, describes how, in December 1707, the people of the neighbourhood prepared the local temple for a ceremony at which drama was performed for three days 'in order to pray to the gods for eternal protection'. The poor people contributed money towards the cost of the occasion. See *Chao Kung-i kung tzu-chih kuan-shu*, 5, 97a. Numerous examples of this kind could be cited. See Tanaka Issei, *Shindai chihō geki shiryō shū*, *passim*.

[3] *Shan-hsi t'ung-chih*, 99, 33a. The god Yao-wang is discussed in Doré, *Recherches, IIème partie*, pp. 724–7.

great country-wide festivals. Du Halde, who has provided us with so much information on Chinese customs, mentions drama as part of the great New Year Festival (*yüan-tan*). He says that, on the second day of the year and the following days, the Chinese 'give demonstrations of extraordinary joy, all the shops are shut up, and every body is taken up with sports, feasts and plays'.[1]

Although the New Year Festival was the people's main time for rejoicing, there were other occasions which gave them the opportunity to enjoy dramatic performances, such as the Avalambana Festival.[2] Another was the feastday of the famous hero of the third century, Kuan Yü, known popularly as Kuan-ti or Kuan-kung, who was worshipped by the people as the God of War. Ku Ts'ai, who was a friend of the famous dramatist K'ung Shang-jen (1648–1718),[3] happened to be visiting Ho-feng in western Hupeh in 1703 and describes how the people there celebrated the feastday of Kuan-kung in one part of the city.

The 13th [of the fifth month] was the feastday of Kuan-kung and dramatic performances were put on at large gatherings in the temple buildings of Hsi-liu. Military officials, guests and other high-ranking persons would all don formal clothing to arrange the sacrifices to him. Among the rural folk there were some who had come 100 *li* to take part in the gatherings. They all drank wine until the 15th day, when [the celebrations] ended.[4]

Drama festivals of this sort were not usually organized by local officials, but these men supervised closely everything that went on. Moreover, the central and provincial organs of government imposed a wide range of restrictions on the content of the drama, the times of performance and other matters.[5]

---

[1] *The General History of China*, II, 166. See the French original in *Description de l'empire de la Chine*, II, 112. The religious nature of the New Year Festival is shown more plainly in *Shan-hsi t'ung-chih*, 99, 27b. There we are told that the drama performed at the festival was linked with the traditional sacrifice offered by the local officials to the god Mang-shen, the clay driver of the earthern ox used to honour agriculture. See also Eberhard, *Chinese Festivals*, pp. 8 ff. The author makes it clear that the New Year Festival was a religious occasion.

[2] For example, see *Ch'ing-chia lu*, 7, 4a.

[3] Aoki Masaru, *Chung-kuo chin-shih hsi-ch'ü shih*, p. 389.

[4] *Jung-mei chi-yu*, p. 8a. See a similar description in *Wu-ch'ü feng-t'u lu*, p. 6a, which refers to Su-chou. On Kuan-kung see Doré, *Recherches*, IIème partie, pp. 54–66.

[5] Wang Hsiao-ch'uan has collected fifty-five documents concerning regional prohibitions on the theatre during the Ch'ing. See *Yüan Ming Ch'ing san-tai chin-hui hsiao-shuo hsi-ch'ü shih-liao*, pp. 88–138.

It was common for drama festivals to last no more than three days, and the example just quoted from Ho-feng is quite typical. In some places the period was fixed not merely by custom but also by law. An order dated the second lunar month of 1725 and applying to Shantung, Chihli, Honan, and other provinces, stipulates that drama should never be performed for more than three days at a time. The local officials are commanded to keep strict watch over everything that happens on such occasions, and if anybody disobeys the order, he is to be tried as a criminal.[1]

It is striking that the Ch'ing government should consider it necessary to place restrictions on the performance of drama and to supervise it so closely. One explanation might be that some officials considered theatrical performances during religious celebrations irreverent. But this does not appear to explain the government's reserve adequately, and we should look more carefully at the restrictions and the reasons for them.

In the first place, dramatic entertainment usually took place in the open air and was very often attended by large crowds of people. This sometimes created congestion in the towns and elsewhere. The regional records of Ning-po report that there were at times so many spectators at the drama that they blocked the streets.[2]

Secondly, dramatic performances sometimes provided the occasion for bad or illegal practices. Many examples of this survive in legal documents. Sometimes the matter was trivial,[3] but occasionally serious crimes were committed during a drama. One case in Shansi involved a monk, Wu-ming. In 1760, he had been sent by his superior from his original monastery to take care of a separate establishment and been given the use of thirty-three *mou* of land. In 1774 he came back to his old habitat to see a drama. During the performance Wu-ming fell into an argument with two of the leading monks who were demanding the return of the thirty-three *mou* of land. A quarrel ensued. Wu-ming picked up a knife and injured one of his antagonists, whereupon

[1] *Fu-Yü hsüan-hua lu*, 4, 46b–47a.

[2] *Ning-po fu-chih*, 4, 37a. Other examples of congestion caused by dramatic performances could be cited. Tung Hsün (1807–92, see Hummel, *Eminent Chinese*, pp. 789–91) writes that a huge audience blocked his way in a town in south-western Shansi when he attempted to pass through it late in 1849 (*Tu-Lung chi*, p. 9b).

[3] For instance, in 1776 in Chekiang a certain Chu Lao-wu went with friends to see a drama and gambled during the performance. See *Po-an hsin-pien*, 8, 2b.

he fled. The other, armed with a stick, immediately set off after him. Wu-ming, afraid that he would be beaten, slashed his pursuer with a knife. The latter died from his injuries about a month later. Wu-ming was tried and sentenced to be strangled.[1]

Sometimes, criminals made use of the crowded surroundings for their own purposes. In 1724 a man called Liu Tzu-yün was fatally wounded while watching a drama in a gathering of 200 to 300 people. In view of the numbers present it proved impossible to discover his murderer.[2]

Crimes of this sort could, according to the authorities, be most easily committed at night. A typical document, referring to Shensi, remarks that, 'When crowds of people gather together, and men and women mix without restraint, it is difficult to tell who is good and who evil. But most of the sexual crimes, gambling, and robbery occur during the night drama. Moreover, sometimes such matters develop into cases involving human life.'[3]

But, to the government, a much more serious threat posed by the dramatic performances was that secret societies could use them as a means of plotting or spreading their influence. This was because they provided an excellent opportunity of meeting for an outwardly innocent purpose and, as at the banquets of the rich, it was not obligatory to concentrate on the drama or to refrain from talking.

An order of 1723 is noted in a collection of Honan legal documents. It prohibits the performance of drama during the spring sacrifices to the gods on the grounds that secret societies were taking advantage of the custom. Various criminals, it alleges, were misleading the people, and when the drama was over, they formed themselves into cliques instead of dispersing. They were thus a menace to society.[4] But despite the order, the danger

[1] Ibid., 19, 7b–8b. Another case occurred in Shantung and was tried in mid-May 1739. On 3 July 1737, there happened to be a performance at a local temple. A boat-puller called Kao Lung passed by. The weather was so hot that he sat down on some matting beneath a tree to enjoy the shade. A drunkard came by, and decided he would like to use the comfort of the matting for a gambling session. He ordered Kao to leave, but the latter refused and a quarrel ensued in which Kao beat his antagonist so savagely that, after a fortnight's illness, he died. The case was taken to court and Kao Lung was sentenced to receive 100 strokes of the rod. Ibid., 19, 3a–b.

[2] *Chao Kung-i kung tzu-chih kuan-shu*, 18, 67a–69a.

[3] *P'ei-yüan t'ang ou-ts'un kao*, quoted in Tanaka Issai, *Shiryō shū*, I, 33.

[4] *Fu-Yü hsüan-hua lu*, 4, 46a–b.

appears to have persisted, for in 1727 the authorities in Honan were still concerned that merchants were meeting at theatrical performances in village temples with subversive and evil intent.[1]

Rebellious elements could also use the drama as a means of propaganda, and to counter this threat the central government imposed strict censorship. Ch'ien-lung set up a commission in 1777 with the task of revising all pieces to suit his rigid moral and political standards. More than 1,000 dramas came under the scrutiny of the censors and their job was not finished until 1782.[2] But this did not solve the problem, since the actors of the popular drama did not necessarily adhere to a prescribed text and could surreptitiously add subversive or bawdy material. The government did its best, at central, provincial, and local levels, to overcome this threat to public security and morality, but its success was very limited.

The reserve with which the government regarded the theatre was due largely to the suspicious nature of many of the Manchu rulers; and it was later to hamper the growth of the Peking Opera.[3] It was related to a wider problem—the obsession of rulers like Yung-cheng and Ch'ien-lung with factionalism and rebellion. It is worth remarking in this context that the Yung-cheng Emperor issued several decrees against factionalism at about the same time as the orders mentioned above against the performance of drama in Honan. He demanded the complete loyalty of his officials and sternly forbade them to split into cliques.[4]

One other reason why the Ch'ing government was never happy about theatrical gatherings was financial. It is true that the great clans often organized dramatic performances for the common people in honour of local or harvest gods.[5] Yet in most cases it was the poor people themselves who paid for routine dramatic performances,[6] and the money used for them was collected from door to door. There was an obvious temptation to abuse the custom to practise extortion. In one text referring to 1742 we read

---

[1] Ibid., 3B, 151a. The date to which the passage refers is given p. 152b.

[2] *YCHFL*, 5, 111–21 and Liu Ts'un-yan, *Buddhist and Taoist Influences on Chinese Novels*, pp. 118 ff.

[3] See below, pp. 211–18.

[4] See Nivison, 'Ho-shen and his Accusers: Ideology and Political Behavior in the Eighteenth Century', in Nivison and Wright, eds., *Confucianism in Action*, pp. 225–8.

[5] See Tanaka Issei, 'Sōzoku engeki', pp. 106–7.

[6] See Tanaka Issei, 'Chihō geki', pp. 147–8.

that 'despite the rules which strictly forbade it, . . . there were some vagabonds and scoundrels who, at the Avalambana Festival every year, . . . would go from door to door demanding [extortionate sums of] money. Such low practices were common in the provinces along the Yangtze.' The money was in theory to be used to cover the costs of the drama.[1]

Sometimes rich families were the victims of the 'vagabonds'. One such case occurred in 1565. Seven wandering musicians went on horseback to Mien-chou in Szechwan province. Their costumes were clean and colourful, their performances of a high standard. Many people came to see them, high-ranking officials, merchants, and the common people of the city. After a few days, the actors asked certain rich families to lend them precious clothes and objects, on the pretext that they would use the material for their performances. They then made their escape, cheating their benefactors of property worth a considerable sum of money. Only one of the seven was found and punished.[2]

The preceding pages show how irreligious practices could become part of what were, after all, religious celebrations. This is exemplified also in the specific dramas put on during the sacrifices and festivals. Despite the occasions on which they were performed, these pieces were not always especially religious in content. One drama constantly put on during festivals in honour of the gods was based on a Buddhist story. This was *Mu-lien*, which tells how Mu-lien, a disciple of the Buddha, descended to hell to rescue his mother.[3] Others rested on secular themes. One text suggests that the famous model judge of the Sung dynasty, Pao Cheng (999–1062), was often the subject of village theatre.[4] Chiao Hsün gives the names of some *hua-pu* dramas performed in the villages.[5] None of them is particularly religious in content.

In one sense it is not surprising that secular dramas should be performed as part of religious celebrations. The peasants rarely watched the drama except on such occasions. It was natural that they should wish to see and hear love-stories and tales about the

---

[1] *P'ei-yüan t'ang ou-ts'un kao*, 14, in Tanaka Issei, *Shiryō shū*, II, 31.

[2] *Huan-yu chi-wen*, pp. 3b–4b.

[3] For examples when *Mu-lien* was performed see *Chao Kung-i kung tzu-chih kuan-shu*, 5, 98b, *T'ao-an meng-i*, 6, 47–8, and the text quoted in note 1 above. On the drama itself see below, appendix C, pp. 254–8.

[4] *Chü-shuo*, 4, 152. For a biography of Pao Cheng see *Sung-shih*, 316, 1a ff.

[5] *Hua-pu nung-t'an*, passim.

heroes of ancient China. Precise distinctions between religious and secular would scarcely worry them.

It is worth pointing out, too, that the ethical basis of the popular drama was mainly Confucian in its inspiration. It is true that certain *literati* placed an extremely heavy emphasis on the moral value of the popular theatre. Liu Hsien-t'ing (1648–95) even described it as 'the great pivot on which illustrious kings changed the world'.[1] Yet such men were very much in the minority and most saw the drama of the masses as a source of evil. In any case, the influence of Confucian morality was not nearly as strong among the common people as among the educated and there were several factors which inhibited the impact of Con-fucianism on the folk drama. One of them 'was simply the demand of audiences . . . for verisimilitude—for believable human situations and conflicts', which ran counter to the idealized Confucian archetypes. As a result, the innumerable warnings and prohibitions of the authorities went to some extent unheard, and their 'efforts to "Confucianize" fiction remained only partly successful'.[2]

A great deal of the material presented here will carry a familiar ring to readers interested in world theatre. The association of the drama with seasonal religious festivals, the suspicion of the government, the secularization of the themes, and other features are found in many civilizations. This is not altogether surprising, since the leisure period of peasants everywhere depends upon the seasons, and individual holidays in almost all pre-industrial societies are religious in their origin. Moreover, the administrators of such societies have almost always preferred to see the people on the job because of the principle that 'the devil finds work for idle hands.' However, it is not my purpose here to establish world-wide patterns of theatrical development or to analyze the reasons for them.

Actors in Society

One implication of a system which made popular dramatic performances concentrated in certain times of the year was that acting companies were often mobile and impermanent. In China,

[1] *Kuang-yang tsa-chi*, 2, 107.
[2] Ruhlmann, 'Traditional Heroes in Chinese Popular Fiction', in Wright, ed., *The Confucian Persuasion*, p. 176.

they would disband after the feastday of Kuan-kung in the fifth month[1] and regroup the following autumn. In the intervening period actors formed other alliances in various parts of the empire, concentrating their attention on the cities or towns. The urban population did not have to worry about the needs of the crops and their leisure was less dependent on the vicissitudes of the elements. In the summer they had more time for the drama than the peasants.

Even during the busiest seasons, when acting companies remained together as a group for several months, they had to move from place to plaçe, taking their equipment with them. This was a necessary consequence of the fact that they could not perform in any place over a long period of time. In provinces well provided with waterways they would usually travel by boat, since this was the most convenient means of transport, but the example just quoted of the visitors to Mien-chou shows that they could also travel on horseback. Naturally, no plans or appointments could be made in advance, and the companies would turn up unexpectedly in a village or town. They would stay at an inn for a few days, give performances for the common people, and then move on to the next place.

It was the responsibility of the leader of the company to recruit new actors. Unwanted children were bought and adopted, a contract being signed with the boy's father. These apprentices were not necessarily treated badly. This is reflected in the eighteenth-century novel *The Scholars*. The actor Pao Wen-ch'ing adopts the son of a failed scholar, for a price, gives him an education and then trains him for the stage. The novelist must have had some actual cases in mind when he wrote that Pao Wen-ch'ing 'loved him more than if he had been his own son, because he came from a respectable family'.[2] On the other hand, historical sources make it clear that many masters treated their apprentices extremely badly. Here are some illustrative stories.

Yin-hua was a *Ch'in-ch'iang* actor of the latter half of the eighteenth century. He came from Kansu and was born into a

---

[1] See *Hang-su i-feng*, p. 8a, which refers specifically to Hang-chou and *Ch'ing-chia lu*, 7, 4a, which concerns Su-chou.

[2] *Ju-lin wai-shih*, 25, 250. I have followed the translation of Gladys Yang and Yang Hsien-yi in *The Scholars*, p. 351. For a short bibliography on this novel see C. T. Hsia, *The Classic Chinese Novel*, p. 395. The work is discussed pp. 203–44.

poor family. He became an orphan quite young and, at the age of eleven, was bought by a man called Chang, who then adopted him as a son and taught him to act. After a few years, however, Chang decided that Yin-hua was no further use to him, so he abandoned the youth leaving him to his own devices. Yin-hua then went to Hsi-an, where he became well known for his stage artistry.[1]

The young child Jen San-tzu of Shansi was not so fortunate. In 1782 he was bought by T'ien Hsüeh-hsin who planned to teach him to act. A contract was drawn up by which he was to be given back to his parents after a certain number of years. However, Jen found the training extremely difficult and could not master the skills demanded of him. In anger T'ien beat him so savagely that he died under the blows. The case was brought to court and T'ien was condemned to be strangled.[2]

If the slave-actor felt some grievance towards his master and teacher, he usually had to suffer in silence unless he could find a sympathetic patron. Certainly it was unwise for him to appeal to the law. This is well illustrated in a case tried in Kiangsu in 1820. T'an T'ien-lin had been sold by his father to an actor from Han-yang, presumably a troupe-leader, on the understanding that he would return home after a certain period. After receiving some training, T'an was resold to another actor named Hao P'an-yüeh and a contract was drawn up according to which he was to be returned after a limited number of years to the seller. The legal document which reports the case adds that 'this was the normal procedure by which actors and others learned drama.' T'ien-lin was apparently unhappy with his new teacher and accused Hao of having taken him by force. The court considered both to be lowly people and refused to recognize any proper master-disciple relationship between them. T'an's accusation was held to be false and he was given eighty strokes of the rod.[3]

It is quite clear that, just as in almost all other countries during most periods, the legal and social status of Chinese actors, whether masters or disciples, was extremely low. They were ranked as slaves and suffered the legal discrimination of that class.[4] They remained objects of contempt until recently and we shall see in

---

[1] *CYHYHP*, pp. 8a–9a.   [2] *Hsing-an hui-lan*, 38, 18a.   [3] Ibid., 47, 13b.
[4] T'ung-tsu Ch'ü has collected some material on the legal discrimination suffered by slaves in his *Law and Society in Traditional China*, pp. 186–200.

later chapters that their position in society was only marginally improved through the great stars of the nineteenth century.

Nowhere is the status of actors better shown than in the laws which forbade them or their families to sit for the official examinations, which, as the main gateway to the bureaucracy, were of the utmost importance in Chinese society. Edicts of 1313 and 1369 had already laid down this rule.[1] In 1652 it was restated and the government declared that if anybody had succeeded in by-passing the prohibition he was to be dismissed from his position.[2] A further decree of 1770 ordered that, since actors were of a menial profession, their sons and grandsons should be excluded from the examinations. It had been found that some people had become adopted by members of a better class to flout the edict of 1652. This was also forbidden to actors or their descendants.[3] These laws remained reasonably effective until 1905, when the examination system was abolished.

It was not only the 'vagabonds' of the wandering companies that suffered contempt and discrimination. The actors of the private companies were likewise excluded from the examinations and looked down upon by the family which they served. We saw earlier how Chiang T'ing-hsi regarded such people. The same attitude is reflected in the novel *The Dream of the Red Chamber*. When the hero Chia Pao-yü consorted with the actor Ch'i-kuan of the mansion, it was considered by his father a crime deserving a savage beating.[4]

Yet there was a degree of social mobility among actors. The lowly wanderer, subordinate to a common troupe-leader, could rise to join a company which performed at the banquets of the educated; and though he was still a virtual slave, at least his master was then a man of standing in society. A few strolling actors even climbed high enough to perform for the Manchu nobility in Peking. One artist, a certain O, began as a member of a wandering company in the countryside and then, as he grew more successful, acted during feasts at the houses of officials. Later he went to Peking where he gave performances for various aristocrats and was even seen in the Imperial Palaces.[5]

[1] Wang Hsiao-ch'uan, *Yüan Ming Ch'ing*, pp. 6, 11.
[2] *Hsüeh-cheng ch'üan-shu*, 43, 1a.   [3] Ibid., 43, 4a.
[4] *Hung-lou meng*, 33, *passim*. See a discussion and bibliography of this novel in C. T. Hsia, *The Classic Chinese Novel*, pp. 245–97, 396–8.
[5] *Chü-shuo*, 6, 209.

But the most outstanding instance of an actor who rose from the bottom to the top of his profession was Ch'en Ming-chih. He came from Su-chou and would act *ching* roles in the villages around the city. On one occasion, a great company of the city, the Han-hsiang, was going to perform at a banquet. At the last minute their *ching* actor was found to be missing. A messenger was sent to find an understudy, but none of the other great companies could help and, since he happened to be in Su-chou at the time, Ch'en acted the part. He won an outstanding ovation and was given a permanent place in the Han-hsiang troupe.

Some time later, when the K'ang-hsi Emperor came to the south and chose some actors to perform at court, Ch'en was among those selected. Twenty years afterwards he returned to the south after a career so brilliant that he was allowed to wear the clothes of an official of the seventh rank; and when he asked permission to build a mansion in Su-chou, the request was readily granted.[1]

Ch'en Ming-chih's was not an isolated case, but in general actors could rarely hope to raise themselves to a respectable position in society. It is natural that works devoted to the drama should mention famous actors, those who had risen to the top of their profession, and so we know more about distinguished than about ordinary actors. But certainly the lives of most of them were full of insecurity and hardship, and the majority took up their profession through necessity rather than choice.

One of the reasons for the generally inferior position of actors in society was that they were considered people of low moral standards. Among male actors, homosexuality was widespread. Public catamites were found in the large cities of both north and south China in the Ming and many of them were actors.[2] Even among the actors of the private mansions and their patrons there was much homosexuality. One known case was the famous actor Chin Feng of Hai-yen, who flourished in the late Ming. He fell into the clutches of Yen Shih-fan, a scurrilous politician noted for his ugliness, who was the son of an equally corrupt but more famous statesman, Yen Sung (d. 1568).[3] Shih-fan fell so deeply in

[1] Ibid., 6, 199–201. A more complete account in English of Ch'en Ming-chih can be found in Waley, *The Secret History of the Mongols*, pp. 85–7.

[2] See Wang Shu-nu, *Chung-kuo ch'ang-chi shih*, pp. 228–30, where quotations are made from primary sources.

[3] See the biographies of Yen Sung and his son in *Ming-shih*, 308, 10a ff.

love with the actor that 'if he was not with Chin during the day he could not eat, and if not with him at night, could not sleep.' After Shih-fan's political eclipse and execution, Chin also fell into decline.[1]

Yen Shih-fan's vice was found also among many educated men of the Ch'ing dynasty. One writer, referring to Peking in the late K'ang-hsi period, claims that 'homosexuality is now widespread enough that it is considered in bad taste not to keep elegant servants on one's household staff, and undesirable not to have singing boys around when inviting guests for dinner.'[2]

The lovers of the young actors included some very eminent men. One of them was Yüan Mei, who is known to have fallen in love with several actors, in Peking and elsewhere.[3] I shall be returning to the question of homosexuality and male prostitution among actors in later chapters.[4]

The prevalence of homosexuality among actors was accentuated by the fact that it was rare to include both men and women in any one theatrical company. Because male companies included no women, the female roles had to be played by men or boys. The need to assume female mannerisms and impersonate women was certainly a factor leading to homosexuality.[5]

The sexual habits of actresses, too, were open to question, for they were normally prostitutes. It was a necessary qualification of a good courtesan to be able to dance and sing. Many of them therefore became extremely fine actresses, despite the fact that

[1] *Chü-shuo*, 6, 201.   [2] *Ching-shih ou-chi*, p. 5b.
[3] See Waley, *Yuan Mei*, pp. 27, 109.
[4] Further material on homosexuality among actors in the early Ch'ing is available in Aoki Masaru, *Hsi-ch'ü shih*, pp. 447–8 and Wang Shu-nu, *Ch'ang-chi shih*, pp. 317–20.
[5] The custom of separating theatrical companies into male and female is very ancient in China. In A.D. 661 the Emperor Kao-tsung (650–84) of T'ang issued an edict forbidding women to perform in comedies. (See *Chiu T'ang-shu*, 4, 9a.) According to Wang Kuo-wei (1877–1927), the foremost authority of recent times on the ancient Chinese theatre, this implies that actresses already belonged to different companies from actors. (See *Ku-chü chüeh-se k'ao*, p. 245.) The *Chiao-fang chi* of 762 records (p. 18) a case of men dressing as women to perform female roles. For later periods only isolated cases of mixed troupes can be found, and even in these there were only one or two women in male companies or *vice versa*. In some places actors and actresses not only belonged to separate troupes, but excelled in different styles of drama. For instance, Ku Ts'ai, referring to Ho-feng, Hupeh, in 1703, records that all actresses were sixteen or seventeen years old and that they first learned *K'un-ch'ü* and later the regional drama of Hupeh. Actors, on the other hand, performed *Ch'in-ch'iang*. See *Jung-mei chi-yu*, p. 5a.

their bound feet severely hampered their mobility. This artificial deformity was, however, one reason why they never formed strolling companies.

The association of the prostitute with acting dates back well before the Ming, and the most famous actresses of the Yüan were also courtesans. The lives and talents of some of them have been recorded by Hsia T'ing-chih in his *Ch'ing-lou chi*.[1]

Like so many other social phenomena connected with the theatre, prostitution was subject to government restrictions. It is true that the Ming founder, Hung-wu, established a system of official prostitution, but this was abolished in the fifteenth century, and officials were forbidden to visit courtesans.[2] The Manchu penal code carried the same prohibition[3] and the Ch'ing emperors issued several edicts against prostitute-actresses.[4] A typical example, dated 1772, directed that they all abandon their profession and return to their home town.[5]

None of these measures was permanently effective. The reversal of the Ming policy resulted in a temporary decline in prostitution, but by the middle years of the Ming it was once again flourishing everywhere. Ta-t'ung in Shansi and Yang-chou, Kiangsu, were famous for their courtesans, but the empire's main centre for the profession was probably Nanking.[6] Similarly, the early Manchu emperors effected a fall in the fortunes of the courtesan, but they appear to have recovered by the late years of the eighteenth century.

A number of courtesans of the Ming and Ch'ing attained considerable fame as actresses, especially in seventeenth-century Nanking. Among the best of them were Li Shih, Pien Sai, Yang Yüan, Ku Mei, and Tung Pai, of whom the first two held the highest reputation for their stage arts.[7] As a courtesan, the best known was probably Ku Mei, whose quarters, called the Mei-lou, were famous among other things for their good food, and banquets were frequently held there.[8]

---

[1] See Waley, *The Secret History of the Mongols*, pp. 89 ff.
[2] See Levy, *A Feast of Mist and Flowers*, pp. 18–20.
[3] See Boulais, *Manuel du code chinois*, p. 691.
[4] See Wang Hsiao-ch'uan, *Yüan Ming Ch'ing*, pp. 18, 20, 23, 26, 44.
[5] *Ta-Ch'ing hui-tien shih-li*, 133, 16a.
[6] Wang Shu-nu, *Ch'ang-chi shih*, pp. 198 ff.
[7] *Pan-ch'iao tsa-chi*, 1, 1b. Levy has presented an annotated translation of this work in *A Feast of Mist and Flowers*, pp. 33 ff.
[8] Ku Mei married as a second wife the distinguished official Kung Ting-tzu

Courtesans often formed themselves into dramatic companies. For this reason, some of them were able to perform both *sheng* and *tan* parts. The actress Yin Ch'un was a case in point.[1] But we know also that male actors were sometimes included among the 'guests' of the courtesans and that they performed in the brothel quarters.[2] It is possible that they sometimes performed together with the inmates of the brothels.

Courtesans also visited the mansions of the rich to perform for them. For example, Chang Tai records that several eminent prostitutes went to his friend's house and took part in a performance with the servants.[3] These actresses seem to have been very popular at banquets. One author writes:

Famed prostitutes and fairy beauties felt deeply ashamed to go up on the stage and perform plays. If the party were filled with musical connoisseurs, they had to be strongly encouraged time and again before they would acquiesce. Their singing voices were modulated and the shadows of their fans blended; the entire party was overwhelmed with admiration. The one in charge (of the party) became greatly excited, gave them money and supplementary gifts, and suddenly increased tenfold (their ordinary recompense).[4]

The most illustrious courtesans were visited primarily by *literati*. It was therefore natural that they should concentrate their efforts mainly on the *K'un-ch'ü* drama. There were, however, acting courtesans who had mastered other styles of drama.[5]

The acting profession was, then, highly varied: it ranged from the wanderers to the permanent servants of the rich and from illtreated slave-boys to much sought-after courtesans. But in general fate did not smile upon Chinese actors and they certainly gave far more pleasure and enjoyment than they themselves received.

(1616–73) of Ho-fei in Anhwei (on whom see Hummel, *Eminent Chinese*, p. 431), but to her great sorrow she remained childless. When she died in Peking, she was widely mourned and her husband wrote a drama in her honour. See *Pan-ch'iao tsa-chi*, 2, 4b ff., translated in Levy, *A Feast of Mist and Flowers*, pp. 58 ff. Wang Shu-nu has collected material on Ku Mei and Tung Pai in *Ch'ang-chi shih*, pp. 211 ff.

[1] *Pan-ch'iao tsa-chi*, 2, 1b.   [2] Ibid., 3, 1b.   [3] *T'ao-an meng-i*, 7, 65.

[4] *Pan-ch'iao tsa-chi*, 1, 2b. I have used Levy's translation of this passage, see *A Feast of Mist and Flowers*, p. 41.

[5] Wang Shu-nu has collected further material on the styles of drama performed by courtesans in *Ch'ang-chi shih*, pp. 277–9.

The rise of regional styles of drama in the Ming helps to explain the universal popularity of dramatic performances. But the converse is an even more important factor: the profound influence of the theatre in the social life of the people undoubtedly gave an added impetus to the spread of regional styles, even to the most remote villages of the empire. It was this that produced the golden age of regional drama in the late eighteenth century, which was itself to exercise so vital an influence on the rise of the Peking Opera.

That the *K'un-ch'ü* became so popular among the educated was due in part to the economic and cultural supremacy of its region of origin. But much of the credit must go also to the famous courtesans who acted and sang it so well and to the social conditions which dictated that private servants could function also as actors. The great volume of trade along the Yangtze and other waterways did much to spread the styles of the *I-yang ch'iang* system. But had there not been among the people so many social occasions which demanded the performance of drama, the system would probably have wilted rather than grown in strength.

The spread of drama and its social aspects would seem to have produced a beneficial effect on one another. As a system of drama became heard in regions outside its original home, it created a form of entertainment which could accompany the major social occasions of the people; and these occasions in turn created the demand for more varied styles, or at least a base on which they might take root. This is why styles originally derived from the *I-yang ch'iang* could add elements from other styles. In short, we may conclude that the reasons for the richness and variety of the Chinese theatre of the Ch'ing were largely social and economic; and that the former were just as important as the latter and probably more so.

The intermingling of economic and social factors in the spread and growth of the drama of all styles and systems can perhaps be best crystallized by explaining in detail the situation of the drama in one specific city. The most appropriate example is Yang-chou in Kiangsu province, and it is to the theatre of that city that the next chapter will be devoted.

III

THE THEATRE IN YANG-CHOU

THE CITY of Yang-chou is of great interest in the history of the Chinese theatre because it demonstrates the impact of merchant patronage with particular clarity. However, there is a much more compelling reason why I have chosen Yang-chou for special treatment. It is the only city, apart from Peking, which has left behind enough material to make a detailed study possible. The principal source is the *Yang-chou hua-fang lu*, a clearly written guide-book to the city by Li Tou, completed in 1794 after some thirty years' preparation.[1] In view of the date of this work, the present chapter will concentrate on the late years of the eighteenth century.

We know enough from the sources to be able to state positively that other cities enjoyed a prospering theatrical life. Not very far from Yang-chou was Su-chou, still the centre of the *K'un-ch'ü* theatre. We shall see in chapter five that many of its actors were invited by the emperor to Peking. At least one company of Su-chou achieved national fame late in the eighteenth century. This was the Chi-hsiu, a somewhat exclusive troupe which sought its clientele from the specialist *K'un-ch'ü* devotee rather than the ordinary theatre-goer. When the Emperor Ch'ien-lung (1736–96) visited the south in 1784, the leading citizens of Su-chou tried to plan appropriate entertainment for him. But in all the city's troupes there was at least one weak point. The eminent *tan* actor Chin Te-hui suggested combining all the best artists of Su-chou, Hang-chou, and Yang-chou into one company. The proposal was taken up and proved such a success that the troupe stayed together after the Emperor left.[2] It was given the name Chi-hsiu and appears to have survived into the nineteenth century. One work of 1825

---

[1] See Hsieh Kuo-chen, *Ming-Ch'ing pi-chi t'an-ts'ung*, pp. 142–5. The *Yang-chou hua-fang lu* (*YCHFL*) has also been published, in greatly abbreviated form, and without the fifth *chüan* on the theatre, under the title *Yang-chou ming-sheng lu*.

[2] *Ting-an hsü-chi*, 4, 19a–20a.

claims that it had disbanded before that year,[1] but other evidence suggests that it was revived: when Chang Chi-liang visited Su-chou in 1827 he was informed that the company had ceased its activities only in the spring or summer of that year.[2]

There were several other renowned troupes in Su-chou[3] and its courtesans included some first-rate actresses. Among the most eminent was Chang Feng-ling who 'was extremely attractive on the stage and could perform to perfection and with genuine feeling both tragic and comic moments; no actor could reach her standards'.[4] Another was Ch'en T'ung-hsiang, born about 1765 in Chekiang. She was extremely unusual among Su-chou's courtesan-actresses in that her prowess lay not in *K'un-ch'ü* but in a form of folk opera popular in coastal Chekiang, one of the many styles known under the general name of *hua-ku hsi*. Ch'en consorted mainly with men of rich and educated families from Chekiang and Kiangsu who were not too keen on this lowly drama, but she would also occasionally visit the villages. The peasants rarely saw their own familiar drama acted by any but the wandering companies, and they would flock in huge crowds to see the performances of this prominent courtesan.[5]

Several other cities were good theatrical centres. Many excellent actors worked in Canton.[6] Hsi-an, too, was favoured with a number of famous drama groups about which a little is known, and I shall be discussing this city briefly in chapter four. According to Li Tou, the best actors came from An-ch'ing,[7] but no doubt many other cities could also boast first-class performers. Nevertheless, the volume of present-day knowledge on the theatre of the cities mentioned is slight by comparison with what can be learned from Li Tou's observations on Yang-chou.

During the Ch'ien-lung period, Yang-chou was a city of central importance both economically and culturally. It was the headquarters of the largest of Manchu China's eleven salt administrations, the Liang-huai, the influence of which extended to the greater part of east central China. This was a government orga-

---

[1] *Lü-yüan ts'ung-hua*, 12, 12b.   [2] *Chin-t'ai ts'an-lei chi*, 2, 6b.
[3] See a stele of 1791 quoted by Ou-yang Yü-ch'ien in 'Shih-t'an Yüeh-chü', in Ou-yang Yü-ch'ien, ed., *Chung-kuo hsi-ch'ü yen-chiu tzu-liao ch'u-chi*, p. 112; see also *Lü-yüan ts'ung-hua*, 12, 12b.
[4] *Wu-men hua-fang lu*, p. 12a.   [5] Ibid., pp. 14a–b.
[6] See Ou-yang Yü-ch'ien, 'Shih-t'an Yüeh-chü', p. 113.
[7] YCHFL, 5, 131.

nization and was managed by a chief salt commissioner, who was a Manchu, and a host of other lesser officials. Some of the salt merchants under its supervision could claim to be among the richest men in China,[1] and the merchants as a whole undoubtedly possessed the largest total capital of any single commercial or industrial group in the empire.[2] The city lay not far north of the junction between the Yangtze River and the Grand Canal and was hence an important stopping-point for vessels engaged in interprovincial trade. Certainly it was a prosperous and populous city and could be counted among the key economic cities of China. Culturally also it was among the richest and most advanced in the empire. It enjoyed an abundance of gardens, temples, and academies, and boasted some very distinguished poets. The 'eight eccentrics of Yang-chou' (*Yang-chou pa-kuai*) were among the most famous painters of their time and two excelled also as calligraphers.[3] All but one of them died in the 1750s or 1760s, but Lo P'in lived until 1799,[4] so that their careers may be said to have spanned the eighteenth century.

The walled city of Yang-chou was divided into two parts. The western third was the Chiu-ch'eng (Old City) and was separated from the eastern sector, the Hsin-ch'eng (New City), by a wall. North of the walls of Yang-chou was the Ts'ao River, the waters of which extended in an arc from the Pei-men (North Gate) of the Old City to a bridge called Kao-ch'iao, where they joined the Grand Canal north-east of the city. Two *li* from the Kao-ch'iao was the Ying-en Bridge and Pavilion. The region between the Kao-ch'iao and the Ying-en Bridge on the two banks of the Ts'ao River was one of the 'eight scenic spots of Yang-chou' and was called Hua-chu ying-en,[5] which means 'welcoming the emperor to celebrate his birthday'.

---

[1] See Ho Ping-ti, 'The Salt Merchants of Yang-chou', *Harvard Journal of Asiatic Studies*, xvii (1954), 150.

[2] Basing himself on the 1806 edition of the *Liang-huai yen-fa chih* (42, *passim*), Ho Ping-ti has calculated that the Liang-huai salt merchants contributed 36,370,968 taels to the imperial treasury between 1738 and 1804. The famous Hong merchants and the salt merchants of Kwangtung and Kwangsi combined gave only 3,950,000 taels between 1773 and 1832. See 'The Salt Merchants', pp. 153–4. It may be added for comparison that in the middle of the eighteenth century, 60,000 or 70,000 taels was considered a large fortune if owned by a private individual. Ibid., p. 150.

[3] See Ch'en Chih-mai, *Chinese Calligraphers and Their Art*, pp. 148, 150.

[4] See Ku Lin-wen, ed., *Yang-chou pa-chia shih-liao*.

[5] YCHFL, 1, 19–20 and *Yang-chou ming-sheng lu*, 1, 5b–6a.

Three of Yang-chou's Buddhist temples are of significance for this chapter. One was the Ch'ung-ning which lay north of the city on a particularly lovely site. It was built in 1783,[1] and was consequently quite new when Li Tou wrote his guide-book. The other two were much older and ranked among the 'eight great Buddhist shrines of Yang-chou'. They were the T'ien-ning Temple, near the Ch'ung-ning Temple just north of the city walls,[2] and the Kao-min Temple, which was some distance south-west of the city beside the Grand Canal not far from the point where it joined the Yangtze River.[3]

The Tien-ning and Kao-min were important temples, for it was there that Ch'ien-lung stayed when he visited Yang-chou.[4] Like his great predecessor K'ang-hsi,[5] Ch'ien-lung travelled to the south six times, the dates of his journeys being 1751, 1757, 1762, 1765, 1780 and, 1784.[6] On each occasion his destination was in or near Hang-chou, Chekiang, but he made a point of visiting Yang-chou during all his tours.

Imperial visitations were, of course, extremely elaborate affairs and Ch'ien-lung's journeys to the south involved the country in considerable economic dislocation.[7] In Yang-chou, as in other places, he was lavishly entertained. Some idea of the scale of the welcome given him may be gauged from the fact that by 1768 the salt merchants of Liang-huai had spent 4,670,000 taels on entertaining the Emperor and his retinue.[8]

One of the ways in which the merchants of Yang-chou endeavoured to please the Emperor was by arranging theatrical performances, of which Ch'ien-lung was known to be extremely fond. When their guest approached from the north, he would enter Yang-chou from the Hua-chu ying-en region. On both

[1] YCHFL, 4, 95.

[2] See YCHFL, 4, 82–4 and Yang-chou ming-sheng lu, 1, 17b–20a.

[3] See YCHFL, 7, 161–2 and Yang-chou ming-sheng lu, 2, 15a–16b.

[4] The Nan-hsün sheng-tien uses the phrase hsing-kung, indicating that the emperor stayed there, for both the T'ien-ning and Kao-min Temples. See Nan-hsün sheng-tien, 97, 7a and 97, 21a. This work, completed in 1766, is a record of Ch'ien-lung's first four journeys to the south.

[5] K'ang-hsi's southern tours are described in Spence, Ts'ao Yin and the K'ang-hsi Emperor, pp. 124 ff.

[6] YCHFL, 1, 1.   [7] See Waley, Yuan Mei, p. 54.

[8] See Ho Ping-ti, 'The Salt Merchants', p. 168. It may be added that when K'ang-hsi landed near Yang-chou on 4 Apr. 1705, he was met by salt merchants and presented with antiques, curios, books, and paintings. See Spence, Ts'ao Yin, p. 144.

sides of the Ts'ao River there were many stages, and in this way Ch'ien-lung could enjoy the drama as the imperial barge drew near the city.[1] Indeed the patronage of the Emperor was a major

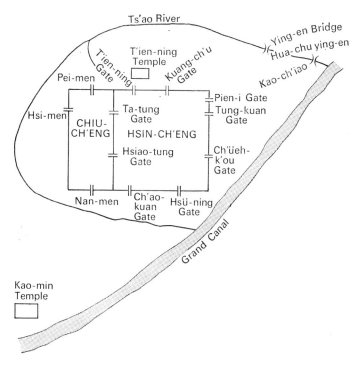

1. Chart of Yang-chou and Surroundings
(This chart is based on *YCHFL*, 9, 186–91 and *Nan-hsün sheng-tien*, 92, 32a–33a).

cause of the prosperity of the theatre in Yang-chou and in its drama it was certainly among China's first cities. The government was keenly aware of its eminence and chose it as the site for the commission of censorship mentioned in chapter two. It is worth remarking, too, that the period of Ch'ien-lung's southern journey was considered by some the heyday of the theatrical life of the south.[2]

Like those of other regions, Yang-chou's drama companies fell into two distinct categories, the *ya-pu* (elegant companies) and the *hua-pu* (flower companies). The former performed the aristo-

[1] *YCHFL*, 1, 20.   [2] *Lü-yüan ts'ung-hua*, 12, 12b.

cratic *K'un-ch'ü* and the latter the more popular styles, of which
a substantial range could be heard in Yang-chou. However, the
most convenient headings under which to discuss Yang-chou's
theatre companies are, firstly, companies attached to the salt
merchant families, and, secondly, companies independent of the
merchants.

Companies Attached to the Salt Merchant Families

Until 1831, when the merchant monopoly of the Liang-huai
Salt Administration was abolished, there were in Yang-chou
thirty head merchants (*tsung-shang*) appointed by the Administration.[1] The Hua-chu ying-en region was divided into thirty
separate areas, each of which was controlled by a head merchant.
Elaborate pavilions were put up as stages, and it was here that the
head merchants and their families welcomed the Emperor with
drama during his southern tours.[2]

The Hua-chu ying-en region was not the only place where the
merchants watched drama. They also attended performances in
the main temples. We know that the T'ien-ning and other
temples were frequented by merchants and that drama was often
performed there.[3] Moreover, a great merchant family could own,
in addition to the family mansion, several gardens scattered
throughout the city and could hold dramatic performances in all
its residences. A case in point is the wellknown merchant Chiang
Ch'un, Yang-chou's most eminent drama patron. He lived in the
Nan-ho hsia Street, which ran along the southern wall of the New
City, and also owned the famous K'ang-shan Garden. In addition,
he had a garden built beside the Ch'ung-ning Temple.[4]

It was taken for granted that the rich of Yang-chou patronized
the theatre. Indeed it was a matter for comment if they did not.
Of one merchant, the famous philanthropist Pao Chih-tao (1743–
1801)[5] from She-hsien in Hui-chou it is reported that he 'did not
have drama performed'.[6] The observation comes immediately
after a long passage on the extravagance of the salt merchants and
implies that Pao Chih-tao was most unusual in his attitude to the
theatre. Not only the head merchants, but the lesser ones and
other rich people ran private companies. Unfortunately, the

---

[1] See Ho Ping-ti, 'The Salt Merchants', pp. 137–8.
[2] *YCHFL*, 1, 20.   [3] *YCHFL*, 5, 107.   [4] *YCHFL*, 12, 274.
[5] See Waley, *Yuan Mei*, p. 108.   [6] *YCHFL*, 6, 150.

details of only a few of them are told us by Li Tou. He does not record the principles on which he has selected companies for description. No doubt he was in a position to comment in detail on only some of them, for his sources of information—personal contact with the families to which the companies were attached, or friends among people with such connections—cannot have extended to every great family. But it is perhaps more likely that he wrote only of the most important companies.

The famous salt merchant families included the Hsü, Hung, Chiang, Huang, Chang, Wang, and Ch'eng.[1] Li Tou gives a list of people who maintained companies. He names in all seven, Huang Yüan-te, Chang Ta-an, Wang Ch'i-yüan, Hsü Shang-chih, Ch'eng Ch'ien-te, Hung Ch'ung-shih, and Chiang Ch'un (Kuang-ta).[2] Information on the actors in the companies of the last four of these are provided in the guide-book.

The company of Hsü Shang-chih was called simply the Hsü company. It is said that its establishment represented the beginning of an era of triumph for *K'un-ch'ü* in Yang-chou, but in view of the city's proximity to Su-chou, we may be sure that the style had enjoyed some popularity there earlier, at least among the rich. Hsü Shang-chih had apparently decided deliberately to found a first-rate *K'un-ch'ü* company, and to this end he had some of the most famous actors of Su-chou brought to Yang-chou and patronized them as a private company in his mansion.[3] Later the Hsü company disbanded and some of its actors returned to Su-chou, where they entered the private company of one of the city's most eminent citizens.[4]

Among the finest actors of the Hsü company was its leader Yü Wei-ch'en. He had earlier been in the service of a rich man in Su-chou, but later fell upon bad days and took up employment with Hsü Shang-chih. Li Tou gives the following sketch of him:

His face was dark, he was heavily bearded, and he loved to drink. He could read both the Classics and the Standard Histories, and was able to explain the musical tablatures [of the *K'un-ch'ü* drama]. He was of a generous nature and took great pleasure in doing kind deeds for others. Once he saw a small beggar boy from Su-chou in the mutton markets

[1] YCHFL, 1, 3.

[2] YCHFL, 5, 107. The name Kuang-ta was the business name of Chiang Ch'un (*Kuo-ch'ao ch'i-hsien lei-cheng*, 457, 6b) and it is possible that the other men mentioned here are called by their business names.

[3] YCHFL, 5, 107.   [4] YCHFL, 5, 125.

at the Hsiao-tung (Small East) Gate,[1] so he took off his fox-skin coat and gave it to the child.[2]

Yü seems to have been better educated than most of his profession and to have retained some affection for his old working-place.

Another distinguished member of the Hsü company was the *ching*[3] Ma Wen-kuan. He was noted for his fine voice and the versatility of his acting: he carried conviction in portraying almost any kind of feeling, anger, amusement, and of course the Confucian virtues of loyalty and righteousness. Above all, he could play not only men's but also women's parts and 'was finer in them than the actresses'.[4] This is a striking statement, for Li Tou seems to be implying that women, and not the male *tan*, were the best executants of female roles. Such an attitude could not have been found in Peking, where good actresses had become a rarity by the late eighteenth century. The contrast between Yang-chou and Peking may perhaps reflect the slightly less rigidly Confucian atmosphere in southern China compared to that in the north.

To the subject of the brothel quarters where Yang-chou's good actresses were found I shall be returning later. In the companies of the salt merchants female roles were of course played by men, and probably the best *tan* in the Hsü company was Wu Fu-t'ien (*tzu* Ta-yu). In his young days Wu had been attached to the superintendent of customs (*chüeh-shih*), T'ang Ying (*c.* 1680–1760), who was in his time the most famous official in charge of porcelain at Ching-te chen.[5] Wu had learned the *pa-fen* style of calligraphy[6] and could recite sections from historical works.

It is the highly educated and not the actors who have written the source material on the theatre. For this reason we are told a great deal about the relations between the *literati* and actors, but

[1] The Small East Gate linked the Old and New Cities. The area nearby in the Old City was famous for its food markets. *YCHFL*, 9, 196.

[2] *YCHFL*, 5, 122.

[3] In *YCHFL*, 5, 123, Ma Wen-kuan is called a *pai-mien*, *erh-mien* or *fu-ching*. A *pai-mien* was a kind of *ching* and *erh-mien* was synonymous with *fu-ching*, itself a kind of *ching*. See also Chou I-pai, *Chung-kuo hsi-chü shih*, pp. 537–8.

[4] *YCHFL*, 5, 123.

[5] See Hummel, *Eminent Chinese of the Ch'ing Period*, p. 442 and Waley, *Yuan Mei*, pp. 159–60.

[6] The *pa-fen* style of calligraphy was devised during the Han period. Examples dating from that time are given by Ch'en Chih-mai in *Chinese Calligraphers*, pp. 41, 43, 45. Tu Fu developed a passion for this kind of writing (ibid., p. 213) and the famous calligrapher of the Ch'ing dynasty, Teng Shih-ju (1743–1805), was an accomplished master of the style (ibid., pp. 150, 152).

very little about relations among the actors themselves. In this respect Wu Fu-t'ien is exceptional, for a short story is recorded about his friendship with the middle-aged Chu Wen-yüan, who belonged to the Hsü company as a *lao-sheng* (an exponent of the roles of old men).

After the Hsü company disbanded, its actors returned to Su-chou, where it happened that a certain customs superintendent managed to force them into the company of his . . . mansion. When the troupe of Hung [Ch'ung-shih] was formed, all the actors followed each other in making their escape [to join it]. Only Wu Ta-yu and Chu Wen-yüan remained to take care of the superintendent's company and were unable to escape. Their families became poorer and poorer, their relationship with one another deeper and deeper. They swore to one another that for the rest of their lives they would never belong to separate companies. After a year, however, Wen-yüan did leave, he entered the Hung company, and remained in it for three years before returning. Ta-yu found out what he was doing through a spy and succeeded in forcing him to come into the superintendent's company and stay there for ten years. By this time Ta-yu's family had gradually become rich, while Wen-yüan was so poor that he would have welcomed death. He induced a friend of Ta-yu's to acknowledge his fault for him. Ta-yu remained resentful that he had gone back on the promise and also knew about his impoverished circumstances, so he asked the customs superintendent to dismiss Wen-yüan.[1]

Wu had certainly nursed his grievance for a long time, and seems to have succeeded in taking his revenge. As it happened, the two never again belonged to the same company. Soon after, Wu moved to Yang-chou where he joined the company of Chiang Ch'un. Hearing of Chu Wen-yüan's reputation, Chiang invited that actor to join his company. Chu readily agreed, but was killed in an accident on the way from Su-chou.

Chu Wen-yüan was not the only actor of the Hsü company who later joined that of Hung Ch'ung-shih. This is clear from the story just related. We are elsewhere told that half the members of the Hung company had formerly belonged to the Hsü. In some cases, actors who had been of only secondary importance in the Hsü company achieved their greatest success when they became attached to the Hung. Chu Wen-yüan himself was one example.[2]

[1] *YCHFL*, 5, 125.   [2] *YCHFL*, 5, 125–6.

Apart from men originally in the Hsü, Li Tou gives the names of over forty actors of the Hung company, including the famous Chin Te-hui whose suggestion had led to the establishment of Su-chou's Chi-hsiu company. This number is much more than he lists for any other company,[1] but he does not deal with any individual in detail. For most actors he writes only very sparse comments. The performer whom he praises most warmly is the *ching* Ch'en Tien-chang, about whom he says that 'in the delicacy and grace of his acting nobody in his generation could compare with him.' Another actor was the *ch'ou* Ting Hsiu-jung, 'who would crack obscene jokes and insert amusing antics causing convulsions of laughter among the spectators'. The Hung family was apparently fairly free from puritanical rigidity. Sometimes Li's comments are derogatory. He says of one actor Chou Wei-pai that 'he could not sing at all, and looked quite worn out. All he could do was to talk in dialogue sections'.

Li Tou has also recorded some comments about the personality of a few actors. For instance, he writes of the *tan* Chu Yeh-tung that 'he was good at writing poetry... and was versed in Buddhist books. He often wanted to buy a small monastery and live there himself.' And of course the company included the usual toper. Shen Wen-cheng 'had an enormous capacity for wine and could drink from sunset to dawn without succumbing to intoxication'.[2] Perhaps the most important example refers to Chou Wei-pai, mentioned above. 'He was a good physician and would dispense medicine without asking for a gratuity. . . . In years of calamity he would give out coffins',[3] presumably for his poor colleagues in the company and their families. Obviously, such a man would be very useful, and Chou's ability as a doctor may have been the main reason why an actor who could not sing was allowed to remain a member of so good a company as that of Hung Ch'ung-shih.

Another patron of the *K'un-ch'ü* was Chiang Ch'un. In 1773 he acted as host at a performance in his mansion of the newly written *Ssu-hsien ch'iu* (*The Four Strings of Autumn*) by Chiang Shih-ch'üan (1725-85), perhaps the most famous Chinese dramatist of the eighteenth century, who was at the time in charge of

---

[1] On the actors of the Hung company see *YCHFL*, 5, 125-9. A list of Yang-chou's actors may be found in Chou I-pai, *Hsi-chü shih*, pp. 540-4.

[2] *YCHFL*, 5, 126-7.   [3] *YCHFL*, 5, 129.

Yang-chou's An-ting Academy.[1] Among Chiang Ch'un's guests on this occasion was the poet Yüan Mei, who was a friend of Shih-ch'üan's.[2] Yüan Mei was apparently very much impressed with the leading *tan* actor, Hui-lang, and wrote a poem on the excellence of his art.[3] Unfortunately we do not know if the company which performed the drama was invited from outside Chiang's mansion or was his private group.

The only *K'un-ch'ü* company known to have been founded and privately patronized by Chiang Ch'un was the Te-yin or Chiang company, established some time after 1773. It became a considerable attraction after its formation and many actors joined it from the Hung company. Yü Wei-ch'en was invited to be its manager, because Chiang Ch'un was highly impressed by his acting and general ability. Chiang would often drink and play cards with Yü and the two men became good friends.[4] The Te-yin company's flourishing condition under these two men is shown by the fact that the group continued to function after its founder's death in 1793. It then came under the patronage of Hung Chen-yüan but its name remained unchanged.[5]

One of the most unusual features of Li Tou's presentation of Yang-chou's drama companies is that he names not only actors but also famous instrumental players of the accompanying orchestras. One of the city's best drummers was Chu Nien-i, who began in the Hsü company and later joined the Hung. Li Tou likens the sounds Chu made on his drum to 'the scattering of rice on a bridal chair or heavy rain drops, tearing cloth or breaking bamboo'. Another fine instrumentalist was Hsü Sung-ju, who played the *ti-tzu* so important in the *K'un-ch'ü*. Like Chu, he began his career as a member of the Hsü company. He later joined Chiang Ch'un's Te-yin company. It is said of him that he had no teeth, a considerable handicap for a flautist. 'He used silver instead and would clamp [his instrument] against his gums; he never played a note out of tune'.[6]

---

[1] Chu Hsiang, 'Chiang Shih-ch'üan', in Cheng Chen-to, ed., *Chung-kuo wen-hsüeh yen-chiu*, p. 471. This article (pp. 467–88) is the principal secondary work on Chiang and was written originally in 1925. The drama *Ssu-hsien ch'iu* is discussed pp. 479–80. See also Waley, *Yuan Mei*, pp. 73, 106–7.

[2] Ibid., pp. 72–4.

[3] *Hsiao-ts'ang shan-fang shih-chi*, 23, 6b. The poem is translated by Waley in *Yuan Mei*, p. 107.

[4] YCHFL, 5, 127.   [5] YCHFL, 5, 107.   [6] YCHFL, 5, 129–30.

Although the merchant families in general claimed to prefer the *K'un-ch'ü* theatre to the *hua-pu*, no doubt partly as a way of declaring their good taste to those more educated than they and hence proclaiming their respectability, there is one known example of a salt merchant who maintained a *hua-pu* company. This was Chiang Ch'un, whom I have already noted as the founder of the Te-yin company. Chiang seems to have taken the task of forming a *hua-pu* company quite seriously. 'Being unable to found it from his own household, he gathered together and invited with presents famous *tan* from all regions, such as Yang Pa-kuan of Su-chou and Hao T'ien-hsiu of An-ch'ing'.[1] The company was known as the Ch'un-t'ai and his two companies, the Te-yin and Ch'un-t'ai, were then called the Inner and Outer Chiang companies.[2]

The Ch'un-t'ai holds a rather special place in the history of Chinese drama. Not only was it the only *hua-pu* company in Yang-chou privately sponsored by a salt merchant, but it was the first known case since the sixteenth century of a private company in the Kiangnan region which did not devote itself to *K'un-ch'ü*. Chiang's need to import actors from outside his household shows clearly how unusual his venture was. Yet it was a symptom of the growing importance of the *hua-pu* to the higher strata of society that so eminent a man as Chiang Ch'un was prepared to devote so much energy to the creation of his own *hua-pu* company. It seems that a number of styles were performed by the Ch'un-t'ai company and some of its best actors had mastered several different regional forms. For instance, Fan Ta, known to connoisseurs as 'the wizard of the theatre', excelled in Clapper Opera, *I-yang ch'iang, lo-lo ch'iang*,[3] and *erh-huang* as well as the elegant *K'un-ch'ü*. However, the styles most emphasized were the *Ching-ch'iang* and Clapper Opera. In fact the Ch'un-t'ai company became a place of fusion of these two styles and its actors took over the best dramas of each into their repertoire. The *Ching-*

---

[1] *YCHFL*, 5, 131.

[2] *YCHFL*, 5, 107. Inner companies performed *K'un-ch'ü*, outer, *hua-pu*.

[3] The origins of *lo-lo ch'iang* are obscure. It is known to have been heard in Peking by 1744, but may be somewhat older. Some scholars, including Chou I-pai (*Hsi-chü shih*, pp. 564–5), consider that it is the same as *ch'ui-ch'iang* and is still heard in some Peking operas under that name or *nan lo-ch'iang*. Others, especially Hsia Yeh, think that *lo-lo ch'iang* is a completely independent style. See *Hsi-ch'ü yin-yüeh yen-chiu*, p. 77.

ch'iang item *Mai po-po* and the well known Clapper piece *Kun-lou*[1] were among those adopted by the Ch'un-t'ai company.[2]

The drama *Kun-lou* was the creation and showpiece of eighteenth-century China's most famous actor, Wei Ch'ang-sheng, whose fascinating career will be considered in chapter four. He arrived in Yang-chou by 1788[3] and became for a time a member of the Ch'un-t'ai company. His influence on its actors was profound, and both Yang Pa-kuan and Hao T'ien-hsiu learned the Clapper Opera from him.[4] Wei appears in fact to have been the prime moving force behind the troupe's adoption of this originally northern form of opera.

Since the Ch'un-t'ai company was largely composed not of Chiang Ch'un's household servants but of visiting stars, its composition was rather more fluid than that of the other troupes of the salt merchants. Moreover, its members did not feel the need to devote all their time to their patron. Wei Ch'ang-sheng, Fan Ta, and Hao T'ien-hsiu were all found frequently in the market-places and the villages outside Yang-chou,[5] and were as popular with the common people as with Chiang Ch'un and his friends. Yet the Ch'un-t'ai company maintained a definite identity and, like the Te-yin, survived its patron's death. Li Tou, who wrote not long after that event, names the company's master as Lo Jung-t'ai.[6]

General Remarks on the Companies of the Salt Merchants

Despite its value as the principal source-book for the foregoing information, Li Tou's work is not without its limitations, some of which will already have become clear. In commenting on actors, the author has strung together interesting facts and episodes and intermingled them with observations based on personal experience or hearsay. In some cases his remarks are limited to the dramas in which the particular actor excelled or to an elegant, but somewhat stereotyped phrase. For no actor can we piece together a plausible biography or write a coherent critique. Any analysis of Yang-chou's companies must therefore be tentative and broad conclusions are in general hard to reach.

One matter that is, however, constantly mentioned is move-

---

[1] These two dramas are discussed below in appendix C, pp. 250-1.
[2] *YCHFL*, 5, 131.   [3] *Yen-p'u tsa-chi*, 2, 17a.   [4] *YCHFL*, 5, 131.
[5] *Hua-pu nung-t'an*, p. 225.   [6] *YCHFL*, 5, 107.

ment from one company to another. There are in all twenty-five cases of recorded movement between Yang-chou's *K'un-ch'ü* companies.[1] Seven are from the Hsü to the Hung, three from the Hung to the Chiang and seven from the Hsü to the Chiang. There is not one case of an actor leaving the Chiang company.

It has already been noted, in the story of Wu Fu-t'ien and Chu Wen-yüan, that when the Hsü company disbanded, its actors left for Su-chou and later came back to Yang-chou to join the newly founded troupe of Hung Ch'ung-shih. Moreover, we know that the Chiang company included among its members a number of actors formerly in the Hung company. It seems, then, that these three companies were not contemporary but rather flourished one after the other. Probably there was, at any one time, only one definitely leading *K'un-ch'ü* company in Yang-chou. The company was not permanent, but might suspend its activities or lose its best members after a few years, and then reappear under the patronage of a different merchant but to a large extent composed of the same actors. There were of course a few actors who did not move with their group: Li Wen-i left the Hung not for the Te-yin but for the famous Chi-hsiu troupe of Su-chou.[2] But the general pattern is fairly clear, and it is that groups of *K'un-ch'ü* actors tended to stay together.

There were, among Yang-chou's private companies, other kinds of movement besides transfer from one patron to another. I have already mentioned several actors who took up residence in nearby Su-chou after leaving Yang-chou and *vice versa*. Interchange of a rather different kind is evident in the way some actors abandoned *K'un-ch'ü* for *hua-pu* or the other way around. The famous *hua-pu* performer Fan Ta had begun his career in *K'un-ch'ü*. A less distinguished example was Yü Mei-kuan who left a *Ching-ch'iang* company to join the *K'un-ch'ü* Hsü company.[3] This sort of mobility was limited, since only a few actors could master more than one style. The important point is that it operated in both directions. This suggests that, despite the rise of *hua-pu*, the elegant theatre had by no means lost its influence. This situation contrasts strongly with that in Peking at about the same time. There, a number of actors transferred their atten-

---

[1] I have listed these examples in 'The Theatre in Yang-chou in the Late Eighteenth Century', *Papers on Far Eastern History* 1 (Mar. 1970), pp. 24–5.
[2] YCHFL, 5, 126.   [3] YCHFL, 5, 123.

tion from *K'un-ch'ü* to the less genteel styles, but few did the reverse.

In Peking, several *K'un-ch'ü* companies were forced to disband owing to lack of interest in their art. But this was probably not the reason for the dispersal of certain troupes attached to the salt merchants of Yang-chou, and other causes must be sought. The death of the patron's father or mother and a consequent mourning period would no doubt often compel a merchant to forego his company. If a patron died himself or fell on evil days financially, his private actors would be forced to seek other masters. It is very striking in this regard that none of the private Yang-chou companies is reported to have devolved upon the son of a patron. This is understandable if financial ruin was the cause, but after Chiang Ch'un's death his two troupes also left his family. Probably the good groups of Yang-chou attained a reputation which was only partly dependent on the fame of the man they served, and sometimes exercised a degree of choice in their patron. The members of each troupe all began as household servants, but those who were especially good in their art came to be regarded first and foremost as actors and tended to lose their identity as servants.

This means, in fact, that members of Yang-chou's private *K'un-ch'ü* companies could enjoy long careers on the stage. All were trained in youth and a few were still acting in old age. Ku T'ien-i, who belonged to Huang Yüan-te's company, and Chang Kuo-hsiang, attached to Chang Ta-an's, both remained competent and active in male roles at the age of about eighty. Li Tou also mentions several performers, such as Hsü T'ien-fu and Ma Chi-mei, both of the Hsü troupe, who took up acting the parts of young women in middle or old age.[1] This can be seen as significant when we consider that in the Anhwei companies of early nineteenth-century Peking (to which I shall be returning in chapter five), *tan* actors were considered old at thirty.[2]

Much of the material presented so far shows the members of Yang-chou's private troupes as an exceptional group of actors. They were unusual also in their social status, which was not nearly as lowly as that of Yang-chou's other known stage-artists. One reason for this was that they were relatively well paid.[2] To be

---

[1] *YCHFL*, 5, 124–5.
[2] The salaries of Yang-chou's actors ranged from 7.3 taels down to 3.6 taels,

sure, the contrast between Wu T'ien-fu's riches and Chu Wen-yüan's poverty, to which reference was made earlier, indicates that not all private actors were equal financially, but in general they enjoyed a greater degree of security than the performers outside the patronage of the salt merchants.

Another important point is that many of the salt merchants' actors had received some education. The reader will recall that Wu Fu-t'ien could recite historical texts, that Yü Wei-ch'en could read the Classics, the Standard Histories and *K'un-ch'ü* musical tablatures and that Chu Yeh-tung could write poetry and had an understanding of some Buddhist books, to mention but a few examples. In short, a number of these actors were far from illiterate, and education was an excellent means of rising in the social scale.

Despite the detailed points told us about such matters as the educational level of the private actors, it is not possible to give more than an approximate indication of the dates when the various companies flourished. Li Tou says that 'Chiang Kuang-ta formed the Te-yin company and again collected *hua-pu* actors to found the Ch'un-t'ai company',[1] and thus suggests that the establishment of the Te-yin company antedated that of the Ch'un-t'ai. Wei Ch'ang-sheng acted in the Ch'un-t'ai company in 1788, so it is clear that both Chiang Ch'un's companies were flourishing by the late 1780s. Furthermore, both were still active when Chiang died in 1793.

I mentioned earlier that the Hung company was formed after the Hsü disbanded but before the formation of the Te-yin. In fact we know from the story of Wu Fu-t'ien's quarrel with Chu Wen-yüan that the Hung lasted at least four years: after the members of the former Hsü company returned from Su-chou to join it, Chu stayed a year in that city and then moved to Yang-chou, acting there in the Hung company for three years. He then lived in Su-chou for ten years before his death on the way back to Yang-chou. This cannot have been later than 1793 since it is reported by Li Tou. Thus the collapse of the Hsü company took place at least fourteen years earlier than 1793, that is in 1779 or

with three grades between the extremes, 6.4, 5.2, and 4.8 taels. These were probably rates given for each performance. The actors in the companies attached to the salt merchant families all received the highest salary of 7.3 taels. *YCHFL*, 5, 122.

[1] *YCHFL*, 5, 107.

before. Probably, then, the Hsü was Yang-chou's principal *K'un-ch'ü* company of the 1770s, the Hung of the late 1770s and early 1780s, and the Te-yin of the 1780s and early 1790s.

The Theatre Outside the Salt Merchant Families

Li Tou's guide-book devotes considerable space to the companies of the salt merchant families and only very little to other kinds of troupes. Yet naturally they were not the only people in Yang-chou who appreciated the theatre. The regional gazetteer of the city and its surroundings records that official families would sometimes give banquets with various kinds of entertainment when engaged in some item of public business. Actors were brought in from distant places and performed all sorts of dramas, songs, and dances. Such events were not particularly common but, when they did occur, were extremely lavish.[1]

Popular companies were also of great importance in and around Yang-chou. Mostly they were made up of local people who themselves took the initiative to form groups. The music, rhythm, costumes, and decoration were, not surprisingly, very crude by comparison with the drama performed in the great mansions. The limited means of the ordinary companies excluded the possibility of their supplying the luxurious costumes and stage properties available to the rich.

A few popular companies performed *K'un-ch'ü*, especially inside the city walls. Yet it was true of Yang-chou as elsewhere that the demand among the ordinary people for the elegant drama was comparatively small. In the fifth lunar month of each year, the popular *K'un-ch'ü* companies disbanded to make way for the actors of other styles.

The *hua-pu* drama was extremely popular both in the city of Yang-chou and in the nearby villages. Inside the city walls it was in the summer that the *hua-pu* companies entertained the people most often. However, as in other places, they regularly performed in the villages during the spring and autumn sacrifices to the gods of the harvest.[2] 'In the second and eighth lunar months, [the troupes] would wander around performing, and all the old peasants and fishermen would gather to enjoy it. This has been so for a long time.'[3]

---

[1] See *Yang-chou fu-chih* (1810 ed.), 60, 8a.
[2] YCHFL, 5, 130.   [3] *Hua-pu nung-t'an*, p. 225.

Popular drama was performed also during festivals. Until the K'ang-hsi period, prostitutes called *yüeh-hu* had given performances at a ceremony to welcome the new year on the day before the New Year Festival, but when the *yüeh-hu* were banned this custom ceased. In later times, drama was regularly performed to celebrate the Lantern Festival. Instead of *yüeh-hu*, it was men who acted and they dressed themselves as women. The festival itself fell on the 15th of the first month, but the celebrations lasted from the 13th to the 18th.[1]

Feastdays of the popular gods also gave the opportunity for dramatic performances. This is made quite clear in a nineteenth-century work on the customs of I-cheng county, just outside Yang-chou city.

The 2nd day of the second month is the feastday of the local god of the soil. The shops that sell paper images cut up paper to make robes [to clothe the images of the god] and then paint them. People buy them as an offering and then put them on [the images in] the public shrines in the large streets and small lanes. In this district they put up many lanterns in front of the images of the god. Some people steal the lanterns to light their womenfolk home so that those who do not easily conceive will become pregnant. If this is successful, [they wait until] the feastday comes round the following year and then return ten lanterns for the one they have stolen. These they place in front of the image. Beside the good-luck shrines near the government offices straw stages are built and local dramas performed for all the crowd to see.[2]

The same work provides a further vivid example.

The 23rd day [of the sixth month] is the feastday of the fire-star (Mars), and at all the temples dedicated to him gatherings are held. In places where there is no temple, dramas are performed for many days on straw stages put up in an open place. Though these structures are called 'straw stages', they are in fact very sturdy. Side platforms are also erected for the onlookers. Everybody takes the opportunity of the feastday to make merry. Worshipping the god is merely the excuse.[3]

---

[1] *YCHFL*, 9, 197–8; *Yang-chou fu-chih*, 60, 9a.

[2] *Chen-chou feng-t'u chi*, p, 2b. There were a great many local gods of the soil. They were quite separate from the more famous and generally worshipped agricultural deities like Hou-t'u. See Doré, *Recherches sur les superstitions en Chine*, IIème partie, *Le panthéon chinois*, pp. 894–9.

[3] *Chen-chou feng-t'u chi*, p. 6b. The five planets Venus, Jupiter, Mercury, Mars, and Saturn were respectively the stars of the five elements: metal, wood, water, fire, and earth. See Doré, *Recherches*, IIème partie, pp. 1211–16, where details on planetary folklore can be found.

The secularization of these religious festivals, to which I referred in chapter two, is here pointed out with special clarity.

The feastdays of Kuan-yin on the 19th of the second, sixth and ninth lunar months were celebrated very splendidly in and near Yang-chou. Large groups of people would gather together and then go to the mountains to make merry. The custom was most popular among the villagers, but the people of 'the wards, shops, streets and alleys' were only slightly less enthusiastic.[1] Although there is no specific record of theatrical performances given during these celebrations in the Ch'ien-lung period, it is known that in later times drama was associated with them, and it is very likely that this was already the case late in the eighteenth century.[2]

The range of drama offered by Yang-chou's *hua-pu* companies was extremely wide. Their repertoire included a large number of items based on Yüan dramas,[3] as well as lighter folk-stories. Chiao Hsün (1763–1820) stresses the ancient ideal of the importance of ethical content in drama by remarking that the themes of many popular operas performed in the Yang-chou region centered on 'loyalty, filial piety, chastity and righteousness'.[4] Among the examples he signals out is the well known piece *Ch'ing-feng t'ing*[5] which records the punishment of an unfilial son. But Chiao frankly admits that many items were somewhat bawdy, and he blames the influence of Wei Ch'ang-sheng for this. He claims that by the second decade of the nineteenth century there had been a gradual return to the older and purer ways,[6] but it is possible that he was describing the situation as he believed it should have been rather than as it actually was.

But more striking than the range of pieces was the variety of styles heard in and near Yang-chou. The style of drama favoured at the Lantern Festival festivities mentioned above belonged to the category of *hua-ku hsi*.[7] This popular form combined with the folk-songs of the area and developed into *Yang-chü*, which is nowadays the most widely loved local opera in the Yang-chou region.[8] In addition, the people of the city and its surrounding

[1] YCHFL, 16, 366; Yang-chou ming-sheng lu, 4, 8b.
[2] See Sung Tz'u, 'Yang-chü', in Hua-tung hsi-ch'ü chü-chung chieh-shao, I, 34.
[3] YCHFL, 5, 130.   [4] Hua-pu nung-t'an, p. 225.
[5] Ibid., pp. 227–9. See also appendix C, pp. 247–9.
[6] Hua-pu nung-t'an, p. 225.   [7] YCHFL, 9, 198; Yang-chou fu-chih, 60, 9a.
[8] An excellent treatment of the development, music and dramatic pieces of Yang-chü may be found in Sung Tz'u, 'Yang-chü', pp. 32–45. Musical notation of

districts could enjoy pieces belonging to the *Ching-ch'iang*,
Ch'in-ch'iang, *I-yang ch'iang*, *lo-lo ch'iang*, or *erh-huang* styles.[1]
Finally, several different styles of 'drum tunes' (*ku-ch'ü*) were
performed in Yang-chou's streets and market-places by the city's
ubiquitous story-tellers.[2]

In the musical styles they performed, the popular theatrical
companies were far more varied than the private troupes of the
salt merchants. In accordance with their more limited financial
means they were, on the other hand, rather more restricted in the
types of actor they contained. Whereas the private companies
included *mo*, *wai*, and various kinds of *sheng*, *ching*, and *tan*, and
were in this respect similar to the companies of the Yüan *tsa-chü*,[3]
the popular Yang-chou groups did not distinguish between *mo*
and *wai* actors and were in other ways much simpler in their
categorization of performers. The most important actors were *tan*
and even in Chiang Ch'un's Ch'un-t'ai company most of the
leading members belonged to this type. *Ch'ou* or clowns were also
significant. 'They were best in bawdy sections. Very prominent
in their parts were confidence tricks or vulgar behaviour, [the
actions of] clumsy women and stupid men and the perverse
accusations of pedlars.'[4] *Sheng* actors also existed in the *hua-pu*
companies but they were in general less prominent than the *tan* or
ch'ou.[5] There is a sharp contrast here between the popular theatre
of eighteenth-century Yang-chou and that of late nineteenth-
century Peking.

Another implication of the financial stringencies of the popular
companies was that they could rarely be sure of access to one
definite place where they could display their art. Like their

---

160 excerpts from this kind of opera is given in Wu Chün-ta, ed., *Yang-chü yin-
yüeh*, pp. 8–221.

[1] *YCHFL*, 5, 107.

[2] *YCHFL*, 11, 253–8. See also Sung Tz'u, 'Yang-chü', p. 38. The art of the
story-teller is nowadays known as *ch'ü-i*, and over 260 different regional styles
can be heard in China. These can be categorized under three headings, stories
spoken in rhythmical prose, spoken jokes, and sung stories. The last of the three
can be further subdivided into two types, those without accompaniment from
musical instruments and those in which it is essential. The latter group is called
ku-ch'ü. See Shen P'eng-nien a.o., *Ku-ch'ü yen-chiu*, pp. 1–2.

[3] *YCHFL*, 5, 122. See also Chou I-pai, *Hsi-chü shih*, pp. 537–8.

[4] *YCHFL*, 5, 132.

[5] Ibid. It may be added that the drama *Liang-lang shan* (discussed below in
appendix C, pp. 264–6) was popular in Yang-chou at this time and its main role
was Yang Yeh, who was a *sheng*. See *Hua-pu nung-t'an*, pp. 226–7.

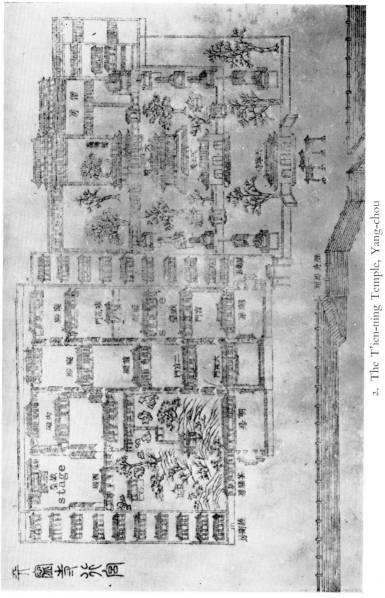

2. The T'ien-ning Temple, Yang-chou

counterparts elsewhere in China, they used market-places, temples, or any open space. The passages on popular festivals I cited earlier in this section show clearly that there was a wide range of temples or other places where stages could be erected. Here the popular companies could put on their performances.[1]

There are records of four temples which maintained permanent stages. One was the Pao-feng Temple where the people 'offered sacrifices to the first ploughman of former generations . . . Outside it a stage was built . . . and the local people would repay him for his favours by having dramas performed there.'[2]

The other three were larger and more grandiose structures. The first of them was the Ch'ung-ning Temple. After its construction, 'a big stage was built and large-scale drama was then transferred to be performed there'. A more important example was the T'ien-ning Temple. According to Li Tou, the temple included a stage in front of a temple hall where pieces on various subjects such as fairies or Buddhas were given.[3] A contemporary chart of the temple (see Illustration 2) shows two stages in the temple precincts. One was large and situated in the north-west corner of the compound. The other was small and lay in front of one of the minor halls of the temple.[4] The third major temple known to have been equipped with a stage was the Kao-min. A chart of the temple (see Illustration 3) shows a walled area in the temple garden with a magnificent stage and large open-air space where the audience sat.[5] None of the stages of these last two temples lay in the main part of the temple. All of them occupied a position west of the largest and most important temple halls which were in the eastern section of the temple.

It is worth noting that these three temples were used not only for the drama of the ordinary people, but also that of the rich and educated classes. The salt merchants would bring their own companies here and officials could be found among the audiences. It has already been mentioned that Ch'ien-lung stayed at the T'ien-ning and Kao-min Temples, and the stages there may well have been built especially in his honour.

Li Tou mentions one other temple where drama was performed, although not whether it was equipped with a permanent stage:

---

[1] More detailed material on Chinese stages in general can be found below in chapter seven.   [2] YCHFL, 1, 29.   [3] YCHFL, 5, 107.
[4] Nan-hsün sheng-tien, 97, 6b.   [5] Ibid., 97, 20b.

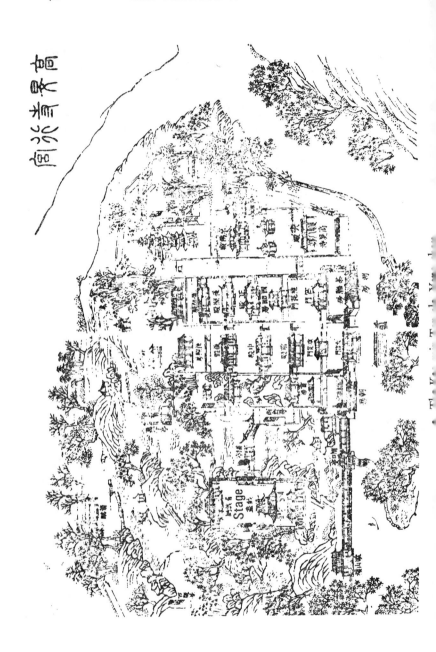

'The general office in control of the theatre was the Lao-lang[1] Shrine, which lay in Su-ch'ang Street[2] within the city walls. Every company that came into the city went first to the Lao-lang Shrine to pray and offer sacrifices . . . It then went to the Ssu-t'u Temple to give a performance.'[3]

This passage implies that government authorities supervised and kept a record of the troupes that visited the city. There is no evidence that either the salt merchants' or the regular *hua-pu* summer companies were bound to visit the Lao-lang Shrine. On the other hand, Li Tou's statement that 'the Liang-huai Salt Administration as a rule arranged for the *ya-pu* and *hua-pu* and prepared large-scale theatre'[4] suggests that the Salt Administration, which was a government organization, exercised some form of control over all Yang-chou's main companies, both the popular ones and those of the salt merchants.

One feature shared by all the types of companies so far discussed was that they were composed entirely of men. But there were also female companies in Yang-chou. Despite the government's disapproval of brothels, courtesans and prostitutes were common in late eighteenth-century Yang-chou and many of these women were famous as actresses.

The beauty of Yang-chou's courtesans had long been famous. As early as the T'ang dynasty, the Poet Tu Mu (803–52) wrote several well known poems on Yang-chou's prostitutes and his feelings towards them.[5] In Ming times, too, the city's prostitutes were among the most noted in all China. Chang Tai writes of the numerous winding alleys away from the main streets in the southwest of the New City, where brothels could be found in large numbers.

[1] Lao-lang was the main patron god of the actors. See below, pp. 222–4.

[2] This street ran east and west and lay in the south-west of the New City. It was called Su-ch'ang because many people who sang (*ch'ang*) in the Su-chou style worked there. *YCHFL*, 17, 422; 9, 190.

[3] *YCHFL*, 5, 122.   [4] *YCHFL*, 5, 107.

[5] The most famous of these poems is 'I-huai' ('In Idle Meditation'):

> Down and out I wander over the waters with a supply of wine,
> The girls here are like the wasp-waisted beauties of Ch'u,
> So light that they could dance on the palm of one's hand.
> For ten years I have lived besotted in Yang Chou,
> And now all that I have to show for it is the reputation for
> a light-of-love in the houses of ill fame.

The translation is that of Jenyns in *Selections from the Three Hundred Poems of the T'ang Dynasty*, pp. 44–5. See the Chinese original in *Ch'üan T'ang-shih*, 524, 5998.

Famous courtesans and ordinary prostitutes could be found living [in the region]. The famous courtesans did not show themselves publicly and a guide was necessary to seek them out. There were some five or six hundred ordinary prostitutes. Every day towards evening they would make themselves up and come out to the entrance of the alleys, lean on the walls and flaunt themselves in front of the teahouses and wineshops ... Wanderers and passers-by went to and fro like shuttles. They watched out keenly and, if any seemed inclined, they would press forward and take him away ... One by one they disappeared until no more than twenty or thirty were left. By the second watch all the lamps and torches were out and the teahouses were dark and silent ... They stood waiting for latecomers singing ... little songs in their charming voices or amusing each other with jokes and laughter, deliberately making a noise to kill the time. But amid the words and laughter their voices gradually became sad. At midnight they could not but go ... and were [probably] starved and beaten by their madams.[1]

It is true that Chang Tai makes no reference to the acting ability of these girls. Yet we know from popular novels that ordinary prostitutes often acted on teahouse-stages. The case of Pai Hsiu-ying in *The Water Margin* is particularly well known.[2] Chang Tai's reference to the charming singing voices of the girls probably permits us to conclude that there were quite a few actresses among them.

We are on firmer ground when we come to the eminent courtesans of the late eighteenth century, for Li Tou has given us some specific information which leaves no doubt that the best actresses in the city were to be found in the gay quarters. In his day most of the famous beauties of Yang-chou lived in the western section of the New City, on both sides of a canal called Hsiao Ch'in-huai which connected the T'ien-ning Gate to the Lung-t'ou area by the Small East Gate.[3]

Among the capable musicians who abounded in the area was

[1] *T'ao-an meng-i*, 4, 31-2.

[2] See *Shui-hu chuan*, 51, 601 ff. The passage describes how Pai Hsiu-ying is killed by one of the guests of the house. The section is translated in Pearl Buck, *All Men Are Brothers*, pp. 910 ff. For a discussion and bibliography on this famous novel see C. T. Hsia, *The Classic Chinese Novel*, pp. 75-114, 392-3.

[3] In Nanking, too, the best brothels were lined along a canal, the Ch'in-huai. This waterway was already famous for its pleasure houses by the T'ang, and Tu Mu wrote a poem about it called 'P'o Ch'in-huai' (*Ch'üan T'ang-shih*, 523, 5980). See Levy, *A Feast of Mist and Flowers*, pp. 9-11. Tu Mu's poem is translated p. 11 under the title 'Stopping at the Ch'in-huai'. The Hsiao Ch'in-huai Canal in Yang-chou was apparently called after Nanking's famous waterway. *YCHFL*, 9, 215.

Liang Kuei-lin whom Li Tou describes in a conventional way. 'She came from Yang-chou and was sold to a brothel at the age of fourteen. She was small in stature, soft and lovely. By nature she was mild and leisurely. She was refined, knew a good deal about music and was a good player of the (three-stringed) *san-hsien*'.[1] Apart from individuals of this kind there were several courtesan theatrical companies in Yang-chou. By far the most important was the Shuang-ch'ing.

The troupe's founder was 'Aunty' (*A-i*) Ku from Su-chou who 'collected some girls to perform *K'un-ch'ü* ... and engaged teachers to instruct them'. Her company was originally housed in the area beside the Hsiao Ch'in-huai Canal, but she later moved to the Shao-yao Alley[2] near the Tung-kuan Gate in the east of the New City.[3]

The members of the company are all named by Li Tou. Two of them, Yü-kuan and Ch'iao-kuan, took *hsiao-sheng* parts (those of beardless young men and scholar-lovers); it is said that, when Yü-kuan performed, she strongly resembled a man. Among the leading actresses was Hsi-kuan, who was the elder sister of another actress, Hsiao-yü. The two often performed together, Hsi-kuan playing the parts of heroines, and Hsiao-yü those of their servant maids. A third member was Ku Mei, who was notable in being the daughter of Aunty Ku.

The company included some extraordinarily young actresses. The *ch'ou* Yü-tzu was only eleven years old. Younger still was Chi-yü, who was ten. Moreover, Li adds that despite her tender years she 'understood the meaning of love-making'.[4] The comment does not prove that she had been defloured, since it was considered important that a good courtesan should be a virgin when she began her career. Chi-yü's profession had clearly been determined for her, and she was acquiring the necessary knowledge and cultural side-skills early in life.

There was only one male performer in the Shuang-ch'ing company and he, paradoxically, played *tan* roles. This actor was Hsü Shun-lung, the son of one of the instructors in the company. The instrumental players were women. One of them, a gong-player called Ssu-kuan, also took acting roles as a *ching*.[5]

The full complement of the Shuang-ch'ing company, apart

---

[1] *YCHFL*, 9, 202.   [2] *YCHFL*, 9, 203.   [3] *YCHFL*, 9, 191.
[4] *YCHFL*, 9, 203.   [5] *YCHFL*, 9, 204.

from the instrumentalists, was twenty-six: nineteen girls,[1] two managers and teachers, one male *tan* actor, and four caretakers in charge of the costumes and other such accessories. The majority of the actresses were *tan*. *Sheng*, *ching*, and *ch'ou* were included, but they were very few, and it may be that male actors from outside sometimes performed together with the company.

The fact that the Shuang-ch'ing company existed at all demonstrates that the bound feet of Chinese women did not prevent them from achieving distinction as actresses. Yet naturally they were not as agile on the stage as their male counterparts. The complicated acrobatics for which Peking Opera became so famous were not important in the *K'un-ch'ü* and were probably beyond the ability of Yang-chou's courtesan-actresses. It is worth remarking that the city was renowned for the smallness of the 'lotus feet' of its women. Since the object of binding girls' feet was to increase their sexual attraction, it is not surprising that in Yang-chou, so famous for its prostitution, the custom should have grown up of binding feet even tinier than usual. The shoes worn by ladies there were smaller and more pointed than those found in most other places and admired everywhere.[2]

The Background of the Prosperity of Yang-chou's Theatre

The foregoing sections leave no doubt about the richness and variety of Yang-chou's theatrical life. Indeed, even though inadequate source-material on other places prevents certainty on the matter, it is quite likely that no other city in China, apart from Peking, could boast such a wealth of drama. How is this to be explained? Why should Yang-chou have been pre-eminent?

One explanation is that Ch'ien-lung visited the city six times. I have already described how it took great trouble to provide the Emperor with fitting theatrical entertainment, and his approval of Yang-chou's theatre must surely have been an important stimulus. Yet Yang-chou was not the only city favoured by Ch'ien-lung's periodic visits and they do not fully explain its flourishing drama.

[1] Li Tou writes (ibid.) that there were eighteen girls in the company. However, he gives in all nineteen names. The actresses of the company are listed by Chou I-pai in *Hsi-chü shih*, pp. 543–4. He includes only eighteen names but has omitted one, that of Chi-yü.

[2] See Levy, *Chinese Footbinding*, p. 56. This work is the foremost on its subject in a Western language and explains in detail the major purpose of binding women's feet. Cf Inoue Susumu, *Shina fūzoku*, III, 422–3.

The main explanations are surely economic and social. Yang-chou's prospering economy was accompanied by certain social factors and together they satisfactorily account for the city's central position in the drama of the period.

I have noted already, in chapter two, the great importance of interregional and interprovincial trade in China at this time. There was a large volume of trade along the Yangtze to and from Yang-chou, and trading vessels carrying produce from the rich Yangtze Valley to the north and Peking passed by the city. Vessels could bring acting companies from a variety of places to Yang-chou and the constant passing through the city of artisans and merchants from other regions created a demand for theatrical styles not native to Yang-chou. These factors were more important for Yang-chou than for most other places simply because of its geographical situation so near the junction of China's two main transport arteries.

Li Tou mentions some specific cases of *hua-pu* styles coming from outside and notes the places whence they were brought to Yang-chou. He says that *erh-huang* came from An-ch'ing, *pang-tzu ch'iang* from Chü-jung, *Kao-ch'iang* from I-yang and *lo-lo ch'iang* from Hu-kuang (Hunan and Hupeh provinces).[1] In fact, *pang-tzu ch'iang* originated in north China and it is most doubtful that *erh-huang* was heard for the first time in An-ch'ing. In these cases and possibly also in that of *lo-lo ch'iang*, Li is referring to the regions from which the styles were introduced directly to Yang-chou rather than to their original birth-places. Only in the case of *Kao-ch'iang* is he stating the town where the style was first heard.[2] *Kao-ch'iang* could have been brought to Yang-chou from any one of numerous places, possibly from one of the provinces of the Yangtze. An-ch'ing was situated on the Yangtze River and was the capital of Anhwei province, Chü-jung was close to Yang-chou in Kiangsu and the great river passed right through the province of Hupeh. Trade along the Yangtze would largely explain the presence of the styles mentioned above in Yang-chou.

The city's most important article of trade was salt which, after

[1] *YCHFL*, 5, 130–1.
[2] I have discussed the places of origin of *pang-tzu ch'iang, erh-huang* and *Kao-ch'iang* in my article 'The Growth of the Chinese Regional Drama in the Ming and Ch'ing', *Journal of Oriental Studies*, ix, no. 1 (Jan. 1971), 67–8, 78 ff.

production in the factories,[1] was taken to Yang-chou where it was handed over to the transport merchants (*yün-shang*) who distributed it.[2] This shipping of salt may have facilitated the spread of various kinds of drama to, and also from, Yang-chou.[3] Moreover—and this is much more significant—the salt trade in Yang-chou attracted many people from other parts of the country to the city and hence gave it a pronounced cosmopolitan atmosphere which inevitably conduced towards the prominence and variety of regional drama. Indeed, according to one account, there had been in the Ming dynasty twenty times as many immigrants in Yang-chou as native people,[4] and the biographies in the *Liang-huai yen-fa chih* and *Yang-chou hua-fang lu* confirm that in the eighteenth century the salt merchants were mostly from districts other than Yang-chou.

Three places in particular provided this inflow of salt merchants. These were the provinces of Shensi and Shansi and the prefecture of Hui-chou in Anhwei. Already in the Ming, many of the salt merchants came from these three regions and as late as 1831, the Hui-chou and Shansi-Shensi groups still largely dominated the Liang-huai salt trade.[5] This must have created a considerable demand for the dramatic styles popular in the two north-western provinces and in Hui-chou, even though many of the immigrant salt merchant families were of long standing in Yang-chou. In view of this demand, we can probably conclude not merely that *pang-tzu ch'iang* and *I-yang ch'iang* were performed in Yang-chou, but that a number of the various styles of these two general systems had established themselves in the city. For instance, even though it is not mentioned in the sources, it may be that one could hear not only '*pang-tzu ch'iang* from Chü-jung', but also from regions in Shensi and Shansi.

[1] There were twenty-three salt factories under the Liang-huai Salt Administration in the late eighteenth century. They are listed with descriptive details in *Liang-huai yen-fa chih*, 27, 13a–25b. For further discussion on them see Ho Ping-ti, 'The Salt Merchants', pp. 131–2.

[2] Up to 1831, the Liang-huai Salt Administration appointed thirty head merchants to supervise the small merchants (*san-shang*). Both the head and small merchants were referred to as 'transport merchants' (ibid., p. 137). The Liang-huai transport merchants of this period numbered about 230 (ibid., pp. 138–41).

[3] According to du Halde (*Description de l'empire de la Chine*, II, 191), salt was transported on rafts, some of which were exceedingly long. These may have assisted in the transportation of wandering dramatic companies.

[4] *Yang-chou fu-chih* (1604 ed.), 1604 preface, p. 3b.

[5] See Ho Ping-ti, 'The Salt Merchants', p. 144.

Social factors like those discussed in chapter two also contributed to the development of Yang-chou's drama. But perhaps the most important social cause of its splendour arose simply from the patronage of the great salt merchants. The arts need patrons. They obtain their patrons from interested rich people. It is therefore highly relevant to consider what kind of men these salt merchants were in order to determine why it was that they patronized the drama so extensively.

Merchants were traditionally considered an inferior class in Confucian China and suffered various disabilities before the law. However, the salt merchants held a much higher position in society than ordinary traders and the Manchu government placed no legal discrimination against them.[1] Yet, though they had no reason whatever to feel inferior to scholars on financial grounds, they still felt at a social disadvantage. They were constantly concerned to compensate for this by showing that they were cultured. They were a class of *nouveaux riches* and great lovers of luxury. Li Tou writes:

Formerly, the salt merchants of Yang-chou vied with one another in extravagance. Each wedding or funeral, with all its expenses for food, clothing and carriage, cost several hundred thousand taels. There was one who insisted on having more than ten meticulously prepared dishes every meal. At dinner time he and his wife were waited upon by a host of servants.[2]

There seems to have been a certain vulgarity about many of the salt merchants, which produced a desire to show off their riches. They loved to invite in their friends and give banquets at which drama would be performed. Another point of interest is that members of salt merchants' families who failed to make a success of any profession often abandoned themselves to a life of pleasure. Yüan Mei writes of one such person that he amused himself with 'music, women, dogs and horses'.[3]

There was a fair degree of social mobility among the salt merchants and some of their families rose to become very respected members of society.[4] One of these, the Hung, of which

---

[1] Ibid., p. 155.

[2] *YCHFL*, 6, 148–50. The passage is quoted by Ho Ping-ti ('The Salt Merchants', p. 155) and I have used Ho's translation.

[3] *Hsiao-ts'ang shan-fang wen-chi*, 26, 6a.

[4] See Ho Ping-ti, 'The Salt Merchants', pp. 156 ff.

Hung Ch'ung-shih was a member, had been engaged in the salt trade since the late years of the Ming. The family owned, north of the city walls, the famous Hung-ch'iao Garden which was, in Li Tou's words, 'a place where literary men gathered and drank'.[1] Its visitors included many distinguished scholars, such as Mei Wen-ting (1633–1721) and Yüan Mei.[2] Another family which rose to a high social position in Yang-chou was the Ch'eng, to which Ch'eng Ch'ien-te belonged. Their Hsiao-yüan lay north-west of the city walls. It was constructed by Ch'eng Meng-hsing[3] after his return to Yang-chou in 1716. Like the Hung-ch'iao it was the haunt of literary men and was famous for its beautiful scenery.[4]

A third family which had risen over a number of generations to a position of very great prestige was the Chiang. The first member of this family to become a salt merchant in Yang-chou was Chiang Kuo-mao of the late Ming era, known for his cultural activities and sense of justice.[5] One of his great-grandsons, Chiang Ch'un, was to become the most cultured head merchant of the late Ch'ien-lung period and the foremost patron of the dramatic arts in Yang-chou.

In view of his importance in the city's theatrical life it is worth while to consider him in a little more detail. Chiang Ch'un's business name was Kuang-ta and his *hao* was Ho-t'ing, the latter name being that by which he is most often called by Li Tou. He came originally from She-hsien in Hui-chou but became a *chu-sheng* (first degree graduate) in I-cheng county outside Yang-chou.[6] He contributed a substantial amount of money to help finance

[1] *YCHFL*, 10, 241.

[2] *YCHFL*, 10, 241–3, and *Yang-chou ming-sheng lu*, 3, 9a–10b.

[3] Ch'eng Meng-hsing passed the *chin-shih* examinations in 1712 and became a compiler of the Han-lin Academy (*pien-hsiu*). He was noted as a poet and, according to Li Tou, 'there was nothing he could not do in artistic matters; he was particularly good at calligraphy, painting, and playing the *ch'in*'. *YCHFL*, 15, 345. The *ch'in* was a flat seven-stringed zither-like instrument, popular with educated Chinese. See especially van Gulik, *The Lore of the Chinese Lute*.

[4] See *YCHFL*, 15, 343 ff., and *Yang-chou ming-sheng lu*, 4, 1a–2a. Notes are given on the Ch'eng family in Ho Ping-ti, "The Salt Merchants", pp. 158–9.

[5] Chiang Kuo-mao 'loved to do chivalrous deeds. Whenever he saw a wrong-doing or injustice in the villages his face would become clouded with anger. Because there was so much at fault in the empire, he would practice horsemanship and archery when at leisure from playing stringed instruments and chanting poetry'. *Liang-huai yen-fa chih*, 46, 6b.

[6] *YCHFL*, 12, 274.

Ch'ien-lung's military campaigns and was indeed quite well known to the Emperor. When he fell into financial difficulties in 1771, the Emperor lent him 300,000 taels because of his earlier assistance. Chiang entertained Ch'ien-lung six times and also attended an imperial banquet,[1] an unusual honour for a merchant.

Chiang Ch'un was interested in a wide range of cultural activities. He was himself regarded as one of the finest poets of his time. He was a good archer and bought some waste land outside the Hsüning Gate, south of the city, where he could indulge this hobby. Chiang Ch'un built at least two beautiful gardens, the most famous being the K'ang-shan, which Ch'ien-lung visited in 1780. He was among the most noted patrons of literature in Yang-chou. Literary men came from all over China to his house, where gatherings of such eminent people were frequently held.[2]

It has been noted that he was the founder of two famous theatrical companies, the Te-yin and the Ch'un-t'ai. But his patronage of the dramatic arts did not stop at this, for he is known to have been interested also in the *ku-ch'ü* of the story-tellers. In his mansion he maintained a permanent group, considered among the best of its kind in Yang-chou, to perform *ch'ing-ch'ang*, the music of which was similar to *K'un-ch'ü* and was accompanied by instruments like the *ti-tzu*, drum, clapper, and *san-hsien*.[3] Another ballad or lyric style to which Chiang took a fancy was *hsiao-ch'ü* or *hsiao-ch'ang*,[4] accompanied only by stringed instruments and clappers. He invited two of Yang-chou's most distinguished exponents of this music, Mou Ch'i and Chu San, to his K'ang-shan Garden to perform it for him.[5]

Chiang died in 1793 at the age of sixty-eight.[6] He left a son, Chen-hung.[7] His most eminent descendant was probably the

[1] *Kuo-ch'ao ch'i-hsien lei-cheng*, 457, 6a–b. The passage in question in this work is in fact an epitaph on Chiang Ch'un written by Yüan Mei.

[2] *Liang-huai yen-fa chih*, 44, 16a.

[3] YCHFL, 11, 254–5.

[4] See also Lo Chin-t'ang, *Chung-kuo san-ch'ü shih*, pp. 230 ff. This style is still popular in Yang-chou under the name *Yang-chou ch'ing-ch'ü*. The texts of six examples may be found in *Yang-chou ch'ing-ch'ü hsüan*, pp. 5–90. Musical scores are given pp. 91–109 and a short explanatory introduction, pp. 1–4.

[5] YCHFL, 11, 257.

[6] *Kuo-ch'ao ch'i-hsien lei-cheng*, 457, 7b. See also Ho Ping-ti, *The Ladder of Success in Imperial China*, p. 288.

[7] YCHFL, 12, 274. Ho Ping-ti has written studies of Chiang Ch'un and his relations in *The Ladder of Success*, pp. 287–9 and in 'The Salt Merchants', pp. 159–61.

famous scholar-official Juan Yüan, who was the son of his daughter.[1]

Chiang Ch'un typifies the cultivated merchant. He stands at the top of a whole host of men who injected into Yang-chou's theatre the life-blood which made it so prosperous. There were such men in other cities, but perhaps the long tradition and enormous scale of the salt trade in Yang-chou may be held chiefly to account for the richness of the city, the cosmopolitan atmosphere of its life, the large number of its merchants, the high degree of education of some of these merchants and the consequent prosperity and variety of the drama in the city.

[1] *YCHFL*, 12, 277. On Juan Yüan see also Hummel, *Eminent Chinese*, pp. 399–402.

IV

THE CH'IN-CH'IANG ACTORS

THE EARLIEST detailed records of *Ch'in-ch'iang* actors date from the late Ch'ien-lung period. They are the *Ch'in-yün hsieh-ying hsiao-p'u* and Wu Ch'ang-yüan's *Yen-lan hsiao-p'u*.[1] The former is of composite authorship; it contains seven sections, four by Yen Ch'ang-ming (1731–87), two by Ts'ao Jen-hu (1731–87) and one by Ch'ien Tien (1744–1806), all from Kiangsu province.[2] This work was completed in about 1780[3] and gives contemporary biographies of six actors and, in addition, short notes on eight others. All of them were known principally for their work in Hsi-an, the capital of Shensi, which had long been a noted centre of *Ch'in-ch'iang* drama. The Clapper actors described by Wu Ch'ang-yüan, on the other hand, flourished primarily over the years 1779 to 1785 in Peking, which before that time seems to have known only little of the *Ch'in-ch'iang* theatre. Though sketches are given on many performers, Wu includes detailed material on the lives of few actors only. One of the men favoured in this way is, however, Wei Ch'ang-sheng, the first of the Szechwanese *Ch'in-ch'iang* actors to win great fame in Peking.

(i) THE CH'IN-CH'IANG ACTORS OF HSI-AN

There were two main styles of *Ch'in-ch'iang* music in Shensi in the late eighteenth century. One was popular chiefly to the

[1] On the *Yen-lan hsiao-p'u* (*YLHP*) and its author see appendix B, pp. 237–9.

[2] See notes on these three authors in Hummel, *Eminent Chinese of the Ch'ing Period*, pp. 907, 828, 156.

[3] The first biography of *Ch'in-yün hsieh-ying hsiao-p'u* (*CYHYHP*) describes the life of Shen Hsiang-lin and is dated 1 Apr. 1778; the second, which deals with San-shou, 2 June of the same year. Probably the various sections were written separately and brought together later. According to a note by Yüan Tsu-chih (1827–98), a grandson of the famous poet Yüan Mei, a manuscript of the *CYHYHP* was dedicated to the memory of Yen Ch'ang-ming's grandfather and became part of a book collection in Nanking. In 1853 the library was burned when the T'ai-p'ing rebels entered the city. This manuscript, however, was carried safely from the holocaust and printed in 1871 (p. 17a). It was later incorporated by Yeh Te-hui into the *Shuang-mei ching-an ts'ung-shu*.

north of the Wei River and the other principally to the south.
Ta-li, a county of T'ung-chou, was the centre of the northern
style, while the major cities for the southern were Wei-nan and
Chou-chih. On the other hand, the Wei was by no means a rigid
border between the two styles. Li-ch'üan, which lay north of the
river, was a popular centre for the southern style,[1] and in Hsi-an
both could be heard.

In the 1770s there were thirty-six famous musical companies in
Shensi's capital. We know the names of only three of them, the
Pao-fu, Chiang-tung, and Shuang-sai companies. Of the three,
the last was considered the finest. It was formed later than the
other two and was given its name, which means 'competing with
both of the two', because it was held to have achieved higher
standards than either the Pao-fu or the Chiang-tung companies.
Later, however, it was renamed Shuang-ts'ai.[2]

It is highly significant that Hsi-an could boast thirty-six famous
companies. There were thirty-five in Peking in 1785, a year which
fell in a period of great prominence in the life of the city's drama.
That Shensi could claim four other major theatrical centres
besides Hsi-an is also striking. It seems that by the late Ch'ien-lung
period this province did not lag behind other regions in the abundance of its drama, even though it was not counted among the
most important cultural or economic areas of the empire.

We know very little about the actors of the Pao-fu or Chiang-
tung companies. The name of only one actor of the former is
recorded. This was Sung Tzu-wen, whose stage-name was
T'ai-p'ing-erh. He, however, had left the stage because of old age
by the early 1770s. The best known actor of the Chiang-tung
company was Fan Yün-kuan, who was known on the stage as
Hsiao-hui.[3] He came from Ta-li and therefore excelled in the
style of *Ch'in-ch'iang* popular to the north of the Wei. Yen
Ch'ang-ming claims that his excellence was recognized in all
parts of Shensi,[4] but is otherwise almost completely silent concerning him.[5]

---

[1] *CYHYHP*, p. 9b.   [2] *CYHYHP*, p. 15h.
[3] Ibid. Hsiao-hui's surname and *ming* are given p. 12b.
[4] *CYHYHP*, p. 9b.
[5] There is a biography of Hsiao-hui in *CYHYHP*, pp. 9b–12b, but it is mostly a
passage of praise for the *Ch'in-ch'iang* and contains very little information on the
actor. Another well known actor of the Chiang-tung company was So-erh
(p. 15b), who is discussed by Yen Ch'ang-ming, pp. 12b–14b.

In view of its pre-eminence, it is not surprising that more is recorded about the actors of the Shuang-sai than those of any other company. By far the most distinguished actors of that troupe were Shen Hsiang-lin and Chao San-kuan, both of whom played *tan* roles.

Shen Hsiang-lin was born into a peasant family about 1755, and spent his early years in Wei-nan, not far from Hsi-an; his childhood name (*hsiao-tzu*) was Kou-erh. One year there was a famine in Shensi, and Hsiang-lin left home to take up lodgings with a neighbour. This man gave him the job of tilling the soil but, thinking him lazy, beat him severely. Hsiang-lin could not stand this treatment and fled into the mountains to the west. Although it was winter, he remained there for several months, begging when he could or living on plants and sleeping in the open. The mountain folk neither liked nor trusted him and, regarding him as a kind of spirit, sometimes even chased him away with knives when he approached.

It became clear that this kind of life could not continue. Hsiang-lin decided to make a thorough study of *Ch'in-ch'iang* and left the mountains for the city of Wu-ch'ang in Hupeh. This was at the time the home of a famous teacher called Hu-tan, from whom Hsiang-lin sought instruction.

The young actor did not find what he needed in Hu-tan. Yen Ch'ang-ming describes his stay in Hupeh as follows:

Hu-tan . . . wanted to live on him but did not want to teach him. He ridiculed him behind his back and then cast him aside in anger. [Shen] took a job in the house of Chin-t'an-erh. Chin-t'an-erh was a famous courtesan of Han-yang.[1] Hsiang-lin served her and watched how she spoke, smiled, behaved, ate and drank, and her very great beauty and fascinating manner both when awake and asleep. Everything went fine. He lived there for a year and then said delightedly, 'Now I can do it'. He again asked to show his skill and the audience were all greatly impressed, just as in the story . . . of Actor Ma recorded by Hou Fang-yü.[2] Two or three months later he was spending the night in an inn when suddenly a naked sword flew in the window towards his head. He managed to dodge it and looked out. It was Hu-tan, and he knew that the place was not safe for him.[3]

Hsiang-lin, who was still only fifteen years old, fled back to

[1] The three sections of the triple city of Wuhan are Wu-ch'ang, Han-yang, and Han-k'ou.
[2] See above, p. 28, note 1.   [3] *CYHYHP*, p. 5b.

Wei-nan, hoping to find his parents still there. Nobody in the town had any clear knowledge of their whereabouts, but one person claimed that they had been seen in Shansi, and Hsiang-lin accordingly set off for that province and acted in P'u-chou and T'ai-yüan. One day he was performing in T'ai-yüan before a local official, Shen Chu-p'ing. It so happened that Hsiang-lin's parents were members of Chu-p'ing's retinue and there the actor became reunited with his family. His old parents were given some land back in Wei-nan and returned to that city, where they remained for the rest of their lives.

Soon afterwards, Hsiang-lin joined the Shuang-sai company in Hsi-an. Yen Ch'ang-ming, his biographer, saw him act there at the mansion of an official called Su Hsien-chih, and he praises highly his ability as an actor. In appearance, Hsiang-lin was very feminine; his demeanour on the stage had a delicacy about it which was very affecting, and Yen was strongly attracted towards him. He was also most impressed by Hsiang-lin's filial search for his parents, and decided that he would like to become Hsiang-lin's patron. When Ch'ang-ming left Hsi-an for the south in 1776, he invited the young actor to accompany him, but Hsiang-lin refused, saying that he wanted to look after his parents in their old age.[1]

We know nothing of Hsiang-lin's life after this point; yet there are few actors about whom so many details are recorded. Yen was in fact asked by Su Hsien-chih to write the actor's biography, for Su had also been very much impressed by the young man's character, especially by his filial piety. His life story, such as we know it, suggests that Hsiang-lin was a man of some determination and ability. His encounter with Hu-tan and Chin-t'an-erh shows that he was not deflected easily from his ambition and he seems to have risen high in his profession with virtually no formal training. He does not appear to have belonged to any company for a substantial period until he joined the Shuang-sai company. In short, his success depended almost entirely on his own talent.

Apart from Hsiang-lin, the best known actor of the Shuang-sai company was Chao San-kuan, whose stage-name was San-shou. He was born in 1762 or 1763[2] and was, like Hsiang-lin, the son of

---

[1] *CYHYHP*, pp. 5b–6a.

[2] San-chou was fifteen years old early in 1778. See *CYHYHP*, p. 6b.

peasants. His birth-place was Mien-chou in Szechwan and his *tzu* was Nan-ju.[1]

San-shou lost his father when still a child, and his mother remarried because she felt unable to make a living as a single woman; but she remained desperately poor and unable to support the boy. It happened that San-shou had an elder brother who was a servant in a family of silk merchants in Ch'eng-tu, and and he went to Ch'eng-tu in the hope that his brother would feed and lodge him. Despite his brother he suffered acutely from hunger that year; but in 1776 he was adopted by a man called Chang from Hsien-yang in Shensi; he then took his new father's name,[2] received training as an actor, and after much travelling around west China with Chang, ended up in Hsi-an.[3]

In Shensi's capital San-shou joined the Shuang-sai company and became successful as an actor; but he was very homesick and missed his mother, so he saved a considerable amount of money to send to her. While in Hsi-an, San-shou was invited to perform at an important banquet held by Kuo Nai-hsüan, an official who had been transferred from Szechwan and was awaiting a post in Shensi. 'During an interval San-shou knelt down [before Kuo] and begged that a letter be posted to his mother to include the money he had saved up. Kuo was sympathetic to him for his sincerity, smiled, granted the request, and wrote for him to his family to inform them.'[4]

The young actor continued to be unhappy in Hsi-an. He felt that the only person who was really profiting from his acting was his adopted father whom he was therefore desperately anxious to leave. He later went to Peking where he joined the ranks of the famous *Ch'in-ch'iang* actors who had followed Wei Ch'ang-sheng to the capital; and there he joined the Shuang-ch'ing company[5] which owed its fame to Wei himself. San-shou is the only one of

---

[1] In *YLHP*, 3, 4a, there is a biography of an actor called San-shou-kuan from Hsi-an. This must be the same actor as *CYHYHP*'s San-chou, since his *tzu* is given both in *YLHP* and in *CYHYHP*, p. 15b, as Nan-ju. Ts'ao Jen-hu states (in *CYHYHP*, p. 6b) that San-chou came from Mien-chou, Szechwan. The author knew the actor personally and his word is therefore more reliable than that of Wu Ch'ang-yüan, who was ignorant of San-shou's early life.

[2] Wu Ch'ang-yüan states (*YLHP*, 3, 4a) that San-shou-kuan's surname was Chang, but does not seem to have known that this was the name of his adopted father, not his real one.

[3] *CYHYHP*, pp. 6b–7a.   [4] *CYHYHP*, p. 7b.

[5] *YLHP*, 3, 4a.

the actors described in the *Ch'in-yün hsieh-ying hsiao-p'u* who is known to have acted in Peking.

Ts'ao Jen-hu describes Chao San-kuan as unusually beautiful on the stage. The actor was apparently very weak physically; he looked like a woman and 'did not make himself up with cosmetics'.[1] But the case of San-shou provides us with a point of comparison between the standards of the theatre in Hsi-an and Peking. In Hsi-an, he was considered one of the finest actors in the city, while in Peking he was of only secondary importance. In Hsi-an his singing was held to be magnificent, but in Peking he was thought a poor singer.[2]

(ii) THE CH'IN-CH'IANG ACTORS OF PEKING

The comparison emphasizes the fact that it was in Peking that the best Clapper actors performed and that it was there that they made their greatest impact.

The most famous of them, Wei Ch'ang-sheng and Ch'en Yin-kuan, dominated the Peking stage of the 1780s and made the city for the first time since the Yüan dynasty the unquestioned theatrical capital of China. From the time of Wei and Ch'en, Peking was to remain the most important centre in the empire for the drama; and in the succeeding decades it witnessed the influx of actors from different provinces performing various styles. Each of these left its mark and the result was the formation of what we know today as the Peking Opera.

The reader will recall that the ninth decade of the eighteenth century was a period of political decline for the Manchu dynasty. Corruption among officials was becoming widespread and the problem was made more serious by the fact that Ch'ien-lung's unscrupulous minister Ho-shen (1750–99),[3] who held a position

[1] *CYHYHP*, p. 6b–7a.

[2] Compare the judgments on San-chou in *YLHP*, 3, 4a and *CYHYHP*, p. 6b. It is true that Ts'ao Jen-hu was prejudiced in favour of San-shou (the biography he wrote suggests that he was in love with the actor). Yet there is no reason to question his assertion that 'the whole audience was thrilled' by his singing.

[3] On Ho-shen and the political decline in China in the late Ch'ien-lung see Hummel, *Eminent Chinese*, pp. 288–90, and Nivison, 'Ho-shen and His Accusers', in Nivison and Wright, eds., *Confucianism in Action*, pp. 209–43. Ho-shen has been harshly judged by historians and many have considered him responsible for the rapid decline of the Ch'ing. The view that the blame can be laid entirely upon Ho-shen is rejected in both the works mentioned above, but it is beyond doubt that the process of dissolution of the Manchu empire, to which Ho-shen certainly contributed, had begun by the 1780s.

of almost total power in the government, was himself as guilty as any of his subordinates.

China as a whole was rather less prosperous in the 1780s than it had been some years earlier. The reverse was true of the Peking stage. In order to clarify the last statement let us begin with a survey of the situation of the theatre in the years leading up to Wei Ch'ang-sheng's spectacular arrival in the capital.

The Peking Stage up to 1779

Three main styles of drama dominated the Peking theatre in the early and middle years of the Ch'ien-lung period. They were *K'un-ch'ü*, *Ch'in-ch'iang*, and *Ching-ch'iang*.

The most important centre for the *K'un-ch'ü* in Peking was the court itself, the theatre of which I shall be discussing in chapter five. Outside the palace, the *K'un-ch'ü* did not find many admirers; according to Wu Ch'ang-yüan, 'it was not liked by the northern-ers.'[1] Nevertheless, there were several companies devoted to performing the *ya-pu* drama, and the most famous of them seems to have been the Pao-ho.

One young actor of the *K'un-ch'ü* became well known to the scholars of the day through his association with the famous scholar-official Pi Yüan (1730–97).[2] This was Li Kuei-kuan (*tzu* Hsiu-chang) from Su-chou, who played *tan* roles.[3] He had been a dancing-master in the mansion of a Chi family in Szechwan, but had become bored with the job and gone to Peking. There he worked as an official musician[4] and also acted in the Ch'ing-ch'eng[5] and other companies. In Peking, he met Pi Yüan and the two were greatly attracted to one another. Li seems to have been tired of acting and to have regarded his affair with Pi Yüan partly as a means of escaping from it. He told his patron, 'Frankly, I am tired of mountebanking on the stage and making a public exhibition of myself.'[6] Li lived for a time as a member of Pi's household and the two devoted themselves to study. There is no

---

[1] *YLHP*, 2, 4a.
[2] Pi Yüan was noted for his contribution to several fields of knowledge, especially history and epigraphy, and for his hospitality to young scholars. See Hummel, *Eminent Chinese*, pp. 622–5.
[3] *YLHP*, 5, 1a.   [4] *Hsiao-ts'ang shan-fang shih-chi*, 21, 4a.
[5] *YLHP*, 5, 1a.
[6] *Hsiao-ts'ang shan-fang shih-chi*, 21, 4a. The translation given above is taken from Waley, *Yuan Mei*, p. 99.

doubt that contemporaries believed the relationship between Pi Yüan and Li Kuei-kuan to be homosexual. In 1760 Pi did extremely well in the *chin-shih* examinations,[1] and at the celebrations which followed his success, Li was treated by the guests just as if he had been Pi's wife.[2]

Some time later Pi and the young actor broke off their connections, and Li went to the south where he lived so extravagantly that he spent all he had saved. In 1767 he met the poet Yüan Mei in Su-chou and told him that he was about to go to Kansu[3] where his former patron Pi Yüan had been posted the same year. He seems to have carried out the plan and to have remained with Pi for some years.[4] We know also that he afterwards met the historian and poet Chao I (1727–1814)[5] in Canton and that the latter wrote a poem in his honour.[6] As an old man Li lived in his native city Su-chou and was still alive in 1803.[7]

The biography of Li Kuei-kuan illustrates two points. In the first place, the fact that Li was so widely travelled shows how varied was the range of regions where *K'un-ch'ü* was heard. Although the elegant drama was not popular everywhere, it was possible for a good exponent of the style to obtain employment in almost any part of China. Officials did not usually serve in their native districts, and even in a province like Kansu, there were administrators from the south who favoured the *K'un-ch'ü*.

Secondly, just as in Yang-chou, many *K'un-ch'ü* actors were educated. That this was so of Li is shown by his devotion to study in Pi Yüan's house. But he was by no means the only example. Wu Ch'ang-yüan writes the following of another *K'un-ch'ü* actor, Liu Kuei-lin-kuan:

He was genial and cultured and quite unlike people in [the usual] acting company. He liked historical and other books and could write the literary style demanded in the official examinations. He was also good at painting orchids (*lan*). [His strokes were] graceful and he had the style of a literary man. In the spring of 1778, I passed by a friend's house

[1] Hummel, *Eminent Chinese*, p. 623.

[2] *Hsiao-t'ang shan-fang shih-chi*, 21, 4a.

[3] Ibid., 21, 4b.

[4] YLHP, 5, 1a. Pi Yüan was given an official post in Shensi in 1771 (Hummel, *Eminent Chinese*, p. 623).

[5] Ibid., pp. 75–6.

[6] *Yen-p'u tsa-chi*, 2, 17a.

[7] *Hua-chien hsiao-yü* (*HCHY*), in *Pei-ching li-yüan chang-ku ch'ang-pien* (*PCLYCK*), p. 7b.

and had a drink with them [my friend and Liu]. I did not realise he was an actor. My friend told me, and treated him just as if he were a scholar.[1]

If our knowledge of the *K'un-ch'ü* and its actors in Peking in the early and middle years of the Ch'ien-lung era is sketchy, even less is known about the *Ch'in-ch'iang* companies of the period before Wei Ch'ang-sheng, and they do not seem to have caught the attention of the scholars who might have described them. One of the leading members of the actors' guild in 1732 came from T'ai-yüan in Shansi[2] and was probably a Clapper performer since very few actors from that province excelled in any other operatic form. It is likely that he and other *Ch'in-ch'iang* artists of this time did most of their work in small and unimportant theatres or in the houses of rich men from the western provinces of Shansi and Shensi, where the Clapper Opera was so popular. There was, in fact, a large number of merchants from Shansi living in Peking during this period[3] and their patronage may well have been the very *raison d'être* of the Clapper companies which performed before Wei Ch'ang-sheng's arrival.

By far the most popular form of drama heard in Peking was the *Ching-ch'iang*, an *I-yang ch'iang* style which had existed in the capital since the sixteenth century. Short extracts from some early *Ching-ch'iang* pieces survive in the *Hsin-ting shih-erh lü Ching-ch'iang p'u*, the preface of which is dated 1684.[4] Although the dramas were derived from *I-yang ch'iang*, they were in fact so

---

[1] *YLHP*, 4, 5a.

[2] See *Pei-ching li-yüan chin-shih wen-tzu lu* (*PCLYCS*), p. 2a. Further confirmation of the existence of these early *Ch'in-ch'iang* companies in Peking is given in Aoki Masaru, *Chung-kuo chin-shih hsi-ch'ü shih*, p. 440.

[3] These included wholesale dye merchants from P'ing-yao, important tobacco-dealers from Chi-shan, Chiang-hsien, and Wen-hsi, and grain and vegetable-oil merchants from Hsiang-ling and Lin-fen. See Katō Shigeshi, *Shina keizai shi kōshō*, II, 581. In discussing these early *Ch'in-ch'iang* companies the contemporary authority Chou I-pai ascribes their presence in the capital to the Shansi bankers in charge of the *p'iao-hao* or draft banks. See *Chung-kuo hsi-chü shih chiang-tso*, pp. 223–4. These banks, which were mainly directed from Shansi, were an important aspect of the Chinese economy in the nineteenth century. However, the oldest *p'iao-hao* cannot be traced back earlier than about 1800. See Yang Lien-sheng, *Money and Credit in China*, pp. 81–4.

[4] The editor of the *Hsin-ting shih-erh lü Ching-ch'iang p'u* was Wang Cheng-hsiang, who compiled a similar work for the *K'un-ch'ü* called *Hsin-ting shih-erh lü K'un-ch'iang p'u*. Neither work contains any musical notation and the texts given show no difference between the *Ching-ch'iang* and *K'un-ch'ü* drama as far as their libretti are concerned.

different from the original that they could scarcely be placed in the same category. For this reason the operatic genre was re-named *Ching-ch'iang*, the style of the capital.[1]

There were six famous *Ching-ch'iang* companies. The best known was perhaps the Great Wang-fu (Princely Mansions) company. The identity of the other five is unfortunately not known for certain, but Li Tou tells us that 'the *Ching-ch'iang* was based on the I-ch'ing, Ts'ui-ch'ing and Chi-ch'ing companies',[2] so that these three were no doubt numbered among the six.

Possibly the three most famous of the *Ching-ch'iang* actors were the *tan* performers, Pai Erh, T'ien-pao-erh, and Pa-ta-tzu. Pai Erh was from Peking and a bannerman. Such people were forbidden even to enter a public theatre, let alone act in one, and I shall be dealing in detail with these prohibitions in chapter seven. However, Pai Erh not only joined the greatest of the *Ching-ch'iang* companies, the Wang-fu, but also achieved great distinc-tion in it. Wu Ch'ang-yüan reports that, when he visited Peking in 1775, he found Pai Erh at the peak of his career; it was not until the arrival of Wei Ch'ang-sheng and Ch'en Yin-kuan a few years later that his popularity declined significantly.[3] T'ien-pao-erh was of the Ch'en family and came from Su-chou. As his place of origin suggests, he had originally played *K'un-ch'ü* dramas, but then gave them up in favour of *Ching-ch'iang*, joining the Ta-ch'eng company. He fell foul of the authorities owing to some misdemeanour and was exiled to Sinkiang, whence, despite efforts made on his behalf, he never returned.[4] Like Pai Erh, Pa-ta-tzu was a bannerman. According to a friend of Wu Ch'ang-yüan's 'he was not particularly beautiful to look at, but his voice, facial expressions and demeanour were calm, refined, dignified, and correct'. The same source claims that he belonged to the Ts'ui-ch'ing company,[5] but the nineteenth-century author Yang Mou-chien asserts that he was a member of the *K'un-ch'ü* Pao-ho troupe.[6] It is true that Yang was writing several decades after Wu and his authority does not carry as much weight in this case. On the other hand, it is also possible that Pa-ta-tzu was like T'ien-pao-erh in transferring his attention from the obsolescent elegant

[1] See Aoki Masaru, *Hsi-ch'ü shih*, p. 439.
[2] *Yang-chou hua-fang lu* (YCHFL), 5, 131.
[3] *YLHP*, 3, 1a.   [4] *YLHP*, 5, 2a–b.   [5] *YLHP*, 5, 3a.
[6] *Ch'ang-an k'an-hua chi* (CAKHC), p. 22a.

drama to the more popular *Ching-ch'iang*. He died in 1774, but so great had his reputation been that even in the 1780s 'his name was still very much on everybody's lips.'[1]

The *Ching-ch'iang* companies reached the height of their fame and popularity in the 1770s. Then an event occurred which caused them to be associated, in the minds of many influential people, with ill luck. Almost immediately afterwards, they suffered an even greater disaster—that of being superseded by other, more appealing, troupes. Tai Lu, writing in 1796, describes what happened:

The six great *Ching-ch'iang* companies had prospered for a long time. In 1778 and 1779 the New Wang-fu company [probably the same as the Great Wang-fu company] reached a particularly high peak. Some gentlemen from Hupeh and Kiangsi were holding a public banquet and the censor Lu Tsan-yüan was among those present. Because a *sheng* actor came late and spoke rudely, he slapped him in the face. Not many days later the censor was dismissed for having disgraced his office. After that, the officials warned each other against engaging the New Wang-fu company. Just then the *Ch'in-ch'iang* [actors] happened to arrive, and the actors of the six great companies lost their jobs.[2]

The stunning popularity of the newcomers was due largely to the ability of their leader, Wei Ch'ang-sheng, and it will be worthwhile to consider his career in some detail.

Wei Ch'ang-sheng

The year of Wei's birth is uncertain but was probably 1744.[3] He came from Chin-t'ang county in Ch'eng-tu, Szechwan

---

[1] *YLHP*, 5, 3a. There were many other famous *Ching-ch'iang* actors besides those mentioned. Pictures were drawn of thirteen of them and publicly displayed. See *Tu-men hui-tsuan, tsa-yung*, p. 33b.

[2] *T'eng-yin tsa-chi*, 5, 7a–b.

[3] See Chou I-pai, *Chung-kuo hsi-chü shih*, pp. 595–6. According to *Jih-hsia k'an-hua chi* (*JHKHC*), 4, 14b. Wei Ch'ang-sheng died in 1802 at the age of fifty-eight (fifty-nine *sui*). This would put his birth in 1744. The author of *JHKHC* was on intimate terms with Liu Ch'ing-jui, one of Wei's disciples during his last years (*JHKHC*, 1, 1a–b). His account is probably the most reliable in this case and is the only one to record Wei's age in any particular year more specifically than in round or approximate numbers. According to Chao I (*Yen-p'u tsa-chi*, 2, 17a), Wei was forty *sui* in 1788; Chao-lien says in his *Hsiao-t'ing tsa-lu* (*HTTL*), 8, 8a, that he was more than thirty *sui* in 1774; and Yang Mou-chien quotes an old servant as putting Wei's age at more than sixty *sui* when the actor returned to Peking just before his death. *Meng-hua so-pu* (*MHSP*), p. 20b.

province,[1] and introduced to Peking the style of *Ch'in-ch'iang* drama popular in the south-west. He was a *tan* actor, his *tzu* was Wan-ch'ing and he was known on the stage as Wei San[2] or Wei San-erh.[3] Like most of his profession he had learned the arts of the theatre when young, but nothing is known of his social origins or how he became an actor. He spent a number of years on the stage in Szechwan, but was always in financial difficulties there.[4]

The passage by Tai Lu, quoted above, implies that Wei Ch'ang-sheng first arrived in Peking in 1779; despite disagreement in the sources over the date, this one is almost certainly correct.[5] Once in the capital, Wei decided to enter the Shuang-ch'ing company, which had up to 1779 performed *Ching-ch'iang* drama. It was considered a second-rate company and Wei clearly regarded it as something of a challenge to join the troupe. He said to its members, 'Let me enter your company for two months and if I cannot increase its prestige for you in that time, I am willing to be punished without any regrets.'[6] He performed the drama *Kun-lou*,[7] the Szechwanese actor Yang Wu-erh acting as his second,[8] and won immediate renown. So great was his reputation that 'every day more than 1,000 people came to see him.'[9] The prestige of the *Ching-ch'iang* companies promptly declined.

Wei's acting was rather bawdy and this created a number of

---

[1] *YLHP*, 3, 8b. Yang Mou-chien claims (*MHSP*, p. 33a) to have heard a story that Wei Ch'ang-sheng came originally from Ch'ang-lo in Kwangtung and later moved to Szechwan. However, he admits that there is no real evidence for it.

[2] *YLHP*, 3, 8b.   [3] *YCHFL*, 5, 132.   [4] *YLHP*, 5, 3b.

[5] According to Chao-lien (*HTTL*, 8, 8a), Wei arrived in 1774; and the author of *JHKHC* (4, 14b) claims to have seen him act in 1775. On the other hand, Wu Ch'ang-yüan (*YLHP*, 5, 3b) quotes an unnamed writer as reporting that Wei's arrival was in 1779 and this date is corroborated by the *HCHY* (in *PCLYCK*, p. 7b). On the surface, the *JHKHC* seems the most reliable report since it is an eyewitness account. However, Wu Ch'ang-yüan, also writing from personal experience, claims that the *Ching-ch'iang* actor Pai Erh was still at the height of his fame in 1775 and notes specifically that this actor's reputation suffered drastically when he had to compete with Wei Ch'ang-sheng in 1780 and 1781 (*YLHP*, 3, 1a). If Wu's account is correct, then we must reject 1774 and 1775 as the date of Wei's first entry into Peking. The author of *JHKHC* wrote in 1805. Therefore, in the present case he was recalling events of many years earlier and could easily have remembered the date inaccurately. Wu Ch'ang-yüan completed his *YLHP* in 1785. Being two full decades closer the time in question, it may be considered a more reliable source. The correct date of Wei's arrival must therefore be 1779.

[6] *YLHP*, 5, 3b–4a.

[7] On this drama see below, p. 251.

[8] *YLHP*, 3, 2b.

[9] *YLHP*, 5, 4a.

enemies for him. One author wrote, in an obvious attempt to depreciate him, 'The whole country went mad about him; I alone did not enjoy his acting.'[1] In the autumn of 1782, Wei Ch'ang-sheng was forbidden to act because his performances were considered to be exercising a harmful influence on the people, and he temporarily left the stage. Soon after, however, he changed the name of his company to Yung-ch'ing and resumed acting. Yet the ban on Wei's performances had succeeded in damaging his reputation and 'he had declined by comparison with earlier days.' Other actors began to take a higher place in the affections of the people. It appears that after 1782 his acting was much less *risqué* than it had been. Wu Ch'ang-yüan wrote in 1785, 'An old concubine in my family recently saw him act the part of a woman chaste till death; his voice and facial expressions were extremely vivid and brought tears to the eyes of the audience'.[2]

Wei's most famous patron during this time was the minister Ho-shen. According to an old man who had seen the two together, the minister and actor were homosexual lovers.[3] In Chang Chi-liang's words, 'Wei Ch'ang-sheng enjoyed from Ho-shen the favour of the cut sleeve (*tuan-hsiu*).'[4] Wei was constantly seen at Ho-shen's mansion, and this seems to have annoyed some of the officials, for on one occasion Wei was met by a certain censor while on his way to Ho-shen's house, and beaten like a criminal.[5] It may be that it was owing to Ho-shen's patronage that Wei continued to act after 1782, but it seems surprising in this case that Ho-shen did not act to prevent the ban in the first place. We know that Ho-shen made a show of disapproving of the *Ch'in-ch'iang* actors, especially Wei Ch'ang-sheng and Ch'en Yin-kuan. The explanation of his curious behaviour over the ban of 1782 must therefore be that he wanted to appear as publicly hostile to the 'obscene' Wei, but privately was disposed very favourably towards him.

Wei had many other friends, including some in high positions. According to Chao-lien, 'among princes and nobles down to

---

[1] *JHKHC*, 4, 14b.   [2] *YLHP*, 3, 9a.   [3] Ibid.

[4] *Chin-t'ai ts'an-lei chi* (*CTTLC*), 3, 5b. The phrase *tuan-hsiu* is commonly used for homosexuality. It is an allusion to a story of the Former Han dynasty. The Emperor Ai-ti (6 B.C.–1 A.D.) was in love with Tung Hsien. One day the two were in bed together and Tung fell asleep with his body across his lover's sleeve. The Emperor had to leave for an audience so, rather than awaken Tung Hsien, he cut off his sleeve with a sword. See van Gulik, *Sexual Life in Ancient China*, p. 63.

[5] *CTTLC*, 3, 5a–b.

ordinary literary men or courtesans, . . . nobody who had not made Wei San's acquaintance could be considered a person of worth.'[1] The actor was also on intimate terms with the Manchu Ch'eng-an,[2] a descendant of Ming-chu (1635–1708), who had been the empire's most powerful official in the 1680s. Ch'eng-an himself was falsely accused by Ho-shen and his family property confiscated.[3]

In view of his aristocratic connections, it is not surprising that Wei Ch'ang-sheng accumulated a great deal of money and property during his stay in Peking. He rode in a carriage like that of a high-ranking official and was able to afford a fine house in the Hsi Chu-shih k'ou, one of the main streets in the north-western sector of the Wai-ch'eng (Outer City), which was itself the name given to the southern walled area of Peking. Wei's residence was indeed in the very centre of the most important theatrical area of the capital. Later it became a banqueting hall where scholars and officials could meet for a meal and watch the drama.[4]

Ch'ang-sheng cannot have lived in this house very long for he left Peking in about 1785. In that year an edict was issued forbidding the performance of *Ch'in-ch'iang* in Peking: the *Ch'in-ch'iang* actors were henceforward to perform only *Ching-ch'iang* or *K'un-ch'ü*. Should anybody prove recalcitrant to the order, 'the *ya-men* is to be contacted, and the guilty person to be arrested, punished, and deported back to his native town'.[5]

The reasons for the ban were three-fold. In the first place the government was upset at the manner in which the *Ching-ch'iang*, formerly so popular with Manchu nobles, and the aristocratic *K'un-ch'ü*, had been supplanted. It was also alarmed at the damaging moral effect which it believed Wei and his followers were producing on all strata of society. But the third cause was probably the most important. The *Ch'in-ch'iang* actors were much less tied to standard scripts than their counterparts in the *Ching-ch'iang* and *K'un-ch'ü*, the texts of which had become stereotyped by decades of close supervision in Peking. Political innuendoes could more easily be inserted into the Clapper Opera to include satire or criticism of the authorities. Ch'ien-lung had tried to enforce censorship of the drama and had caused many

[1] *HTTL*, 8, 8a.   [2] *HTTL*, 8, 8b.
[3] Hummel, *Eminent Chinese*, p. 577.   [4] *CTTLC*, 3, 5a–b.
[5] *Ta-Ch'ing hui-tien shih-li*, 1039, 15b–16a.

books to be listed as seditious.[1] He could hardly tolerate a form of theatre so difficult to censor, especially in the very seat of his government.

Apparently Wei Ch'ang-sheng obeyed the order against the *Ch'in-ch'iang* for we hear no more of him in Peking for the time being. According to Chao-lien, he returned home to Szechwan.[2] In 1788 he was acting in Yang-chou as a member of the Ch'un-t'ai company of Chiang Ch'un.[3] He seems to have been extremely highly regarded, for Li Tou reports that 'he was given 1,000 taels for one scene he performed.' Indeed so popular was he in the city that he drew crowds wherever he went, even outside the theatre. 'On one occasion he went boating on a lake; as soon as they heard the news, the sing-song girls all came out in their own boats [to see him].'[4] His influence was very great among the ordinary people and everywhere in Yang-chou one could hear his tunes played and sung.[5]

Despite his success in the area, Wei was not without his critics. Away from Peking, he had reverted to his less decorous style of acting. Chiao Hsün says, 'After the Szechwanese Wei San-erh started singing his lewd songs and low and ridiculous words, a generation of actors in the market-places ... have imitated him and have all been infected [by his influence].'[6] This particular condemnation is made all the more serious by Chiao's known appreciation of the popular theatre.

At about this time, Wei went also to Su-chou, where his impact was apparently similar in kind and extent to that which he had exerted in Yang-chou. Shen Ch'i-feng, writing in 1791, complains strenuously of his ribaldry but is forced to add that actors do not share his antipathy: 'The companies of the popular theatre (*luan-t'an*) have copied him enthusiastically; even among the *K'un-ch'ü* actors there are some who have turned their backs on their teachers and learned from him.'[7] A shocking state of affairs indeed!

In 1792 Wei Ch'ang-sheng went back to his native province.

[1] See Goodrich, *The Literary Inquisition of Ch'ien-lung.*
[2] *HTTL*, 8, 8a.
[3] *Yen-p'u tsa-chi*, 2, 17a.
[4] *YCHFL*, 5, 132.
[5] *YCHFL*, Hsieh Yung-sheng's preface, p. 7.
[6] *Hua-pu nung-t'an*, p. 225.
[7] *Hsieh-to*, 12, 1a.

He wrote a letter to one of his best known admirers and friends, the Szechwanese scholar and official Li T'iao-yüan (1734–1803).[1] Very little else is known about Wei's years at home, but we may assume that he was popular as an actor among his fellow Szechwanese. There is a tradition that at the end of the eighteenth century he established a shrine in Ch'eng-tu and dedicated it to the actors' chief patron god, Lao-lang.[2]

Late in 1800 Wei returned to Peking.[3] He was no longer criticized for coarseness and naturally lacked the fascinating appearance which had earlier won him fame. For the first time we find him also praised for his 'military arts' (wu-chi) which involved complicated acrobatics.[4] Wei's acting seems, then, to have changed somewhat since his first stay in the capital. Ch'ang-sheng still commanded a considerable following. Yang Mou-chien quotes his old servant as saying that 'he still had his own style and whenever he was on the stage the sound would be ten times better [than normal].'[5] He was indeed unusual among Chinese actors in being recorded as making a successful return to Peking. It would be interesting to know if there were any other actors at this period who tried to follow his example, but without success. It is a pity that the sources cast no light on this question.

Yet although 'many people made friends with him because of his great reputation', Wei Ch'ang-sheng was a desperately poor man by the time of his final visit to Peking. He had squandered all his vast savings and no longer lived in a fine house.[6] It may indeed have been the hope of making another fortune that drove him back to Peking. But if this is true, Wei did not succeed, for he died not long after his return to the capital.

One day he was performing in the drama *Piao ta-sao pei wa-tzu*,[7] when he suddenly felt faint and left the stage.[8] He returned

---

[1] See *Chung-kuo ku-tien hsi-ch'ü lun-chu chi-ch'eng*, VIII, 33.

[2] See Kalvodová, 'The Origin and Character of the Szechwan Theatre', *Archiv Orientální*, xxxiv (1966), 512.

[3] *JHKHC*, 4, 14b. According to Chao-lien (*HTTL*, 8, 8a–b), the date of Wei's return to Peking was 1801. However, the *JHKHC* is an earlier work and the author is writing from personal experience about a recent event.

[4] *JHKHC*, 4, 14b–15a. In the traditional Peking Opera specialists in acrobatics are still called *wu-hang*. See Scott, *The Classical Theatre of China*, p. 184. *Wu-sheng, wu-ching, wu-ch'ou*, and *wu-tan* actors, that is the military *sheng, ching, ch'ou*, and *tan*, must also be competent in acrobatics. See ibid., pp. 66, 75, 77, 73.

[5] *MHSP*, p. 21a.   [6] *HTTL*, 8, 8b.

[7] See below, appendix C, p. 252.   [8] *MHSP*, p. 21a.

to the inn where he was staying and died soon afterwards, on
1 May 1802. His possessions were too meagre to cover the costs of
a burial, so friends arranged mourning ceremonies for him and
had his body taken back to Szechwan.[1] A sad end for one who
had earlier been so rich!

As an actor Wei Ch'ang-sheng was an important innovator,
and was never content to perform old dramas. Two specific points
of his dress on the stage were unknown or rare before his time.
One was his hair-style; the other the false foot worn under the
foot and tied to the leg with a cotton bandage, enabling the actor
to imitate the gait of a woman's bound feet (ts'ai-ch'iao).[2] One
author of the nineteenth century wrote of Wei's innovations:

Tan actors were commonly called pao-t'ou ('wrap the head') because
formerly they all wore netting over their heads. Nowadays they all
comb their hair in the 'water' style exactly like women,[3] but they still
retain the name pao-t'ou. An empty name! I heard an old person say that
the combed 'water' hair-style and the walking on false feet so usual in
the singing-houses were both originated by Wei San, and did not
exist before him . . . Nowadays [all actors] learn these arts, but almost
everybody has forgotten who invented them.[4]

Yet naturally they had not gone unnoticed in Wei's own time, at
least in the case of the ts'ai-ch'iao. A friend of Wu Ch'ang-yüan's
commented that 'in former times there were no more than two or
three scenes in which the false tiny feet were used . . . but after
Wei San had all the fame to himself, there was none without the
tiny feet'.[5]

Although he was so renowned as an actor, very little is known
about Wei Ch'ang-sheng as a man. He certainly had a family
despite his homosexuality. A grandson born about 1790 accompanied him to Peking during his final visit there. Wei would
take the boy to the theatres every day, holding him by the
hand.[6]

The sources offer occasional glimpses into Wei's character.
Chao-lien says that 'although he was an actor he was rather
magnanimous in disposition.' His relations with Ch'eng-an show

---

[1] HTTL, 8, 8b.
[2] The ts'ai-ch'iao are discussed by Scott in The Classical Theatre, pp. 143–4.
[3] For a detailed description of the hair-style used by tan actors see ibid., pp. 162–6.
[4] MHSP, p. 10a.   [5] YLHP, 5, 5b.
[6] MHSP, p. 21a.

him to have been a loyal friend. When Ch'eng-an fell from favour and lost all his money, Wei gave him comfort and help.[1] Another story showing his sympathetic nature is told by Chang Chi-liang. A certain scholar from Szechwan was once sitting at Wei's gate in a state of utter destitution; Wei found out about it and gave the man lodgings. He also obtained the assistance of an influential friend to have the scholar given a post as the magistrate of a county.[2]

Like many others of his profession, this great actor was somewhat superstitious. In 1780 there occurred in the south of Peking a devastating fire which lasted a month and destroyed 2,000 or 3,000 houses.[3] When Wei visited a fortune-teller at this time, he was told that the catastrophe had been due to an evil spirit which had struck up from south-west China. He immediately had a temple built to Wen-ch'ang (the God of Literature) in the hope of warding it off.[4]

It will be clear from his biography that Wei Ch'ang-sheng's career as an actor was long. He started acting when young and was still on the stage just before his death at the age of fifty-eight. No other known actor in Peking at this time could claim so long a life on the stage. Furthermore, Wei acted in a number of different parts of China. It was natural, therefore, that he should influence other actors. During his first stay in Peking he instructed a number of disciples. Those known to have been taught by him include Chiang Ssu-erh, who belonged to Wei's Yung-ch'ing company,[5] and Ch'en Chin-kuan from Chungking in Szechwan, who joined the Yü-ch'ing company.[6] In Yang-chou, both Hao T'ien-hsiu and Yang Pa-kuan learned the art of Ch'in-ch'iang from him.[7] The great actor also took on disciples during his final stay in the capital. The two young Pekingese, Huang K'uei-kuan of the Shuang-ch'ing company[8] and Liu Ch'ing-jui of the San-ch'ing,[9] were numbered among them.

Among Wei's disciples, there was one who overshadowed by far all his fellow-students and achieved a reputation equal to that of his great master. This was the young *tan* actor Ch'en Yin-kuan.

[1] *HTTL*, 8, 8b.   [2] *CTTLC*, 2, 5a–b.   [3] *HTTL*, 10, 25a.
[4] *HTTL*, 8, 8b. On Wen-ch'ang see Doré, *Recherches sur les superstitions en Chine*, IIème partie, *Le panthéon chinois*, pp. 29–44.
[5] *YLHP*, 2, 8a.   [6] See *MHSP*, p. 21a and *YLHP*, 2, 5b.
[7] *YCHFL*, 5, 131.   [8] *JHKHC*, 4, 6b.   [9] *JHKHC*, 1, 1a.

Ch'en Yin-kuan; Wei Ch'ang-sheng's Successors

Ch'en Yin-kuan came from Ch'eng-tu and his *tzu* was Mei-pi.[1] Nothing is known of his childhood or the circumstances under which he became an actor. At the age of sixteen he went to Peking where he joined the Shuang-ch'ing company.[2] We know that he was with Wei Ch'ang-sheng in that company in 1780 and 1781[3] and probably arrived in Peking in the former year or shortly before. We may hence place his birth in 1763 or 1764.

Ch'en was deeply influenced by his master. He, too, was considered lewd on the stage and loved to make bawdy jokes. He carried on Wei's custom of wearing false feet on the stage, was short and attractive, and had developed to perfection the art of copying female garb.[4] Like his master, he was especially famous for his performance in one particular drama. In Ch'en's case it was *K'ao-huo*, which relates the story of a girl noted for her fidelity and chastity.[5]

Yet Ch'en Yin-kuan quickly developed a reputation in his own right, and when Wei was forbidden to act in 1782, his disciple left him and joined the I-ch'ing company,[6] which had given up performing *Ching-ch'iang* in favour of *Ch'in-ch'iang*. Ch'en's popularity even began to overtake his former master's, and he became the most noted actor of the day. According to Yü Chiao, 'the *literati* and officials also rose up in crowds to cheer him, and the audiences were unhappy if he was not acting in a drama.'[7]

As befitted his fame and popularity, Ch'en Yin-kuan became very rich. High-ranking officials would offer him precious gifts for his performances and within two or three years he collected many thousands of pearls, pieces of gold, jade, and silk.[8] Though hardly twenty years old, he was able to afford a residence in Tung Ts'ao-ch'ang,[9] a street in the north-eastern region of the Outer City, and a house in Sun-kung yüan, in its north-western sector, where he lived near Ch'en Chin-kuan.[10]

Ch'en was known personally to a great many people. He was welcomed by the rich families and made a number of friends among them. He also developed the habit of mixing socially in a restaurant at the end of each performance and offering drinks to

---

[1] YLHP, 2, 1b.   [2] *Ch'iu-p'ing hsin-yü*, in PCLYCK, p. 10a.
[3] YLHP, 2, 1b.   [4] *Ch'ing-yüan meng-han tsa-chu*, in PCLYCK, pp. 8a–b.
[5] See below, appendix C, pp, 252–3.   [6] YLHP, 2, 1b.
[7] *Ch'ing-yüan meng-han tsa-chu*, in PCLYCK, p. 8b.   [8] Ibid.
[9] CTTLC, 3, 2a.   [10] MHSP, p. 21a.

his admirers. His circle of acquaintances thus became very wide indeed, and it was fashionable among the *literati* to seek invitations to his house in Sun-kung yüan.[1]

But the best known relationship Yin-kuan contracted was with the official Li Tsai-yüan. The latter had heard of his fame and been persuaded by friends to visit him in his residence. The two quickly became intimate and would eat and drink together. They were seen in each other's company so often that their friendship was the subject of much talk throughout Peking.

The young actor's affection for his patron is illustrated by the following story:

In 1786 Tsai-yüan wanted to take the examinations in Chihli province. But because he had been very extravagant and contracted many debts, it was difficult for him to leave Peking. So Ch'en arranged a big banquet for him and gave a performance in the I-ch'ing t'ang [one of the best restaurants in Peking]. He greeted all the guests very politely and they were all happy to contribute money. In this way he raised 1,000 taels and also paid back two or three of the creditors out of his own money. Tsai-yüan was then able to leave with his debts cleared.[2]

So intimate did the two men become that it was rumoured that their relationship was homosexual. One writer, pen-named Fou-ch'a san-jen, who knew Tsai-yüan well, made bold to ask him directly if there was any truth in the tale. Tsai-yüan replied that Ch'en constantly came to his house to chat. At night he would urge the actor to go home, but Ch'en frequently refused. The two would then approach one another like lovers. Tsai-yüan continued: 'Our necks and legs touch and we fondle one another. Although we are both aroused, we have no sexual connection. He has often wondered at my restraint, but I have never changed my behaviour.' On hearing this, Fou-ch'a san-jen 'smiled and did not ask again'.[3]

It is very striking that such material could be printed despite Ch'ien-lung's censorship, and the author's reluctance to write under his surname and *ming* is not surprising. Certainly the story seems to be much more that mere rumour and, despite Li's 'restraint', shows clearly that Ch'en Yin-kuan had strong homosexual leanings. Just as with many other actors, this did not prevent him from being married or keeping concubines,[4] but unfortu-

---

[1] *Ch'iu-p'ing hsin-yü*, in *PCLYCK*, p. 9a.   [2] Ibid., p. 11a.
[3] Ibid., pp. 10b–11a.   [4] *Ch'ing-yüan meng-han tsa-chu*, in *PCLYCK*, p. 8b.

nately we know nothing at all about the women in his life or whether they meant anything to him.

Only one incident in Ch'en's career is recorded in detail. It is an interesting episode and gives an insight into this actor's character. Wu Ch'ang-yüan records it as follows:

I have heard that a year or more ago a certain actor met a high-ranking guest in a theatre, who invited him out to a restaurant and praised him for his marvellous beauty and talents. He ordered his servants to hand him two silver pieces which he gave to him [the actor]. The latter asked where he lived, but he would not tell, saying only that he was a prefect (*t'ai-shou*) from Kwangtung and had come to the capital to await transfer as an intendant (*kuan-ch'a*) [a higher post]. He would be leaving the capital within a few days so they would not be seeing much of each other. The next day the actor was in a different theatre and the guest also went there. He again invited him for a drink and gave him silver as on the previous occasion. Before leaving, the actor insisted on his coming to his house for lunch on a certain day. The other hesitated [and declined] time and again [but then agreed] saying [the actor] must not spend much and prepare only one or two dishes. They could chat a little and that would be all. On the appointed day the man came with a big retinue and specially gave him 1,000 taels. At sunset he wanted to go, but [the actor] insisted on his staying the night, so he sent his servants back, saying they need not come too early the next day. The actor invited him into his bedroom where they chatted very cordially, and he told [his guest] where all his boxes and coffers were. About midnight everybody was asleep except for the two, who were still chattering incessantly. Next morning, when the household got up, they saw that the doors, windows, boxes, and coffers were all open, and that only the actor was lying on the bed. They called him, but could not induce him from sleep. They hurriedly applied water to him after which he woke up. Only then did he realise that the robber had rolled up [all his goods] and escaped over the walls.[1]

The possibility that this story is pure fabrication cannot be overlooked, especially since Chinese theatrical circles have always bristled with rumours, but it is, after all, entirely plausible. Moreover, it is recorded by two authors besides Wu Ch'ang-yüan, both of whom mention that the actor in question was Ch'en Yin-kuan. One of them was Fou-ch'a san-jen[2] who, as we have

[1] *YLHP*, 5, 7a–b.

[2] *Ch'iu-p'ing hsin-yü*, in *PCLYCK*, pp. 9a–10a. Fou-ch'a san-jen adds quite a few lurid details not given by Wu Ch'ang-yüan, especially regarding the bedchamber scene. The other version is *Ch'ing-yüan meng-han tsa-chu*, in *PCLYCK*, pp. 8b–9a.

seen, was on good terms with Li Tsai-yüan. As Ch'en's lover, Li would have been in an excellent position to know the full details and would certainly have wanted to deny the story to Fou-ch'a san-jen had it been untrue.

Certain traits of Ch'en Yin-kuan's personality are crystallized in this incident and they are striking as a reflection of the kind of men successful actors were at the time. The story confirms that Ch'en was a homosexual. He was somewhat naive and very susceptible to flattery and gifts. Finally, he was a social climber. Though he had lived in Peking less than five years, he was drunk with success and very hasty in making intimate friends with high-ranking people. He seems, in fact, to have been not unlike a high-class male prostitute, easily used for the benefit of others, and equally easily deceived.

It is not surprising that a man so morally careless and so rich and successful despite his youth should have made enemies as well as friends. His ribald acting offended many people. He grew increasingly vain and sometimes refused to finish a performance when his audience was not large enough to satisfy his pride. He also completely ignored the edict of 1785 prohibiting the performance of *Ch'in-ch'iang*. It was inevitable that he should eventually be forced to leave the capital.

As it happened, it was Ho-shen himself who brought about Ch'en's departure. He accused the actor of misleading the public[1] and was apparently furious at his refusal to obey the edict, for Ch'en Yin-kuan did not enjoy his master's favour with Ho-shen. Soon after, Yin-kuan was unfortunate enough to come across the carriage of a city supervisory censor (*hsün-ch'eng yü-shih*). This was Ho-shen's opportunity! Ch'en was arrested and the cangue of a criminal placed around his neck. He was about to be banished to the frontiers, but he still had influential friends and the sentence was commuted: he was ordered instead to return to Ch'eng-tu. On his way back he passed through Lu-ch'eng, Chihli, some

---

[1] The *Ch'iu-p'ing hsin-yü* (in *PCLYCK*, p. 11b) says that 'a man with great power' slandered Ch'en Yin-kuan and goes on to describe the circumstances of his arrest and banishment. Since we know from Chao-lien (*HTTL*, 8, 8a) that Ho-shen was responsible for Ch'en's arrest, we may conclude that the 'man with great power' was Ho-shen himself. Clearly Fou-ch'a san-jen sympathized with Ch'en Yin-kuan and, since Ho-shen was still in power in 1792 when he wrote his account, it would have been dangerous to mention Ho-shen by name. By the time *HTTL* was written, Ho-shen was safely dead and degraded.

distance south of Pao-ting. His friend Li Tsai-yüan had taken up an appointment in Lu-ch'eng and he was able to tell his former patron the sad story of his exile, and make a final farewell. At this point, Ch'en disappears entirely from history.

The exact date of Yin-kuan's exile is not certain. However, after Ch'en had raised money to pay Li Tsai-yüan's debts, the latter went to Pao-ting and, soon after, Lu-ch'eng. The date of his departure from Peking was 1786. Yang Mou-chien records that 'when Ch'en Yin-kuan was at the height of his career, people inviting [friends] for a drink would always go to the Chin-ling lou'[1] and it is known that this theatre closed down temporarily in the autumn of 1786.[2] There could well have been a connection between Ch'en's departure and the suspension of business at the Chin-ling lou. This would mean that Yin-kuan left Peking in 1786. In any case we are told directly that 1789 was the year in which Fou-ch'a san-jen gleaned his information on Ch'en's exile from Li Tsai-yüan in Lu-ch'eng.[3] The actor must therefore have left Peking in or before that year.

Ch'en Yin-kuan was the most distinguished of the 'four beauties' (*ssu-mei*)[4] who took Wei Ch'ang-sheng's place in the affection of the Peking populace in the wake of that great actor's decline. The other three were Liu Erh-kuan, Liu Feng-kuan, and Wang Kuei-kuan, all of whom played *tan* roles. All three had reputations not far short of Wei Ch'ang-sheng's. Yet we know much less about them than about Wei or Ch'en and can construct only sketchy biographies of them.

Liu Erh-kuan's *tzu* was Yün-ko and he came from Yunnan. He joined the Ts'ui-ch'ing company as a *Ch'in-ch'iang* actor, probably early in the 1780s, and was still on the stage in 1785. It is not known whether or not he obeyed the prohibition against *Ch'in-ch'iang* of that year. He was tall and graceful, but is said to have been rather scornful and high-handed in his treatment of others.[5] His only known disciple was Man-t'un-erh from Shensi.[6]

Like Liu Erh-kuan, Liu Feng-kuan was a member of the Ts'ui-ch'ing company. He came from Hunan and his *tzu* was T'ung-hua. He learned to sing when young and spent some time

---

[1] *MHSP*, p. 6b.   [2] *MHSP*, p. 3a.
[3] *Ch'iu-p'ing hsin-yü*, in *PCLYCK*, p. 11b.
[4] The term *ssu-mei* is used of the four actors under discussion here in *YLHP*, li-yen, p. 1b.
[5] *YLHP*, 2, 2b.   [6] *YLHP*, 3, 5b.

in Kwangtung and Kwangsi. This is significant, for he must have known the local styles of provinces other than Szechwan before he went to the capital. He arrived in Peking in the winter of 1783 from Kwangsi and immediately became famous. His voice was as 'melodious as that of a young phoenix' and he was endowed with the usual good looks, but, unlike Wei or Ch'en, he was not accused of coarseness on the stage.[1]

The best known of the three was Wang Kuei-kuan (*ming* Hsiang-yün) from Hupeh, also a member of the Ts'ui-ch'ing company. In the same way that Wei Ch'ang-sheng's showpiece was *Kun-lou* and Ch'en Yin-kuan's *K'ao-huo*, Wang was particularly famous for his performance in *Mai po-po*.[2] As an actor he was versatile and took up the study of *K'un-ch'ü* while still noted as a *Ch'in-ch'iang* performer.[3] In appearance he was rather like Ch'en Yin-kuan;[4] in disposition good-natured and retiring.[5]

Like most of the best actors of his time, Wang had a great many friends among scholars and officials. Wu Ch'ang-yüan, indeed, was so keen on this actor that he devoted the whole of the first *chüan* of his *Yen-lan hsiao-p'u* to poems about him. This led some to the conclusion that the relationship between the two men was homosexual, but Wu indignantly denies the rumour.[6]

Apart from his excellence on the stage, Wang was known for his magnificent drawings of orchids. His general ability seems to have made him very rich, for a certain eminent person sold him some of the buildings of his mansion to repay his debts.[7] Wang had two houses, one in Fen-fang Street, the other in Kuo-tzu Alley,[8] both in the western area of the Outer City. His worldly goods enabled him to give up acting, probably about the time of the 1785 edict against the Clapper Opera, and to set up business as a merchant. He apparently did well in his trade and was still living a prosperous and successful life in the second decade of the nineteenth century.[9]

The Ch'in-ch'iang Theatre—Its Impact and the Reasons for its Success

The five *Ch'in-chiang* actors of Peking mentioned so far were

---

[1] *YLHP*, 2, 3a–b.
[2] *YLHP*, 2, 2a–b. On *Mai po-po* see below, appendix C, pp. 250–1.
[3] *YLHP*, 1, 2a.   [4] *YLHP*, 2, 2a.   [5] *HTTL*, 8, 8b.
[6] *YLHP*, 1, 2b.   [7] *HTTL*, 8, 8b–9a.   [8] *CTTLC*, 3, 2a.
[9] *HTTL*, 8, 9a.

but the most important of a whole crowd of fine exponents of the style. In its two *chüan* on the *hua-pu* actors of Peking, the *Yen-lan hsiao-p'u* provides notes and information on forty-four actors, of whom the great majority appear to have performed *Ch'in-ch'iang*. No doubt there were, apart from these forty-four, many other good actors of the style in the capital. A large number of companies were devoted to performing *Ch'in-ch'iang*. Of the forty-four actors, twelve belonged to the Ts'ui-ch'ing company, ten to the I-ch'ing, five to the Yü-ch'ing, four each to the Chi-ch'ing and Yung-ch'ing companies, and nine to other groups.[1] The five mentioned were merely among the most prominent of the *Ch'in-ch'iang* companies. Under the year 1785 a stele found in the Ching-chung Temple in the centre of Peking's Outer City lists thirty-five theatrical companies outside the court,[2] and almost all of them appear to have performed predominantly *Ch'in-ch'iang* dramas.

As the biographies of Liu Erh-kuan, Liu Feng-kuan, and Wang Kuei-kuan show, the *Ch'in-ch'iang* actors were not all Szechwanese. It is true that Wei Ch'ang-sheng and other leading actors were from Szechwan, but they very quickly attracted natives of other provinces to their ranks. Of the forty-four *hua-pu* actors mentioned by Wu Ch'ang-yüan, only thirteen were Szechwanese. Of the remaining thirty-one, twelve were from Peking or its surroundings, six from Chihli, two each from Shensi, Shansi, and Shantung, and one each from Yunnan, Hupeh, Hunan, Kweichow, Honan, Kiangsu, and Kiangsi.[3] We know also that there were actors from Kwangtung in Peking at the time.[4] Musical and stylistic elements might thus have been absorbed from various regions into the *Ch'in-ch'iang* drama of Peking. This becomes all the more possible because a teacher from one province could instruct a disciple from another; the example of Liu Erh-kuan and

---

[1] See also Chou Chih-fu, *Chin pai-nien ti Ching-chü*, p. 17.

[2] The text of the stele is given in *PCLYCS*, pp. 3a–b. The Ching-chung Temple was dedicated to the famous Sung patriot Yüeh Fei and is discussed in *T'eng-yin tsa-chi*, 5, 9b–10a.

[3] Figures given by Aoki Masaru and P'an Kuang-tan differ slightly from mine. According to them, thirteen of the actors came from Peking, five from Chihli, twelve from Szechwan, and three from Shensi. In the latter case the discrepancy is easily explained since I have included San-shou-kuan as a native of Szechwan, not Shensi (see above, p. 85). In the former, Aoki Masaru made a slight and unimportant error; possibly P'an Kuang-tan followed him without checking the material. See Aoki Masaru, *Hsi-ch'ü shih*, p. 452 and P'an Kuang-tan, *Chung-kuo ling-jen hsüeh-yüan chih yen-chiu*, pp. 77–8.

[4] *CTTLC*, 3, 5b.

M'an-t'un-erh is a case in point. Peking, for the moment dominated by *Ch'in-ch'iang*, became in this way a true meeting-place
for various styles from all over China.[1]

Of the *hua-pu* actors who came to Peking from 1779 on, only
one is known to have been associated with a regional style other
than *Ch'in-ch'iang*. This was Hsieh Ssu-erh from P'u-chou in
southern Shansi, who performed *kou-ch'iang*. This music was
special to Shansi, and Wu Ch'ang-yüan describes it as rather like
a cross between *K'un-ch'ü* and *Ching-ch'iang*.[2] Shansi had long
been a bastion of the Clapper Opera, which had probably
influenced *kou-ch'iang*. Yet Hsieh Ssu-erh's accompanists could
easily have included *ti-tzu* players, such as often perform in the
Clapper music of Shansi nowadays, and it was probably this
factor that led Wu Ch'ang-yüan to liken *kou-ch'iang* to *K'un-ch'ü*.
In any case, this Shansi style seems to have been absorbed into
the predominant *Ch'in-ch'iang* music of Wei Ch'ang-sheng and
lost its separate identity. Certainly it was virtually extinct in
Peking by 1829.[3]

There were, then, some points of divergence among the actors
described by Wu Ch'ang-yüan. Yet there is one very striking
attribute shared by all of them. Each of the forty-four was a *tan*.
Our study of the Peking theatre of the 1780s is therefore severely
limited, for a drama included parts for various types of roles.
However, about the famous *lao-sheng*, *ching*, *hsiao-sheng*,[4] or *ch'ou*
of the period we know virtually nothing.

Yet, despite this serious gap in our knowledge, it is possible to
suggest some general characteristics of the *Ch'in-ch'iang* dramatic
pieces performed by Wei Ch'ang-sheng and his followers. Wu
Ch'ang-yüan gives the names of nineteen pieces other than
K'un-ch'ü.[5] Seven of them, including *Mai po-po*, *Hsiao kua-fu
shang-fen*, *Piao ta-sao pei wa-tzu*, and *K'ao-huo*,[6] survived into the
present century. It is striking that all were small theatre and
comedy. None included important *lao-sheng* parts, and none was
noted for roles which demonstrated great skill and staying-power

---

[1] See also Chou Chih-fu, *Ching-chü*, pp. 16–17.

[2] *YLHP*, 3, 3a–b.   [3] *CTTLC*, 2, 4b.

[4] P'eng Wan-kuan performed *hsiao-sheng* as well as *tan* roles (*YLHP*, 2, 4b).
The types of actors in Peking Opera are treated extensively by Scott in *The
Classical Theatre*, pp. 66 ff.

[5] These are listed in Chou Chih-fu, *Ching-chü*, pp. 18–19.

[6] See below, appendix C, pp. 250–1, 252–4.

in singing. Since Wu Ch'ang-yüan deals exclusively with the *tan* artistry, the lack of references to *lao-sheng* roles is not surprising. Nevertheless, it is striking that he should record the names of no dramas with large singing-roles for *tan* performers. Moreover, the famous drama-collection *Chui pai-ch'iu* includes no *Ch'in-ch'iang* pieces with major singing-parts for the *tan* or *lao-sheng* and confirms the impression given by Wu. It seems, then, that the *Ch'in-ch'iang* of Peking was far more important for its acting than for singing.[1]

This characteristic of the *Ch'in-ch'iang* was noticed by contemporaries of Wei Ch'ang-sheng. One of them, an unnamed friend of Wu Ch'ang-yüan, commented harshly upon it. '[In the *Ch'in-ch'iang* music] there is no differentiation in the pitch of the notes and it is just like talking. The *tan* actors who do not sing are just using this as a way to hide their incompetence.' He goes on to remark that when Kao Ming-kuan performed in *Hsiao kua-fu shang-fen*, there was one section where he did not hear a word. 'It was as if puppets had come on the stage.'[2] This listener seems to have been offended by the rapid movement and lack of flowing melody of the *Ch'in-ch'iang*. He was no doubt used to the smooth and slow tunes of the *K'un-ch'ü*.

He comments also on the orchestra used to accompany the *Ch'in-ch'iang* drama. 'There is no *sheng* (reed-organ) or *ti-tzu* used. The main instrument is the *hu-ch'in* and the secondary the *yüeh-ch'in*'.[3] To the *K'un-ch'ü* devotee, the substitution of melodious woodwind by stringed instruments must have made the music sound a little harsh, especially in the case of the bowed *hu-ch'in*, which is popular among the common people and not particularly delicate in tone. It is therefore not surprising that some educated people looked down on the *Ch'in-ch'iang*.

Despite the critics, the Clapper actors undoubtedly produced a tremendous impact on the Peking theatre. Many of its positive aspects will already have become clear in this chapter. In a short time many *Ch'in-ch'iang* actors and companies appeared, acting standards seem to have reached an unusually high level, and the drama took an unprecedented hold on the imagination of people of all strata in Peking.

---

[1] See also Chou Chih-fu, *Ching-chü*, p. 19.   [2] *YLHP*, 5, 5b–6a.
[3] *YLHP*, 5, 5b. On the instruments used in Peking Opera see Scott, *The Classical Theatre*, pp. 41 ff. The *hu-ch'in* is discussed pp. 42–4 and the *yüeh-ch'in*, p. 44.

Though the edict of 1785 certainly dealt a heavy blow to the *Ch'in-ch'iang* actors, many elements of their art lasted. Their dramas were absorbed into the repertoire of the Peking Opera. For example, the Peking operas *Mai yen-chih* and *K'ao-huo* betray by their music their origin as *Ch'in-ch'iang* pieces.[1] Lasting elements of Wei Ch'ang-sheng's dress on the stage have already been mentioned.

But the magnitude of the impact of the *Ch'in-ch'iang* actors can be gauged also by their effect on the other styles of drama, *Ching-ch'iang* and *K'un-ch'ü*.

Although it recovered to some extent in later years, possibly as a result of the 1785 edict, the *Ching-ch'iang* became virtually defunct as an independent style after 1779, except at court. The *Ching-ch'iang* actors lost their patrons. We are told that 'hardly anybody took any interest in the six great companies.'[2] Their actors 'competed in going over to the *Ch'in[-ch'iang]* companies so as to earn a living and avoid cold and hunger'.[3] The great *Ching-ch'iang* actor Pai Erh became regarded as *passé* and joined the Yung-ch'ing company[4] which performed *Ch'in-ch'iang*. Companies which had formerly been so popular because of their excellence in the performance of *Ching-ch'iang* dramas now turned their attention to *Ch'in-ch'iang*. We have already seen that the I-ch'ing and Ts'ui-ch'ing companies, once among the most famous of the *Ching-ch'iang* groups, attracted some of the greatest of the new actors to their ranks and owed their popularity not to *Ching-ch'iang* but to *Ch'in-ch'iang*. The New Wang-fu company is also listed on the 1785 stele found in the Ching-chung Temple, but had probably followed the other troupes in transferring its attention to the newly arrived opera.

The *K'un-ch'ü*, too, declined seriously after 1779. The Ch'ing-ch'eng company, to which Li Kuei-kuan had belonged, had apparently disbanded by that time and there are no references to it for the 1780s. In the fourth *chüan* of his *Yen-lan hsiao-p'u*, Wu Ch'ang-yüan gives details of twenty *ya-pu* actors. It is not clear exactly how many of these were still performing *K'un-ch'ü* in 1785, but four are listed as belonging to companies known to have

---

[1] See Chou I-pai, *Chiang-tso*, p. 226. Some details on the pieces named are given below in appendix C, pp. 249–50, 252–3.
[2] *YLHP*, 3, 9a.   [3] *T'eng-yin tsa-chi*, 5, 7b.
[4] *YLHP*, 3, 1a.

been devoted chiefly to *Ch'in-ch'iang*.[1] One of the four, Wu Ta-pao, had begun his career by learning *K'un-ch'ü*. However, he lived with the Szechwanese actor P'eng Wan-kuan and also tried to learn *Ch'in-ch'iang*.[2] It is quite possible that the other three had also partly given up *K'un-ch'ü* in favour of the Clapper Opera.

The remaining sixteen *ya-pu* actors described by Wu belonged to five companies, the Chi-hsiang, Ch'ing-ch'un, Tuan-jui, T'ai-ho, and Pao-ho. Of these, only the last three are listed on the Ching-chung Temple stele of 1785. The others must therefore have disbanded by then. The Tuan-jui company was apparently quite unimportant. Only one actor mentioned by Wu Ch'ang-yüan belonged to that company. This was Liu Kuei-lin-kuan, and he had returned to Su-chou and was dead by 1785.[3] The T'ai-ho company also had only one known *K'un-ch'ü* member (Yao Lan-kuan from Kiangsu).[4] Three other members named by Wu were all *hua-pu* actors.[5] The company was therefore mixed and cannot have done much to maintain the sagging popularity of the *K'un-ch'ü*.

After 1779 there was only one *K'un-ch'ü* company of any eminence. This was the Pao-ho, to which eleven of Wu Ch'ang-yüan's twenty actors belonged. It was large enough that its managers found it expedient to divide it into two groups. Following one of the basic traditional categorizations of the Chinese theatre, they formed a civilian (*wen*) section, which performed mostly love-stories, and a military (*wu*), emphasizing heroic battle scenes. Yet there is evidence that this double company did not greatly promote the prestige of the *K'un-ch'ü* in Peking. Its only *ya-pu* actor who was still in his prime was Chang Fa-kuan, a member of the civilian section. At twenty-three he was much the youngest performer in the company. Nearly all the others were old and behind the times. Moreover, in 1784

---

[1] The four are Wu Ta-pao (*YLHP*, 4, 1a) of the I-ch'ing, Hsi-ling-kuan (p. 3b) and Li Hsiu-kuan (p. 7b) of the Yung-ch'ing, and Chin Kuei-kuan (p. 7b) of the Ts'ui-ch'ing companies.

[2] *YLHP*, 4, 1a.   [3] *YLHP*, 4, 5a.   [4] *YLHP*, 4, 3a.

[5] These were Chang Lien-kuan and Hsieh Ssu-erh from Shansi (*YLHP*, 2, 5a; 3, 3a), and Yang Pao-erh from Kweichow (p. 6b). Wang Chih-chang implies that the T'ai-ho was a *kou-ch'iang* company because Hsieh Ssu-erh performed that Shansi style and Chang Lien-kuan came from the same province. See *Ch'iang-tiao k'ao-yüan*, pp. 32b–33a. However, he has overlooked the other two actors I have named, the presence of whom suggests that the T'ai-ho could perform several different styles.

it became a mixed company which performed both *K'un-ch'ü* and *Ch'in-ch'iang*.[1] One of its members, Cheng San-kuan of the military section, was a native of Su-chou and had begun his career as a *K'un-ch'ü* actor. After his arrival in Peking in 1783 he learned *Ch'in-ch'iang* music.[2]

Though the impact of Wei and his followers on the *K'un-ch'ü* was neither as sudden nor as radical as that which they produced on the *Ching-ch'iang*, there is little doubt that the Clapper actors came near to monopolizing the Peking stage.

But the effect of the *Ch'in-ch'iang* companies was by no means limited to the changes they wrought in Peking's dramatic music. Their influence on the social aspects of the theatre was also profound. It was they who brought to maturity customs which were to remain features of the Peking theatre until recent times.

During the Ming and early Ch'ing, China's dramatic companies had been of three basic types: the courtesan troupes, the wandering companies, and the private groups. The *Ch'in-ch'iang* troupes belonged to none of these three categories. Many of the actors who belonged to them probably played a social role as male prostitutes, but there were no women in the Clapper troupes. It is worth pointing out that female prostitutes were not important in the development of the Peking theatre in the later half of the Ch'ing, and very few indeed excelled as actresses.[3] The Clapper companies were permanent in the sense that they did not move constantly from one town or village to another, and they were public in that they were not the servants of any particular family and frequently performed in public places.

This does not mean that the *Ch'in-ch'iang* actors did not perform at the banquets of the rich. They were still hired and some actors had special patrons. The reader will have noticed constant references throughout this chapter to the enjoyment which rich men and *literati* found in the arts of Wei and his followers. But no individual or group could claim any special right over the *Ch'in-ch'iang* companies.

Peking's Clapper troupes of the 1780s were divided from other companies mentioned earlier in this work in that they performed not in temples, market-places, brothels, or private mansions, but in public theatres with permanent stages and arrangements for

---

[1] *YLHP*, 4, 8a–b.   [2] *YLHP*, 2, 4a.
[3] See Wang Shu-nu, *Chung-kuo ch'ang-chi shih*, pp. 285–7.

seating spectators. Moreover, many of these theatres catered for the enjoyment not merely of the gentry and wealthy members of society, but also for the ordinary people.

The *Ch'in-ch'iang* companies were not the first public and permanent male troupes. Some of the *Ching-ch'iang*, for instance, appear to have belonged to the same type.[1] Moreover, theatres were not new to Peking in the 1780s. But there can be no doubt at all that the *Ch'in-ch'iang* performers stimulated greatly the system whereby the major theatrical companies of Peking performed frequently not only for one family and its friends, but also for a wider range of people. Henceforth, great theatrical events which all could attend would take place all the year round and not just at certain festivals and seasons.

Why was it that the *Ch'in-ch'iang* actors were able to take the capital by storm and influence it so deeply?

For some time the number of dramatic styles and actors had been increasing all over China and standards of performance were high. Social and economic factors had, by the late Ch'ien-lung period, produced a real golden age of the theatre in many regions of the empire. Since Peking was the political and administrative capital of the country, it was natural that the city should attract talent from all over China. If the Chinese theatre of the Ch'ien-lung era can be compared to a pyramid, then Peking stands at the pinnacle. It was the last of China's major cities to become a great theatrical centre, but when it eventually did so, it completely outstripped its rivals.

It has been suggested that there was a specific occasion which prompted Wei to go to Peking. The seventieth birthday of Ch'ien-lung (by Chinese reckoning) fell in 1780 and it is known that he celebrated his eightieth with great theatrical festivities.[2] It is quite likely that Wei Ch'ang-sheng's arrival in 1779 was connected with Ch'ien-lung's birthday celebrations.[3] Unfortunately, however, there is no direct evidence for this assumption in the primary sources.

---

[1] The name of the Wang-fu company, which means 'the company of the princely mansions', suggests that the troupe performed chiefly for the aristocracy. But there is no record that any of the other *Ching-ch'iang* companies was the private possession of an individual or group and probably they were public troupes.

[2] See below, p. 124.

[3] See Chou I-pai, *Hsi-chü shih*, p. 595.

Both *Ching-ch'iang* and *K'un-ch'ü* had, to a greater or lesser extent, been in vogue in Peking for a long time and both were losing popularity even before Wei Ch'ang-sheng's arrival. Their decline created a vacuum in the theatrical life of the city. The time was ripe for the population of the capital to welcome a new style.

The fact that the *Ch'in-ch'iang* companies were public and permanent was another reason for their success. Private troupes often performed before large audiences. But a family's friends are always limited in number. The Clapper companies, on the other hand, could act for very large groups of spectators. Being permanent, they had time to establish a greater reputation than a wandering troupe could ever hope to enjoy. The combination of the two factors just mentioned must have contributed enormously to the influence they were able to wield over the people of Peking.

There were good reasons in the nature of Peking society itself why many people should be receptive to a style such as that which Wei offered. Chao-lien summarizes them thus:

> The scholars and gentry did not like [the *Ching-ch'iang*] because it was too disorderly and clamourous. They were in need of theatrical entertainment of a more colourful kind ... The words [of *Ch'in-ch'iang*] were rustic and coarse, but people found its abundance of music and hurried rhythm very affecting. Moreover [Wei Ch'ang-sheng's] lewd appearance on the stage was something which people had rarely seen; his reputation thus had a great impact on the capital ... At the time, the officials and rich were by habit very wasteful. The two actors [i.e. Wei and Ch'en] were therefore able to captivate their minds.[1]

Chao-lien's is a reasonable view. It is not surprising that *Ch'in-ch'iang* should appeal to the scholars and officials of Peking because of its novelty, its colourful, or at any rate unusual, music and bawdy acting. Furthermore, it is to be expected that as such people became more corrupt and spent increasing sums of money on entertainment and pleasure, they should welcome a style like the *Ch'in-ch'iang*. And where the influential members of society take the lead in establishing a fashion, the common people will readily follow.

Finally, the simplest and one of the most important reasons for the success of the *Ch'in-ch'iang* actors lay in the magnificence of

[1] *HTTL*, 8, 8a.

their artistry and skill. The sources give the impression that the Clapper actors, and not merely those few already mentioned in these pages, were possessed of considerable artistic and personal magnetism, which made them very difficult to resist. No previous Chinese actors were praised in the extravagant terms applied to Wei and his followers. The people of Peking may have been receptive to a new type of acting, but without the superlative skill of the new actors, the *Ch'in-ch'iang* could scarcely have made so powerful an impression or won such popularity and fame.

It will be clear that the reasons for the success of Wei, Ch'en, and the other Clapper actors were social and cultural rather than economic. There is no evidence that they were specifically following a trade route. They did not arise in Peking as the direct result of a prospering economy. Unlike Yang-chou, where flourishing trade and industrial production nurtured the gradual rise of a theatrical tradition, Peking was favoured with the sudden appearance of a host of splendid actors whose arrival coincided with the beginning of a general decline. The decay of Manchu China was to continue and to be accompanied in Peking by a dramatic life which retained its vigour for over a century. It hardly needs to be pointed out that while economic prosperity favours the development of the arts, there are many historical precedents to show that they can flourish also in times of deterioration.

In this chapter, four distinct styles of *Ch'in-ch'iang* have been mentioned. They are the northern and southern styles of the actors of Hsi-an, that performed in Peking before the arrival of Wei Ch'ang-sheng, and the style of Wei and his followers. These four *Ch'in-ch'iang* forms all belonged to the general system of Clapper Opera and there were consequently similarities among them. They were not, however, identical to each other.

Shensi was almost certainly the original home of the Clapper Opera. The two *Ch'in-ch'iang* styles of Hsi-an were thus probably the earliest, or among the earliest, of the system. Shansi appears to have accepted the new style quickly. As mentioned earlier, it is likely that it was from Shansi that the *Ch'in-ch'iang* heard in Peking before 1779 was derived.

It was recognized immediately in Peking that the style of drama which Wei performed there from 1779 on belonged to the system of Clapper Opera. Wu Ch'ang-yüan comments that the music Ch'ang-sheng introduced to the capital was in fact *pang-tzu ch'iang* or Clapper Opera.[1] Furthermore, the name *Ch'in-ch'iang* (the style of Shensi) betrayed the fact that the new music had originated in the western province of Shensi.

It is, however, not clear when or how the Clapper Opera spread from Shensi to neighbouring Szechwan. One suggestion is that Li T'iao-yüan was responsible for its introduction into his native province.[2] But this is surely most improbable, since Li himself mentions the presence of *Ch'in-ch'iang* in Szechwan and then immediately quotes with explicit approval another author who claims that not much can be known about the Clapper Opera.[3] Moreover, to establish a tradition fine enough to produce a whole galaxy of magnificent actors would have needed time, and Li was not born until 1734, less than fifty years before Wei's entry into Peking. A more plausible explanation is that the rebel Li Tzu-ch'eng (1605?–45),[4] who came from Shensi and is believed to have been keen on Clapper music,[5] brought some *Ch'in-ch'iang* companies with him when he moved his base of operations to Szechwan in 1637 and thus popularized there the music he himself loved.[6] But I think it most likely that, early in the Ch'ing period, wandering companies from Shensi introduced the Clapper Opera to Szechwan in the normal course of their work.

Whatever the truth on these questions, we know that by the time Wei Ch'ang-sheng performed in Peking, the music he sang had undergone certain changes from the original *Ch'in-ch'iang*.

[1] YLHP, 5, 4a.
[2] See Hsi Ming-chen, *Ch'uan-chü chien-t'an*, pp. 20–1.
[3] *Chü-hua*, 1, 47.
[4] See Hummel, *Eminent Chinese*, pp. 491–3.
[5] See Chou I-pai, *Chung-kuo hsi-ch'ü lun-chi*, pp. 220–1. Chou's source is a short biography by the seventeenth-century writer Lu Tz'u-yün, who claims his material to be historical, of the beautiful Ch'en Yüan-yüan. Her story is too well known to require restatement here. Suffice it to say that she fell into the hands of Li Tzu-ch'eng, who ordered her to sing for him. She performed a *K'un-ch'ü* item, but this did not satisfy Tzu-ch'eng and he commanded a group of actresses to sing *hsi-tiao*, 'the tunes of the west', that is of Shensi. 'They took up a *juan* [i.e. the *yüeh-ch'in*, which is used in Clapper music], and a *cheng* [a flat, stringed, zither-like instrument], and beat the *fou* [a clay percussion instrument]. He himself clapped his hands in time to the music, the sound of which was bright and clear.' See *Yüan-yüan chuan*, p. 15b.
[6] See Meng Yao, *Chung-kuo hsi-ch'ü shih*, p. 655.

For example, the orchestras used to accompany the two styles were slightly different in composition.[1] This is not surprising, since each region could produce its own effect on any given style of theatrical music.

There is still today a form of drama called *Ch'in-ch'iang*. It is popular principally in Shensi and must be the descendant of the *Ch'in-ch'iang* heard in Hsi-an in the eighteenth century. What is today called *Ch'uan-chü* or Szechwanese Opera is a combination of a variety of styles including one named *t'an-ch'iang*, which is a form of Clapper Opera. Probably *t'an-ch'iang* is the descendant of the style Wei Ch'ang-sheng performed in Peking, especially since the Clapper Opera was already called *luan-t'an* in Szechwan before 1779.[2] It may be that the Szechwanese *t'an-ch'iang* is as close as any current style to Wei's *Ch'in-ch'iang*. But since there are no precise records of how Wei's music sounded, this is a matter about which we cannot be sure.

[1] The main stringed instrument in the early *Ch'in-ch'iang* of Shensi and Szechwan was the *yüeh-ch'in* (see p. 114, note 5 and *Chü-hua*, 1, 47), whereas that of the Peking *Ch'in-ch'iang* was the *hu-ch'in*, the *yüeh-ch'in* being its secondary instrument.

[2] Ibid.

V

THE COURT AND THE ANHWEI
COMPANIES TILL 1830

THE HISTORY of Wei Ch'ang-sheng and his followers shows that Ch'ien-lung took a decidedly biased attitude in his patronage of the theatre. He was keen to see the *K'un-ch'ü* flourish in the south; not too enthusiastic about the popular *Ch'in-ch'iang* actors in the capital. Where Peking was concerned, he concentrated his efforts to promote the opera not in the streets and alleys where the commoners lived, but in a place even nearer home—his own court.

The Court Theatre

Many emperors of earlier dynasties were known as patrons of the palace drama—Ming-huang (712–56) of T'ang and Chuang-tsung (923–6) of Later T'ang were particularly famous examples—and the first Ch'ing rulers followed this precedent.[1] After the Rebellion of the Three Feudatories was suppressed in 1681,[2] the K'ang-hsi Emperor even went to the length of arranging a public banquet early in 1683 to celebrate this great victory. Special stages were built and the drama *Mu-lien* performed. One work records that 'live tigers, live elephants, and real horses were used' to render the occasion truly spectacular.[3]

However, it was not until the reign of Ch'ien-lung that the imperial house took any active and serious steps to encourage the court theatre. At the beginning of his reign he ordered the official Chang Chao (1691–1745)[4] to rearrange some old dramas

[1] See Chou I-pai, *Chung-kuo hsi-chü shih*, p. 667.

[2] In 1673 the ruler of south-west China, Wu San-kuei, repudiated Manchu authority and induced most of south China to follow his lead. The country was thrown into a prolonged civil war, known as the Rebellion of the Three Feudatories. See Hummel, *Eminent Chinese of the Ch'ing Period*, pp. 879–80. Effective Manchu rule had never really been felt all over the south and it was only after Wu's forces and those of his successors had been crushed that the whole country could be considered united under Manchu administration.

[3] *Ch'un-hsiang chui-pi*, 3, 19a.   [4] See Hummel, *Eminent Chinese*, pp. 24–5.

for the court's entertainment and to supervise the establishment of a court troupe to perform them. Chao produced some five pieces, including the *Ch'üan-shan chin-k'o*, which deals with the story of Mu-lien. Yin-lu (1695–1767),[1] the sixteenth son of the Emperor K'ang-hsi, was commanded to assist in Chang's task and re-arranged the stories of the Three Kingdoms into the *Ting-chih ch'un-ch'iu*.[2]

Around 1740 a special organization was set up to control the court theatre.[3] It was called Nan-fu after its site, which lay not far south-west of the south-western corner of the imperial palaces.[4] It consisted of several sections, including an office called Ch'ien-liang ch'u in charge of costumes and stage-sets[5] and five schools. The three most important of these were initially placed under the presidency of Chin Chin-chung (1682–1754)[6] and came to be known as inner schools (*nei-hsüeh*). The actors trained there were eunuchs, and all were drawn from within the court itself—hence the name 'inner'. They contrasted with the performers from outside the palaces, who were placed under the tutelage of two outer schools (*wai-hsüeh*).[7] These establishments, however, did not come into being until about a decade after the *nei-hsüeh*.

The emperor's decision to include actors from outside the court

[1] Ibid., pp. 925–6.

[2] *Hsiao-t'ing hsü-lu*, 1, 4a–b.

[3] See Wang Chih-chang, *Ch'ing Sheng-p'ing shu chih-lüeh*, pp. 6–7. Wang's is the most authoritative secondary work on the court drama of the Ch'ing. Much of his information for the period before the earliest court annals (1806) is based on steles, including a few discovered in a cemetery, set aside especially for the members of the Nan-fu, outside the Fu-ch'eng Gate in Peking's western suburbs. See also Hsü Mu-yün, *Chung-kuo hsi-chü shih*, p. 82.

[4] Wang Chih-chang, *Ch'ing Sheng-p'ing shu*, p. 584.

[5] The functions of the Ch'ien-liang ch'u are stated in the court theatre annals. The passage refers specifically to 27 October 1821 but can probably be applied also to the earlier period. It is quoted by Chou Chih-fu in his *Ch'ing Sheng-p'ing shu ts'un-tang shih-li man-ch'ao*, 3, 1a. Chou's work is a collection of extracts from the surviving volumes (*ts'e*) of court theatre annals, which number over 500. They are the most important sources for the court drama of the nineteenth and early twentieth centuries and their titles are listed by Chou Chih-fu in the closing section of his book. In 1924 the volumes were sold by some former court eunuchs to a book-dealer. They were bought by Professor Chu Hsi-tsu who, in 1932, gave them to the then Peiping Library (Wang Chih-chang, *Ch'ing Sheng-p'ing shu*, p. 3). The originals are not easily accessible and Chou's work can be regarded as a primary source.

[6] Wang Chih-chang, *Ch'ing Sheng-p'ing shu*, pp. 8, 331.

[7] The various sections under the Nan-fu are listed in the Ching-chung Temple stele of 1785. See *Pei-ching li-yüan chin-shih wen-tzu lu* (*PCLYCS*), p. 3a.

was a direct result of his first visit to the south in 1751.[1] He had
been greatly impressed by the standards of acting he witnessed in
Su-chou and Yang-chou, and determined to take some of these
cities' actors for his own entertainment. The machinery for their
dispatch to the north was formal and well organized. The
nineteenth-century author Ku Lu writes that in Su-chou all drama
troupes 'must first register their names in the Lao-lang Temple;
the temple is under the control of the Imperial Silk Office, so all
the people needed to supply the Nan-fu must be chosen by that
office.'[2] With one important difference, the system of registration
was very similar to that which prevailed in Yang-chou. As noted
in chapter three, it was the Liang-huai Salt Administration which
supervised the drama troupes there, and no doubt that organization chose the actors for the emperor.

The influx of southern actors into the court created administrative problems for the Nan-fu. Many of the southerners had
already established their reputation and did not mix at all well
with the court eunuchs. Accommodation at the Nan-fu also
required much rearrangement. The emperor therefore set up
another organization. Its site was at Ching-shan, a large mound
just north of the imperial palaces, and, like the Nan-fu, it took the
name of the place where its headquarters lay.[3] By 1785 there were
three outer schools and a Ch'ien-liang ch'u attached to the Ching-
shan,[4] and it was here that most of the actors from Yang-chou and
Su-chou taught, learned and prepared their performances for the
emperor. In 1788 Wu Ch'ang-yüan described their compound
briefly as follows: 'In the north-west corner of the inner walls of
the Ching-shan there are more than 100 rooms together, where
live the actors from Su-chou who perform for the court. It is
commonly called Su-chou Lane. Inside the main gate there is a
temple with a main and two side halls ... In front there is a
pavilion which is a place for rehearsals.'[5]

[1] See Chou I-pai, *Hsi-chü shih*, p. 668 and Wang Chih-chang, *Ch'ing Sheng-
p'ing shu*, p. 8.

[2] *Ch'ing-chia lu*, 7, 4a.

[3] Wang Chih-chang, *Ch'ing Sheng-p'ing shu*, p. 24. Ching-shan was also the
site of an official school for the sons and younger brothers of certain high-ranking
bannermen. The school had been founded by K'ang-hsi and was still functioning,
in a different part of the Ching-shan enclosure, when the theatrical organization
was set up. See *Ta-Ch'ing hui-tien shih-li* (*TCHT*), 1200, 11a–14b. Ching-shan is
famous as the place where the last Ming Emperor committed suicide.

[4] *PCLYCS*, p. 3a.   [5] *Ch'en-yüan shih-lüeh*, 16, 38b.

The dramas which the Nan-fu and Ching-shan actors offered the court belonged to the *Ching-ch'iang* and *K'un-ch'ü* styles. The influence of the *Ch'in-ch'iang* did not penetrate into the palaces, which resisted the bawdy popular opera firmly. There is an oral tradition that the southern actors brought back to the court by Ch'ien-lung included some who could sing *erh-huang*.[1] This cannot be confirmed from early written records, and even if it is true, the style does not seem to have made much impression at court until the Manchu rulers of the late nineteenth century began taking an interest in Peking Opera.

The Ch'ien-lung period was the heyday of the Ch'ing court theatre, and there were well over 1,000 actors providing entertainment for the imperial family. Under Chia-ch'ing this number declined sharply. According to the court annals of 21 February 1821, 'there are now more than 300 students and others from outside in the Nan-fu and Ching-shan, but this is less than half the figure in 1799.'[2] The number of *wai-hsüeh* in the Ching-shan had fallen from three to two (called 'the Great and Small companies'), the loss being compensated by a rise from two to three in the Nan-fu. But, though the overall total of *wai-hsüeh* remained at five, there were now only two *nei-hsüeh* instead of the three which had functioned under Ch'ien-lung.[3]

These reductions were only the prelude to the much more drastic action taken in the 1820s. Within a few months of Tao-kuang's accession in 1821, the outer schools numbered only 183 students and ten leaders.[4] Moreover, it was declared on 1 July that 'the Great and Small companies of the Ching-shan must be absorbed into the Nan-fu, and the name Ching-shan never mentioned again.'[5] And on 26 September the order came that there should henceforth be only one inner and one outer school under the Nan-fu.[6]

In 1827 Tao-kuang moved against the southern actors once more. 'On 3 March there was an imperial decree that every

---

[1] Ch'i Ju-shan, *Ching-chü chih pien-ch'ien*, pp. 24a–b. The story was told to Ch'i by the actor Sheng Ch'ing-yü, then aged seventy-five, who had heard it in his youth from old actors.

[2] Chou Chih-fu, *Ch'ing Sheng-p'ing shu*, 3, 2b.

[3] Wang Chih-chang, *Ch'ing Sheng-p'ing shu*, p. 40.

[4] *TCHT*, 1218, 1a.

[5] Chou Chih-fu, *Ch'ing Sheng-p'ing shu*, 3, 1b.

[6] Ibid., 3, 2a.

single one of the Nan-fu's students from outside should be sent away and return to his native town.'[1] The custom of importing actors from Su-chou and Yang-chou was suspended. On the same day the Nan-fu was abolished and a new organization, called Sheng-p'ing shu, set up to replace it.[2]

The sharp fall after 1800 in the number of court actors, especially those from the south, suggests that Chia-ch'ing was not as keen on the theatre as Ch'ien-lung had been; and Tao-kuang seems to have been even less interested. But another reason for the cuts was possibly the emperor's fear for the security of the palace after it was stormed by members of the T'ien-li chiao in 1813. A third motive for Tao-kuang's ferocity against actors has been suggested. There is a tradition that an ambassador from outside Peking once brought Chia-ch'ing three sable coats as a gift. The future Tao-kuang wanted them himself, but his father gave him only one; the others he presented to his favourite southern actor. Tao-kuang is said to have felt extremely humiliated at seeing a mere actor preferred to himself and to have nursed a grudge against the performers from outside. The story cannot be checked, but is certainly plausible and would go some way towards explaining the Emperor's attitude.[3]

The official who presided over the changes on the Emperor's behalf was Li Lu-hsi and his name appears constantly in the court theatre annals of the Chia-ch'ing and Tao-kuang periods. Born in 1782 near Peking, he had entered the court as a eunuch trainee at the age of ten, and in 1801 became a leader of the inner schools. In 1803 he was promoted to the position of president of the schools and appears to have retained this office until 1827, apart from one

[1] Ibid., 3, 2b.   [2] Ibid.

[3] See Wang Chih-chang, *Ch'ing Sheng-p'ing shu*, pp. 31–2. Wang accepts the story largely because an event in 1827, recorded in the court theatre annals and veritable records of 9 December (see ibid. and *Ta-Ch'ing Hsüan-tsung Ch'eng huang-ti shih-lu*, 128, 14a–15b) suggests that there was much hard feeling between actors and Tao-kuang. In that year Mien-k'ai (1795–1839, see Hummel, *Eminent Chinese*, p. 573), Tao-kuang's younger brother, was charged with hiding a fugitive eunuch actor, a crime for which he was temporarily degraded. Mien-k'ai was an enthusiast of the theatre and Tao-kuang was upset at the way he associated with actors to the neglect of higher pursuits. The evidence for Tao-kuang's alleged grievance is extremely flimsy, especially since the actor concerned in the attempted escape was a court eunuch and not a member of the *wai-hsüeh*. Nevertheless, it is impossible to reject the oral tradition out of hand. It is described in detail and accepted unreservedly by Lei Hsiao-ts'en in 'P'i-huang chü chih shih ti chin-chan', *Wen-hsüeh shih-chieh chi-k'an* 20 (1958), p. 2.

interval in the late Chia-ch'ing period. When the Sheng p'ing shu was set up in 1827, he became its president and retained this function until he retired on 8 December 1856. He died four years later on 1 January 1861.[1]

But whatever the talents or otherwise of the officials who ran the organizations guiding the palace actors, the theatre remained important to the court and played a definite role in its life. In the first place, it was a useful aid towards impressing foreigners. The emperors would invite envoys from abroad to watch dramatic performances as a way of entertaining them and showing forth their own splendour. The Earl of Macartney, who visited China in 1793, attended several sessions during his stay, including one in September at the emperor's famous summer residence in Jehol.[2] To judge from Sir George Staunton's account, the British party was more impressed by the stages they saw there than by the dramas performed upon them, but in any case the purpose of the afternoon spent watching the opera was partly to provide Macartney with an additional opportunity of meeting the courtiers. Staunton wrote that 'Between the acts, many of the spectators went into the Embassador's [sic] box, to see and converse with him.'[3]

Another significant function fulfilled by the drama was that of companion to various kinds of celebrations, some of which occurred regularly, others only occasionally. Chao-lien specifies that the dramatic companies 'performed at all festivals' in the Ch'ien-lung period,[4] and the court theatre annals provide abundant testimony that all the main popular festivals, like the Feastday of Kuan-ti, and the New Year, Lantern, Dragon Boat, and Mid-Autumn festivals, were similarly celebrated during the nineteenth century.[5] Of course days of special significance for the imperial family also provided the opportunity for enjoying operas with

---

[1] Wang Chih-chang, *Ch'ing Sheng-p'ing shu*, pp. 332–51.

[2] The construction of the summer palaces at Jehol, about 120 miles north-east of Peking, was begun in 1703 by K'ang-hsi, who visited the city every year from 1683 until his death. They were greatly expanded under Ch'ien-lung, during whose reign they enjoyed their heyday. See Hummel, *Eminent Chinese*, p. 330 and especially Hedin, *Jehol*.

[3] Sir George Staunton, *An Authentic Account of an Embassy from the King of Great Britain to the Emperor of China*, II, 265.   [4] *Hsiao-t'ing hsü-lu*, I, 4a.

[5] Chou Chih-fu, *Ch'ing Sheng-p'ing shu*, I, *passim* and Wang Chih-chang, *Ch'ing Sheng-p'ing shu*, pp. 58–9. The New Year, Lantern, Dragon Boat, and Mid-Autumn Festivals are discussed in Eberhard, *Chinese Festivals*.

appropriately auspicious themes. The birthday of the Emperor, his mother, wife, or main concubine, and the wedding of an Emperor or prince were among the many joyous events which called for such entertainment.[1] The place of the theatre in court life was strikingly similar to that it held in other social strata.[2]

No less wide than the variety of festivals which called the court actors to their work was that of the sites where the performances were actually given.[3] The particular hall, courtyard, or garden depended mainly on the occasion or season, and a stage would be built temporarily if need be. Yet there were two locations within the Forbidden City compound which were favoured as theatres above all others. One was the Ch'ang-ch'un kung, one of the most imposing of the side-palaces; it lay in the central-western quarter of the Forbidden City and was the home of many famous imperial concubines. The other was the Ning-shou kung, in its north-eastern area, whither Ch'ien-lung retired after his abdication; it later became the abode of the Empress Dowager Tz'u-hsi. The enclosure contained the largest stage in all the palaces of Peking or its environs, the three-tiered Ch'ang-yin ko.[4]

There were also several places outside the city of Peking where the court actors could live, rehearse and perform. One was the so-called Old Summer Palace, Yüan-ming yüan, not far north-west of Peking. It was built under K'ang-hsi, beginning in 1709, and was intended for the enjoyment of his fourth son, the future Yung-cheng Emperor.[5] Before its destruction by British and

---

[1] Wang Chih-chang, *Ch'ing Sheng-p'ing shu*, pp. 89–134 and Chou Chih-fu, *Ch'ing Sheng-p'ing shu*, 2, 1a–14a.

[2] The celebration of popular festivals in Peking is described in the *Yen-ching sui-shih chi*, written by Tun Ch'ung in 1900. An annotated translation of this work has been written by Derk Bodde under the title *Annual Customs and Festivals in Peking*. Tun describes the feastday of Kuan-ti thus: 'Every year, beginning from the eleventh day of the fifth month, the temple [of Kuan-ti] is opened for three days, during which time actors come each year to perform according to invariable custom'. See *Yen-ching sui-shih chi*, p. 65. I have followed Bodde's translation here. See *Annual Customs*, p. 49.

[3] See Chou I-pai, *Chung-kuo chü-ch'ang shih*, pp. 21–4.

[4] See Chou I-pai, *Hsi-chü shih*, pp. 694–9 and especially Ts'ao Hsin-ch'üan, 'Ch'ien-Ch'ing nei-t'ing yen-hsi hui-i lu', *Chü-hsüeh yüeh-k'an* ii, 5 (May 1933), pp. 7–8. A good picture of the Ch'ang-yin ko can be found in Osvald Sirén, *The Imperial Palaces of Peking*, II, pl. 92. This work, in three volumes, contains 274 plates of Peking's palaces, including those outside the city, and a short historical introduction.

[5] See Malone, *History of the Peking Summer Palaces under the Ch'ing Dynasty*, p. 43.

French forces in 1860,[1] this large compound of gardens and palaces boasted a fine stage within a square courtyard. It was called T'ung-lo yüan and here Yung-cheng and succeeding emperors before T'ung-chih frequently watched the opera.[2] The famous three-tiered stages of the more recent Summer Palace, I-ho yüan, were built by the Empress Dowager Tz'u-hsi and will be discussed in the next chapter. During the Tao-kuang period there were usually resident actors at the Yüan-ming yüan.[3] This seems to have been partly because Li Lu-hsi believed that his subordinates could rehearse more efficiently there than in the Nan-fu or Ching-shan, owing to the calmer atmosphere away from the central court.[4]

But a far more important site for the imperial drama was the summer palaces at Jehol. Under Ch'ien-lung the splendour of the city's court opera hardly lagged behind Peking itself, and its main theatre was larger than any in the capital. The poet and historian Chao I has left us the following vivid description of a performance in Jehol:

The actors of the court's theatrical companies are greatest in number. Their robes, tablets, armour and stage-sets are [more magnificent than] anything those outside the court ever see. I happened to see them at the palaces in Jehol. The emperor had gone to Jehol for the autumn hunt [which did not begin until after the Mid-Autumn Festival[5]], and all the Mongol princes were there to pay their respects. Two days before the Mid-Autumn Festival was the emperor's birthday. Therefore large-scale dramas were performed from the sixth day of that month [the eighth] until the fifteenth, and stories about immortals and spirits . . . were put on. They were chosen to be mythical in order not to offend anybody and, moreover, so that passages could be inserted. Many people were led on and the whole show was designed to be spectacular. The stage was nine bamboo mats wide and there were three tiers. Among those dressed up as wizards or four-legged demons, there were some who would descend from above or spring out from below, and even the two wings were made into the dwellings of fairies. Some [actors] rode camels or danced on horses and even filled the courtyard

---

[1] This is described ibid., pp. 177–93.

[2] See ibid., pp. 94–5. On p. 95 there is a reproduction of a picture which includes the theatre courtyard. See also Ch'en-yüan shih-lüeh, 11, 22a and Chou Chih-fu, Ch'ing Sheng-p'ing shu, 6, passim.

[3] See Wang Chih-chang, Ch'ing Sheng-p'ing shu, pp. 586–92.

[4] Chou Chih-fu, Ch'ing Sheng-p'ing shu, 4, 9a.

[5] See Hedin, Jehol, pp. 162–4.

[which separated the stage from the emperor's seat]. Sometimes spirits would gather, and there were hundreds or thousands of *ching* actors, not one looking the same as another. Before the immortals came out, Taoist acolytes of eleven or twelve years old would come on the stage in groups, and, after them, some of fourteen, fifteen, sixteen or seventeen, each group containing dozens of people all of identical height. I have given but one example, so the others can be gauged.[1]

A colourful picture indeed! The emperor Ch'ien-lung certainly did things on a lavish scale.

The Anhwei Companies: The Position of Erh-huang

The audiences at performances such as the one just described were restricted to members of the imperial retinue. But celebrations including drama were sometimes held to honour imperial birthdays not only within the various courts but also outside them, where the common people could join in the festivities. On the twenty-fifth of the eleventh lunar month (which corresponded to 11 January), 1752, Ch'ien-lung's mother, the Empress Hsiao-sheng, had her sixtieth birthday and there were great celebrations held.[2] We are told that 'over the ten or more *li* from the Hsi-hua Gate [in the western wall of the Forbidden City] to the Kao-liang Bridge outside the Hsi-chih Gate [in the western wall of Peking city] . . . there were stages every twenty or thirty paces. On them, both northern and southern tunes were performed.'[3] Similar celebrations were held for the Empress Hsiao-sheng's eightieth birthday in 1772.[4]

At least one such occasion was to exercise a profound influence on the history of the Peking theatre. In 1790 various companies came to Peking to celebrate the eightieth birthday (by Chinese reckoning) of Ch'ien-lung. These were the so-called Anhwei companies, some of which were to survive for more than a

---

[1] *Yen-p'u tsa-chi*, 1, 11b–12a. It may be added, too, that many of the mansions inhabited by Ch'ien-lung during his southern tours were equipped with fine stages. This is shown by charts in the *Nan-hsün sheng-tien*, 97, 6b and 20b (Yang-chou); 99, 1b (Su-chou); 101, 1b (Nanking); and 102, 2b and 3b (Hang-chou). The stages are similar in architecture to the other buildings in the residences.

[2] Empress Hsiao-sheng was born on the 25th of the eleventh month (1 January) 1693. See Hummel, *Eminent Chinese*, p. 369. Her sixtieth birthday in Chinese reckoning fell, on the same day of the lunar year, fifty-nine (not sixty as in Western reckoning) years later.

[3] *Yen-p'u tsa-chi*, 1, 10a.

[4] Ibid., 1, 11a.

century and function as the principal instruments for the rise and development of the Peking Opera.

There are five principal sources on the actors of these and other *hua-pu* troupes of Peking from 1790 to the late 1820s. They are the *Jih-hsia k'an-hua chi*, the *P'ien-yü chi*, the *Chung-hsiang kuo*, the *T'ing-ch'un hsin-yung* and the *Chin-t'ai ts'an-lei chi*.[1] These works were completed in 1803, 1805, 1807, 1810, and 1829 respectively and their contents refer, in the main, to the period of composition. Like the *Yen-lan hsiao-p'u*, they describe almost exclusively *tan* actors. The first four deal with many actors, but their language is highly literary and they do not provide enough information about any single actor to enable us to construct a detailed biography. The *Chin-t'ai ts'an-lei chi*, though its style is clearer than that of the earlier works, deals with only few actors and the scope of the material if offers about them is somewhat disappointing. Nevertheless, the existence of five works dealing with slightly different periods does permit us to trace the development of the actors and companies of Peking. In this respect the first four are particularly useful. Because their methods of presentation are similar and the time-span of their composition short, it is possible to make informative comparisons of their contents and hence learn something about the progress of the Peking stage.

At the head of the companies which arrived in 1790 was the San-ch'ing, led by Yü Lao-ssu.[2] By 1793 this troupe included the famous *tan* actor Kao Yüeh-kuan (*tzu* Lang-t'ing).[3] Li Tou believed that Kao was actually the founder of the San-ch'ing company. He wrote that Kao 'combined the *hua-pu* of An-ch'ing with *Ch'in-ch'iang* and *Ching-ch'iang* and called his company the San-ch'ing (the company of the three *ch'ing*). Consequently, the former I-ch'ing, Ts'ui-ch'ing and Chi-ch'ing disappeared.'[4] However, there is little doubt that the San-ch'ing company existed before 1790,[5] and later writers have rejected Li's implica-

---

[1] I have discussed the *Jih-hsia k'an-hua chi* (*JHKHC*), *T'ing-ch'un hsin-yung* (*TCHY*) and *Chin-t'ai ts'an-lei chi* (*CTTLC*) in appendix B.

[2] *Hsin-jen kuei-chia lu* (*HJKCL*), p. 10a.

[3] *Hua-chien hsiao-yü* (*HCHY*), in *Pei-ching li-yüan chang-ku ch'ang-pien* (*PCLYCK*), p. 8a.

[4] *Yang-chou hua-fang lu* (*YCHFL*), 5, 131.

[5] The Chi-ch'ing is not listed in the 1785 stele (*PCLYCS*, pp. 3a–b) and must therefore have disbanded before then. This fact is in itself evidence against Li Tou's report. Furthermore, a marginal note by the son of the Manchu Wu-la-na

tion.[1] Yet this does not significantly lessen Kao's importance as an innovator and he was the first person recorded in the primary sources as performing in Peking the dramatic style *erh-huang*,[2] which has remained popular there ever since his time.

Much less is known about Kao Yüeh-kuan than Wei Ch'ang-sheng. Yet his impact on the music of the Peking theatre was more lasting and he became as much a legend as did his Szechwanese counterpart. The names of Wei and Kao are linked together as though the two actors were of comparable greatness. In one text of the early nineteenth century we read that 'the [author of the] *Yen-lan hsiao-p'u* regarded Wan-ch'ing [Wei Ch'ang-sheng] as the prince of his generation among actors; this verdict may be rightly applied also to Lang-t'ing.'[3] It is noted of the actor Wu Lien-kuan, who flourished about 1810, that 'he had the beauty of style of Wei Wan-ch'ing and the magnificent expression of Kao Lang-t'ing.'[4]

The precise date of Kao Yüeh-kuan's birth is not known, but it was a few years before or after 1770.[5] He came originally from Pao-ying, a county of Yang-chou, but as a boy lived also in Hang-chou. He moved afterwards to Anhwei[6] and it was probably there that he learned the style with which his name became so closely associated, the *erh-huang*. He later lived and acted also in Yang-chou and it seems to have been from there that he went to Peking.[7]

By 1800, Kao Yüeh-kuan was past his prime.[8] In 1803 he was

(see Ch'i Ju-shan, *Pien-ch'ien*, p. 49a) on Yüan Mei's *Sui-yüan shih-hua* records that 'to celebrate the emperor's birthday . . . there was an order to take the San-ch'ing company to Peking'. (See Chou I-pai, *Hsi-chü shih*, p. 607). This suggests that it existed as a separate entity *before* its arrival in Peking.

[1] See Yang Mou-chien's *Meng-hua so-pu* (*MHSP*), p. 6b and *HJKCL*, p. 10a. In the former work Yang specifically rejects the notion, apparently held by some of his contemporaries, that there was a connection between the name San-ch'ing and the three companies, I-ch'ing, Ts'ui-ch'ing, and Shuang-ch'ing.

[2] See *JHKHC*, 4, 14a.   [3] Ibid.   [4] *TCHY*, *pieh-chi*, p. 4a.

[5] *JHKHC*, written in 1803, says (4, 14a) that Kao was twenty-nine. This would make his birth-year 1774. On the other hand the *Chung-hsiang kuo*, written in 1806–7, claims (p. 15b) that he was more than forty. If this is true, Kao was born in 1766 or earlier.

[6] *JHKHC*, 4, 14a–b.

[7] Li Tou records (*YCHFL*, 5, 131) that Kao went to Peking. The fact that this author should mention his existence and his entry into the capital suggests that he acted in Yang-chou and went from there to Peking.

[8] *HCHY*, in *PCLYCK*, p. 8a.

already regarded as a veteran (*ch'i-su*). Yet he was the leader of the San-ch'ing company and his reputation was still great. He was unsurpassed in the performance of *erh-huang* drama and it was said of him that he was so good in the portrayal of female parts that 'the spectators forgot that he was not really a woman.'[1] His most noted drama was *Sha-tzu ch'eng-ch'in* (*The Fool Completes a Marriage*),[2] the title of which suggests that it was a light comedy.

Even in 1807 Kao had not left the stage completely. However, his appearances were rare,[3] and he probably stopped performing altogether not long afterwards. Certainly, the *T'ing-ch'un hsin-yung* of 1810 makes no mention of him as a current actor.

Kao Yüeh-kuan may well have worked as a teacher long after his retirement from the stage. We know that he was active in the main actors' guild, which had become an important feature of the Peking theatre. A stele found in the Ching-chung Temple lists him as the head of the guild in 1816. In 1826 his name was still to be found among the leading figures of the guild. He was in the forefront of its activities the following year and was among the members in charge of founding a cemetery for actors.[4] However, we hear no more of the great actor after 1827 and he may have died at about that time.

The *erh-huang* music which Kao had helped to make popular in Peking probably included *hsi-p'i* as well, and even today the term *erh-huang* is used to cover both the *erh-huang* and *hsi-p'i* styles.[5] Consequently, we may say that Peking Opera, as known today, arose no later than the early 1790s, for already its two major styles were heard in the capital. *Erh-huang* had been accompanied in the middle of the Ch'ien-lung period by the *hu-ch'in*[6] and this is still the case today.[7] However, there is a tradition that, early in his reign, the Chia-ch'ing Emperor prohibited the use of the *hu-ch'in*, declaring that it should be replaced in the new drama by the *ti-tzu*; not until about 1862 was the *hu-ch'in* reinstated as the chief

[1] *JHKHC*, 4, 14a.   [2] *TCHY*, *pieh-chi*, pp. 4a–b.
[3] *Chung-hsiang kuo*, p. 15b.
[4] *PCLYCS*, pp. 5a–6a.
[5] See Chou Chih-fu, *Chin pai-nien ti Ching-chü*, pp. 3–5: Tsou Wei-teng, '"Ssu ta Hui-pan" yü Ching-hsi', *Ming-pao yüeh-k'an* iii, 6 (1968), p. 56. According to Chou Chih-fu, it is common to refer to a Peking opera as *erh-huang* even if it is in fact made up exclusively of *hsi-p'i* music.
[6] *Chü-hua*, 1, 47.
[7] See Liu Chi-tien, *Ching-chü yin-yüeh chieh-shao*, pp. 32 ff. On *erh-huang* music see pp. 91 ff., and on *hsi-p'i*, pp. 177 ff.

accompanying instrument of the style.[1] Whether or not there is substance in this story, it is clear that the *erh-huang* music sung by Kao Yüeh-kuan during his first years in Peking was accompanied principally by the *hu-ch'in*, since he arrived before the accession of Chia-ch'ing.

Although Kao and the San-ch'ing company were the most famous early performers of the *erh-huang* style in Peking, there were other large and important troupes which made their way to Peking at about the time of the Emperor's eightieth birthday. According to the son of the Manchu Wu-la-na, 'following on [the San-ch'ing company] other troupes came [to the capital]. They included the Ssu-hsi, Ch'i-hsiu, Ni-ts'ui, Ho-ch'un and Ch'un-t'ai. None had less than 100 *hsiao-tan* actors. Most of these can be seen described in the songs of the *literati*.'[2] Probably the writer has exaggerated the number of *tan* in the troupes, but it would no doubt be fair to assume that they were fairly large.

The original homes of these companies are not known for certain. Wu-la-na's son suggests that it was the salt administration in Chekiang which had arranged for the San-ch'ing company to move to Peking for the birthday celebrations and thus implies that the group originated in that province. However, we shall see later that, by 1803, most of the *tan* members of the new companies came from Kiangsu, not a single known actor being a native of Chekiang. Even though these *tan* enjoyed but a short career, we should expect to find among a hundred at least one who survived beyond 1800. The key to this problem may lie in the fact that many young actors were taken from Su-chou to Chekiang and a number could sing *erh-huang*[3] as well as *K'un-ch'ü*. Possibly some

---

[1] This information is based on an oral tradition told to Ch'i Ju-shan. He heard it separately from two old actors, Shang Ho-yü and Sheng Ch'ing-yü. Both had themselves heard it when young from actors who had flourished in the early decades of the nineteenth century. Apparently, these performers knew people who could remember the ban. See Ch'i Ju-shan, *Pien-ch'ien*, pp. 24a–b. See also Wang Chih-chang, *Ch'iang-tiao k'ao-yüan*, p. 24a. Wang claims that the flute was originally the principal instrument of the *erh-huang* orchestra. However, this is most unlikely since it conflicts with the authority of Li T'iao-yüan (*Chü-hua*, 1, 47). Moreover, the tradition mentioned by Ch'i Ju-shan is quite unknown among the actors of Kiangsi who believe that *erh-huang* (called *erh-fan* in *Kan-chü* of Kiangsi) has always been accompanied by the *hu-ch'in*. See Li Hsiao-ts'ang, 'Kan-chü chu-ch'iang ti lai-yüan yü yen-pien', *Hsi-ch'ü yen-chiu* 2 (1957), p. 96.

[2] See Chou I-pai, *Hsi-chü shih*, p. 607 and Ch'i Ju-shan, *Pien-ch'ien*, p. 49a.

[3] *Hang-su i-feng*, p. 8a. This text refers to *Hui-tiao* (tunes of Anhwei). Chou Chih-fu points out (*Ching-chü*, p. 10) that the term is not necessarily synonymous

of them had joined the San-ch'ing company in Chekiang and gone from there to Peking. The Ssu-hsi company may also have gone to Peking from Chekiang, since one of the main troupes of Hang-chou was called Ssu-hsi,[1] but there is insufficient evidence to prove it. The Ch'un-t'ai company mentioned by Wu-la-na's son was probably not the same as the famous troupe of that name in Yang-chou. As noted in chapter three, this was still flourishing in its home city in 1793. The name was quite a common one for the theatrical groups of the time—there was also a famous Ch'un-t'ai company in Anhwei[2]—and it is quite unnecessary to conclude, as some scholars have done, that this parallel in names shows an identity of troupes.

Among the best companies, then, none is known to have come from Anhwei. Yet already that province was regarded as the foremost centre of *erh-huang* actors[3] and had become associated in the popular mind with the style. Consequently, although the membership of the new companies in Peking was predominantly from provinces other than Anhwei, the term *Hui-pan* (Anhwei companies) was used to refer to them.

According to a stele found in the Lao-lang Temple in Su-chou, a proscription was issued in 1798 against various styles, including *Ch'in-ch'iang* and *erh-huang*,[4] and the actors of such drama strongly condemned in the usual terms: 'Their voices are thoroughly licentious and the parts they perform are either utterly depraved and dirty or else ridiculous and seditious. They are harmful in their effect on the customs and feelings of the people.' The edict goes on to bemoan the decline of the *K'un-ch'ü*, especially in Su-chou and Yang-chou, where actors have been 'suppressing the old and enjoying the new'. Naturally the established styles,

---

with *erh-huang*. But since this latter style was perhaps the most popular of those from Anhwei, we may probably conclude that the *Hui-tiao* just mentioned included some *erh-huang* tunes. For greater detail on the *Hui-tiao* see Liu Ching-yüan, 'Hui-hsi ti ch'eng-chang ho hsien-k'uang', in *Hua-tung hsi-ch'ü chü-chung chieh-shao*, III, 59–64.

[1] According to Fan Tsu-shu (*Hang-su i-feng*, p. 7b), the four major companies of Hang-chou were called Hung-fu, Heng-sheng, San-yüan, and Ssu-hsi.

[2] See steles of 1780 and 1791 quoted Ou-yang Yü-ch'ien, 'Shih-t'an Yüeh-chü', in Ou-yang Yü-ch'ien, ed., *Chung-kuo hsi-ch'ü yen-chiu tzu-liao ch'u-chi*, pp. 111–12.

[3] *YCHFL*, 5, 130–1.

[4] The edict does not actually name *erh-huang*, but mentions Anhwei, along with Shensi, as one of the two sources of the obscene theatre. The reference to *erh-huang* is quite plain.

K'un-ch'ü and *I-yang ch'iang* are exempted from the ban. In Peking the duty of its enforcement fell on Ho-shen, and in the provinces on local bodies like the Imperial Silk Office in Su-chou and the Liang-huai Salt Administration in Yang-chou.[1]

This proscription is thoroughly typical of its kind, but appears to have been directed especially against the actors of the Anhwei companies, whose recent successes in Peking had been rather impressive. We do not know how long the ban was effective. However, its date is very striking. Ho-shen died in 1799, the year after it was issued, and Chia-ch'ing immediately called for denunciations against him. While it is true that the Emperor did not dismiss all the powerful men of Ho-shen's entourage and left the former minister's influence to some extent intact,[2] there is no record that any official was appointed to replace Ho-shen in suppressing the *erh-huang* drama in Peking. Probably it was not affected long by the 1798 proscription and Chao-lien remarked tersely in about 1815 that 'although banned by imperial decree, its tunes could still not be stopped.'[3]

There may have been one other restriction concerning the *erh-huang* style. It is said that within a year or two of Chia-ch'ing's accession, a certain censor sent a memorial to the throne remarking on the similarity between the sound of the name *erh-huang* 黃 and the phrase *erh-huang* 皇 meaning 'two emperors'. The censor suggested that the title of the musical style was blasphemous and should be changed. Chia-ch'ing agreed with the proposal. The name *erh-huang* was no longer used, and the style was suspended at court for the time being.[4]

This story is based on oral tradition and is therefore not wholly reliable. But whether it is true or not, no reader of the sources on the theatre of the period can avoid being struck by the extreme rarity with which the term *erh-huang* occurs. Moreover, among the dramatic pieces mentioned there, very few are known to have belonged specifically to the *erh-huang* style. The *T'ing-ch'un hsin-yung* records the titles of sixty scenes for which the actors of the

---

[1] The text of this stele is quoted in Chou I-pai, *Chung-kuo hsi-chü shih chiang-tso*, pp. 231–2.

[2] See Nivison, 'Ho-shen and his Accusers', in Nivison and Wright, eds., *Confucianism in Action*, pp. 240–3.

[3] *Hsiao-t'ing tsa-lu*, 8, 7a.

[4] See Ch'i Ju-shan, *Pien-ch'ien*, pp. 24a–b. This information was told to Ch'i by the old actors Shang Ho-yü and Sheng Ch'ing-yü.

Anhwei companies were noted. Of these, thirty were certainly *K'un-ch'ü*. Of the remainder, most were *Ch'in-ch'iang* pieces and only two are known to have been *erh-huang*.[1]

How is this curious lack of *erh-huang* scenes to be explained? One possibility is that the *erh-huang* style died out almost completely owing to the 1798 edict. This is, however, highly improbable. It runs directly counter to the evidence of Chao-lien quoted above. Furthermore, the Anhwei companies which made the style popular in Peking showed no signs of leaving the capital. Another possibility is that *erh-huang* scenes were indeed performed, but are not listed. In view of the apparent stigma attached to the name *erh-huang*, this can be accepted as the most likely explanation. Many dramas formerly performed in a different style were adapted by the Anhwei companies into *erh-huang* items. One concrete example of a piece acted during the Chia-ch'ing period in two distinct styles is reported. *Hsiang-shan*[2] was performed a little differently by the *Ch'in-ch'iang* and Anhwei companies. 'The costumes and adornments for the Anhwei companies' version [of this drama] were imposing and solemn, but the *Ch'in-ch'iang* companies wore only sleeveless blouses [while performing it].'[3] No doubt the music was also different.

Nevertheless, the Anhwei companies were extremely adaptable and could perform styles other than *erh-huang* and *hsi-p'i*. Several actors mastered more than these two styles. For instance, Ch'en Kuei-lin from An-ch'ing 'belonged to a *hua-pu* company [the Ch'un-t'ai] and yet was highly proficient in *K'un-ch'ü*'.[4] Chiang Chin-kuan from An-ch'ing is another example. He was a member of the San-ch'ing company, but could perform *K'un-ch'ü* and *Ch'in-ch'iang* as well as *erh-huang*.[5] There must have been many other members of the Anhwei companies who were similarly versatile.

The Peking Theatre up to 1820

Although the *Ch'in-ch'iang* drama became to a large extent

---

[1] See Chou I-pai, *Hsi-chü shih*, pp. 611–12. Chou has listed fifty-nine scenes performed by the Anhwei companies as recorded in *TCHY*. He has, however, omitted one, *Chao-ch'in* (*Entering a Wife's Family in Marriage*), which is coupled with a *Ch'in-ch'iang* scene and probably belonged to that style. See *TCHY, pieh-chi*, p. 9b.

[2] On *Hsiang-shan* see below, appendix C, p. 258.

[3] *TCHY, hsi-pu*, pp. 6a–b.   [4] *JHKHC*, 2, 2b.   [5] *JHKHC*, 2, 3a.

absorbed by the Anhwei companies and consequently continued to be popular, the number of troupes devoted primarily to it fell off seriously after the edict of 1785. Only two of the famous companies of the 1780s are known to have survived after 1790. These were the I-ch'ing and the Shuang-ch'ing. In 1793 there was a famous actor called Wang Te-erh of the I-ch'ing[1] while Lo Jung-kuan and Yü San-yüan, both of whom are described by Wu Ch'ang-yüan as members of the I-ch'ing in the 1780s,[2] continued to act after 1790. However, the decline of the I-ch'ing company is obvious from the fact that both these two actors left it for the Shuang-ch'ing.[3] Meanwhile, three other actors had entered the ranks of the Shuang-ch'ing: Huang K'uei-kuan, a disciple of Wei Ch'ang-sheng, Ch'en San-kuan of Su-chou and Shih Pao-chu of Tientsin.[4] However, the Shuang-ch'ing company had disbanded by 1803.[5]

The fate of the two *Ch'in-ch'iang* companies did not signal the total disappearance of *Ch'in-ch'iang* troupes in Peking. Even in 1793 another Clapper company had begun its ascent in the capital. This was the Ta Shun-ning.[6] One of the earliest actors of this group was Han Ssu-hsi who is said to have been on a par with Wei Ch'ang-sheng.[7] Han was born in 1786 and came from Peking. He had joined the Ta Shun-ning company by 1803[8] and was still a member in 1810.[9] Although he was the only man known to have belonged to the Ta Shun-ning company in 1803, the *P'ien-yü chi* of 1805 lists three actors of the company.[10] Meanwhile there was another *Ch'in-ch'iang* group by 1803, the Shuang-ho, which was considered the best of the Clapper companies of the time.[11] The *T'ing-ch'un hsin-yung* devotes its second *chüan* entirely to the actors of the *Ch'in-ch'iang* companies and in it twelve actors are described. In the third and final *chüan* of this work, there are notes on four more actors of the *Ch'in-ch'iang* companies.[12] Of the

[1] HCHY, in PCLYCK, p. 8a.   [2] Yen-lan hsiao-p'u, 3, 6a and 2, 6b.
[3] JHKHC, 4, 13a–b.   [4] JHKHC, 4, 6b–8b.   [5] JHKHC, 4, 13b.
[6] HCHY, in PCLYCK, p. 8a.   [7] TCHY, pieh-chi, p. 13a.
[8] JHKHC, 3, 6a.   [9] TCHY, pieh-chi, p. 13a.
[10] These three were Ho Wan-yüeh, Han Ssu-hsi, and Ts'ao Fu-lin. A list of all the actors to whom poems are dedicated in the *P'ien-yü chi* may be found in the table of contents (*t'i-tseng chu-jen*) of that work. The *Chung-hsiang kuo* (pp. 14a, 13a) of 1806–7 lists Ho Wan-yüeh and Han Ssu-hsi as members of the Ta Shun-ning company. It omits Ts'ao Fu-lin, but adds an actor called Ma Feng (p. 15a).
[11] JHKHC, 2, 4a.
[12] The actors to whom sections are devoted are listed at the beginning of each *chüan*.

sixteen actors, nine belonged to the Ta Shun-ning company, six to the Shuang-ho and one to a third company, the Ching-ho, the existence of which is not noted in earlier sources. By 1816, the Ta Shun-ning had disbanded. A stele of that year lists nineteen of Peking's theatrical companies and of them only three are known to have been devoted to Clapper Opera: the Shuang-ho, Ching-ho, and Shun-li.[1]

One striking feature of the actors of the *Ch'in-ch'iang* companies of the Chia-ch'ing period is that Szechwan was no longer the principal source for their actors. Of the sixteen described in the *T'ing-ch'un hsin-yung*, five were native to Peking, four had come from Yang-chou, two each from Shensi and Szechwan, and one each from Chihli, Shansi, and Shantung. The high proportion of Pekingese may perhaps be partly explained by the fact that Clapper actors had been performing in the capital for some time and had thus been able to attract young inhabitants of the city to their art.

Despite the continued presence of *Ch'in-ch'iang* companies, it is plain that by the turn of the century, the Anhwei companies had achieved a dominant position on the Peking stage. Apart from the companies which we know to have arrived in the capital in 1790 or soon after, the San-ch'ing, Ssu-hsi, Ch'i-hsiu, Ni-ts'ui, Ho-ch'un, and Ch'un-t'ai, we find among pre-1803 actors a member of one other Anhwei company, K'ung T'ien-hsi of the Pao-hua.[2]

Some idea of how these drama companies were faring can be gleaned through their composition as shown in the *Jih-hsia k'an-hua-chi* (1803). The sixty-three Anhwei actors who were recorded in that work as still performing in 1803 were spread over eleven companies, as indicated in the following table.[3]

Ch'un-t'ai	20	San-to	4	Ch'ing-yüan	1
San-ch'ing	14	Ni-ts'ui	3	Fu-ch'eng	1
Ssu-hsi	8	Yü-ch'ing	3	Hsin-ch'ing	1
Chin-yü	6	Chi-hsiu	1	Unknown	1

It appears that three Anhwei companies, the Ch'un-t'ai, San-ch'ing, and Ssu-hsi, had emerged as the most distinguished in Peking. Conspicuously absent from this list are three of the eight

---

[1] See *PCLYCS*, pp. 5a–b.   [2] *JHKHC*, 4, 12a.
[3] See also Chou Chih-fu, *Ching-chü*, p. 21. The figures given by Chou are slightly different from mine because his calculations include actors who had left the stage by 1803.

companies of the pre-1803 stage, the Pao-hua, Ch'i-hsiu, and Ho-ch'un. The first two disappear from history at this point. The Ch'i-hsiu is, indeed, mentioned in the *Jih-hsia k'an-hua chi*, but only because two actors had left it. These were Chiang T'ien-lu, who had joined the Ssu-hsi company, and Ch'ien Yüan-pao, who had become a member of the San-to.[1] The Ho-ch'un company is the only one of the three which eventually rose to a position of prominence.

The *P'ien-yü chi* (1805) devotes considerable space to actors of the Ho-ch'un company. The following table shows the number of actors in eight Anhwei companies as recorded in that work.

San-ch'ing	14[2]	Ssu-hsi	7	Sung-shou	3
Ho-ch'un	10	Ch'ing-ning	4	San-to	2
Fu-hua	9	Ch'un-t'ai	3		

In view of its later prominence, it is doubtful that the Ch'un-t'ai company had declined as much as is suggested by the small number of its members mentioned in the *P'ien-yü chi*. Probably, however, it is fair to assume that the Ho-ch'un company had come to occupy a place of great importance among the Anhwei companies.

The Ni-ts'ui and Yü-ch'ing companies of 1803 appear to have declined. Two actors of the Ni-ts'ui company in 1803, T'ao Shuang-ch'üan and Chiang Chin-kuan from Su-chou, had left it by 1805, T'ao for the San-ch'ing and Chiang for the Fu-hua. We know of one member of the Yü-ch'ing company in 1803 who had abandoned it by 1805. This was Chang Hsi-lin who joined the Ssu-hsi troupe. Both the Ni-ts'ui and Yü-ch'ing companies had disappeared by 1816 for neither is listed on the stele of that year. If the above tables are a reliable guide, the Ch'ing-yüan, Fu-ch'eng and Hsin-ch'ing companies had likewise failed to advance. They too are lacking in the 1816 stele.

The *Chung-hsiang kuo* and *T'ing-ch'un hsin-yung* suggest that the relative importance of the Anhwei companies changed again in the following years. The lists below show the composition of these companies as recorded in those works, which provide sections on sixty-four and seventy Anhwei actors respectively.

[1] *JHKHC*, 4, 3a–b.
[2] There are actually fifteen actors listed in the San-ch'ing company but one (T'ien Hsiang-ling) had returned to the south by 1805. See *P'ien-yü chi, t'i-tseng chu-jen*, p. 1b.

Chung-hsiang kuo (1806–7)

San-ch'ing	20	San-ho	9	San-to	3
Ho-ch'un	11	Ssu-hsi	6		
Ch'un-t'ai	10	Ch'ing-ning	5		

T'ing-ch'un hsin-yung (1810)

Ho-ch'un	22	Ssu-hsi	14	San-ho	9
San-ch'ing	15	Ch'un-t'ai	9	Chin-yü	1

One striking feature of these tables is the inclusion of the San-ho company, which is mentioned neither in the earlier texts nor in the stele of 1816. Another point of interest is the reappearance by 1810 of the Chin-yü company. It had probably persisted as a minor company throughout the first decade of the nineteenth century. It was still performing in 1816 and ranked among the leading seven companies of the early Tao-kuang.[1]

The Fu-hua company of 1805 appears to have been short-lived. Several of its members, including Wang Kuei-lin[2] and Chiang Chin-kuan[3] had left it by 1807 and it is not among the companies listed on the 1816 stele. Neither, indeed, are the Sung-shou, Ch'ing-ning, or San-to companies mentioned there. The first of these had apparently declined between 1805 and 1807, the last two in the following years.

The above lists are not a certain guide to the relative prominence of the Anhwei companies. Although the Ssu-hsi troupe does not rank at the top there, we are told directly that it was the foremost of the Anhwei companies.[4] It is possible that there are other respects in which the statistics are misleading. Yet they are the best the sources can offer, and are interesting for one major reason. They leave the impression that the various groups of actors were competing keenly among each other for popularity, the minor companies enjoying in general only a short life while the major became increasingly dominant. Within a few years of the Anhwei companies' entry into Peking, four among them had already asserted themselves above all the others. These were the

[1] *Liang-pan Ch'iu-yü an sui-pi*, 2, 60.

[2] Wang Kuei-lin was a member of the San-ch'ing company by 1807 (*Chung-hsiang kuo*, p. 7a) and was the leader of the Chin-yü in 1810 (*TCHY*, *pieh-chi mu-lu*, p. 1b).

[3] Chiang Chin-kuan belonged to the San-ho company in 1806–7 (*Chung-hsiang kuo*, p. 8a) and to the Ho-ch'un in 1810 (*TCHY*, *pieh-chi mu-lu*, p. 1a).

[4] *TCHY*, *Hui-pu*, p. 17b.

San-ch'ing, Ssu-hsi, Ch'un-t'ai, and Ho-ch'un, which were later known simply as the 'four great Anhwei companies'. They attracted most of the best actors and retained their reputation and commanding position for many decades. Kao Yüeh-kuan's leadership of the San-ch'ing company was no doubt an important cause for its rise, and the other three, too, were possibly led with similar energy and ability.

There is one other aspect of the Anhwei companies upon which a considerable amount of material is available. In most cases the sources report the places of origin of Peking's actors. Below are three tables, based on the *Jih-hsia k'an-hua chi*, *P'ien-yü chi*, and *T'ing-ch'un hsin-yung*, showing the native places of Peking's Anhwei actors.[1]

Jih-hsia k'an-hua chi (1803)

Kiangsu	36	(Yang-chou 19, Su-chou 15)	Shensi	1
Anhwei	21	(An-ch'ing 20)	Unknown	1
Peking	4			

P'ien-yü chi (1805)[2]

Kiangsu	17	(Su-chou 13, Yang-chou 2)	Peking	1
Anhwei	2	(An-ch'ing 2)		

T'ing-ch'un hsin-yung (1810)

Kiangsu	50	(Yang-chou 36, Su-chou 13)	Hupeh	2
Anhwei	14		Chihli	1
Peking	2		Hunan	1

The above lists make it plain that, like the *wai-hsüeh* of the court, the Anhwei companies drew most of their membership from Yang-chou and Su-chou. Anhwei also provided a significant number, but other places yielded comparatively few actors who moved to Peking to perform there. The reason for this overwhelming importance of Kiangsu and Anhwei will become clear later in this chapter.

Despite the availability of such statistical material, it is not possible to find out much about particular actors of the Anhwei companies, since the sources are distressingly silent about their lives. Even the most famous actor of the early 1800s, Liu Ch'ing-

---

[1] The author of *Chung-hsiang kuo* made a deliberate policy of omitting the place of origin of actors (*fan-li*, p. 1a), hence its absence here.

[2] The *P'ien-yü chi* (*t'i-tseng chu-jen*) gives the place or origin of only twenty-two actors of the Anhwei companies. Of these, two had left Peking by 1805.

jui, is treated only scantily. His principal biographer writes of him as follows:

Ch'ing-jui's surname is Liu and his *tzu* is Lang-yü. He is twenty years old and comes from Huang-ts'un in Ta-hsing [county], Peking. He belongs to the San-ch'ing company and was a disciple of Wei Ch'ang-sheng. In his younger days he became famous through [the lyric or ballad style] *hsiao-ch'ü*. He is elegant and radiant and [endowed with a] loveliness without parallel. In demeanour he is dignified and correct and his voice is clear and beautiful . . . He is not used to false feet[1] and his waist is thin and delicate. He does not go in for head ornaments, yet his coiffure is like a fairy's [in its beauty]. In *Yen-chih (Cosmetics)* and *K'ao-huo (Stoking a Fire)*, his performance is charming and tasteful and does not depend on obscenity for its appeal; in *Ch'uang-shan (Hastening up a Mountain)* and *T'ieh-kung yüan (Marriage Through a Steel Bow)*, it is beautiful without being lewd. Liu is quite equal to the girl in the old saying who 'drew the attention of the city with one smile'.[2] . . . At the end of spring, 1801, I went with [a friend pen-named] Hsiao-fan chü-shih to see Liu perform in this piece [*Pieh-ch'i, Parting from a Wife*]. We both praised him for his excellence. The next day he performed in *Sung-teng (Sending a Lantern)*[3] and it was just like meeting the goddess of the Lo River [the daughter of the mythical emperor Fu-hsi, Mi-fei, who was drowned in the Lo][4] . . . Last spring [1802] I went to visit him with Hsiao-fan and he was just like a scholar. He did not say much, yet he was very clever, and avoided seeming dull without being frivolous. At one of the many elegant gatherings he attended he brought with him a copy of his own new songs on the peony and begged for a preface for them from [a writer pen-named] Wei-hsien chü-shih . . . Recently he has wanted to learn calligraphy, and his strokes are elegant and strong. He is really among the finest persons in theatrical circles. Formerly Mei-pi [Ch'en Yin-kuan] was the best disciple of Wan-ch'ing [Wei Ch'ang-sheng], and there was a saying that he was even more magnificent than his teacher. Is the temperament, beauty and talent of the later elegant [actor from] Huang-ts'un in any way a decline compared with these former masters?[5]

There are several aspects of this passage which call for comment.

[1] See above, p. 97.

[2] A quotation from Li Pai's 'Kan-hsing'. See *Ch'üan T'ang-shih*, 183, 1864.

[3] The stories of *K'ao-huo* and *Yen-chih* may be found in appendix C. Those of *Ch'uang-shan*, *T'ieh-kung yüan* and *Sung-teng* are given in T'ao Chün-ch'i, *Ching-chü chü-mu ch'u-t'an*, pp. 145, 436, 446. For the text of *Pieh-ch'i* see *Chui pai-ch'iu*, XI, 3, 143–8.

[4] See Doré, *Recherches sur les superstitions en Chine, IIème partie, Le panthéon chinois*, pp. 784–5.

[5] *JHKHC*, I, 1a–b.

In the first place its style is utterly typical of the works on the theatre of its period. Concrete and relevant information is sparse and the literary flavour makes the author's remarks seem highly subjective. Interesting stories, such as the robbery of Ch'en Yin-kuan, are not recorded about the actors of the early nineteenth century.

The phrases used are strikingly similar to those found in works on eminent courtesans. Liu Ch'ing-jui himself followed women of this kind in that he began to acquire an education and wrote poetry. On the other hand, he seems to have resented the more unseemly habits which the social patterns of his time imposed upon *tan* actors. This is suggested by his attempts to steer clear of licentiousness on the stage and by the comment of one writer that he 'tried to avoid the suspicion of the cut sleeve [homo-sexuality]'.[1] Yet the manner in which certain *literati* regarded him indicates that this was no easy task.[2]

A third point of interest is that Liu can be seen from the quoted notes to have been predominantly a Clapper actor. The music of *Ch'uang-shan*, *T'ieh-kung yüan*, and *Sung-teng* is entirely *Ch'in-ch'iang*,[3] and the reader will recall that *K'ao-huo* was Ch'en Yin-kuan's *pièce de résistance*. Apart from those mentioned above, the only scene associated with the name of Liu Ch'ing-jui was *Pei-wa*,[4] the item Wei Ch'ang-sheng was performing when a sudden feeling of faintness forced him to leave the stage just before his death. Since Liu was the disciple of the greatest of the Clapper actors, it was natural that he should have been heavily influenced by the *Ch'in-ch'iang* music. Yet as a member of Kao Yüeh-kuan's San-ch'ing company he cannot have remained aloof from the *erh-huang* drama recently introduced into Peking. He was, for instance, skilled in acrobatics,[5] a feature much more prominent in *erh-huang* than in early Clapper Opera. It was only under the influence of the Anhwei actors that Wei himself had learned this art.

Ch'ang-sheng did not return to Peking until 1800. Liu Ch'ing-jui's greatest successes must consequently have belonged to the first years of the nineteenth century. His career was very short. He

---

[1] *JHKHC*, 4, 19b.   [2] See also *JHKHC*, 4, 17b–18a.
[3] Chou I-pai, *Hsi-chü shih*, p. 612.
[4] *JHKHC*, 4, 17b–18a. This piece is discussed in appendix C, p. 252.
[5] *JHKHC*, 4, 14b–15a.

is mentioned with enthusiasm in a work of 1806–7,[1] but is not to be found in the lists of the *T'ing-ch'un hsin-yung* of 1810 and had almost certainly left the stage by then.

The Popular Theatre of the 1820s

Very little indeed is known about the popular Peking theatre in the second decade of the nineteenth century. Apart from steles, only one work on the subject survives from the period, and it is both short and uninformative.[2] In the second decade, however, the silence of the historical sources is once again broken. Because of the death of the Chia-ch'ing Emperor in 1820, all actors suspended their performances, which were not resumed until early in 1823. By that time, the dominance of the San-ch'ing, Ch'un-t'ai, Ssu-hsi, and Ho-ch'un troupes was secure enough for contemporaries to describe them as 'the four great Anhwei companies' (*ssu ta Hui-pan*) or 'the four great famous companies' (*ssu ta ming-pan*). In addition, three further groups contained some outstanding actors: the Ch'ung-ch'ing, Chin-yü, and Sung-chu.[3] Of these three, only the Chin-yü is included in the 1816 stele, and the others must have been fairly new.

Chang Chi-liang is our chief source for the Anhwei companies of the third decade of the nineteenth century. He went to Peking in 1826 and there contracted many friendships with actors. He claims that the Ch'un-t'ai and San-ch'ing were by then the two most prominent of the four great Anhwei companies,[4] and it seems that many actors were leaving their original company to join one of these two.[5] The Ssu-hsi company was declining in popularity, apparently because it placed too much emphasis on the obsolescent *K'un-ch'ü*. To correct this adverse trend its members began performing fewer 'elegant' pieces, eventually replacing them entirely with operas of the various *hua-pu* styles.[6]

By far the most eminent actor of the Ch'un-t'ai company was Mi Hsi, commonly called Mi Hsi-tzu, whom Chang does not appear to have known personally. He began acting when very

---

[1] *Chung-hsiang kuo*, p. 6b.

[2] This is the *Ying-hua hsiao-p'u*, written in 1819. It consists, apart from introductions, of a list of thirteen actors of the Ssu-hsi company (author's preface, p. 1a), stating their names and places of origin, and thirteen short poems, one dedicated to each actor.

[3] *Liang-pan Ch'iu-yü an sui-pi*, 2, 60.   [4] *CTTLC*, 1, 4a.

[5] *HJKCL*, p, 4b.   [6] *CTTLC*, 1, 2b.

young and became so famous that 'there was nobody, in distant places or near at hand, who did not know of the existence of Mi Hsi-tzu. Those who came to court to give tribute from Korea or the Ryukyu Islands and students had all heard [his name] and sought to make his acquaintance.'[1] He continued to act in the company even when no longer young and became quite rich, drawing a yearly income of 700 taels. However, he never adopted the practice, usual among performers of his kind, of buying small boys to instruct in his profession.[2]

Hsi-tzu was known not only as an actor but also as a physician. Yet he does not appear to have taken great care of his own health. He was a desperately hard worker and set up in his house a large mirror in front of which he would practise day and night. His tireless labours made him fall seriously ill and he began coughing blood. Nothing could be done to effect his recovery, even though his most intimate disciple Ting Ssu waited on him hand and foot,[3] and he died in 1832 at the age of about forty.[4]

Mi Hsi-tzu's most famous role was Kuan Yü, the great general of the third century. The story goes that on one occasion a censor of Peking engaged Mi to perform the role of Kuan Yü in *Chan Ch'ang-sha* at a *t'ang-hui*.[5] When Mi came on the stage he was covering his face with his sleeve, but he then threw down his hand, revealing his face. At this, the whole audience stood up involuntarily, for so magnificent was Mi's expression and feeling that he seemed to be possessed by Kuan Yü's spirit. After this time no one dared to perform the part of Kuan Yü for more than thirty years.[6]

Ting Ssu proved an able successor to Mi; once when he performed as an understudy for his master it took the audience some time to realise that they were not watching Mi himself.[6] In one important respect the two actors are unique among the known performers of the time. They are the only famous actors mentioned in the sources who performed the *lao-sheng* roles of bearded old men. With only a few exceptions, every other actor

---

[1] *Ch'ang-t'an ts'ung-lu*, in PCLYCK, p. 13a.   [2] Ibid., p. 13b.

[3] MHSP, p. 29a. This information was told to Yang Mou-chien by his friend Ch'en Hsiang-chou.

[4] *Ch'ang-t'an ts'ung-lu*, in PCLYCK, p. 13b.

[5] *Chan Ch'ang-sha* is discussed below, pp. 261–2 and *t'ang-hui*, pp. 198–9.

[6] See Ch'i Ju-shan, *Kuo-chü man-t'an*, I, 54; MHSP, p. 29a.

[7] Ibid.

known to us from this period was a *tan*. Mi and Ting were indeed the first of a long series of great *lao-sheng* actors who later came to the Peking stage, and their emergence foreshadowed the close of the period when the *tan* reigned supreme.

The two leading *tan* actors of the Ch'un-t'ai company were Chou Hsiao-feng and Ch'en Ch'ang-ch'un. Chou came from An-ch'ing and was famous in his profession by 1823.[1] In 1827 he contributed some money towards the upkeep by his guild of a cemetery for Peking's actors.[2] Ch'en, too, was a native of An-ch'ing and was a skilled performer not only of the *erh-huang* and *hsi-p'i* styles for which the Ch'un-t'ai company was noted but also of *K'un-ch'ü*.[3] He was known as a teacher and built a house to instruct his many disciples.[4] Like Chou, he was active in the actors' guilds, and in 1837 was among the most generous of all donors in a project to found a cemetery for the actors of the Ch'un-t'ai company.[5]

In Peking, both Chou Hsiao-feng and Ch'en Ch'ang-ch'un were patronized by the scholar Chu To-shan from Hai-yen in Chekiang and became rivals for his affection. It is said that Ch'en presented the scholar with a large sum of money, hoping thereby to monopolize his attention. Chou was extremely annoyed at this attempt to humiliate him, so when Chu's father came to Peking, Hsiao-feng demanded a large amount of money from his patron. If the scholar had refused him, Chou apparently intended to cause a scandal. But Hsiao-feng's plan was successful: he was given the money and promptly left his patron.[6]

Chu To-shan turned all his attentions to Ch'en Ch'ang-ch'un. In 1825 and 1826 he did extremely well in the official examinations. His affair with Ch'en was public knowledge and was instantly compared with that between Pi Yüan and Li Kuei-kuan, to which I referred in chapter four. Ch'en Ch'ang-ch'un was treated by Chu's friends just as if he had been the latter's wife. Unlike Pi Yüan's, however, To-shan's success in the government was short-lived. Soon after his triumph in the examinations, he became involved in a criminal affair and was dismissed from his office; and although he was accepted back into the civil service a few years later, he never attained great distinction.[7]

---

[1] *Yen-t'ai chi-yen*, p. 6b.　　[2] *PCLYCS*, p. 7a.　　[3] *CTTLC*, I, 3b; 2, 7b.
[4] *HJKCL*, p. 21a.　　[5] *PCLYCS*, p. 8b.　　[6] *CTTLC*, I, 3b.
[7] *HJKCL*, p. 21a.

Despite the reputation which Ch'en Ch'ang-ch'un and Chou Hsiao-feng enjoyed as actors in the 1820s, they were by no means the only popular *tan* in the Ch'un-t'ai company at that time. Another was Meng Ch'ang-hsi from Yang-chou whose fine acting was marred by his somewhat unpredictable character. Chang Chi-liang writes: 'He is carefree and addicted to wine. When drunk he used to swear rudely [at the audience] over and over again. He cursed a certain Han-lin academician who [responded by having] his house destroyed; Ch'ang-hsi gave up his job in a fury and now . . . he does not see visitors.'[1]

Wine makes the mind oblivious of the consequences likely to follow upon a daring deed. Yet there must have been many actors who yearned to follow Meng Ch'ang-hsi's example and tell the condescending officials, either by word or action, exactly what was in their minds. They knew perfectly well that most highly educated men despised them, regarding them as nothing more than a source of enjoyment or pleasure. It is inconceivable that they should all have accepted this without resentment.

Among the most interesting personalities in the *tan* acting circles of the early Tao-kuang period was Yang Fa-ling (or Fa-lin), who belonged not to the dominant Ch'un-t'ai company, but to the Ssu-hsi. He arrived in Peking from his hometown, Yang-chou, in 1819,[2] at which time he was still only a boy of eight. According to Chang Chi-liang, Yang did not enjoy acting; he was retiring and abstemious by nature and longed for the peace of his native city. Chang also depicts Yang as very filial. He quotes the actor himself as expressing a desire to buy a shop, field and private house and spend his days with his mother there. She did not want him to give up his career, however, and not until 1827 did she allow him to return home. Yang went back to Yang-chou in the autumn of the following year.[3] A few years later he was back in the capital and on close terms with Yang Mou-chien. He told his patron that

[1] *CTTLC*, 1, 5b.

[2] Yang is mentioned in the *Ying-hua hsiao-p'u* (pp. 1b–2a) of 1819, where he is called Yang Fa-lin, his *hao* being given (*mu-lu*, p. 1a) as Hui-ch'ing and Yün-hsiang. In *Yen-t'ai chi-yen* (p. 1a) there is a record of a Yang Fa-lin whose *hao* were Hsün-ch'ing or Yün-hsiang. Chang Chi-liang says (*CTTLC*, 1, 1a) that his *ming* was Fa-ling and his *tzu* Yün-hsiang. Finally, Yang Mou-chien refers (*HJKCL*, p. 8b) to an actor called Yang Fa-ling, whose *tzu* was Hsün-ch'ing. Despite the discrepancies in the names, there appears no doubt that each of the four sources is referring to the same actor.

[3] *CTTLC*, 1, 1a.

he had given all his money away to his parents, relatives, and friends,[1] and it was presumably the hope of further riches that drove him back to Peking.

According to Yang Mou-chien, Fa-ling did not like taking on apprentices because they demanded too much time and energy. Yet he was regarded by some as a magnificent singer. Chang Chi-liang writes quite ecstatically of his skill in this art. He says, 'Once, on a snowy day, he sang alone outside. There were several hundred people listening, including some who were passing by in carriages. All the horses looked up, frothed at the mouth, neighed sadly and would not move.'[2]

The name of Yang Fa-ling is associated with the founding of a *K'un-ch'ü* company. It will already be clear that 'elegant troupes' had been few and unimportant in Peking during the Chia-ch'ing period, except at court. The influence of *K'un-ch'ü* music was felt only through the Anhwei companies which performed it in many pieces. By the early Tao-kuang, the Anhwei companies had become less adept in the *K'un-ch'ü*. They played it less often than in earlier years and, according to Chang Chi-liang, the standard of their performance was poor.[3]

It was in these circumstances that a group of actors of the Ssu-hsi company, and in particular Yang Fa-ling, chose to establish their own *K'un-ch'ü* troupe.[4] The precedent in their minds was the famous Chi-hsiu company of Su-chou,[5] to which I referred in chapter three, and they gave their own group a name with a similar meaning, Chi-fang 'collecting fragrance' (the phrase *chi-hsiu* can be rendered as 'collecting elegance'). Liang Shao-jen comments that the company existed when he visited Peking in 1826,[6] but it is not known how long it had been functioning before that year. The sources disagree as to how successful the company was. Yang Mou-chien writes:

At first [the Chi-fang company] put up notices everywhere, telling the *literati* of the capital [about its existence]. The scholars all awaited its performances eagerly and struggled to get in first to hear the drama. On the day of the performance the number of spectators in the seats was usually reckoned at about 1,000. They listened with such rapt attention that even the shoals of fish in the ponds [i.e. the people in the *ch'ih-tzu*

---

[1] *HJKCL*, pp. 8b–9a.   [2] *CTTLC*, 1, 1a.   [3] *CTTLC*, 2, 4a.
[4] *CTTLC*, 1, 2a.   [5] *Ching-ch'en chü-lu*, p. 1a.
[6] *Liang-pan Ch'iu-yü an sui-pi*, 2, 60–1.

discussed in chapter seven] were quite silent and did not dare make a sound.[1]

In contrast, Chang Chi-liang, who, unlike Yang Mou-chien, appears to have actually seen the Chi-fang company perform, leaves the impression that it aroused comparatively little interest. In any case the company disbanded in 1828, for it was unable to survive the departure of Yang Fa-ling for the south.[2]

Although the early Tao-kuang period saw the brief formation of a *K'un-ch'ü* company, no names of *Ch'in-ch'iang* troupes are preserved. There is, however, no reason to suppose that the Shuang-ho, Ching-ho and Shun-li groups had ceased their activities. In 1823 a censor sent a memorial to the Emperor suggesting that the *Ch'in-ch'iang* be banned,[3] but his proposal does not seem to have resulted in effective action since the Anhwei companies still performed the style in the late 1820s and to some extent it replaced *Kun-ch'ü* in the repertory of the Ssu-hsi company.

Another style heard in Peking during the early years of the Tao-kuang was *Ching-ch'iang*, which appears to have recovered to some extent from the blow dealt it by Wei Ch'ang-sheng's arrival in the capital in 1779. The Ssu-hsi company occasionally put on this kind of drama[4] and, as we shall see in chapter six, the Ho-ch'un was noted for the *Ching-ch'iang* performances it gave to the princely families. Furthermore, there were several companies devoted especially to the style. They included the Ch'ing Sheng-p'ing, En-ch'ing, Ch'ung-ch'ing, An-ch'ing, and Fu-ho.[5] These five groups were attached to aristocratic families and did not perform for the ordinary people. None is listed on the 1816 stele where it is stated specifically that all Peking's companies (presumably meaning public troupes) are included.[6] The popularity of the *Ching-ch'iang* can be seen to have been for the most part limited to the nobility.

Yet the *Ching-ch'iang* companies were undoubtedly very active in the 1820s. This is obvious from their wide repertoire. There survives from the year 1824 a list of the dramas performed by the Ch'ing Sheng-p'ing company, at the time led by Shen Ts'ui-hsiang, and it includes no fewer than 272 titles.[7] Probably the

[1] *MHSP*, pp. 26b–27a. Cf. also *Ch'ang-an k'an-hua chi* (*CAKHC*), p. 8b.
[2] *CTTLC*, 1, 2a–b.   [3] *CTTLC*, 3, 5a.   [4] *CTTLC*, 1, 2b.
[5] Chou Chih-fu, *Ching-hsi chin pai-nien so-chi*, p. 1.
[6] *PCLYCS*, p. 5a.   [7] Chou Chih-fu, *So-chi*, pp. 4–7.

other troupes could boast a substantial repertory too, since members did not necessarily remain in the same company forever and could therefore help enlarge the range of dramas offered by troupes other than their original one. An example of this mobility is the Mongolian *ch'ou* actor, born on 25 December 1813, who became known as Huang San-hsiung. In the decade or so following his début in about 1821, he acted at one time or another in all the *Ching-ch'iang* companies I have named.[1]

Huang later achieved great fame as a *ch'ou* in several of the popular Anhwei companies of Peking, in particular the Ho-ch'un and Ch'un-t'ai.[2] By that time, however, he had transferred most of his energies to the Peking Opera. His case is therefore no evidence that the recovery of the *Ching-ch'iang* drama ever percolated into the lower strata of society again. High and low may have shared some tastes in common, but sharp differences remained.

The Boy-Actors and the Success of the Anhwei Companies

One point of special importance to emerge from the preceding sections is the extreme youth of Peking's actors in the early nineteenth century. Kao Yüeh-kuan was considered a 'veteran' by the time he was thirty.[3] Although the sources of the period tend to be uncommunicative on the life story of any particular actor, they very often record his age. Of the sixty-three Anhwei actors reported in the *Jih-hsia k'an-hua chi* to be still on the stage, the oldest was Su Hsiao-san of the San-ch'ing company, and he was only thirty-two.[4] The youngest was Chu Ch'i-lin of the San-to, who was eleven.[5] The ages of all sixty-three actors are given and their average was about eighteen. The *P'ien-yü chi* records the ages of twenty-one actors still on the Peking stage and the average of these was nineteen. In the *T'ing-ch'un hsin-yung* the ages are given for twenty-one Anhwei actors. They range from a minimum of twelve (Chang Yü-mei)[6] to a maximum of twenty-two (Lu Chen-fu),[7] with an average of sixteen. The *Ch'in-ch'iang* actors listed in the *T'ing-ch'un hsin-ying* were even younger. The oldest, Tai Fei-lai-feng, was twenty-three,[8] the youngest, Chang Te-lin, was eleven,[9] the average, fifteen. The *tan* actors of the

[1] Ibid., p. 1.
[2] See Ch'i Ju-shan, *Ch'ing-tai p'i-huang ming-chüeh chien-shu*, p. 122.
[3] *JHKHC*, 4, 14a.   [4] *JHKHC*, 3, 4b.   [5] *JHKHC* 4, 2b.
[6] *TCHY, Hui-pu*, p. 13b.   [7] *TCHY, pieh-chi*, p. 6b.
[8] *TCHY, pieh-chi*, p. 13a.   [9] *TCHY, hsi-pu*, p. 8a.

1820s were also very young, and Yang Fa-ling, who was only eight when he arrived in Peking, was quite typical.

The reason why the famous *tan* actors in Peking were so young is closely associated with a method of recruiting which grew up towards the end of the Ch'ien-lung period and developed further still during the Chia-ch'ing. This method was to buy boys from the south, take them to Peking and train them as actors. Chang Chi-liang explains the process in some detail. He writes:

Most of the actors noted in the *Yen-lan hsiao-p'u* were from the north or west and were regarded as famous actors at the age of thirty. The remainder were about twenty, but few were children. Nowadays they are all from Su-chou, Yang-chou and An-ch'ing. When they are seven or eight years old, their teacher gives their parents a certain amount of money and arranges a bond of a limited period, [which is specified in] years and months. The teacher then takes the child to the capital ... He dresses him in pretty clothes, brushes off the dust and gives him wine to drink, as if he were about to try and do business at a market. If a rich man buys the child out before the bond has expired, it is called *ch'u-shih* and he must pay up to 2,000 or 3,000 taels.[1]

Several points raised in this interesting passage require elaboration. In the first place, Chang is talking specifically about one city, Peking, at a particular time. Yet practices similar to the one he describes were by no means new in the early nineteenth century. The material given in chapter two leaves no doubt about this. What was new was the extent of the trade and the bulk transportation of children from the south to Peking. Moreover, this was not the only city in China to receive indentured boy-actors from Kiangsu. Many were destined for Hang-chou, where Su-chou children ranging in age from ten to fifteen were commonly seen on the stage,[2] and no doubt other places as well.

Chang's observation that the boys were bought at seven or eight years old also deserves comment, for other sources give a slightly different account. There is a reference to the trade in young performers in the famous novel *P'in-hua pao-chien*, first printed in 1849,[3] and although this book is fictional it probably reflects fairly well the social conditions of the boy-actors around whom the plot revolves. One character remarks: 'In Peking there are four great famous companies. At their request a teacher goes

[1] *CTTLC*, 3, 1b.   [2] *Hang-su i-feng*, p. 8a.
[3] See Liu Ts'un-yan, *Chinese Popular Fiction in Two London Libraries*, pp. 132–8.

to Su-chou and buys ten children. None is more than thirteen or fourteen and some are eleven and twelve.'[1] A third version is given in a nineteenth-century work on Peking where it is recorded that the boys began their careers as actors at twelve or thirteen.[2] Probably most boys were nearer seven than fourteen when actually indentured. They then spent several years as trainees, until they were about twelve, before being allowed to play important roles in public. After that they could acquire a reputation of their own, even though still contracted to a master who might continue to train them.

Yet there seem to have been no hard-and-fast rules concerning these ages. For instance, Hsü Kuei-lin of the San-ch'ing company did not arrive in Peking until he was thirteen.[3] On the other hand, Chang Chi-liang relates a touching story about an actor from Su-chou called Chang Ch'ing-hsiang, a member of the San-ch'ing company.[4] When he was only eight his father took him to a tea-house, where a strange man produced twelve or thirteen strings of cash to buy the child. A contract was signed on the spot and Ch'ing-hsiang taken away to Peking without even being allowed to say good-bye to his mother.[5]

Chang Ch'ing-hsiang's case raises yet another problem related to Chang Chi-liang's remarks quoted above: how much were the twelve or thirteen strings of cash really worth? This is a difficult question to answer, since the value of money varied widely from time to time and place to place. In theory a string of cash contained 1,000 cash, but in practice sometimes very much less.[6] However, it is clear that the sum was not large, and no parent could hope for much reward by indenturing his son as an actor. A string of cash was less valuable than a tael. When the government issued notes to represent taels of silver and copper cash in 1853, the rate of exchange was established at one tael of silver to 2,000 cash.[7] The twelve or thirteen strings of cash can be seen to pale into insignificance before the 2,000 to 3,000 taels required to buy a child out of his bond. The teachers always stood to make a profit from any transaction.

This sale, purchase, and transportation of boys explains why so

---

[1] P'in-hua pao-chien, 1 (hui 2), 5b.   [2] Yen-ching tsa-chi, p. 7a.
[3] CTTLC, 1, 1b.   [4] CTTLC, 1, 4a.   [5] CTTLC, 3, 1b.
[6] Yang Lien-sheng, Money and Credit in China, pp. 34–7.
[7] Ibid., p. 68.

many of Peking's *tan* actors came from Kiangsu or Anhwei. The three places Chang Chi-liang mentions as sources, Su-chou, Yang-chou, and An-ch'ing, were all in those provinces. In the light of his remarks on the recruiting of actors, it can hardly be doubted that the great majority of Peking's best actors had entered their profession through the system of indenture.

The route used to take the children from the south to Peking was the Grand Canal. 'The boy-actors ... go to Tientsin in grain-junks; old actors then buy them and teach them to sing and dance.'[1] The *P'in-hua pao-chien* also makes reference to the method of transportation: 'On the Canal, the grain-junks are very congested, so it takes them more than four months to get to Peking. Every day the boys can be seen learning drama.'[2] Despite basic agreement, there is a slight difference between these two accounts. The first implies that instruction did not begin until after the journey was over, the second states clearly that it commenced during the voyage itself. No doubt the matter was dictated by the circumstances of each individual boat-load. But in either case the children had already left home before they started learning to act.

This rather significant fact explains one striking feature of the Anhwei actors. Although a large proportion of them came from Su-chou, the home of the *K'un-ch'ü*, they did not effect a great revival of that style in Peking. Until the late Ch'ien-lung, it could usually be taken for granted that an actor from Su-chou excelled principally in the elegant drama. After the trading system began, such an assumption would have been a great mistake; the boys no longer acquired their skills in *K'un-ch'ü* territory, and their teachers were probably more interested in Peking Opera than in *K'un-ch'ü*.

Once arrived in Peking the boys sometimes joined a training-school (*k'o-pan*). A few of the major companies ran their own schools, but these did not exist independently early in the nineteenth century. It was only in later times that *k'o-pan* unattached to any troupe could be found in Peking.[3] The earliest and most famous of the new-style schools was the Hsi-lien-ch'eng, where many famous actors like Mei Lan-fang received their training.

1 *Yen-ching tsa-chi*, p. 7a. Cf. also *Ts'e-mao yü-t'an*, p. 2b.
2 *P'in-hua pao-chien*, I, (hui 2), 5b.
3 See Chou Chih-fu, *Ching-chü*, pp. 50–5.

However, this institution was not founded until 1903 and is therefore not important in the present context.[1]

By far the most widespread system of training in the early period was private instruction. Having arrived in the capital most of the boys were resold to already established actors. Most such men adopted two or three boys as their sons and personal disciples. Upon them fell the duty of lodging, feeding, and looking after the children. In particular they were responsible for ensuring that their charges were properly trained in the arts and skills of the theatre.

These boy-actors were known in Peking as *hsiang-kung*, a phrase which occurs constantly in the *P'in-hua pao-chien*. The term is frequently found in Chinese historical works as a polite designation for a *tsai-hsiang* (chief minister), but had come to be applied also to actors as early as the tenth century.[2] By the eighteenth, boys in the regions of the lower Yangtze were commonly called *hsiang-kung* and it is this factor which led to the use of the phrase to describe Peking's boy-actors, the great majority of whom came from the south.[3]

Every *hsiang-kung* lived in his master's dwelling, and such places were colloquially called *hsiang-kung t'ang-tzu* (the houses of the *hsiang-kung*). Fortunately the names and positions of quite a few of them have been preserved. At the end of his notes on each actor, Yang Mou-chien has given this information about the *t'ang-tzu* where the performer in question resided.[4] The houses were concentrated in the region just west of Ta Sha-lan outside the Cheng-yang Gate. The name of a *hsiang-kung t'ang-tzu* was very often used also to refer to the senior actor who lived and taught there. This was called his *t'ang-ming*.[5] For instance, Liu T'ien-kuei kept a number of disciples at his house, the Ch'uan-ching t'ang by the Yü-huang Temple, and he was commonly called Ch'uan-ching t'ang. Possibly his best known student was Yang Fa-ling,[6] whom I have already discussed.

The life the *hsiang-kung* led in these houses was extraordinarily luxurious. We are told that 'the dwellings where they resided

---

[1] Mei Lan-fang has described this school in his *Wu-t'ai sheng-huo ssu-shih nien*, I, 54 ff. See also Scott, *Mei Lan-fang*, pp. 27–34.

[2] *Pei-meng so-yen*, 6, 51.

[3] See also Chou Chih-fu, *Ching-chü*, p. 58.

[4] See *HJKCL*, *CAKHC* and *Ting-nien yü-sun chih*, *passim*.

[5] See Chou Chih-fu, *Ching-chü*, pp. 59–61.

[6] *MHSP*, p. 18a; *HJKCL*, p. 9a.

were as good as the mansions of the rich'. The main room was splendidly decorated with embroidered curtains as well as 'Chou libation cups and Han bronze tripods'; and the bedroom was also magnificently adorned. Furthermore, the boys were favoured with the attention of servants.

When they travelled the *hsiang-kung* rode in a fine carriage drawn by strong horses. 'Even the sons of high-ranking people did not live so luxurious a life.'[1] That many actors rode in carriages is confirmed by Chang Chi-liang. He records that in the main theatrical region of Peking, Ta Sha-lan just outside the Cheng-yang Gate, there were so many actors' carriages that it was almost impossible to move there.[2]

For the *hsiang-kung*, there was one somewhat disappointing feature of all these luxuries—they were provided on sufferance by the masters. The children themselves possessed virtually nothing of their own. One character in the *P'in-hua pao-chien* complains that even the clothes he wears belong to his teacher.[3] The comfortable life a master gave his apprentices was a lever to force them to do his will.

The boy-actors worked hard. The more famous among them sometimes performed at more than one banquet in a day, moving from one to another in their carriage. They received handsome payment for their services, but usually had to hand it over to their teacher. Often they were paid in the form of money, and might receive ten taels for acting at a banquet. Sometimes they were given two or three taels, and, in addition, other rewards in kind such as jade, pearls, sable coats, or elegant cloth.[4]

Such gifts are in fact what one might have expected a delighted audience to present to a female performer. In fact, the *literati* took it for granted that the *hsiang-kung* could be used as boy-lovers and it was no accident that the famous Liu Ch'ing-jui should have been depicted in terms appropriate for a beautiful woman. The sources abound in references to love-affairs between scholars and actors and suggest strongly that an adult homosexual seeking a partner would be able to find one among the *hsiang-kung*. It is not surprising that the *t'ang-tzu* came to be regarded as somewhat unsavoury places.[5] In fact, the reputation of the young actors

---

[1] *Yen-ching tsa-chi*, p. 7a. [2] *CTTLC*, 3, 5a.
[3] *P'in-hua pao-chien*, 3 (*hui* 23), 19a. [4] *Yen-ching tsa-chi*, p. 7a.
[5] See Chou Chih-fu, *Chen-liu ta-wen*, p. 47.

as catamites was probably one reason why most of the authors of our sources forbore to attach their surname and *ming* to their work. Even today many of these writers are known only by their pen-name.

Many authorities have gone one step further and equated the *hsiang-kung* system with male prostitution.[1] There are several reasons for accepting this proposition. One is the titles of some of the books which describe the boys. The names *Jih-hsia k'an-hua chi* and *Ch'ang-an k'an-hua chi* both mean 'Records about Watching Flowers in Peking', and the term 'flower' (*hua*), here clearly referring to the young actors who are the subject of the works, is a common euphemism for a prostitute. Moreover, the houses where the boy-actors lived were frequently termed *hsia-ch'u*,[2] which can also mean 'brothel'. Another argument is a remark made by Yang Mou-chien: 'To take a stroll into a brothel is called *ta-ch'a-wei* (holding a tea-gathering), to go to an actor's home for a chat is also called *ta-ch'a-wei*'.[3] Finally, the evidence of a scholar pen-named Shu-hsi ch'iao yeh can be cited. In a work on the *hsiang-kung*, he bemoans that the female prostitutes of Peking are so unattractive and that satisfaction cannot be derived from them; for real beauty, he adds, one has to resort to the members of the acting companies.[4] The scholars of the nineteenth century do not seem to have been in doubt that the boy-actors were the same as male prostitutes.

However, not all experts have been prepared to accept this equation. Ch'i Ju-shan (1877–1962), the greatest of recent authorities on the Peking theatre, comments on two main factors which, in his view, make it unfair. Firstly, nobody but friends could visit the home of an actor, let alone spend the night there; secondly, money was never given in advance to a *hsiang-kung* for his service.[5] The first of these points is very important. On the other hand, the sources give the very strong impression that an educated man rarely found it difficult to befriend an actor he desired and could thus gain access to the latter's house. Moreover it should be pointed out that the best courtesans were also quite difficult of access. Chi's second point is also of doubtful validity

---

[1] For instance see Wang Shu-nu, *Chung-kuo ch'ang-chi shih*, pp. 322 ff.
[2] *MHSP*, p. 5a.   [3] *MHSP*, p. 19b.
[4] *Yen-t'ai hua-shih lu*, preface, p. 1a.
[5] Ch'i Ju-shan, *Kuo-chü man-t'an*, I, 36–7.

since the *literati* lavished material rewards on the *hsiang-kung* they patronized, even though such gifts usually ended up with the masters.

The boy-actors can best be compared not to ordinary prostitutes but to high-grade courtesans. Certainly they were not available just to any comer but could to some extent pick and choose. Their friends were usually *literati* and they were themselves well educated and refined. Their chief interest lay in cultural matters, especially music and the theatre, and the sale of their bodies was only of secondary importance.

Yet because their appeal as actors depended to some extent on physical attraction, the *hsiang-kung* enjoyed but short careers. Most of them left the *t'ang-tzu* when they lost their appeal, at about the age of twenty.[1] If a youth decided to remain in the theatre after reaching that age, he became regarded as an 'old actor' and it was then his turn to buy younger people to instruct. Possibly some of them became *sheng* performers after this time. In any case it appears that there was a significant minority who did not return home.

The main reason for the expansion of the trade in boy-actors which led to their being taken to Peking in large numbers lay in the economic deterioration of China from the late Ch'ien-lung period onwards. China's population had been growing steadily for many years and appears to have reached the point where it could produce the greatest economic welfare for the people some time between 1750 and 1775.[2] After that time their standard of living began to fall. Economic problems due to overpopulation were assuming serious proportions by the 1790s.[3] It is not surprising that more and more peasants and other poor people began to find that they had more children than they could afford to support. By selling children for a limited period, such people could make a certain amount of money and, at the same time, rid themselves of a serious economic burden. It is to be expected that there were many unscrupulous men quite willing to take advantage of the

[1] See *CTTLC*, 3, 1b and *Yen-ching tsa-chi*, p. 7a. Cf. *P'in-hua pao-chien*, 3 (*hui* 18), 1a.

[2] See Ho Ping-ti, *Studies on the Population of China*, pp. 270 ff. Ho estimates that China's population in the early 1760s was about 250,000,000.

[3] It was during this decade that the 'Chinese Malthus', Hung Liang-chi (1746–1809, see Hummel, *Eminent Chinese*, pp. 373–5) expounded his theories on the 'population explosion'. See Ho Ping-ti, *Studies*, pp. 271–2.

plight of the poor. It would be easy for them to explain to a boy's father what a luxurious and colourful life his son would lead in the capital, and keep him happy through an assurance that the boy would be able to return home later.

The social phenomenon of the boy-actors is closely related to the success of the Anhwei companies. In this chapter certain similarities between the *Ch'in-ch'iang* and Anhwei companies will have become obvious. Both were successful, both were affected by proscriptions. Yet in some ways the progress of the *Ch'in-ch'iang* and *erh-huang* styles in Peking was very different. The *Ch'in-ch'iang* actors created a sudden impact which then dwindled. A flood of *Ch'in-ch'iang* performers came to Peking from Szechwan and other places. The stream then ebbed as dramatically as it had flowed. The Anhwei companies, on the other hand, made no such sudden impression. There is no evidence that Kao Yüeh-kuan took the capital by storm in the way that Wei Ch'ang-sheng had done. On the contrary, the growth of the Anhwei companies in Peking appears to have been fairly gradual. Unlike the supply of *Ch'in-ch'iang* actors, however, that of the Anhwei performers did not fall off. A steady flow of new actors continued to come to Peking from the south. The effect of the Anhwei companies was therefore more lasting in some ways than that of the *Ch'in-ch'iang*. While the Clapper Opera had passed its apex within a few years, the Peking Opera continued to be popular and remains so to this day. The companies of the *Ch'in-ch'iang* of the 1780s had all disbanded within two decades; the Anhwei companies lasted well over a century.

It was the custom of buying boys in the south and selling them as actors in Peking that ensured the continuous supply of Anhwei actors. It must therefore be held to be the principal reason why the Anhwei companies survived and grew in strength. Prosperity had earlier promoted the rise of the drama in the south. Subsequent economic decay may not have been of overall assistance to the theatre of Kiangnan but, by favouring the practice of selling boys, it certainly contributed to the development of the Peking Opera.

VI

THE CONSOLIDATION OF THE PEKING OPERA

THE FORTUNES of the theatre in Peking entered a new phase late in the 1820s, and significant changes took place both in the popular and court drama. In the ordinary playhouses of the Outer City, the influence of actors from Hupeh was felt for the first time about 1830, while in the palaces, the old office in charge of the imperial theatre was abolished in 1827 and the Sheng-p'ing shu set up to replace it. The importance of the Hupeh artists will become apparent later in this chapter. The patronage of the court was not without its impact on the Peking Opera, and it will be appropriate to begin this discussion with a brief survey of developments in the imperial drama after 1827.

The Court Theatre

Although the Sheng-p'ing shu took over the site of its predecessor, it was a smaller, simpler, and more compact organization than the one it replaced. The seven departments of the Nan-fu in its last years were reduced to only four. The total number of court actors in the Sheng-p'ing shu fluctuated between 60 and 110,[1] even the higher number being less than one tenth of that of the actors in the palaces in the time of Ch'ien-lung.

Yet the basic functions remained the same as those of the Nan-fu and the occasions which called for theatrical performances were unchanged: the birthday of an emperor or empress, festivals, and so on. There were also regular half-monthly sessions. The preliminaries to these have been vividly described by Katharine Carl, who was commissioned to paint a portrait of the Empress Dowager Tz'u-hsi in 1903 and took up residence in the palaces for the purpose:

On the first and fifteenth of the month, the Imperial players were at

[1] See Wang Chih-chang, *Ch'ing Sheng-p'ing shu chih-lüeh*, p. 53.

the Theater. On these days, the Emperor, instead of returning to his own Palace, would accompany the Empress Dowager and the Ladies from the Audience Hall to the Theater. The Imperial Hymn was played on Their Majesties' entrance into the court of the Theater, and when they had entered the Imperial loge, the players would come in a body on the stage and "kow-tow." Then the actors, splendidly gowned, would make the customary wishes for the Imperial Peace, Prosperity, Longevity, after which there would be a posture-play in costume, and then the plays for the day would begin.[1]

When the Sheng-p'ing shu was first set up, a list of rules was drawn up to govern it on 3 March 1827. The salaries and ranks of members were fixed and the general administrative structure laid down.[2] On 23 March further rules and some prohibitions were issued. Actors were forbidden to gamble, conduct any kind of commerce inside the palace compound, or fish in any of the lakes in the Imperial City or Yüan-ming yüan. The leaders of the Sheng-p'ing shu were particularly anxious to prevent their subordinates from leaving the palace without permission. They directed that 'any eunuch who escaped but then gave himself up should be given forty strokes of the rod, sent back to his employment in his original department and not allowed to apply for leave of absence for three months'. Those who were caught or repeated their escape were to be sentenced to heavier penalties.[3] Presumably this was a security measure designed to prevent the possibility of attacks on the palace such as those of the T'ien-li chiao in 1813.[4]

The affairs of all four departments in the court office fell under the supervision of a president (tsung-kuan). Below him was a hierarchy of leaders (shou-ling) in the various departments and other lesser officials. All these people, from the president down, were eunuch actors. In theory the president was an official of the seventh rank,[5] that is on par with a district (hsien) magistrate in the provinces.[6] In practice, however, most presidents were able to

[1] Katharine A. Carl, *With the Empress Dowager of China*, p. 191.

[2] Chou Chih-fu, *Ch'ing Sheng-p'ing shu ts'un-tang shih-li man-ch'ao*, 3, 2b–3a.

[3] Wang Chih-chang, *Ch'ing Sheng-p'ing shu*, p. 46.

[4] This rule was not the result of the famous incident in 1827 (referred to in chapter five, p. 120) when Mien-k'ai was charged with hiding a fugitive eunuch, since his misdemeanour was not discovered until later in the year.

[5] *Ta-Ch'ing hui-tien shih-li*, 1218, 3a.

[6] See T'ung-tsu Ch'ü, *Local Government in China under the Ch'ing*, p. 8. A *hsien* magistrate in the capital was sixth rank (ibid).

enjoy a higher status. Li Lu-hsi had been an official of the sixth rank before 1827 and, although his appointment as president of the Sheng-p'ing shu involved a demotion to the seventh, he was placed back in his old grade within a few years and rose to the fifth rank shortly before his retirement in 1856. His successor, An Fu, was promoted from the seventh to the sixth rank immediately on his appointment in 1856 and was still in the same grade at the time of his death in 1865. Pien Te-k'uei came to the office in 1877 in the sixth rank and rose to the fifth in 1881, retaining both the post and the rank until his death in 1889.[1]

The most important department in the Sheng-p'ing shu was the *Nei-hsüeh* (Inner School) where the actors were trained. The leadership of this section could be regarded as a sort of stepping-stone to the presidency, and every single *tsung-kuan* of the Sheng-p'ing shu had been a *shou-ling* of the Inner School at one time or another. Just as in the time of the Nan-fu, the performers who received their instruction there were court eunuchs. Like most other Chinese actors they began their training young. Before the Hsien-feng period few were more than twelve or thirteen when they entered the *Nei-hsüeh*. Indeed, the emperors felt they had the right to the services of the youngest eunuchs, and any that were twenty or more when they embarked upon learning the arts of the theatre were handed over to the Court of the Imperial Clan (*Tsung-jen fu*) which dealt with all matters connected with the emperors' relations. As time went on, however, the supply of boys tended to fall off, with the result that the imperial court was forced to be content with older trainees. By the first decade of the present century many of them were over twenty.

When a boy entered the Sheng-p'ing shu, his age and place of origin were noted down in the annals and the direction of his ability tested. After that, he was assigned to one of the four departments, and if acting and drama were his *forte*, he was put into the *Nei-hsüeh*.[2] The type of actor he would be, *sheng, tan, ching,* or *ch'ou*, was the decision of the leaders of the *Nei-hsüeh* and president, who handed him over to an appropriate teacher. He normally received instruction twice a day, morning and evening, but sometimes only once in the hot season. After he had mastered all the motions, song and dialogue sections of any particular

[1] See Wang Chih-chang, *Ch'ing Sheng-p'ing shu*, pp. 51–2, 333–61.
[2] Ibid., pp. 52–3.

drama, he was examined thoroughly, first by the *shou-ling* and later by the president. Only when he had proved his competence in that drama was he allowed to show his skill in the imperial presence.[1]

Yet despite this careful training, the eunuchs proved inadequate to satisfy the demands of the courtiers, and Tao-kuang's policy of forbidding established actors from outside to teach and perform in the palaces lapsed under the Emperor Hsien-feng. The court annals of 1860 record the names of twelve teachers and thirty students from the city of Peking who were working at court in June.[2] Moreover, some of the major companies of the capital began performing in the palaces. They included two of the four great Anhwei companies, the San-ch'ing on 23 July and the Ssu-hsi five days later.[3] The purpose of these visits was to contribute to the celebrations for the Emperor's thirtieth birthday, which fell on 26 July 1860.[4]

This revival of the old practice whereby the actors of the people came to offer their services to the emperor is very striking. It differed from its eighteenth-century parallel in two main respects. In the first place, the actors came not from Su-chou or Yang-chou but from Peking itself. Moreover, not all stayed permanently at court, and the greatest and most popular performers of the day were prepared to come for isolated performances. The obvious conclusion is that many courtiers and members of the imperial family wanted to see the Peking Opera and the artistry of its famous exponents. Unlike Clapper Opera, which had never penetrated the walls and moats of the Forbidden City, the Peking Opera had broken down the barriers which forbade the highest aristocracy from admiring the popular opera.

However, this first attempt to bring the drama of the ordinary populace into the court proved short-lived. When the British and French armies were approaching Peking, the Emperor fled to Jehol on 22 September 1860 and died there on 22 August the following year.[5] In the normal way, all theatrical performances

[1] Ibid., p. 55.
[2] Chou Chih-fu, *Ch'ing Sheng-p'ing shu*, 3, 4b–5a.
[3] Ibid., 3, 10a.
[4] See Hummel, ed., *Eminent Chinese of the Ch'ing Period*, p. 378. Hsien-feng was born on the 9th of the sixth month (17 July) 1831. The same day in 1860 corresponds to 26 July.
[5] Ibid., pp. 380–1.

were then suspended for the mourning period. Under Hsien-feng's successor, T'ung-chih, a gigantic effort was made to restore governmental authority, and it was part of the new and stricter attitude of the Restoration leaders to dismiss the actors from outside. For them, the very idea of bringing the vulgar Peking Opera to the imperial presence was extremely shocking. On 4 September 1863 the Grand Secretariat (Nei-ko), one of the country's highest political bodies, sent a memorial to the Emperor, part of which read:

It is now the third year since the Emperor Wen-tsung [Hsien-feng] departed from us. In the tenth month of this year (11 November to 10 December) it will be time to discard our mourning clothes ... In the established precedents of our dynasty, the Emperor should hold all the ceremonies in order after taking off his mourning garb ... After the imperial coffin has been laid to rest for ever, the Sheng-p'ing shu should, awaiting your commands, carry out its annual duties according to precedent. All those actors brought in from outside in the tenth year of Hsien-feng (1860) should be eliminated from court for ever. The Emperor gave his approval.[1]

The policy put forward in the name of T'ung-chih, who was in fact still only a small child, lasted until his mother, the Empress Dowager Tz'u-hsi, won a position of virtually total power in the reign of her nephew Kuang-hsü, T'ung-chih's successor. Tz'u-hsi was an avid enthusiast of the Peking Opera and the theatre generally. The following remarks by Katharine Carl on theatrical performances given to celebrate Kuang-hsü's birthday is ample testimony to her interest: 'Finally, there was the first gala performance at the Theater. Her Majesty occupied her loge nearly all day, overlooking every detail, sending now and then to the stage one of her eunuchs to transmit her Imperial commands as to the speaking of certain lines or the using of certain postures.'[2]

The occasion used by the Empress Dowager to reinstitute the custom of bringing artists from the city to the court was her fiftieth birthday in 1884.[3] From that time until 1910 they arrived in an uninterrupted stream. Some came to take up residence as

---

[1] Chou Chih-fu, Ch'ing Sheng-p'ing shu, 3, 5b–6a.

[2] Katharine A. Carl, With the Empress Dowager, pp. 59–60.

[3] Tz'u-hsi was born on the 10th of the tenth month (corresponding to 29 November) 1835. See Hummel, Eminent Chinese, p. 295. Her fiftieth birthday in Chinese reckoning fell on the 10th of the tenth month (27 November) 1884.

4. Stage in the Summer Palace, outside Peking (Photographed from Chou I-pai, *Chung-kuo chü-ch'ang shih*, p. 22)

teachers and actors, others for isolated performances.[1] Until 1900 a whole company would sometimes enter court to demonstrate its prowess as a group, but after the Boxer Uprising only individual actors were invited. Yet the actors from the city dominated the court theatre over the whole period, and the court eunuchs tended to lose their appeal. In the imperial palaces themselves, the 'elegant' drama yielded in importance before the sweep of the popular Peking Opera.

In accordance with her love for the drama, the Empress Dowager ensured that there should be several buildings suitable for performances in the New Summer Palace, I-ho yüan. This complex of palaces and beauty spots was built over the years 1886 to 1891 on part of the site occupied by the Yüan-ming yüan before its destruction in 1860. The money used for the Summer Palace had been intended for the building of a modern navy, but the Empress Dowager was doubtful about the value of such a venture and preferred to channel the funds into a project which would yield her more immediate enjoyment.[2] The stages she built were an excellent means towards this end. The largest was called the I-lo tien.[3] It was three-tiered and, apart from the great structure at Jehol and that in the Ning-shou kung, was the biggest stage in the palaces of the Manchu emperors. It lay not far from the main entrance of the I-ho yüan. Somewhat smaller was the T'ing-li kuan, on the other side of the K'un-ming Lake. 'This was where drama was [next] most often performed and in the summer there was a particularly large number of pieces given at the T'ing-li.'[4] It is true that the range of sites available in the Forbidden City was somewhat wider, but the Summer Palace did not lag too far behind.

The Empress Dowager has been given much of the credit for the growth to maturity of the Peking Opera,[5] and her patronage

[1] Chou I-pai has listed eighty-two of these actors, together with their age at the time of entry to court, their place of origin, the date they entered the imperial service and the date they left it. See *Chung-kuo hsi-chü shih*, pp. 676–81. See also Meng Yao, *Chung-kuo hsi-ch'ü shih*, pp. 538–44. Some stories of actors at court during this period and other historical details have been collected by Hsü Mu-yün in *Chung-kuo hsi-chü shih*, pp. 77 ff. See also Ts'ao Hsin-ch'üan, 'Ch'ien-Ch'ing nei-t'ing yen-hsi hui-i lu', *Chü-hsüeh yüeh-k'an* ii, 5 (May 1933), pp. 6–7.

[2] See Carroll Brown Malone, *History of the Peking Summer Palaces under the Ch'ing Dynasty*, pp. 194–218.

[3] A picture of the I-lo tien is given, among other places, ibid., p. 202.

[4] Ts'ao Hsin-ch'üan, 'Ch'ien-Ch'ing nei-t'ing', p. 8.

[5] See Chou Chih-fu, *Chin pai-nien ti Ching-chü*, pp. 33–5.

was undoubtedly an important factor. Yet much had happened outside the court even before her ascendancy, and the remainder of this chapter will be devoted to the major companies and actors contributing to the progress of the *Ching-chü* down to the time of the T'ung-chih Restoration.[1]

The Companies of Peking

During the Tao-kuang period, the 'four great Anhwei companies' and the Sung-chu held by far the most important place on the Peking stage. A text of the time records that no company was more expensive to watch than the Ch'un-t'ai, San-ch'ing, Ssu-hsi, and Ho-ch'un and that 'only the Sung-chu charged as much as the four great companies.'[2] However, there were other less important Anhwei companies, and the Clapper groups were still on the stage. These did not usually perform at important theatrical occasions and were rarely patronized by people of good family. A guide-book of Peking in 1845, the *Tu-men chi-lüeh*,[3] mentions eight troupes which may be taken as the most important in Peking at that time. They are the four great Anhwei companies, the Sung-chu, Chin-yü, Shuang-ho, and Ta Ching-ho.[4] The Chin-yü was a minor Anhwei company which had been first formed about 1803. It is said to have been recently resurrected in 1845,[5] and must therefore have disbanded some time before. The Shuang-ho is called a *pang-tzu ch'iang* company and had been devoted to the Clapper Opera since its inception about 1803. It will be recalled that the Ta Ching-ho, which had been formed before 1810, had also been a *Ch'in-ch'iang* company, but seems to have transferred its attention to *erh-huang* and *hsi-p'i* by 1845.[6]

The number of actors, as listed in these eight companies in the *Tu-men chi-lüeh* of 1845, is as follows:

---

[1] I have considered the later period in *The Chinese Theatre in Modern Times*, chapters four and five.

[2] *Meng-hua so-pu (MHSP)*, p. 3b.

[3] Updated versions of the guide-book followed in 1851, 1864, 1872, 1876, 1880, 1887, and 1907. These works are discussed by Hsieh Kuo-chen in *Ming-Ch'ing pi-chi t'an-ts'ung*, pp. 125–7 and by Chou Chih-fu in *Tu-men chi-lüeh chung chih hsi-ch'ü shih-liao*, pp. 1–8. The latter work contains extensive quotations from the versions of 1845, 1864, 1876, 1880, 1887, and 1907; it may be regarded almost as a primary source in itself.

[4] Ibid., pp. 112–21.

[5] Ibid., p. 50.

[6] Ibid., p. 9.

Chin-yü	12	San-ch'ing	9
Ssu-hsi	11	Ch'un-t'ai	8
Ta Ching-ho	10	Shuang-ho	7
Ho-ch'un	9	Sung-chu	7

Although these numbers suggest that the three minor troupes were no less favoured with good actors than the five major ones, their social status appears to have been much lower. Very little is known about their members, and Yang Mou-chien, who records details of the lives of nearly seventy Peking actors, devotes himself almost exclusively to the five main troupes.

The *Tu-men chi-lüeh* of 1851 lists two companies not included in the 1845 version of the work. They are the Ch'ung-ch'ing and the Shuang-k'uei.[1] The former was already functioning during the 1820s and had no doubt been recently revived by 1851. The latter may have been the same company, under a different name, as the Ho-ch'un, which is not included in the 1851 edition. This suggestion was made in the 1920s by a Japanese scholar,[2] but is thrown into doubt by the fact that not a single actor noted in the Ho-ch'un troupe in 1845 is listed in the Shuang-k'uei six years later. The 1864 version of the guide-book reveals further changes and shows that only four of the companies of 1845 and 1851 had survived: the San-ch'ing, Ch'un-t'ai, Sung-chu and Ssu-hsi. The others had vanished or been replaced by new groups.[3]

The sources also give information concerning the relative fortunes of the five main companies. As remarked in chapter five, the Ssu-hsi company had lost a number of its members to other troupes in the early years of the Tao-kuang period. The early 1830s witnessed a further decline, and many of those who remained in the company were 'white-haired old men',[4] who showed no sign of originality or of adapting their art to the needs of the times. However, the company gained new life in the following years. According to one writer, 'Since early in the spring of 1837, there have often been as many in the audience [during performances] by the Ssu-hsi company as those of the Ch'un-t'ai. On no day are there fewer than 700 or 800. This is about double what

---

[1] See Wang Chih-chang, *Ch'iang-tiao k'ao-yüan*, pp. 17a–20a, where the original is quoted in full.
[2] See Hatano Kenichi, *Ching-chü erh-pai nien chih li-shih*, p. 19.
[3] See Chou Chih-fu, *Tu-men chi-lüeh*, pp. 112–21.
[4] *Ch'ang-an k'an-hua chi (CAKHC)*, p. 8b.

there had been a year or two before.'[1] The reason for this revival will become apparent later in this section.

In the first years of the 1830s, the Sung-chu company fell into decline. Its best members left it, and it was forced to disband. However, the teachers of the troupe tried to resuscitate it by attracting younger actors. They met with a great deal of success and one of the best performers of the period, Lin Yün-hsiang, joined the Sung-chu company. The newly formed group rose quickly to new heights of proficiency and fame. It played regularly to full houses and the people found difficulty in obtaining seats. According to Yang Mou-chien, theatre-goers always tried first for entrance to the performances of the Sung-chu company and would go to see the Ch'un-t'ai or San-ch'ing only if seats were unavailable for the Sung-chu.[2]

This statement is certainly exaggerated. Both the Ch'un-t'ai and San-ch'ing were doing well. Yang himself makes this clear by the space he devotes to actors of these companies. The Ch'un-t'ai was led by three artists, T'an T'ien-lu, Yin Pien-chih, and Ch'en Ssu.[3] T'an was one of Peking's most distinguished performers and Yin had been well known for some time, since he occupies the fourth place in a list of fifty-five actors on a stele dated 1827.[4] Furthermore, referring to the year 1837, Yang says specifically that the San-ch'ing company abounded in splendid *hsiao-sheng* actors; it was led by Tung Hsiu-jung and Ch'en Chin-ts'ai, both of whom were among the most revered teachers in Peking.[5]

Like the Sung-chu, the Ho-ch'un company disbanded early in the 1830s,[6] possibly for the same reason: decline in membership. It had revived by 1837, for details are recorded of several actors who were performing in it in that year.[7] Of the four great Anhwei companies it was the least durable and had certainly disbanded permanently by the time of the T'ung-chih Restoration.

---

[1] *Ting-nien yü-sun chih*, p. 7a.

[2] *Hsin-jen kuei-chia lu* (*HJKCL*), pp. 4a–b.

[3] *HJKCL*, p. 19b.

[4] *Pei-ching li-yüan chin-shih wen-tzu lu* (*PCLYCS*), p. 6b.

[5] *Ting-nien yü-sun chih*, p. 14b. Tung Hsiu-jung and Ch'en Chin-ts'ai are referred to by their *t'ang-ming*, Ching-i t'ang and Pao-shan t'ang. See *HJKCL*, pp. 13a–14a; Chou Chih-fu, *Ching-chü*, p. 59.

[6] *MHSP*, p. 15a.

[7] For example, Su-hsiang (*CAKHC*, p. 17b) and Wu Chen-t'ien (p. 18b) were members of the Ho-ch'un company in 1837.

The other three enjoyed longer lives. The San-ch'ing disbanded in 1887, being re-established briefly in 1892 and again in 1896. Both the Ch'un-t'ai and Ssu-hsi companies suspended activities at the time of the Boxer Uprising in 1900, the Ch'un-t'ai permanently. The Ssu-hsi revived once more for a very short period in 1910.[1]

The four great companies of the Tao-kuang period had definite characteristics. The San-ch'ing is reported to have performed long dramas in episodes, rather like a lengthy scroll being unfolded scene by scene. Yang Mou-chien says of the company that 'all the dramas of its repertoire are newly arranged pieces. It continues performing the same item on successive days, and the *literati* approve of this.'[2] We know that during the T'ung-chih period the highlight of the Peking theatre was a complete performance by the San-ch'ing company of the dramas based on the novel *The Romance of the Three Kingdoms*.[3] No doubt stories from the famous popular novel *The Water Margin* were also performed in this way.

At the time, the most usual practice was to perform short scenes individually, so that items put on at one sitting did not necessarily present a connected story. Sometimes two, three, or several scenes might form a single episode. The lists of performed dramas in the *Tu-men chi-lüeh* of 1845[4] suggest that it was not normal to concentrate entirely on one piece for several days, and items given there for the San-ch'ing company do not differ in this respect from those of other companies. Probably, then, the San-ch'ing staged extended dramas in many instalments only on special occasions, rather than as a normal rule.[5]

The Ch'un-t'ai company is said to have been called *hai-tzu*

---

[1] See Chou Chih-fu, *Ching-chü*, pp. 73–4 for details of the lives of the four great companies.

[2] *MHSP*, p. 6a.

[3] Ch'i Ju-shan, *Ch'ing-tai p'i-huang ming-chüeh chien-shu*, pp. 4–5. On the San-kuo yen-i see appendix C below, pp. 259–63.

[4] See Chou Chih-fu, *Tu-men chi-lüeh*, pp. 13ff., 124 ff.

[5] The *tsa-chü* of the Yüan were comparatively short and could be fitted into one session without difficulty. However, the *ch'uan-ch'i* of the Ming were extremely long and sometimes ran for excessive periods. Acting companies naturally began to confine themselves to a few key scenes of a drama. This is obvious from texts of popular plays from the Ming and Ch'ing. See Wang Ku-lu, *Ming-tai Hui-tiao hsi-ch'ü san-ch'u chi-i* and the famous Ch'ien-lung collection *Chui pai-ch'iu*. Only for very exclusive circles, like the court (see Chou Chih-fu, *Ch'ing Sheng-p'ing shu, 6, passim*) and *literati*, was it still possible to perform an extended drama complete. See also Chou I-pai, *Chung-kuo hsi-chü shih chiang-tso*, pp. 234–7.

(children), because of the youth of its members.[1] The statement is curious for, as was remarked in the last chapter, all actors began their careers when still very young. In the 1830s, the period to which the record specifically refers, all companies contained boy-actors and there is nothing to suggest that those of the Ch'un-t'ai were any younger or finer than those of the other companies. The same can be said of later years. A work of 1867 notes details of a number of famous boy-actors, who belonged not only to the Ch'un-t'ai but also the San-ch'ing and Ssu-hsi troupes.[2] Another work, of 1873, records the names of many young performers, and they too belonged to various companies.[3] Finally, the *Tu-men chi-lüeh* of 1845 and later years give no indication that the Ch'un-t'ai company was in any way noted for scenes which emphasized boy-actors.[4] The explanation of the Ch'un-t'ai's reputation for its child actors may be that the boys of that company were seen publicly on the stage even younger and more often than those of other troupes. In some scenes numerous minor characters are needed to enhance the atmosphere of the drama. It may be that the Ch'un-t'ai company could provide more children than other troupes for scenes of this sort.

There were several points of special interest in the life of the Ho-ch'un company. In the first place, its members were particularly noted for their skill in the military theatre. They displayed remarkable dexterity in dancing with swords and in wielding the various weapons used on the stage of the Peking Opera.[5] After midday they would perform scenes based on the stories of *The Romance of the Three Kingdoms* and *The Water Margin*.[6] Other companies, too, were adept at the acrobatics for which the military drama was especially famous, but apparently none of them reached the superb standards of the Ho-ch'un.

It has been suggested by the contemporary scholar Chou I-pai that the prevalence of warlike themes in the drama was a reflection of the unsettled conditions of the time. Travelling officials or merchants were constantly attacked and robbed despite the presence of professional bodyguards. Incidents of highway robbery

---

[1] *MHSP*, p. 6a.   [2] *Ming-t'ung ho-lu, passim.*
[3] *Chü-pu ch'ün-ying (CPCY), passim.*
[4] See Chou Chih-fu, *Tu-men chi-lüeh*, pp. 22–31.
[5] For a treatment of the weapons used in the Peking Opera see Scott, *The Classical Theatre of China*, pp. 172 ff.
[6] *MHSP*, p. 6a.

were absorbed, in adapted form, into the repertory of wandering story-tellers. Acting companies saw in these strollers a ready source of material for their dramas and an opportunity to reflect actual events in their art.[1] On the other hand, stories based on civil wars, such as those of the third century, had also been popular for a long time, and dramatized versions of these events came to form a large part of the Peking Opera repertory.

A second characteristic of the Ho-ch'un company was that it was associated in a special way with the Manchu aristocracy. Although not considered as fine in its standards as the famous companies of the princely mansions of the Ch'ien-lung era, it was the only one of Peking's major troupes which performed regularly in the houses of the Manchu nobles.[2]

Yet the privilege of acting for members of the ruling clan was not entirely denied to other great companies, even in the 1830s. For example, the eighth son of Ch'ien-lung, Yung-hsüan (1746–1832),[3] invited the Sung-chu to his mansion in 1831.[4] But evidence that the Ch'un-t'ai, Ssu-hsi, or San-ch'ing were similarly honoured by the Manchu aristocracy is lacking for this period. It was only later in the nineteenth century that they were found frequently in the houses of the nobility. One instance was in September 1885, at about the same time as the Empress Dowager was starting to introduce large numbers of city actors into the court, when the Ssu-hsi company collaborated with some members of other groups to give performances at the mansion of Prince Kung (1833–98) during a t'ang-hui.[5]

Throughout the Ch'ien-lung and later periods the relations of the Manchu emperors were noted patrons of the theatre. This was natural since the drama was an excellent means of alleviating the boredom of their lives: they were rarely allowed to leave Peking, and their contacts with Han officials and scholars were extremely limited. Many Manchu nobles ran their own private companies, which they sometimes allowed to perform outside their own residences. Perhaps the most famous company of the princely

[1] Chou I-pai, Chiang-tso, pp. 239–40.

[2] HJKCL, p. 4b.

[3] See Hummel, Eminent Chinese, pp. 963–4.

[4] HJKCL, p. 4b.

[5] See Chou Chih-fu, Ching-hsi chin pai-nien so-chi, p. 66. See Prince Kung's biography in Hummel, Eminent Chinese, pp. 380–4 and especially Mary Wright, The Last Stand of Chinese Conservatism, passim.

houses in the Chia-ch'ing period was the En-ch'ing, which belonged to Prince Yung-hsing (1752–1823),[1] the brother of Yung-hsüan. There were also well known troupes attached to the royal princes later in the dynasty. Among the best of them was the Ch'üan-fu of Prince Kung, which was led by Tu Tieh-yün, and later by Ch'en Shou-feng. Towards the end of the Ch'ing we even find members of the royal family who could act.[2] By far the most famous was P'u-t'ung, a great-great-grandson of Yung-hsing. P'u-t'ung was highly regarded not only for his stage skills but also for his wide academic knowledge of the Chinese drama, and he at one time taught the subject at Tsinghua University in Peking.[3]

In accordance with the age-old rule which demanded that aristocrats should despise the drama of the people, the companies of the princely houses performed *K'un-ch'ü* and *Ching-ch'iang*, at least until after the T'ung-chih Restoration. The Ho-ch'un company, too, carried on this tradition. Its actors were quite versatile and probably restricted themselves to the more high-class styles when their audience was of noble extraction. Yet the company could also perform *Ch'in-ch'iang*[4] and the pieces it gave in the major playhouses of the Outer City were mostly Peking Operas.[5]

If the Ho-ch'un troupe differed from the other main Anhwei companies in its prowess in *Ching-ch'iang*, the special characteristic of the Ssu-hsi company was the emphasis it lay on *K'un-ch'ü*. Yang Mou-chien writes of this troupe, 'The Ssu-hsi is called *ch'ü-tzu*. It preserves the style of the former generations . . . and does not perform lewd songs.'[6] This stress on *K'un-ch'ü* had, as we have seen, undergone variations. According to Chang Chi-liang, the Ssu-hsi troupe had given up performing this old style completely by 1829.[7] However, during the following years it again began performing *K'un-ch'ü*, and this seems to have been the reason for the decline in its popularity in the early 1830s. Yang records that the audiences of the Ssu-hsi company 'listened attentively, nodded

[1] See Hummel, *Eminent Chinese*, pp. 962–3.

[2] See Chou Chih-fu, *Ching-chü*, pp. 30–2.

[3] See Ch'en Yen-heng, *Chiu-chü ts'ung-t'an*, pp. 4b–5a and Hummel, *Eminent Chinese*, p. 378.

[4] *CAKHC*, p. 17a.

[5] See Chou Chih-fu, *Tu-men chi-lüeh*, pp. 43–4.   [6] *MHSP*, p. 6a.

[7] *Chin-t'ai ts'an-lei chi (CTTLC)*, 1, 2b.

their heads and smiled; the situation was completely different from the roaring sound of laughter and talking among the audiences at performances by the Ch'un-t'ai and San-ch'ing.'[1]

The recovery of the Ssu-hsi company late in the 1830s was apparently due to the famous actor Hu Hsiao-t'ien-hsi, who reached the apex of his career about 1837. Yang Mou-chien wrote: 'Recently the best actor in the performance of *K'un-ch'ü* has been [Chang] Chin-lin but with T'ing-hsiang's [Hsiao-t'ien-hsi's] appearance, Chin-lin has been overshadowed.' The source of Hu's reputation was apparently his singing, which was sometimes loud enough 'to impress a deaf man' and yet could be 'so sad that it penetrated the heart and really made people listen'.[2]

It is worth pointing out here that, just as the Ho-ch'un had no monopoly of the military drama or the Ch'un-t'ai of child actors, the Ssu-hsi was by no means the only troupe which included good *K'un-ch'ü* actors in the 1830s, depite its reputation for the style. Chang Chin-lin, for instance, belonged to the Ch'un-t'ai troupe,[3] and so did Hsiao-t'ien-hsi's own brother Lien-hsi, who was also a good exponent of *K'un-ch'ü*.[4] Moreover, when the actors from Su-chou and Yang-chou were expelled from the court in 1827, many of them moved to Peking's Outer City, where they joined not only the Ssu-hsi but all the main Anhwei companies.[5]

The Ssu-hsi company's special prominence in the elegant tunes does not seem to have lasted long. The lists in the *Tu-men chi-lüeh* of 1845 do not show it as interested especially in the *K'un-ch'ü*. Hsiao-t'ien-hsi is not mentioned there[6] and, as we shall see later, its leader Chang Erh-k'uei was famed for his performance of *hsi-p'i*, not for *K'un-ch'ü*. Later versions of the guide-book confirm that the trend was in favour of the Peking Opera.[7]

The last spate of popularity for the *K'un-ch'ü* among the public was apparently heavily dependent on Hsiao-t'ien-hsi's artistry for, by the end of the Tao-kuang period, it was rarely performed outside the court or private mansions of the rich. We find the names of occasional *K'un-ch'ü* actors, but few of them created much impression. Chu Lien-fen was perhaps the best known. He was born on 17 January 1837[8] and forced by his elder brother to go to

---

[1] *CAKHC*, p. 8b.   [2] *Ting-nien yü-sun chih*, p. 6b.   [3] Ibid., pp. 5b–6a.
[4] *CAKHC*, pp. 18b–19a.   [5] *CTTLC*, 3, 6a.
[6] See Chou Chih-fu, *Tu-men chi-lüeh*, pp. 31–3.   [7] Ibid., pp. 33–43.
[8] *CPCY*, p. 26a.

Peking when still a child. He was a *tan* and, though famous by 1852,[1] was still a noted exponent of such roles as Kuan-yin in *Hsi Mu-lien* in 1873.[2] Yet even Chu did not greatly enhance the prestige of the dying elegant drama, and he began devoting much of his time and energy to the Peking Opera.[3] In Su-chou itself the old *K'un-ch'ü* tradition was virtually killed by the wars and economic catastrophe resulting from the T'ai-p'ing uprising.[4]

Naturally, people could still be found even in the present century who regretted the passing of the *K'un-ch'ü* in the capital and its replacement by the Peking Opera. Chen-chün, writing in 1907, comments bitterly on the popularity of the *Ching-chü*. He remarks, 'Its sounds are higher and more hurried than I[-*yang ch'iang*, i.e. *Ching-ch'iang*]. Its words are uneducated and vulgar, and lack the elegance either of *K'un*[-*ch'ü*] or *I*[-*yang ch'iang*].'[5] The ordinary people, however, had grown to love the new Peking Opera, and even a personage as high-ranking as the Empress Dowager gave it her blessing. Its popularity was not confined to Peking, for it spread through most of China and by the middle of the present century had become a kind of national drama.

Actors of the Middle Tao-kuang Period

Against this background of developments in Peking's major companies, let us turn to consider a few of the most significant and interesting actors of the 1830s, beginning with the earliest exponents in the capital of the opera of Hupeh, called *Ch'u-tiao*, which was similar to the music of the Peking Opera already there in being dominated by *erh-huang* and *hsi-p'i*.[6]

The first actors known to have performed *Ch'u-tiao* in Peking were the *lao-sheng* Wang Hung-kuei and Li Liu. Unfortunately, the earliest reference to these men, written in 1832, confines itself to one rather uninformative remark: 'The capital honoured the *Ch'u-tiao*; some actors in the drama companies, like Wang Hung-kuei and Li Liu, excelled in the new music and were praised by those of the time.'[7] In the *Tu-men chi-lüeh* of 1845

[1] *T'an-po*, p. 2a.   [2] *CPCY*, p. 26a.   [3] Ch'i Ju-shan, *Chien-shu*, p. 61.

[4] The fall of the *K'un-ch'ü* and the reasons for it are discussed by Yao Hsin-nung in 'The Rise and Fall of the K'un Ch'ü', *T'ien Hsia Monthly*, ii, 1 (Jan. 1936), 80 ff; Josephine Huang Hung, *Ming Drama*, pp. 240–2.

[5] *T'ien-chih ou-wen*, 7, 27a.

[6] I have discussed the origins and history of the Hupeh Opera in *The Chinese Theatre*, chapter nine.

[7] *Yen-t'ai hung-chao chi*, pp. 10a–b.

Wang Hung-kuei is listed first among the actors of the Ho-ch'un company and he was especially noted for his performance as Liu Chang in *Jang Ch'eng-tu*. Li Liu is given second among the members of the Ch'un-t'ai troupe.[1] Neither actor is mentioned in later versions of the guide-book.

Although the earliest known *Ch'u-tiao* actors in Peking were *lao-sheng*, the artists of the 1830s about whom we know most were still *tan*. This is because our sources were written mainly by scholars who described performers to whom they were personally attracted and with whom they had in many cases some special liaison. The first of the *tan* reported to have taken up the performance of *Ch'u-tiao* in Peking was Wang I-hsiang.

Wang's *ming* was Ch'üan-lin[2] and he came from Peking. He was a member of the Ch'un-t'ai company and was fair, slender, and elegant. Like other actors, he began his career on the stage very young. His elder brother, Yün-hsiang, also in the Ch'un-t'ai, was born in 1815.[3] He himself must therefore have been born later than that and would have been no more than sixteen at the time of his greatest success, which was early in the 1830s. I-hsiang was not popular among his colleagues, since he was very arrogant and inclined to look down on others.

One writer, whose *nom de plume* was Su-hai an chü-shih, has left a short description of his artistic talents. 'I-hsiang learned [the *Ch'u-tiao*] from them [Wang and Li] and came to be just as good as they. [His singing] was equally good in high or low passages, his actions perfectly natural, and his enunciation clear ... People found him very moving and he was without rivals.'[4]

Probably I-hsiang's career was fairly short. It is reported on a stele of 1837 that he contributed a small sum of money towards the building of a cemetery for the members of the Ch'un-t'ai company.[5] However, the *Tu-men chi-lüeh* of 1845 makes no reference to him and he may by then have retired from the acting profession.[6]

---

[1] See Chou Chih-fu, *Tu-men chi-lüeh*, pp. 43, 22. On the drama *Jang Ch'eng-tu* see below, appendix C, p. 262.

[2] *Yen-t'ai hung-chao chi*, p. 6a.

[3] Ibid., pp. 9b–10b. According to this source, Wang Yün-hsiang was thirteen years old in 1828.

[4] Ibid., p. 10b.   [5] *PCLYCS*, p. 9a.

[6] On Wang I-hsiang see also Chou Chih-fu, 'Tsao-ch'i p'i-huang ming-tan k'ao', *Ta-Hua* 39 (Oct. 1967), p. 19.

Wang Hung-kuei, Li Liu, and Wang I-hsiang are the only actors who are reported directly as having excelled in the *Ch'u-tiao* during this early period. Yet the extent of the Peking Opera's development as shown in the *Tu-men chi-lüeh* of 1845 suggests that others had followed their lead, and it is likely that both the actors described later in this section were already familiar with the music of Hupeh in the 1830s. Indeed, the fact that Wang I-hsiang, who came from Peking, already saw fit to study it then suggests that Wang Hung-kuei and Li Liu were very quick in spreading its influence.

It is true that the *Ch'u-tiao* was a branch of the larger system of *erh-huang* and *hsi-p'i* drama, so that Wang Hung-kuei and Li Liu did not bring to Peking anything as radically new as Wei Ch'ang-sheng's or Kao Yüeh-kuan's music. Yet the Hupeh Opera was by no means identical to the *erh-huang* of Kao; some scholars have even suggested that the melodies sung by the early Anhwei companies included no *hsi-p'i* and that the 'new music' of Wang and Li means specifically *hsi-p'i*.[1] In any case, it is very striking that the primary sources refer so little to the *Ch'u-tiao*. Su-hai an chü-shih is the only author of the period to mention it and the two great *lao-sheng* who introduced it came across as extremely nebulous figures.

Unlike the Anhwei actors of the earlier period, those from Hupeh arrived as individuals, not as groups. They did not bring new companies with them, but joined the troupes already flourishing in Peking. Their impact was much more gradual than that made by Wei Ch'ang-sheng or Kao Yüeh-kuan. They added to, but in no sense superseded, the music of Anhwei which had already become so popular in the capital.

The principal sources for the actors of Peking during the 1830s are the works of Yang Mou-chien. He relates a good deal of biographical information and has much to say about the habits and characteristics of his subjects. Unfortunately, he seems to have been unaware of the significance—or even existence—of the *Ch'u-tiao*. His interest in the actors he describes was personal, and his concern with their artistry was quite secondary. It is therefore

[1] See, for instance, Chou I-pai, *Chiang-tso*, p. 247. Though of separate origin, *erh-huang* and *hsi-p'i* quickly came to the associated closely with one another, and in present-day regional styles the one is virtually never found without the other. Chou Chih-fu (*Ching-chü*, pp. 3–5) points out also that the term *erh-huang* is used to cover *hsi-p'i* as well. Chou I-pai's suggestion is therefore unlikely.

virtually impossible to assess the influence of the Hupeh Opera on the performers he admired.

In Yang's estimation, the best of the *tan* actors of the time was Lin Yün-hsiang[1] of the Sung-chu company.[2] Lin was born about 1818[3] in Su-chou. At the age of fourteen or so he was sold by his father on a three-year contract, and taken to Peking where he became the disciple of a certain Liu Cheng-hsiang.[4] Yün-hsiang worked extremely hard and, after very little training, became very popular among theatre-goers in the capital. It appears that he rarely rested and fulfilled so many engagements that his health was affected.

In 1834 Lin's contract with his master expired and he was hoping to be allowed to return to Su-chou. Liu Cheng-hsiang, however, had other plans. He was profiting extensively from Yün-hsiang's work and wanted to keep the youth under his tutelage. He therefore sent a messenger to Su-chou to persuade the actor's father to come to Peking. When the latter arrived, Liu lodged him in a different house so that his son, who had not been told that he was in Peking, would not see him. Liu then set about persuading Yün-hsiang's father to renew the period of apprentice-ship for another three years, and, to encourage him to agree to the request, presented him with 800 taels. The old man signed the contract and it was not until after this that Yün-hsiang found out what was happening.

The young actor was, not surprisingly, extremely upset at what had been done behind his back. Although in other ways he appears to have been of a mild and rather weak character, he determined on this occasion to resist. He raised from various of his admirers the sum of 3,000 taels. All of this he gave to his master, who therefore released him from the contract.[5]

The incident is interesting for the light it throws on two aspects of the young boy-actors' lives. Firstly, it shows that masters did not, in general, break their contract with impunity. Had Liu felt that his power over Yün-hsiang was total, he would hardly have gone to the trouble and expense of bribing the boy's father to

[1] *CAKHC*, p. 8a.
[2] *HJKCL*, p. 8a.
[3] Lin was seventeen at the beginning of 1835 (*HJKCL*, p. 6a).
[4] *MHSP*, p. 18a. Liu Cheng-hsiang was the son of Liu T'ien-kuei, the master of Yang Fa-ling, whom I discussed in chapter five.
[5] *HJKCL*, p. 5a.

renew the contract, but would simply have ignored the fact that it had expired. Secondly, the incident suggests that a master could, in fact, usually impose his will on his charge. It was only because Lin was able to raise such a large sum of money that he was able to buy his way out of the contract. If Liu was hoping to gain financially from his ploy with the actor's father, he succeeded admirably and made a considerable profit from it. As I noted in chapter five, 2,000 to 3,000 taels was the normal price for buying an actor out of a contract. In practice few of the boys could have found so much in a short time, especially since they had to give their masters the money they earned in the course of their work, so we may assume that it would have been difficult for most actors to resist the wishes of a master who behaved in the way displayed by Liu.

After his release from the contract, Yün-hsiang decided to remain in Peking, presumably because his father was there. He set up his own house and *hsiang-kung t'ang-tzu* in a building beside the Yü-huang Temple, west of the Ta Sha-lan in the Outer City. This place was called the Mei-ho t'ang and there Lin lived in some comfort. His father stayed in the capital and took employment with him as a cook. The Mei-ho t'ang became a well known eating-place and was noted for its fine delicacies. People would forgather there to enjoy the tea, melons, and good conversation for which it became famous.[1]

It was at this time that Yün-hsiang, though still only seventeen, arranged to be married. A certain Kao Ch'ing-lin, or Kao Shuang-lin, had a daughter who was coming of age and whom he promised in marriage to Lin. He later regretted his decision, possibly because of the social stigma which was still attached to actors, and she was engaged to someone else. A man called Ku Hsi-yü of Hang-chou then intervened on Yün-hsiang's behalf. Ku was an admirer of the actor and it is said that he kept a portrait of the boy in his house and would display it during banquets. Ku's intervention proved successful and Kao again promised his daughter to Yün-hsiang. As it happened, however, the actor never married because he died before the wedding could take place.[2]

[1] *HJKCL*, p. 5a–b.
[2] *HJKCL*, p. 8a and *MHSP*, p. 17b. In the former text the girl's father is called Kao Shuang-lin, in the latter Kao Ch'ing-lin.

Lin's death occurred in the following way. After he moved to the Mei-ho t'ang, Yün-hsiang fell ill. A friend recommended to him the practice of smoking opium as an escape from his sorrows. Lin became addicted to the drug, but this of course only exacerbated his illness. It appears to have been a combination of opium and natural sickness which killed him. Lin realised his mistake too late and, just before his death, prayed to the Buddha for good health. He swore that if his prayer was granted he would give up opium for ever. Unfortunately the entreaty went unanswered and Lin died in January 1835. Ironically, the friend who had recommended the drug to him also died from excessive addiction at about the same time as Lin.[1]

Yang Mou-chien writes quite ecstatically about this boy's character. He paints Lin as quiet and dignified, always correct in his speech, modest and unassuming. His description leaves no doubt that his liking for the actor went a good deal beyond ordinary admiration.[2] Unfortunately, it is possible to observe the relationship between the two only from Yang's point of view. Whether or not the feeling was reciprocal we do not know, but in this regard Lin's plan to marry may be significant.

Lin was unworldly and differed from most *t'ang-tzu* owners in that he did not try to become rich. He never amassed a large private fortune,[3] even though his ability to raise 3,000 taels at short notice proves that he could have done so. His house seems to have been modest and there is no evidence that he lived in great splendour. It is true that he maintained a permanent servant, but this was by no means a sign of great opulence in those days. Lin's servant was called Liu Erh and came from Ho-chien in Chihli. He outlived the actor by many years and would talk to Yang Mou-chien about his late master.[4]

As a performer Lin was unsurpassed and appears to have been responsible for the meteoric rise of his company, the Sung-chu, around 1833 and 1834. He performed *hsiao-sheng* roles as well as *tan*, and the hero Chia Pao-yü of *The Dream of the Red Chamber* was among his most popular roles. Yang says that he was elegant and natural in the part, and that one seemed to be meeting Pao-yü himself.[5] The styles of drama Lin sang are not known for certain. Presumably he was principally concerned with *erh-huang* and

[1] *HJKCL*, pp. 5b–6a.　　[2] *HJKCL*, p. 7a.　　[3] *HJKCL*, p. 7b.
[4] *MHSP*, p. 18a.　　[5] *HJKCL*, p. 7b.

hsi-p'i, since these were the main styles of the Anhwei companies, but he may well have studied *K'un-ch'ü* too. His attitude to the newly arrived Hupeh Opera is not recorded, but he cannot have escaped its influence entirely.

Another very famous *tan* actor of the period was Ch'en Feng-lin, whose *tzu* was Luan-hsien.[1] He came from Anhwei[2] and had become known as an actor in Peking by the early 1830s. He was a disciple of Tung Hsiu-jung,[3] one of the leaders of the San-ch'ing company, and was a member of that troupe until about 1837.[4] However, it is recorded on a stele of that year that he contributed a small sum of money towards the costs of constructing a cemetery for the Ch'un-t'ai company,[5] and he had presumably joined this group by then. The *Tu-men chi-lüeh* of 1845 notes the names of two *tan* actors called Feng-lin, one belonging to the Ch'un-t'ai, the other to the Ssu-hsi,[6] and it is likely that the former was Ch'en Luan-hsien.[7] Like other important actors, he ran his own *hsiang-kung t'ang-tzu*: the Ou-hsiang t'ang near Ta Sha-lan, where he took up residence in April 1836.[8] However, he later grew tired of his profession and left the capital for Han-k'ou, probably some time after 1845. He had become quite wealthy and set up a business in his new home, thus gaining a respectable living.[9]

Ch'en was skilled in arts other than acting and singing. He was a good painter and his drawings of orchids were especially fine, though he was unable to devote much time to practising this art owing to his social and theatrical engagements.[10] He could also play the *p'i-p'a* with some skill.[11] As a man, however, he was not popular, since he was somewhat arrogant and inclined to be supercilious towards ordinary actors.[12] He drank a good deal, but could not stand a large quantity and frequently got inebriated. He received quite a number of scholarly patrons at the Ou-hsiang t'ang and was a close friend of Yang Mou-chien's.

As a *tan* actor Ch'en was first-rate. He was graceful in his laughter, very beautiful in appearance, and endowed with a

---

[1] The *ming* of this actor is given in *Yen-t'ai hung-chao chi*, p. 8b and *Huai-fang chi*, p. 3a as Feng-lin and in *CAKHC*, p. 5b as Feng-ling.
[2] *Huai-fang chi*, p. 3a.   [3] *CAKHC*, p. 12a.   [4] *CAKHC*, p. 6b.
[5] *PCLYCS*, p. 9a.   [6] See Chou Chih-fu, *Tu-men chi-lüeh*, pp. 23, 33.
[7] See Chou Chih-fu, 'Ming-tan k'ao', p. 19. In the *Tu-men chi-lüeh* of 1851 there is also a Feng-lin in the Ch'ung-ch'ing company. See Wang Chih-chang, *Ch'iang-tiao k'ao-yüan*, pp. 17a–20a. This could have been Ch'en Luan-hsien.
[8] *CAKHC*, p. 6a.   [9] *Huai-fang chi*, p. 3b.   [10] *CAKHC*, p. 6a.
[11] *Yen-t'ai hung-chao chi*, p. 8b.   [12] *Huai-fang chi*, p. 3a.

magnificent voice which Yang compares to the sound of a *p'i-p'a*. Feng-lin showed considerable versatility in the moods of his acting and could perform tragic or coquettish parts.[1] But we know also that he played the *hsiao-sheng* role of Chou Yü in *Ch'ün-ying hui* (*The Meeting of Many Heroes*),[2] which has traditionally been a favourite part for *hsiao-sheng* actors. The text which records his skill as Chou Yü dates from 1876 and primary sources of the thirties do not mention that he performed the role. However, Ch'en's master, Tung Hsiu-jung, was known for his skill as a *hsiao-sheng* and it may be that Ch'en had learned to play Chou Yü from Tung.[3] On the other hand, it is equally possible that, as he neared the end of his career on the stage, he tired of acting only as a *tan* and transferred some of his attention to male parts.

The Three Great Lao-sheng Actors

The previous section makes it clear that the combination of the music of Anhwei and Hupeh, which is the basis of Peking Opera, was already a feature of the Peking stage in the 1830s. Meanwhile, three really great *lao-sheng* actors were building up their reputations and were to dominate the stage in the following decades. These were Ch'eng Chang-keng, Yü San-sheng, and Chang Erh-k'uei. They consolidated the work of earlier artists and established varying schools of the Peking Opera. If Wang Hung-kuei and Li Liu blazed the trail by familiarizing the populace of Peking with the Hupeh music, it was Ch'eng and his colleagues who blended the Peking Opera into the magnificent art known today.

The sources for our knowledge of these three actors are quite different in kind from earlier books mentioned in these pages. They were written by men who appreciated the acting of their subjects, but did not necessarily know them personally. Their time of composition was not normally contemporary with the period under discussion. They record stories about actors, often showing some moral virtue or failing, but only in exceptional

---

[1] *CAKHC*, pp. 5b–6b.

[2] *Huai-fang chi*, p. 3a. For an account of the *Ch'ün-ying hui* see Scott, *The Classical Theatre*, pp. 186–92, and for a translation with comments see Arlington and Acton, *Famous Chinese Plays*, pp. 201–10.

[3] See Chou Chih-fu, 'Ming-tan k'ao', p. 19.

cases are such anecdotes based on personal first-hand observations. The private side of the actors' lives is virtually ignored.

The first of the three great *lao-sheng* actors, Ch'eng Chang-keng (*tzu* Yü-shan), was probably the most famous exponent of the Peking Opera in the nineteenth century. He was born in Ch'ien-shan county, An-ch'ing, in 1812,[1] but went to Peking when very young. It is said that he ran a small business there, selling musical instruments.[2] However, his maternal uncle, who was an actor, was very fond of him and encouraged him to go on the stage. Ch'eng was enthusiastic about the suggestion and underwent training, but the road to success turned out to be more difficult than he imagined:

When he made his [first public] appearance, his performance was not yet polished and the audience laughed at him. Chang-keng was deeply ashamed. He locked his house and sat in a special room for three years and was not heard in public.[3] One day a certain noble held a large banquet attended by princes of the blood, high-ranking ministers and eminent subjects. He tried out all the actors in the drama *Chao-kuan*. All at once Chang-keng appeared as Wu [Tzu-] hsü.[4] His robustness in wearing the cap and carrying the sword, the nobility of his voice and rhythm, and his wonderful and chivalrous air made him seem absolutely like a god. The several hundred people in the audience were all very surprised. They rose up and shouted madly, shaking heaven. The host was very pleased and got all his guests to drink toast after toast to Chang-keng, calling him Chiao-t'ien (shouting to heaven). After that, the name of Chiao-t'ien spread everywhere in the capital. Princes, dukes, and eminent subjects gave each other banquets and if Chang-keng did not come, the whole audience would be displeased.[5]

By 1845, Ch'eng Chang-keng was the principal actor in the San-ch'ing company and he remained the leader of that troupe

---

[1] See Chou Chih-fu, *So-chi*, p. 57.   [2] Inoue Susumu, *Shina fūzoku*, II, 457.
[3] According to Ch'i Ju-shan, *Kuo-chü man-t'an*, I, 54, Ch'eng learned from the famous *lao-sheng* Mi Hsi-tzu after this first disaster. As in most other cases, Ch'i gives no source for his statement. However, he had access to reliable oral information on Ch'eng Chang-keng, as indeed on many other matters concerning the theatre. Ch'eng had a nephew who came to be regarded as his son. This nephew had three sons, all of whom learned German together with Ch'i Ju-shan. See Ch'i Ju-shan, *Chien-shu*, p. 5. It may be added that Ch'i's version is not necessarily inconsistent with that quoted above, since the statement that 'he sat in a special room for three years' is clearly a manner of speaking.
[4] For a brief summary of the story of *Chao-kuan* in English see Elizabeth Halson, *Peking Opera*, pp. 89–90 or Cecilia Zung, *Secrets of the Chinese Drama*, pp. 233 ff.   [5] *I-ling chuan*, p. 1a.

until his death. Successive versions of the *Tu-men chi-lüeh*, those of 1845, 1851, 1864, 1872, and 1876, list him first among members of the San-ch'ing.[1]

Ch'eng was among those actors from the Outer City who performed at court in 1860, and he made a profound impression on the Hsien-feng Emperor. The latter decided to grant him an unusual honour and remarked: 'Ch'eng Chang-keng has much merit in the performance of drama. We ought to reward him with the rank of a sixth-degree official.' Hsien-feng's opinion was conveyed to the actor. Ch'eng pointed out that actors were not allowed to enter the government service. He felt that he should therefore not accept the offer. He was, however, eventually persuaded that it would be unseemly to refuse a compliment paid by the Emperor. He went before Hsien-feng and 'thanked him for his favour'.[2] Ch'eng Chang-keng was indeed unique among actors of this time (other than court eunuchs) in being favoured by the Emperor in this way.

In his later years, Ch'eng made arrangements for the succession of the San-ch'ing's leadership after his death. He tried to persuade the amateur Sun Chü-hsien (1841–1931) to become his 'heir-apparent', but the latter declined the invitation saying that he was too incompetent to succeed the great actor, and later managed the affairs of the Ssu-hsi. His refusal was certainly not intended as a slight to Ch'eng, for he copied Chang-keng's style of leadership in his own troupe. After failing to interest Sun, Ch'eng Chang-keng chose as his successor the *lao-sheng* Yang Yüeh-lou, who was the father of the famous *wu-sheng* Yang Hsiao-lou (1877–1938).[3] Yüeh-lou duly became the San-ch'ing leader upon Ch'eng's demise and remained so until his death; it was the failure to find another leader that led the company to disband in 1887.[4]

Ch'eng Chang-keng's active life took its toll upon his health. His career on the stage ended when he fell seriously ill after a particularly strenuous series of performances at a party gathering (*t'ang-hui*). He died a few months later in 1879 or 1880.[5] Chang-

---

[1] See Chou Chih-fu, *Tu-men chi-lüeh*, p. 13; Wang Chih-chang, *Ch'iang-tiao k'ao-yüan*, pp. 17a–b; and *Tu-men hui-tsuan, tsa-chi*, p. 28a.

[2] Ch'i Ju-shan, *Ching-chü chih pien-ch'ien*, p. 54b.

[3] I have discussed Sun Chü-hsien and Yang Hsiao-lou in *The Chinese Theatre*, chapters four and five.　　[4] Hatano Kenichi, *Ching-chü erh-pai nien*, pp. 14–15.

[5] Chou Chih-fu, *So-chi*, pp. 57–8. The date 1879 is given by Hatano Kenichi (*Ching-chü erh-pai nien*, p. 8), who quotes the authority of Mu Ch'en-kung, a well known journalist and drama critic.

keng left no sons. However, he had adopted the actor Ch'eng Chang-pu,[1] whose son Chi-hsien was born in April 1874 and later became known as a *hsiao-sheng*.[2] Chang-keng also had another 'grandson', called Shao-t'ang, who entered the government service and was for a time attached to the Foreign Ministry under the Republic.[3]

Ch'eng Chang-keng founded a branch of Peking Opera called *Ch'eng-p'ai* or *Hui-p'ai* (the Anhwei school).[4] The latter name suggests that the main characteristic of his singing was its emphasis on the music of Anhwei. His influence remained strong even after 1880, since he was noted not only as an actor but also as a teacher. His disciples included Yang Yüeh-lou and T'an Hsin-p'ei,[5] who was the greatest and most famous of his successors.

Ch'eng's knowledge of the drama was unparalleled by any of his contemporaries. His repertoire was wide and included the parts of Liu Chang in *Jang Ch'eng-tu* and Kuan Yü in *Chan Ch'ang-sha*.[6] Chang-keng was also extremely versatile. He mastered several styles, not merely Peking Opera, but also *K'un-ch'ü* and *Ching-ch'iang*. His skill in the former apparently improved his enunciation of words, which was unusually clear.[7] In addition, he could play not only *lao-sheng* but also *tan* and *hsiao-sheng* roles, both types indicating his ability to sing falsetto.

---

[1] Ch'i Ju-shan, *Chien-shu*, p. 5.

[2] Chou Chih-fu, *So-chi*, p. 49. This text calls Ch'eng Chi-hsien Chang-keng's grandson; Ch'en Yen-heng (*Chiu-chü ts'ung-t'an*, p. 24a) refers to Chang-pu as Chang-keng's eldest son; and finally Inoue Susumu claims that Ch'eng divided his wealth between two sons, see *Shina fūzoku*, II, 462. In view of Ch'i Ju-shan's friendship with members of the Ch'eng family (see above, p. 177), we may accept his statement that Chang-pu was only an adopted son. This is confirmed by Ch'en Tan-jan (*I-ling chuan*, p. 2b). The suggestion that Chang-keng had two sons may be explained by the fact that his nephew was regarded as a son (p. 177).

[3] Hatano Kenichi, *Ching-chü erh-pai nien*, p. 16.

[4] Hsü Chiu-yeh, *Li-yüan i-wen*, p. 1a; Ch'en Yen-heng, *Chiu-chü ts'ung-t'an*, p. 1b.

[5] *I-ling chuan*, p. 2a. I have discussed T'an Hsin-p'ei in some detail in *The Chinese Theatre*, chapter four.

[6] For a list of dramas in which Ch'eng Chang-keng was famous see Chou Chih-fu, *Tu-men chi-lüeh*, p. 13. On the dramas *Jang Ch'eng-tu* and *Chan Ch'ang-sha* see below, appendix C. It will be recalled that Kuan Yü in *Chan Ch'ang-sha* was the role in which Mi Hsi-tzu had made so great an impression that other actors did not play the role for more than thirty years. In this connection it is striking that the *Tu-men chi-lüeh* of 1845 does not list *Chan Ch'ang-sha* among Ch'eng's dramas. The piece appears under his name only in the versions from 1864 to 1876.

[7] *Li-yüan chiu-hua* (*LYCH*), p. 2b.

As a *hsiao-sheng* he could equal the finest exponents of the day, as the following story demonstrates.

The acknowledged master in the San-ch'ing company of *hsiao-sheng* parts was Hsü Hsiao-hsiang from Su-chou, who, in contrast to his leader, was of a free and easy nature. He was also quite rich and wanted to give up acting and return home. Ch'eng refused him permission, so he made his own plans and escaped back to Su-chou. Chang-keng then arranged with a high-ranking friend to have his main *hsiao-sheng* brought back to Peking, and devised a way to shame him into remaining in the San-ch'ing company. He told Hsü: 'You have put our company's rules into confusion, despised our contract and escaped. You seem to think that if you do not appear, then we shall have nobody to perform our *hsiao-sheng* dramas. Tomorrow I shall act them myself, and I ask you to watch.' Ch'eng duly did as announced, and Hsiao-hsiang was so impressed by the standard of his leader's artistry that he repented his hastiness and agreed to stay on as the San-ch'ing's leading *hsiao-sheng*.[1]

Apart from giving some indication of Ch'eng Chang-keng's extraordinary ability, this incident provides an insight into his personality. It is in fact one of the many recorded in the sources which can help form a picture of this remarkable man. He emerges as a Confucian type of character—moral and upright—totally different from the great actors of earlier days.

It is clear from his confrontation with Hsü Hsiao-hsiang that Ch'eng was a strict man. He imposed rigid discipline on the members of his company. The rather easy-going atmosphere which allowed actors not on stage to laugh and chat during the performance was total anathema to him.[2] He also made all his apprentices call him 'master' and would not allow them to watch more experienced actors from the wings of the stage. This was a usual custom whereby boys observed and learned from their

---

[1] See Hatano Kenichi, *Ching-chü erh-pai nien*, p. 10. As it happened, Hsü retired to Su-chou in 1880 and died soon after. Chou Chih-fu, *So-chi*, p. 61. One other confrontation between Hsü and Ch'eng is recorded. When the leader was already old, Hsü dropped a hint that Chang-keng was aware of his own decline and of his dependence upon Hsü. Ch'eng immediately countered with an equally clear hint that he regarded Hsiao-hsiang's suggestion as thoroughly impertinent. See Ch'i Ju-shan, *Hsi-chieh hsiao chang-ku*, p. 34. For further material on Hsü, see especially Chou Chih-fu, *Chen-liu ta-wen*, pp. 19–23 and Hatano Kenichi, *Ching-chü erh-pai nien*, pp. 145–8.

[2] Ch'en Yen-heng, *Chiu-chü ts'ung-t'an*, p. 24a.

elders. Ch'eng argued that, since the audience could see them clearly in the wings, they constituted a distraction when they stood there. He therefore obliged them to watch and listen from behind the curtain at the back of the stage, even though this made their task of learning much more difficult.[1]

It is clear from his behaviour towards the Emperor during his audience in 1860 that this actor was able to overcome any fear he might feel in front of high-ranking persons. This characteristic is quite consistent with his strictness and obvious self-respect. It is said that he once refused, in polite but extremely firm words, to act for Prince Kung, even though that eminent minister had given him instructions to do so.[2]

Yet, though he was strong and able to stand up even to the most powerful of people, and was undoubtedly well aware of his popularity, he always remained serious-minded and never succumbed to vanity—a sharp contrast with earlier actors like Ch'en Yin-kuan. He even seems to have been rather annoyed that so many people came to see not the drama itself but a famous actor like himself. One rather charming incident which took place towards the end of Ch'eng's life illustrates his devotion to the theatre for its own sake and not for the indulgence of his vanity.

Chang-keng had come to act less and less, and the audiences of the San-ch'ing company fell off drastically. The situation became very grave and the financial loss to the troupe was such that its members were threatened with starvation. Ch'eng was implored to perform again. He agreed to do so and the following day the house was packed out. Instead of being flattered Ch'eng was furious, because the audience seemed to care only about the fame of the day's actor, and refused to act. This happened several times before Chang-keng eventually gave his performances. When it was later announced in advance that Ch'eng would appear, the people believed that he would repeat his ploy, and on the first day only about 100 spectators turned up. Chang-keng was highly indignant and told his audience: 'Every time I have come on stage, the house has been full. But the reason for this is because everybody admires the name of Ch'eng Chang-keng. But all you gentlemen who have condescended to come today are genuine lovers of the theatre. I should like to repay your appreciation for

[1] *Ts'e-mao yü-t'an*, p. 17a.
[2] *I-ling chuan*, pp. 3a–b.

music by performing two pieces, and, to acknowledge your kindness, I beg you all to instruct me to give whichever ones you like.' The audience then conferred and chose two items which Ch'eng, as agreed, immediately performed.[1]

The fact that Chang-keng was willing to come out of semi-retirement for the financial benefit of his company, even though he himself was quite well off, suggests a concern for the poorer actors of the troupe. This is shown also in his attitude to the custom of *wai-ch'uan*. In Peking at this time it was the practice that whenever there was a celebration arising from an event such as a birthday, a gathering would be held at which drama was performed. At large-scale occasions of this sort, a distinguished actor might be engaged to perform together with actors of a company other than his own, and this was termed *wai-ch'uan*. Ch'eng Chang-keng, however, always refused to act with any company but the San-ch'ing. He claimed that it was unfair that he should be paid individually when the other actors of the San-ch'ing were receiving no remuneration.[2] The following story is ample testimony to the strength of his conviction and corroborates that he did not fear people with power.

In a certain year the Court of Censors held a New Year's party. They invited the Ssu-hsi company to perform and wanted Chang-keng to give one item as a guest actor. Chang-keng refused. A certain member of the imperial family further urged him to come, but even despite that he refused. The crowd got angry and seized Chang-keng, locking him under the stage pillar and insulting him. They asked why he would not sing, but Chang-keng replied flippantly that he had a sore throat. Later, a busybody inquired into the real reason. Chang-keng replied, very seriously: 'How could locking me up frighten me? What I feared was that I should not be able to face my brothers in the San-ch'ing. What shame is there in being locked below the pillar? It only shows the unreasonable attitude of the Court of Censors.' The crowd was more and more moved by Chang-keng's honesty and lack of meanness.[3]

Ch'eng's fearlessness, strength of character and concern for the well-being of his subordinates were coupled with unusual generosity and persistence. His reaction to the difficult times

---

[1] Inoue Susumu, *Shina fūzoku*, II, 461–2.   [2] *LYCH*, p. 18a.

[3] Chang Tz'u-hsi, *Yen-tu ming-ling chuan*, p. 1a. Despite Ch'eng's disapproval of guest acting, we know of one occasion when he performed in *Chan Ch'eng-tu* together with Yü San-sheng and Chang Erh-k'uei, both of whom belonged to different companies. See below, p. 186, note 3.

which followed the death of the T'ung-chih Emperor in 1875 provides some evidence of this. The mourning for a deceased sovereign included the cessation of dramatic performances for an extended period. However, because the economic situation of China was in such bad straits, actors could not afford to suspend activities for so long, and they were therefore given special permission to act in restaurants outside the city. The company leaders, however, felt that it would be impossible for them to earn money there to continue supporting large groups of actors, so most companies disbanded and individual actors were left to fend for themselves. But the San-ch'ing, under the direction of Chang-keng, remained together as a unit and moved to a different centre. Ch'eng performed every day, shared his personal earnings among all the company members and kept for himself only what was absolutely necessary. In this way, the San-ch'ing company succeeded in surmounting the crisis.[1]

Finally, Ch'eng Chang-keng's high principles are reflected in his passionate concern with the political events of his time:

When the British entered Kwangtung with opium in 1838 and the Yangtze River in 1842,[2] Chang-keng was so annoyed that he felt like dying. In the Hsien-feng period, the Tai-p'ing, Nien, Hui, and Miao rebellions spread all over China,[3] but the aristocrats all went on holding banquets as usual. Chang-keng closed his house and would not come out. Somebody blamed him for this but he wept bitterly and said: 'The capital [is supposed to be] a model, but if it is like this I do not know where to rest.' He then chose some worthy disciples, and supervised and taught them . . . In the tenth year of Hsien-feng (1860), the British and French allied armies entered Peking and the Emperor Hsien-feng went hunting in Mu-lan;[4] Chang-keng wept bitterly . . . The following year Hsien-feng died. T'ung-chih ascended the throne as a child, the two Empresses Dowager acting as regents,[5] and the court returned

[1] *LYCH*, pp. 17b–18a.

[2] The Treaty of Nanking, which ended the First Opium War, was finally forced on the Chinese by the conquering advance by the British fleet up the Yangtze in mid 1842. The treaty was signed on 29 August the same year. See Hummel, *Eminent Chinese*, p. 131.

[3] For a brief account of the rebellions of this period, see Mary Wright, *The Last Stand*, pp. 96–124, 335–44, where many further sources are quoted.

[4] Mu-lan was the imperial hunting district, just north of Jehol. See Hedin, *Jehol*, p. 161.

[5] These two were Tz'u-an (1837–81) and Tz'u-hsi. After a power struggle following Hsien-feng's death, these two women formed a joint regency and Prince Kung was invited to advise them. See Hummel, *Eminent Chinese*, p. 296; Mary Wright, *The Last Stand*, pp. 16–17.

to the capital ... The nobles banquetted as before. Chang-keng had lost [his possessions during the] confusion, so he was poor and once more took up his old trade. Though alone, sad and depressed in spirit, his singing was nobler than ever. He only liked performing dramas about the heroes of ancient times or the creators of states, like Chu-ko Liang [181–234] or Liu Chi [1311–75].[1] He showed great depth of feeling and was very imposing. The audience found him awe-inspiring, and when he played characters who were loyal, upright, brave and virtuous, their tears would moisten their garments and there was nobody who did not weep.[2]

The greatest of the *lao-sheng* actors of the nineteenth century is, then, depicted in the sources as a magnificent and versatile performer, and a man with firm, upright convictions and a character patriotic, unselfish, strict but just, strong yet not vain. In short he was the model of a truly virtuous actor. I have found reference to only one failing—that Ch'eng smoked opium.[3] One could perhaps place an unkind interpretation on the moralisms of the sources and call him stubborn and self-righteous. But this seems quite unnecessary, especially since opium-smoking was extremely widespread and there is no evidence that he indulged in it to excess. It is quite beyond doubt that Ch'eng was respected and loved by most people who had dealings with him. The legend that grew up around him could easily have made his biographers emphasize his good points and forget his failings, but there is no reason at all to think that Chinese and Japanese writers have come to distort their image of his character radically in his favour.

The second of the three great *lao-sheng* actors, Yü San-sheng, presents in some ways a striking contrast to the serious-minded and meticulous Ch'eng Chang-keng. Unfortunately, much less is known about him. Yet his impact on the Peking stage was also profound and his popularity great.

Yü San-sheng came from Lo-t'ien in Hupeh, and was the son of a merchant.[4] It is not clear when he first became famous on the

---

[1] Chu-ko Liang and Liu Chi were both famous heroes and both helped create states; Chu-ko Liang assisted Liu Pei is the setting up of Shu, and Liu Chi was active in driving the Mongols from China and in aiding the first Ming emperor to consolidate his power. For the biographies of these two men see respectively *San-kuo chih*, 35, 911 ff., and *Ming-shih*, 128, 1a ff.

[2] *I-ling chuan*, pp. 1b–2a.

[3] Hatano Kenichi, *Ching-chü erh-pai nien*, p. 29.

[4] Ibid., p. 21.

stage. However, his name appears at the head of the Ch'un-t'ai company in the *Tu-men chi-lüeh* of 1845,[1] so he was no doubt the most important actor of the company by that year. In the 1851 version of the guide-book, his name still appears first among the members of the Ch'un-t'ai,[2] but is not found in the 1864 edition. He is listed on a stele of 1857,[3] and presumably gave up acting some time between that year and 1864.

Like Ch'eng Chang-keng, Yü had no sons, but did adopt one. This was Yü Tzu-yün, who had been a disciple of the famous *tan* performer Mei Ch'iao-ling (1842–*c*.1881), the grandfather of Mei Lan-fang (1894–1961).[4] San-sheng thought very highly of Tzu-yün and took the young actor into his care. The two then lived together as if they were really father and son. Tzu-yün himself had four sons, the third of whom was the famous *lao-sheng* actor Yü Shu-yen (1890–1943).[5]

It is certain that San-sheng was no longer alive by 1876.[6] The fact that he adopted a son provides us with a further clue concerning the time of his death. Tzu-yün was born on 19 August 1855[7] and must have been at least ten years old when Yü took him as his son since he had already been Mei Ch'iao-ling's disciple. Therefore, San-sheng died no earlier than 1865 and probably some time later. No doubt it would be correct to assume that his death took place in the first half of the 1870s. His departure from the stage by 1864 does not therefore imply that he had died.

Yü San-sheng was the founder of a school of acting. It was called *Yü-p'ai* or *Han-p'ai* (the school of Hupeh).[8] The latter name implies that the school laid particular emphasis on the *Ch'u-tiao*. Yü retained the influence of the music of Hupeh all his

---

[1] See Chou Chih-fu, *Tu-men chi-lüeh*, p. 22.

[2] See Wang Chih-chang, *Ch'iang-tiao k'ao-yüan*, pp. 17a–b.

[3] *PCLYCS*, p. 10a.

[4] For a comprehensive biography of Mei Lan-feng in the pre-Communist period see his autobiography, *Wu-t'ai sheng-huo ssu-shih nien*. Scott has written a biography in English based on this work: *Mei Lan-fang*.

[5] Ch'i Ju-shan, *Chien-shu*, pp. 6–7. Other sources call Tzu-yün Yü San-sheng's 'son'. For example, see Chou Chih-fu, *So-chi*, p. 24 and Yü Shu-yen's principal biographer, Sun Yang-nung (*T'an Yü Shu-yen*, p. 2). However, since San-sheng and Tzu-yün lived together as father and son, it would be easy to mistake an adopted son for a real one.

[6] *LYCH*, p. 1a.

[7] Chou Chih-fu, *So-chi*, p. 24.

[8] Hsü Chiu-yeh, *Li-yüan i-wen*, p. 1a; Ch'en Yen-heng, *Chiu-chü ts'ung-t'an*, p. 1b.

life and, like many Peking Opera actors of his and later times, sang with a Hupeh accent. In contrast to Ch'eng Chang-keng, he never mastered *K'un-ch'ü*.[1]

San-sheng was particularly noted for his great knowledge of the novel *The Romance of the Three Kingdoms* and the dramas about the heroes of the third century.[2] He was famous in the role of Huang Chung in *Ting-chün shan*. However, he played the parts of other heroes of the period too, such as Ch'en Kung in *Cho-fang Ts'ao* and Ma Ch'ao in *Chan Ch'eng-tu*.[3]

Yü's characteristics as a performer were quite unlike those of Ch'eng. His voice was higher than Ch'eng's and his acting included more acrobatics. Furthermore, he was much less meticulous about his performances and would often improvise. Once, Yü was performing with his younger brother, Ssu-sheng, a *ching* actor, who was addicted to opium and somewhat unreliable. On this occasion he missed his entry. San-sheng improvised for some time while he waited for his brother to come on the stage.[4] Other stories of this kind survive and show Yü as a clever man with extraordinary presence of mind.

Yü had a keen sense of humour and would occasionally use his improvising skill to insert an amusing interlude. Sometimes his jokes were at somebody else's expense. One story is recorded to illustrate this, showing at the same time how much less tactful and serious-minded than Ch'eng Chang-keng he was.

It happened that Ssu-sheng was not only an opium addict, but was also given to gambling. Owing to this habit he fell into debt and pawned some clothes and other belongings with his more famous elder brother to enable him to pay his debts. The two brothers were both performing together in *Cho-fang Ts'ao*. San-sheng used this occasion to laugh at his debtor. During the drama he inserted the remark, 'Look at this man; you can tell by looking

[1] Ch'i Ju-shan, *Chien-shu*, p. 6.
[2] *LYCH*, p. 3a.
[3] See Chou Chih-fu, *Tu-men chi-lüeh*, p. 22 and *LYCH*, pp. 3a–b. Ma Ch'ao is not the main character in *Chan Ch'eng-tu*. Yet it is said that once Yü San-sheng played in the drama together with Ch'eng Chang-keng and Chang Erh-k'uei and that he rather stole the show by the magnificence with which he played the part of Ma Ch'ao. *Ting-chün shan*, *Cho-fang Ts'ao*, and *Chan Ch'eng-tu* are discussed in appendix C.
[4] Ch'i Ju-shan, *Chien-shu*, p. 6. Ch'i records that this incident was told to him by the famous actor Ch'en Te-lin (1862–1930, see Chou Chih-fu, *So-chi*, pp. 38, 123), who could remember even the improvised words.

at him that he loves to gamble.' This caused great mirth among those members of the audience who understood the situation.[1]

Even less material is available about Chang Erh-k'uei than about Yü San-sheng. His place of birth is given differently in various sources, but was probably Peking.[2] Chang came from a family of officials, and he and his elder brother held minor positions in the government service.[3] When he decided to go on the stage as an amateur his brother was angry and tried to prevent him, but without success. Erh-k'uei gave several performances as a guest artist in the Ho-ch'un company and was well received. He then took up acting full-time, much to the dismay of his brother, who was dismissed from his job for his connections with so disgraceful a profession as that of the theatre.[4] The *Tu-men chi-lüeh* of 1845 describes Chang Erh-k'uei as a 'young' actor[5] and lists him first among the members of the Ssu-hsi company.[6] By 1851 he had forsaken the Ssu-hsi for the Shuang-k'uei troupe, of which he was the head.[7] However, his career in the theatre turned out to be short and he died in 1860.[8]

Chang was of powerful build and his voice was loud and clear. According to Wu Tao, most of the dramas he sang used the *hsi-p'i* style.[9] His roles included Yang Ssu-lang in *T'an-mu*[10] and Ch'en Kung in *Cho-fang Ts'ao*,[11] and he was particularly good at playing the parts of ancient emperors.[12]

---

[1] Ch'en Yen-heng, *Chiu-chü ts'ung-t'an*, p. 21b. This incident was told to Ch'en by an old friend, Liang Yu-lan.

[2] According to Wu Tao (*LYCH*, p. 2a), Chang Erh-k'uei came from Chekiang, but this is unlikely since very few of Peking's actors at this time came from that province. Wang Meng-sheng claims in his *Li-yüan chia-hua*, p. 58, that Erh-k'uei was from Anhwei. However, this is an extremely unreliable source. Chou Chih-fu has pointed out numerous errors in Wang's book in his *Chen-liu ta-wen*, pp. 32–40. A third source (Ch'en Yen-heng, *Chiu-chü ts'ung-t'an*, p. 27a) claims that Chang was born in Peking, and this has been accepted by modern scholars like Chou Chih-fu (*Ching-chü*, p. 25) and Chou I-pai (*Chiang-tso*, p. 253).

[3] Ch'i Ju-shan, *Kuo-chü man-t'an*, I, 63; Hatano Kenichi, *Ching-chü erh-pai nien*, p. 18.

[4] Ibid., pp. 18–19.   [5] See Chou Chih-fu, *Tu-men chi-lüeh*, p. 12.

[6] Ibid., p. 31.   [7] See Wang Chih-chang, *Ch'iang-tiao k'ao-yüan*, pp. 17a–b.

[8] Hatano Kenichi, *Ching-chü erh-pai nien*, p. 19.   [9] *LYCH*, p. 3b.

[10] *T'an-mu* has been translated into English by Scott in *Traditional Chinese Plays*, I, 33–91. Background material on the story of the drama and the costumes used in it may be found pp. 21–31.

[11] See Chou Chih-fu, *Tu-men chi-lüeh*, p. 31.

[12] Hatano Kenichi, *Ching-chü erh-pai nien*, p. 19. The Ming and Manchu penal codes actually forbade the representation of emperors on the stage (Boulais, *Manuel du code chinois*, p. 704; Wang Hsiao-ch'uan, *Yüan Ming Ch'ing san-tai*

Like Ch'eng and Yü, Chang Erh-k'uei was the founder of a special school of performing. It was called the *K'uei-p'ai*.[1] Authorities differ over the central characteristic of this school. In Ch'i Ju-shan's view, it was developed from the *p'i-huang* style brought through the merchants of Shansi and Shensi to Peking from southern Shensi and Hsi-an.[2] There is no reason to doubt Ch'i's assumption that merchants had been instrumental in introducing theatrical music from Shensi and Shansi. This drama was like the *hsi-p'i* in belonging to the Clapper system, but the name *hsi-p'i* was of southern origin and was used to refer to music which had come from the south to Peking.[3] The style introduced directly from the western provinces was called *Ch'in-ch'iang*. Therefore, Wu Tao's statement that Chang's dramas were mostly *hsi-p'i* casts doubt on Ch'i Ju-shan's interpretation of the *K'uei-p'ai*.

Other scholars have suggested a different theory to explain the significance of the *K'uei-p'ai*. Chou Chih-fu, like Ch'en Yen-heng, claims that the distinctive feature of the school was that it adapted the words of the *erh-huang* and *hsi-p'i* dramas to suit the need of the Peking dialect.[4] According to this interpretation, Chang, being a native of Peking, was able to adopt the Anhwei style of singing of Ch'eng Chang-keng and the Hupeh type of Yü San-sheng and 'blend them with the words of the north'.[5] Chou's theory seems to me more plausible than Ch'i Ju-shan's. The adaptation of the provincial dramas to suit the ears of the populace of Peking, especially as regards the dialect of their libretti, must have been a problem of great importance and it is not surprising that one of the great actors should have directed special attention towards it.

These three *lao-sheng* were the most famous of the early Peking Opera actors. Yet the decades preceding the T'ung-chih Restoration saw the birth of a number of men who became supreme exponents of the new style of drama. Some of them, such as Hsü Hsiao-hsiang, Chu Lien-feng, Mei Ch'iao-ling, Yang Yüeh-

---

chin-hui hsiao-shuo hsi-ch'ü shih-liao, pp. 10, 31), but this rule was not enforced and nobody observed it.

[1] Hsü Chiu-yeh, *Li-yüan i-wen*, p. 1a.
[2] Ch'i Ju-shan, *Chien-shu*, pp. 134–5.
[3] See my article 'The Growth of the Chinese Regional Drama in the Ming and Ch'ing', *Journal of Oriental Studies*, ix, no. 1 (Jan. 1971), 83–4.
[4] See Chou Chih-fu, *Ching-chü*, pp. 26–7.
[5] Ch'en Yen-heng, *Chiu-chü ts'ung-t'an*, p. 1b.

lou, T'an Hsin-p'ei, and Yü Tzu-yün, have already been mentioned in these pages. The apex of these actors' careers belong in the main to a period later than the heyday of the three *lao-sheng* actors described in this chapter and it is beyond the scope of the present work to consider their lives in detail.

The consolidation of the Peking Opera in the middle years of the nineteenth century was due mainly to the introduction of the Hupeh music and to the emergence of the great *lao-sheng* actors. Since the *lao-sheng* themselves strengthened the influence of the *Ch'u-tiao*, we may say that the central factor in the development of the Peking Opera at this time was the rise of the art of *lao-sheng* acting which, though not new, had played no major role in the theatre of Peking between 1770 and the 1820s.

There can be no doubt that the impact of Ch'eng Chang-keng and his colleagues upon the history of Peking Opera was of the profoundest importance. So great was Ch'eng's influence that he has come to be called the father of Peking Opera.[1] It therefore seems appropriate to conclude this chapter with a brief enquiry into the reasons why the *lao-sheng* actors became so popular and why their impression upon the capital was so great.

One reason was the lack of balance in the art of the Peking Opera down to the middle years of the Tao-kuang period. Most of Peking's best actors of that time had been *tan*. This fact imposed considerable limits upon the range of stories which the theatrical companies could perform. It hardly needs emphasizing that many plays include not only major female roles but also important parts for men. This must in itself have created a great demand for good actors who could portray men. The point carries all the more weight when we remember that many of China's most popular stories concern military heroes of the past. Dramas based upon popular novels, like *The Romance of the Three Kingdoms*, *The Water Margin*, and *The Romance of the Yang Family Generals*, were more or less closed to companies which lacked magnificent *sheng* actors. Since these novels had been popular long before the eighteenth century, it could only be a matter of time before the people of Peking should demand to see them dramatized. It followed naturally that great actors should arise to perform the parts of the illustrious warriors who were the subjects of these operas.

[1] See Scott, *The Classical Theatre*, p. 37.

The period leading up to the T'ung-chih Restoration was a singularly appropriate time for a resurgence in the popularity of heroic drama. At few other periods of history had the Chinese sense of patriotism been so outraged as it was then. To the insult of being ruled by a foreign dynasty was added that of being humiliated by the might of the Western powers. If Ch'eng Chang-keng himself felt that this was a good reason for performing dramas about courage and patriotism, it is not surprising that he should have met with enthusiastic responses from his audiences.

In other ways, too, the young *tan* actors of the previous era were found to be inferior to the great *lao-sheng* performers. It followed from their youth that their acting lacked maturity. They could not possibly be endowed with a personality as powerful as that of a man like Ch'eng Chang-keng. Moreover, the shortness of their careers imposed severe restrictions upon the influence they could wield. Wei Ch'ang-sheng and Ch'en Yin-kuan had been able to make a tremendous impression in a short time, but they were assisted by the novelty of their art and were in any case exceptional. The boy-actors of the following period could not hope within their brief period of glory to attain the dominating position of Ch'eng Chang-keng or his colleagues. Many of these men were extremely durable, and could persist as actors for decades; they could grow in stature as they became more experienced, and there was much less danger that their careers would be cut short. The boy-actors continued to be popular, even though the T'ai-p'ing rebellion cut off the supply from the south, forcing Peking itself to provide most of the apprentice actors.[1] Henceforward, however, their influence upon the people was but slight compared with their older and more experienced colleagues.

In response to the demand for a more balanced theatre, the training of actors became more developed and varied. The *hsiang-kung t'ang-tzu* remained significant and training-schools grew in number and in their output of actors. But there was

[1] See *Huai-fang chi*, p. 9b. The statement can be checked through a comparison of two works, one written about boys who came to Peking before or in the early stages of the rebellion, the other after it had been suppressed. The *Fa-ying pi-chi* of 1855 lists sixty-two boy-actors, of whom forty came from Su-chou, eleven from Peking, eight from Anhwei, and three from Yang-chou. The *Yen-t'ai hua-shih lu* of 1876 gives, in its first *chüan*, short notes on a number of boy-actors and records the place of origin of twenty-seven. Of these, twenty-one came from Peking or its surroundings, three from neighbouring Chihli, only two from Kiangsu, and one from Kwangsi.

another method of recruitment which became important at this time. This was the *p'iao-yu* system, by which actors began their careers as amateurs. There had of course been non-professionals in China before 1800,[1] but it was not until the mid nineteenth century that they became truly significant.[2] Chang Erh-k'uei was but one among many famous exponents of the Peking Opera who was a *p'iao-yu*.[3] There is an important implication in the rise of amateur acting, namely that many men came to the stage through choice rather than necessity. Boys who were contracted into the acting profession before they were ten had hardly chosen their career themselves, and it is to be expected than many of them lacked the zeal of those who had made a deliberate decision to devote their lives to the theatre.

But, as has so often been the case with the dramatic arts, the key to the success of the *lao-sheng* actors lay in the audiences who watched and listened to them. As the Peking Opera grew, so also did the importance of Peking's theatres. These, in turn, gave added impetus to the success of the *p'i-huang* drama, especially since they were open to all classes of society. By the middle years of the nineteenth century, the theatres of Peking were perhaps the city's most popular public places of relaxation and they played an increasingly important role in the social life of the people.

There were, in fact, many ways in which the theatre and actors of Peking became linked with the society of their time. Some of them have already been considered. It remains in the last chapter to examine more closely the connections between society on the one hand and the theatres and acting profession on the other; and to show how this relationship affected the growth of the Peking Opera from the time of Wei Ch'ang-sheng down to the T'ai-p'ing rebellion.

[1] See P'an Kuang-tan, *Chung-kuo ling-jen hsüeh-yüan chih yen-chiu*, p. 33.

[2] The earliest nineteenth-century actor recorded in primary sources as being a *p'iao-yu* was the *lao-sheng* Hsieh Yin-hsüan. In the *Tu-men chi-lüeh* of 1845, he is listed first among the actors of the Chin-yü company, and under his name is inserted the character *p'iao*. His repertoire appears to have been very large and more dramas are associated with his name than any other actor mentioned in the *Tu-men chi-lüeh* of 1845. See Chou Chih-fu, *Tu-men chi-lüeh*, pp. 50–1. Amateurs were trained in special schools called *p'iao-fang* (see Chou Chih-fu, *Ching-chü*, pp. 63–4) and their instruction was much less strict than that given in training-schools. See also Ch'i Ju-shan, *Kuo-chü man-t'an*, I, 52–3.

[3] See Ch'i Ju-shan, *Chien-shu*, pp. 134–52, and Chou Chih-fu, *Ching-chü*, pp. 62–3.

VII

THE THEATRE AND THE ACTING PROFESSION IN PEKING

THE LINK between the drama and the life of the people has always been much tighter in China than it is today in the West. I described in chapter two how village drama was closely associated with religious activity and with harvesting, and this association persisted to a greater or lesser degree until quite recently. The Peking Opera was also important not only as a form of art but as a social phenomenon. However, its relationship with society was of a kind quite different from that of the village drama, and was centred much less on religion than on the theatres where it was performed.

The Theatre and the Stage: Historical Background

In its first definition of the word 'theatre', *The Concise Oxford Dictionary* gives the meaning 'building for dramatic spectacles', and an English-speaking person will normally expect a 'theatre' to include both a stage and arrangements for seating the spectators. Although the performance of dramatic entertainment of one sort or another can be traced back in China well before the time of Christ, the earliest definite reference to a theatre with both a stage and seating does not occur until the Later Han period (A.D. 25–220). The second-century poet Chang Heng writes that 'the Emperor went to P'ing-lo' where he 'favoured an ... arena with his presence'.[1] A note by Li Shan[2] explains that the P'ing-lo kuan was an amusement centre.[3] Chang Heng's *fu* goes on to record the

---

[1] *Hsi-ching fu*, p. 42. See also Erwin von Zach's translation in *Die chinesische Anthologie*, p. 14.

[2] Li Shan was a scholar of the early T'ang. He is most famous as the commentator to the great literary collection *Wen-hsüan*. See *Hsin T'ang-shu*, 202, 4b. Li's memorial presenting the commentary to the Emperor is contained in the *Wen-hsüan*, just after the first preface, and is dated 658.

[3] Chou I-pai has collected some information on the P'ing-lo kuan in his *Chung-kuo chü-ch'ang shih*, pp. 2–3.

items which the Emperor witnessed, and since these included dramatic pieces, the 'arena' may be considered a kind of theatre.

There is evidence also of theatres in the Six Dynasties, Sui, and T'ang periods,[1] but it was not until the Sung that theatres became important in society. It is only then that we find positive proof of large numbers of theatres frequented by all classes of the populace.

In the capital of the Northern Sung (960–1127), K'ai-feng, there were, from the beginning of the twelfth century, amusement centres known as *wa*, *wa-tzu* or *wa-she*. Here all kinds of people, whether scholars or commoners, went to enjoy themselves and the entertainment was often somewhat improper. Apparently the sons of good families loved to visit these places.[2] Bad weather was no obstacle to the patrons of the *wa-tzu* and we are told that 'no matter whether it was windy or rainy, cold or hot', one could see people every day in all the constructions of the *wa-tzu*.[3]

Among the buildings of the *wa* were theatres called *kou-lan*. There could be fifty or more of them in one *wa-tzu* and the largest could accommodate several thousand people.[4]

The *wa-tzu* of Hang-chou during the Southern Sung (1127–1279) were an even more important feature of society than their Northern Sung counterparts. They were built there originally because many members of the army came from regions outside Chekiang and the government found it necessary to amuse them. According to one source, there were seventeen *wa-tzu* in Hang-chou,[5] but another lists six others in addition. Of all the amusement centres the richest in *kou-lan* was the Pei-wa which boasted thirteen theatres.[6] As in K'ai-feng, the *wa-tzu* were frequented by the sons of noble families, and one work records that they were the occasion of even more misbehaviour among such people than those of the Northern Sung.[7]

The *kou-lan* were also extremely important during the Yüan (1280–1368) and they are mentioned in the *tsa-chü* of the time.[8] One of these dramas makes several references to the gate of the *kou-lan* and adds that it could be opened or locked.[9] There were

[1] Ibid., pp. 3–5.   [2] *Tu-ch'eng chi-sheng*, p. 95.
[3] *Yu-lan chü-shih Tung-ching meng-hua lu*, 5, 30.
[4] Ibid., 2, 14.   [5] *Meng-liang lu*, 19, 298.
[6] *Wu-lin chiu-shih*, 6, 440–1.   [7] *Meng-liang lu*, 19, 298.
[8] See collected texts on the *kou-lan* in Ch'en Wan-nai, *Yüan Ming Ch'ing chü-ch'ü shih*, pp. 177–80.
[9] *Han Chung-li tu-t'o Lan Ts'ai-ho*, 1, 1b, 5a. On this drama see Lo Chin-t'ang, *Hsien-ts'un Yüan-jen tsa-chü pen-shih k'ao*, pp. 409–11.

also doors to the stage where the actors could enter or leave, and behind them was an area called a 'theatrical room' (hsi-fang)[1] where the actors made ready or waited to go on stage. The fourteenth-century writer T'ao Tsung-i reports a tragic incident concerning a kou-lan in Sung-chiang, Kiangsu province:

When they heard the sound of the drum at the kou-lan, [the people] would go in. On this day, they had not been inside for long when there was a splitting sound in the building. The crowd was frightened and dispersed, but when nothing happened they later gathered again. Shortly after, the building (p'eng) collapsed on them ... killing forty-two people ... Only one person, the actor T'ien-sheng-hsiu, got away with his entire family uninjured.[2]

Several important points emerge from this information on the kou-lan. Firstly, they included seating arrangements for an audience, sometimes a large one. Secondly, they were frequently none too sturdy. This is suggested by the use of the word p'eng, which refers to a flimsy building, not only in the story just told, but in other texts about the kou-lan.[3] Probably they were not built to last very long. On the other hand, they were not temporary in the sense of being erected for a specific occasion and then dismantled. It would otherwise be very strange to state that there were thirteen kou-lan in the Pei-wa. Finally, these theatres were at least partly roofed. The fact that rain did not prevent enjoyment at K'ai-feng's wa-tzu implies that the buildings were covered. The story quoted above confirms that the audiences in the kou-lan were protected from the elements by a roof, otherwise the collapse of the theatre might not have killed so many spectators. But the fact that an actor was unharmed suggests that the stage was separate from the auditorium and may have been covered by a different roof. It is indeed possible that part of the theatre was open-air.

However, it has not always been normal in China to perform dramas in a theatre with a stage and seating arrangements. Throughout the ages, stages were erected wherever a suitable place could be found, and from the Sung on, it was customary to perform popular drama at a temple.[4] This had become the most usual practice by the Ming, since the kou-lan, as known in the

---

[1] T'ai-ho cheng-yin p'u, 1, 54. [2] Cho-keng lu, 24, 345–6.
[3] For example, see Wu-lin chiu-shih, 6, 441.
[4] See Chou I-pai, Chü-ch'ang shih, p. 6.

Sung, had gone out of fashion and were now more important as brothels than as theatres.[1]

There were, of course, other places besides temples where drama could be put on. Many passages in the sources relate that performances were held in market-places or other unoccupied parts of the cities,[2] and in villages which possessed no temple the actors would simply use any open area.[3] Since dramatic pieces could be performed in such a variety of places, it was natural for most stages to be temporary. Usually they were set up for the occasion and then pulled down when the performances were over. There was nothing undignified about such structures. When the Chinese officials arranged a session of dramatic performances on a temporary stage near Tientsin for the British ambassador Earl George Macartney (1737–1806),[4] they certainly regarded it as an honour.

Audiences at shows of this kind enjoyed no protection from the vagaries of the weather. The people simply sat round the stage or, especially in the well-watered Yangtze Valley, watched from boats. The following passage written by Chang Tai provides a vivid example:

The elders of my family had a . . . boat-building put up . . . The day it was finished was the 15th of the seventh month [the Avalambana Festival, see appendix C] and everybody gathered [to celebrate], men and women, young and old from my grandfather down. A stage was built out of several layers of wooden rafters and drama performed. The people came from the city and villages to watch in more than 1,000 large or small boats. After midday a strong wind blew up, large waves were everywhere and it poured with rain . . . When the wind calmed down, they finished the drama and the people dispersed.[5]

When the wealthy families held banquets for their friends or

[1] In the late Yüan we find references to courtesan-actresses performing in *kou-lan*. For example, see *Ch'ing-lou chi*, pp. 24, 38, 40. In the famous novel *Shui-hu chuan* (51, 601 ff) there is a story about a prostitute-actress called Pai Hsiu-ying who dances and sings in a *kou-lan* where there is a stage. For a translation into English of the relevant section, which describes how Pai Hsiu-ying is killed by one of the *kou-lan's* patrons, see Pearl Buck, *All Men Are Brothers*, pp. 910 ff.

[2] For example, see *Ning-po fu-chih*, 4, 37a.

[3] See, for example, *Chen-chou feng-t'u chi*, p. 6b, translated above, p. 66.

[4] Staunton, *An Authentic Account of an Embassy from the King of Great Britain to the Emperor of China*, II, 30.

[5] *T'ao-an meng-i*, 8, 69.

high-ranking guests, they did not usually need a stage at all for the operas that accompanied the party. A level space in a large room, courtyard, or garden was perfectly adequate, and a mat was laid out to mark the space where the actors performed. Only at very large banquets when guests were numerous was it necessary to raise the actors above the audience.

Permanent stages were the exception rather than the rule in the villages, cities and mansions. They did, however, exist and properly constructed stages of the Sung, Chin, Yüan, Ming, and Ch'ing can be found in many parts of China. These are pavilions inside or outside a temple compound or mansion and are separate from the main temple or residential halls. Inscriptions and other records prove the existence of many more such stages.[1]

The construction of these permanent stages calls for some comment. In the north, the tendency was to build a fairly high base which would separate the stage from the ground, while in the south the lowest platform was only slightly raised.[2] Everywhere in China these structures were rectangular or square and included, in addition to the stage itself, rooms where the actors could prepare for the performance or wait while they were off-stage. Most had, like the stages of the Yüan *kou-lan*, two stage doors, one for the actors to make their entrances, the other for their exits. They were built according to four basic shapes. The oldest were simple rectangles with the *hsi-fang* (also called *hou-tai* 'backstage') behind, but as time went on, more complex patterns were used, and the green-rooms might lie in two distinct sections on either side of the main platform, with a small corridor directly behind it linking the two parts to the stage and to each other (see opposite).[3]

Permanent stages were not, however, merely raised platforms. The area where actors performed was in fact part of a hall, which could be of varying shape or size.[4] The temple stages were covered by a roof which was supported by wooden columns. Normally, two of these rose up from the front of the stage, so that the vision of some of the spectators was partly blocked.

Occasionally, permanent stages were double-tiered. One example is that in the Temple of the City God in Wu-kung

[1] See, for instance, Mo I-p'ing, 'Chi chi-ko ku-tai hsiang-ts'un hsi-t'ai', *Hsi-chü lun-ts'ung* 2 (1957), pp. 203–6, where there is a discussion of some ancient stages in Shansi.
[2] See Chou I-pai, *Chü-ch'ang shih*, pp. 15–16. [3] Ibid., p. 13.
[4] See examples of different styles in ibid., pp. 16–20

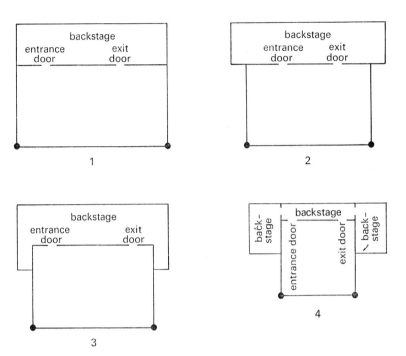

5. The Four Shapes of Ancient Chinese Stages (Based on Chou I-pai, *Chung-kuo chü-ch'ang shih*, pp. 14–15)

county, western Shensi province (see overleaf). The most famous stages with more than one tier are those in the palaces of Peking and Jehol. These have already been discussed in chapters five and six; having been designed specifically for imperial use, they can hardly be counted as typical.

Theatres in Peking

Although public playhouses were not fashionable in the Ming dynasty, the Ch'ing period witnessed a revival in the building of theatres, especially in Peking. There, three different types functioned simultaneously. They catered for different sections of the community and distinct customs were practised in each of them.

One kind was the *hsi-chuang*. Theatres of this sort 'were called such-and-such a *t'ang* or *hui-kuan*, and they were places where the

6. Stage in the Temple of the City God, Wu-kung, Shensi (Photographed from Chou I-pai, *Chung-kuo chü-ch'ang shih*, p. 20)

gentry got together to celebrate a birthday or entertain guests'.[1] Parties of this kind were termed *t'ang-hui* and they were similar to those of earlier times when educated or rich men held banquets with drama in their own mansions. In nineteenth-century Peking, a private house was still a normal venue for such a gathering, but the *hsi-chuang* were designed specifically to cater for the *t'ang-hui*; they were equipped with a permanent stage or at least a large space planned to be seen conveniently by the guests.

T'ang-hui were formal occasions at which people from the same province or town, or scholars who had passed the examinations in the same year would get together to celebrate. Family events, like a birthday or wedding, could also call for a party.[2] Arrangements had to be made well in advance, formal invitations issued and an appropriate theatrical company engaged. Usually, only the five principal Anhwei companies could be granted an invitation, since the well-to-do tended to look down on the minor troupes and the

[1] *Meng-hua so-pu (MHSP)*, p. 2b.
[2] See Ch'i Ju-shan, *Hsi-pan*, pp. 44a, 73a–b.

Clapper companies. Great emphasis was laid on good manners and ceremonial during the party itself, which normally lasted most of the day until sunset. Just as at the banquets of the rich in earlier times, the programme was chosen by the guests themselves. The repertoire of the actors was handed round on a piece of red paper and each guest would tick the items he wished to see. He would also leave a monetary gift for the actors.[1]

Although *t'ang-hui* were usually organized by a scholar or rich person, actors themselves were sometimes the hosts at such gatherings. One particularly large banquet was held by the *tan* performer Fan Hsiu-lan, who came from Su-chou. The occasion lasted two days, 8 and 9 May 1836, and took place in the Yen-hsi t'ang, which was in the Pei Hsiao-shun hu-t'ung in the north-east sector of the Outer City. Six or seven hundred guests, almost all of good family, were invited to attend, and the best actors of the five most famous companies were selected into one group to perform.[2]

Including the Yen-hsi t'ang, there were ten famous *hsi-chuang* in Peking, all in the Outer City. Possibly the best known of them was the Hui-kuan of Wen-ch'ang (the God of Literature) which was near the Ts'ai-shih (Vegetable Markets) in the centre of the Outer City's western section.[3] Very close to it was the Hui-kuan of Ts'ai-shen (the God of Wealth), also a popular *hsi-chuang*.[4]

Another kind of theatre-restaurant was the *tsa-shua kuan*

---

[1] *MHSP*, pp. 2b–3a, 8a. In Ming times, too, guests would give actors money after a party at which drama had been performed. See an example in *Chin P'ing Mei tz'u-hua*, 72, 15b and Egerton, *The Golden Lotus*, III, 316. The *t'ang-hui* are discussed further in my book *The Chinese Theatre in Modern Times*, chapter two and in Scott, *Mei Lan-fang*, p. 46.

[2] *Ch'ang-an k'an-hua chi* (*CAKHC*), p. 2b.

[3] *MHSP*, p. 4a. This Wen-ch'ang hui-kuan is quite separate from another place of the same name in Liu-li ch'ang (north-west section of the Outer City). This latter Wen-ch'ang hui-kuan was a guild-hall where Peking's booksellers sacrificed to their patron god Wen-ch'ang. See Katō Shigeshi, *Shina keizai shi kōshō*, II, 580.

[4] See *Tu-men hui-tsuan, tsa-chi*, pp. 25a–b. Ts'ai-shen and other gods of wealth are discussed by Doré in *Recherches sur les superstitions en Chine, IIème partie, Le panthéon chinois*, pp. 956–65. One kind of restaurant similar to the *hsi-chuang* was the *chiu-chuang*. Such places could be called *t'ang* and were intended for people who liked to invite guests to dinner. There was plenty of food and wine, but the *chiu-chuang* differed from the *hsi-chuang* in that no drama was performed there. Many parties could take place at one time and each group would sit in a separate room divided off by screens (*MHSP*, pp. 2b–3a). There were a number of well known *chiu-chuang* throughout the city in the nineteenth century. Possibly the most famous was the I-ch'ing t'ang, so closely associated with the name of Ch'en Yin-kuan. Another was the Yen-ch'ing t'ang in Ta Sha-lan (*MHSP*, p. 5a).

(variety houses). These were similar to the *hsi-chuang* in that meals could be bought and eaten there. However, they differed in several important respects. Firstly, they were found not only in the Outer City, but also in the Inner, where indeed the three most famous lay—namely the Ching-t'ai yüan, T'ai-hua yüan, and Wan-hsing yüan.[1] Secondly, they were much less formal and were open to everybody, whatever his social or financial status. Finally, the theatrical entertainment offered in a *tsa-shua kuan* was much smaller in scale than that found in the *hsi-chuang*. The artists who visited the variety houses were amusing story-tellers who roamed round in small groups called *tang-tzu pan*. They sang and acted out much the same historical episodes as the main dramatic companies, but lacked their complex equipment.

Among the main kinds of story-telling were two called *pa-chiao-ku* and *shih-pu-hsien*.[2] Neither is of ancient origin, dating back certainly no earlier than the Ch'ien-lung period. The *pa-chiao-ku* was accompanied mainly by stringed instruments and included a great deal of buffoonery. There were several forms, of which the most popular still surviving is called *k'uai-shu* and is noted for its swiftly moving rhythm. The *shih-pu-hsien* was performed by a *tan* and *ch'ou*, but no *sheng*. It lost its popularity after the T'ung-chih period, but did not die out entirely and can still be heard in Peking.[3]

By far the most important theatres during this period were the *hsi-yüan*. These places were called 'such-and-such a *yüan, lou* or *hsüan*'. They were very informal and all kinds of people could go there. The *hsi-yüan* were very noisy. Yang Mou-chien writes, 'One can hear a constant noise of gongs, drums and people shouting approval. It is just like 10,000 crows cawing in competition.'[4] Also in contrast to the *hsi-chuang*, large dinners were not

---

[1] See *MHSP*, pp. 4a–b. The *Tu-men hui-tsuan* (*tsa-chi*, pp. 25a–b) lists the ten main *hsi-chuang* and these three places under the same heading, which states that dinner parties and drama could be enjoyed there. The *Tu-men chi-lüeh* of 1864 refers to the three as *tsa-shua kuan*. See Chou Chih-fu, *Tu-men chi-lüeh chung chih hsi-ch'ü shih-liao*, p. 152.

[2] *MHSP*, pp. 8b–9a.

[3] See *Yen-ching sui-shih chi*, p. 89, translated in Bodde, *Annual Customs and Festivals in Peking*, pp. 96–7. See also Fu Hsi-hua, *Ch'ü-i lun-ts'ung*, pp. 184–93, where further details about the music and specific items of these two story-telling forms can be found. The *shih-pu-hsien* is mentioned as one of the ballad forms performed at the time of the Lantern Festival in the streets of Peking, especially in Ta Sha-lan and its surroundings, during the late Ch'ien-lung period. See *Ti-ching sui-shih chi-sheng*, pp. 8–9.　　[4] *MHSP*, p. 2b.

provided. 'In the *hsi-yüan*, there will always be tea and refreshments, but no wine or full meals, so they are called *ch'a-lou* (tea-houses).'[1] Though the *hsi-yüan* were, then, more for popular theatre than the *hsi-chuang*, standards of performances were not necessarily low. In the big *hsi-yüan*, the main Anhwei companies were seen constantly, and some performances there were among the most important dramatic occasions of the time. On the other hand, in the smaller *hsi-yüan*, the minor Anhwei and the Clapper companies took it in turns to perform.[2]

A great deal is told us about the structure of the *hsi-yüan*, especially by the two nineteenth-century writers, Chang Chi-liang and Yang Mou-chien. It will be worthwhile discussing it in some detail, since it gives considerable insight into the social place of the theatre at the time when the Peking Opera was developing towards maturity.

There were seats both upstairs and downstairs in the larger *hsi-yüan*, the former being for the rich, the latter for the poor. Of all the categories of seats in the theatres, the dearest was the 'official seats' (*kuan-tso*). Yang Mou-chien writes, 'Upstairs at the very back [measured from the door of the theatre, not the stage] and near the stage, the seats to the left and right are separated by movable door-screens into three or four groups and are called *kuan-tso*. This is where the high-ranking spectators gather.'[3] Chang Chi-liang adds that 'the *kuan-tso* on the right balcony [seen from the stage] are called "entrance seats" (*shang-ch'ang men*), those on the left "exit seats" (*hsia-ch'ang men*).'[4] The second group of *kuan-tso* on the left-hand balcony contained the most expensive seats in the theatre.[5]

During the Chia-ch'ing period the official seats were covered with red cushions,[6] this being the colour symbolizing first- and second-degree officials. Later, however, only blue cloth was used for cushions in the *hsi-yüan*. The seats within the screens were not all equally comfortable. In front there were short couches where the rich sat, while behind them were placed higher cushioned tables, also for the rich. At the back were tall benches for their servants.[7]

---

[1] *MHSP*, p. 3a.   [2] *MHSP*, p. 2b.   [3] *MHSP*, p. 7a.
[4] *Chin-t'ai ts'an-lei chi* (*CTTLC*), 3, 4a.   [5] *MHSP*, p. 7a.
[6] *Tu-men chu-chih tz'u*, in *Pei-p'ing li-yüan chu-chih tz'u hui-pien* (*PPLYCC*), p. 2a.
[7] *MHSP*, pp. 7b–8a.

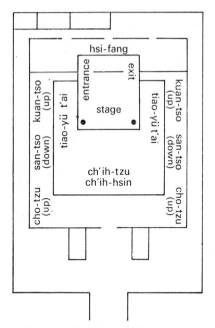

7. Diagram of a *Hsi-yüan* (Based on Aoki
Masaru, *Chung-kuo chin-shih hsi-ch'ü shih*,
p. 513)

Another kind of seat was the 'tables' (*cho-tzu*), which lay
behind the official seats as seen from the stage. As their name
implies, these were short tables arranged in rows. Though not as
comfortable as the *kuan-tso*, they were fairly expensive, owing to
their situation in the exclusive upper section of the theatre.[1] The
people sat at three sides of the table, leaving the fourth one,
nearest the stage, vacant so that all could see the actors. Meanwhile,
they drank tea, ate refreshments suitable to the season, and frequently chatted together,[2] for a friendly conversation was just as
much a part of theatre-going as watching the drama itself.

The poor sat in a more crowded and less salubrious area but
could also choose among different sections of the ground floor.
Directly under the *kuan-tso* were the 'scattered seats' (*san-tso*).

[1] *MHSP*, p. 7a.
[2] See Chou Chih-fu, *Chin pai-nien ti Ching-chü*, p. 69. Compare also the comments of Mgr Favier in *Péking*, p. 334.

'Downstairs are long benches spread all round in big circles, on which spectators all perch together. They are called *san-tso*. Behind them are placed high seats. By standing on tiptoe against the walls, one can gain a bird's-eye view.'[1] These *san-tso* were the cheapest seats in the theatre and their price was one-seventh that of a seat in the *kuan-tso*. Children paid one-half the full price.[2] There were other variations in the sum of money demanded for a seat too. Prices were highest if one of the five major companies was performing, but less for a minor Anhwei or Clapper troupe.[3] It was also possible to obtain for extra money a pot of tea and a cushion.[4] All seats and other facilities were purchased by direct transaction, not through tickets bought in advance; these were not used in Chinese theatres until the last few years of the Ch'ing.[5]

Downstairs, in front of the stage, was the 'pond' (*ch'ih-tzu*), also called 'the centre of the pond' (*ch'ih-hsin*). This was also for the poor, although children did not sit there.[6] 'In the centre of the auditorium they put up tables, just as [elsewhere] downstairs. The people who sit there are all pedlars from the market-places, brokers, servants or menials, and the place is called *ch'ih-tzu*. I have said that this sea of a myriad people is really just like a shoal of fish.'[7] The name 'pond' was apparently quite appropriate.

The last kind of seat was in the 'fishing platform' (*tiao-yü t'ai*). This was just to the side of and below the stage. The seats near the exit door were quite expensive, but those near the entrance were not so popular. This was because the orchestra was very close and the continual noise of the gongs produced a deafening effect upon the ear.[8]

The stage was usually square and raised about four feet above the ground. At the front, to the left and right, were two large round pillars which were useful to actors performing acrobatics, but could be very inconvenient to the spectators and obstruct their view. At the back was a wall with two openings, one on the right and one on the left, where the actors went in and out. They came in through the right door (seen from the stage) which was called

[1] *MHSP*, p. 7a.   [2] *CTTLC*, 3, 4a–b.
[3] *MHSP*, p. 3b.   [4] *MHSP*, p. 8a.
[5] Ch'i Ju-shan, *Hsi-chieh hsiao chang-ku*, p. 182; see also Mei Lan-fang, *Wu-t'ai sheng-huo ssu-shih nien*, I, 45–6.
[6] *CTTLC*, 3, 4a.   [7] *MHSP*, pp. 7a–b.   [8] *MHSP*, p. 7b.

'door for entrance' and went off through the left, which was called 'door for exit'. Behind the wall was the room where the actors got ready for the performance.[1] The construction of the stage in the *hsi-yüan* can be seen to have resembled that of others in north China.

One French observer of the turn of the twentieth century described Peking's main theatres as 'badly built, badly kept and dirty'.[2] Certainly they did not measure up to the great opera-houses of Europe in durability and were built mainly of wood. They were also badly ventilated, a feature not peculiar to Chinese theatres, and stiflingly hot in the warm season. Yang Mou-chien tells an amusing story which illustrates this point. At the height of summer, he was once at the Kuang-te lou, one of the big *hsi-yüan*, watching the Ch'un-t'ai company perform. It was extremely hot and he was 'sweating like an oar'. He looked down at the 'thronging sea of people below who were laughing and talking noisily. Air rose up [through the theatre] like steam from a cauldron.' The actors started to play *Mai yen-chih*[3] and he felt very happy. Yang continues: 'I undid my belt and hung it over the balustrade. I took off my clothes down to the waist, waved a fan and ate water-melons. In this way I was able to get cool after a while. Ten thousand eyes, both upstairs and downstairs, started looking at me and, whether they knew me or not, all said, "This man is insane."' The story spread throughout the neighbourhood, and the following day a man came to see him, saying that he should not behave in this way.[4] The tale shows also that people did not hesitate to talk or laugh during performances at *hsi-yüan*, and the same is to some extent true of other theatres. Even today, Chinese like to talk during theatrical performances.

It can be seen from the above that much more is known about the *hsi-yüan* than about Peking's other theatres. It is possible also to trace their development. Public theatres existed in Peking from the early years of the Ch'ing dynasty. They are mentioned in an edict of 1671 where they are called *hsi-kuan*.[5] One of the oldest of them was called Cha-chia lou, a very imposing building which seems originally to have been the private stage of a Ming dynasty

---

[1] Aoki Masaru, *Chung-kuo chin-shih hsi-ch'ü shih*, pp. 514–15.
[2] Favier, *Péking*, p. 334.
[3] See below, appendix C, pp. 249–50.
[4] *MHSP*, pp. 30a–b.
[5] *Ta-Ch'ing hui-tien shih-li* (*TCHT*), 1039, 14b.

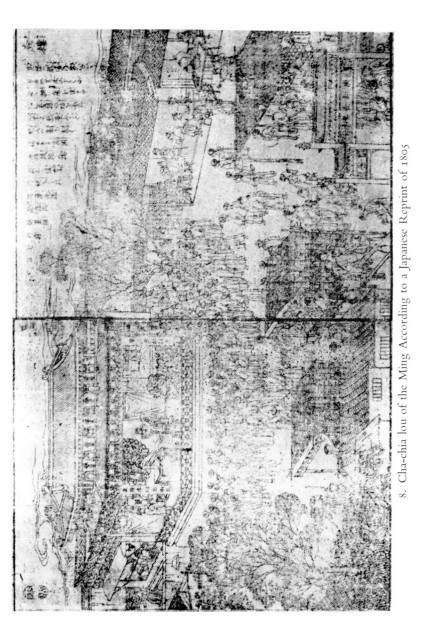

8. Cha-chia lou of the Ming According to a Japanese Reprint of 1805

family.[1] Another very old theatre was the Yüeh-ming lou.[2] Tradition has it that this place was privately visited by the K'ang-hsi Emperor[3] and it must have belonged to one particular individual. Other *hsi-yüan* which had been converted from stages in private mansions included the Ch'ing-lo yüan, Chung-ho yüan, and probably also the Fang-hu chai.

With the arrival of the *Ch'in-ch'iang* actors, some old *hsi-yüan* were repaired[4] and a number of others built. The 1785 stele lists eight *hsi-yüan*, the Kuang-ho lou, Chung-ho yüan, Ch'ing-lo yüan, Wan-chia lou, Yü-hsing yüan, Ch'ang-ch'un yüan, T'ung-ch'ing yüan, and Ch'ing-feng yüan.[5] The last five of these are not mentioned in earlier texts and appear to have been new. The Cha-chia lou had been renamed Kuang-ho lou[6] and was known also as Chin-ling lou. This was Ch'en Yin-kuan's favourite theatre[7] and it closed down temporarily in 1786.[8] The Fang-hu chai, though not listed on the stele, was still flourishing at the end of the eighteenth century.[9]

By 1816 the number of Peking's *hsi-yüan* had grown considerably. A stele referring in the relevant section to that year names twenty-one of them and specifies that the list is complete.[10] No new *hsi-yüan* is known to have been built after this time. A Peking guide-book of 1872 gives a list of *hsi-yüan*, which includes only fourteen names,[11] the smaller number implying probably a greater concentration of business on the main *hsi-yüan* rather than a decline in popularity of the theatre.

---

[1] A picture of the Cha-lou or Cha-chia lou, as it was in the Ming dynasty, survives through a Japanese reprint of 1805. It shows a large, permanent stage and other structures, some of which appear to have been temporary. The scene is quite crowded and many of the spectators are women. Cf. Ch'en Wan-nai, *Chü-ch'ü shih*, pp. 415–16 and Chou I-pai, *Chung-kuo hsi-chü shih*, pp. 734–5. A reproduction of the picture may be found above, facing p. 204.

[2] *T'eng-yin tsa-chi*, 9, 4b.

[3] *MHSP*, pp. 2a–b. This tradition was told by Yang Mou-chien by his old servant Yang Sheng.

[4] *T'eng-yin tsa-chi*, 5, 7a.

[5] *Pei-ching li-yüan chin-shih wen-tzu lu* (*PCLYCS*) pp. 3a–b.

[6] *T'eng-yin tsa-chi* 5, 7a. On this theatre see also Mei Lan-fang, *Wu-t'ai sheng-huo ssu-shih nien*, I, 44 and Scott, *The Classical Theatre of China*, pp. 221–2. A picture of the theatre's stage c.1898 may be found ibid., facing p. 161.

[7] *MHSP*, p. 6b.

[8] *MHSP*, p. 3a.

[9] *T'eng-yin tsa-chi*, 9, 4b.

[10] *PCLYCS*, pp. 5a–b.

[11] *Tu-men hui-tsuan, tsa-chi*, pp. 25b–27a.

I give below the names and situations of the nine largest and most important *hsi-yüan* in nineteenth-century Peking.[1]

San-ch'ing yüan	Ta Sha-lan	Chung-ho yüan	Liang-shih tien
Kuang-te lou	Ta Sha-lan	Kuang-ho lou	Jou-shih
Ch'ing-ho yüan	Ta Sha-lan	Yü-hsing yüan	Hsien-yü k'ou
Ch'ing-lo yüan	Ta Sha-lan	T'ien-lo yüan	Hsien-yü k'ou
T'ung-lo hsüan	Ta Sha-lan		

The large theatrical centres of Peking were, then, all in the region just south of the Cheng-yang Gate (Ch'ien-men). Ta Sha-lan and Liang-shih tien (Grain Shops) crossed each other at right angles just west of the main street which led south from that gate dividing the Outer City down the middle. The Jou-shih (Meat Markets) and Hsien-yü k'ou (Fish Markets) lay east of the street (see opposite).

The area round the Meat Markets was in fact one of the main pleasure centres of the city. There were many wine-houses there and, despite the foul smell from the markets, Yang Mou-chien tells us that he would take companions to the area to drink and eat. Just to the south was the Chin-yüan lou which was frequented by merchants from west China. Yang writes that 'in this theatre there are no elegant seats and [good] actors never show their faces there.'[2] Presumably the dramas performed were mainly *Ch'in-ch'iang* pieces.

There were other areas with *hsi-yüan*. Indeed, except for the Inner City, where *hsi-yüan* were forbidden, all the main regions of Peking were provided with them. But those away from the Ta Sha-lan area were all small and unimportant:

There were two in the southern city, one outside the Ch'ung-wen Gate called Kuang-hsing, and one outside the Hsüan-wu Gate called Ch'ing-shun; one in the eastern city outside the Ch'i-hua [Ch'ao-yang] Gate called Fang-ts'ao; one in the western city outside the P'ing-tse [Fu-ch'eng] Gate called Fu-ch'eng; and one in the northern city outside the Te-sheng Gate called Te-sheng. The main Anhwei companies do not go to these places, although the Sung-chu may sometimes be found there.[3]

---

[1] Ibid. All nineteenth-century versions of the *Tu-men chi-lüeh* list the same major *hsi-yüan*. See Chou Chih-fu, *Tu-men chi-lüeh*, pp. 141 ff.

[2] *MHSP*, pp. 6b–7a. 'Chin' is a common name for Shansi province.

[3] *MHSP*, p. 4b. The positions of these gates may be seen from the map of Peking (p. 268) It may be added that the Ch'ing-shun yüan is mentioned in the

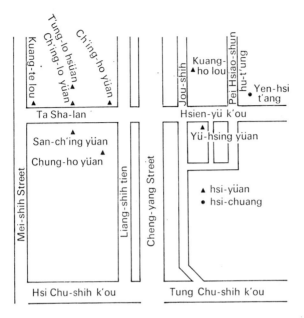

9. The Ta Sha-lan Area of Peking South of the Cheng-yang Gate

The Systems of Rotation in the Hsi-yüan

It was the practice for various companies to take it in turns to perform at the different *hsi-yüan* of Peking. The 18th of the third lunar month was a special day for actors, being the feastday of their patron god, and it was from this day that the year's drama was counted.[1] Before that time the managers of the main theatres would arrange a roster with the companies. The time-table would stipulate which company would perform at which theatre on the various days of the lunar months of that year. The major companies invariably performed in the major *hsi-yüan* outside the Cheng-yang Gate. The smaller companies also performed in the large theatres when they got the chance; but they could not afford to refuse to perform elsewhere. There was considerable competition over the arrangements, for the managers of the big

Tu-men chi-lüeh of 1845 and 1864, but not in later versions, and that all nineteenth-century editions list one other *hsi-yüan*—the Lung-ho yüan outside the Ch'ao-yang Gate. See Chou Chih-fu, *Tu-men chi-lüeh*, p. 151.

[1] See Ch'i Ju-shan, *Ching-chü chih pien-ch'ien*, p. 10b.

theatres did not willingly engage minor companies to perform in their *hsi-yüan* if they could possibly have the better ones. For this reason lesser troupes acted in the main theatres only if no better one could be found. This general system obtained for many decades but died out with the Boxer Uprising in 1900, when several of Peking's major *hsi-yüan* were burnt down.[1]

Below I give examples to illustrate the working of the system. The first table shows the *hsi-yüan* where the San-ch'ing company performed during the months of the year 1845.[2]

1st to 4th days	San-ch'ing yüan	17th to 19th days	Ch'ing-lo yüan
5th to 8th days	Ch'ing-lo yüan	20th to 23rd days	Chung-ho yüan
9th to 12th days	Ch'ing-ho yüan	24th to 27th days	Kuang-te lou
13th to 16th days	Kuang-te lou	28th to 30th days	Kuang-ho lou

The following table shows the roster for the same company, the San-ch'ing, in 1872.[3]

1st to 4th days	San-ch'ing yüan	17th to 19th days	Chung-ho yüan
5th to 8th days	Kuang-te lou and Ch'ing-lo yüan	21st to 23rd days	Ch'ing-ho yüan
		24th to 27th days	Kuang-te lou
9th to 12th days	Ch'ing-ho yüan	28th to 30th days	Chung-ho yüan
13th to 16th days	Kuang-te lou		

The month was divided up into groups of three or four days and the roster arranged according to short periods of several rather than single days. The main companies rarely had a day with no performances. In the above lists it is striking that in 1845 the San-ch'ing company enjoyed no holiday and in 1872 only one, the 20th of the month. At the same time it was possible for the company to split into two, since naturally not every member was needed for a day's performance, and leading actors could perform at one theatre in the morning and at another later in the day.[4] From the 5th to the 8th days in 1872, some members of the San-ch'ing performed at the Kuang-te lou, others at the Ch'ing-lo yüan. Possibly some actors performed in both theatres at different times of the day. It is worth noting also that the most famous theatres rarely closed even for a day. For example, the roster of the Kuang-te lou for 1872 shows the month completely booked

[1] The roster system of the late Ch'ing is discussed by Ch'i Ju-shan in *Hsi-pan*, pp. 68a–69a. See also Chou Chih-fu, *Ching-chü*, pp. 64–8.

[2] See Chou Chih-fu, *Tu-men chi-lüeh*, pp. 153–4.

[3] *Tu-men hui-tsuan, tsa-chi*, pp. 25b–26b.

[4] A work of 1805 records that the San-ch'ing company would, at that time, often split up into several parts and perform in different places at once. *P'ien-yü chi*, p. 8b.

up.[1] Less famous theatres, on the other hand, did have unoccupied periods. The Yü-hsing yüan, for instance, was free in 1872 from the 5th to the 12th, from the 17th to the 23rd, and again from the 28th to the 30th of each month.[2] The minor *hsi-yüan* were not affected by the roster system and accepted what business they could find.

The main reason for these rosters was the weakness of communications in those times. It was necessary to inform the populace well in advance which company was to perform when and where. Consequently, performances were usually well advertised. The signs were called *pao-t'iao* and were put up in various places. In the time of Wei Ch'ang-sheng and his followers, the entrance of the *hsi-yüan* was the most normal place.[3] A poem of 1813 says that the signs were stuck up on the walls of market-places.[4] And, referring to the late Tao-kuang period, Yang Mou-chien writes, 'Nowadays, large signs called *pao-t'iao* are put up on the main roads everywhere saying, "On such-and-such a day of the month, such-and-such a company will perform certain dramas in a certain theatre." The old custom is still followed in this respect.'[5] It seems, then, that not only was the roster arranged beforehand, but, at least in the Tao-kuang period, the specific pieces to be performed were to some extent planned and made known in advance. The programmes, however, remained vague. Yang Mou-chien tells us that actors sometimes told their friends all the details of the performances,[6] but most people in the audience had no clear idea of what piece or actor to expect next. Contrary to the practice in the *hsi-chuang*, nobody in the audience could choose which drama the company would perform.

---

[1] The roster of the Kuang-te lou for 1872 was as follows:

1st to 4th days	Ch'un-t'ai	17th to 19th days	Shuang Shun-ho
5th to 8th days	San-ch'ing	20th to 23rd days	Ssu-hsi
9th to 12th days	Ch'un-t'ai	24th to 27th days	San-ch'ing
13th to 16th days	San-ch'ing	28th to 30th days	Ssu-hsi

See *Tu-men hui-tsuan, tsa-chi*, p. 25b.

[2] Ibid., p. 26b.

[3] *Yen-lan hsiao-p'u*, 5, 6a.

[4] *Tu-men chu-chih tz'u*, in PPLYCC, p. 1b.

[5] MHSP, p. 3b. Compare also Favier, *Péking*, p. 334, where it is claimed that the signs were stuck on the walls of the city.

[6] MHSP, p. 8a. Developments in advertising the dramas of the day are discussed in Ch'i Ju-shan, *Chang-ku*, pp. 52, 128–9, 188–9. See also my book, *The Chinese Theatre*.

Many scenes were acted in a day at each theatre. Performances began in the morning and normally finished at sunset. Chang Chi-liang describes how the system worked in the 1820s:

In the performances of the Peking theatre, first three or four separate, unconnected scenes are put on, then three or four more scenes. This [second] group is called the middle phase (*chung chou-tzu*). Then there are one or two more unconnected items followed by three or four other scenes. This [last] group is called the main phase (*ta chou-tzu*).[1]

Yang Mou-chien, referring to the 1830s, gives a slightly different picture:

Nowadays, the custom with theatrical performances is to divide the day into three phases. At the early phase (*tsao chou-tzu*), very few spectators have gathered and the performance is rather careless. There are then three disconnected scenes, all put on by beautiful [i.e. boy] actors. The scene after this middle phase is called *ya chou-tzu* and includes the finest actor. After that is the main phase. Every drama performed during the main phase is a complete and new piece. It is put on in sections over a number of days, and may take ten days to finish.[2]

These quotations are to be taken as referring not to universal custom among all companies and on all days in the Peking drama of the nineteenth century, but to general, changeable rules. We saw in chapter six that the San-ch'ing company was noted for complete dramas, and may even sometimes have performed connected scenes of a whole drama all day.

During the Chia-ch'ing era, the days performances did not finish even with the main phase, for after that the *tang-tzu pan* would come on the stage and sing *shih-pu-hsien* or other humorous songs. By the Tao-kuang period, the *tang-tzu pan* no longer performed in the *hsi-yüan*. They did, however, continue to be popular in private houses, as well as in *tsa-shua kuan*.[3]

Regarding the phases of the day's theatre, Yang Mou-chien tells us some interesting details of the habits of Chinese audiences at the time. He says that the high-ranking members of the audience would listen to the early phase and then, during the middle one,

---

[1] *CTTLC*, 3, 4b.

[2] *MHSP*, pp. 8a–b. The two quotations given above show that the way the *chou-tzu* functioned had changed slightly between the 1820s and 1830s. There were further changes later in the Ch'ing period. See Chou Chih-fu, *Ching-chü*, p. 46.

[3] *MHSP*, pp. 8b–9a. See also *Tu-men chu-chih tz'u* of 1813, in *PPLYCC*, p. 1b.

go round the theatre chatting to their friends. By the time the *ya chou-tzu* was finished they were ready to go home. The air was full of the sound of carriages moving and people talking. He claims that it was mainly the common people of the market-places who stayed for the final, main phase, since they liked the connected scenes and loved to follow a story from beginning to end. However, in view of Yang's own remark (noted in chapter six) that it was the scholars who approved of the performance of entire dramas by the San-ch'ing company, it is difficult to believe that there were no members of this class in the theatre during the *ta chou-tzu*. Very often, people would go from theatre to theatre to follow one story through.[1]

Yang's remarks confirm that the *hsi-yüan* of eighteenth- and nineteenth-century Peking were used just as much for meeting friends and chatting as for watching drama. They were tea-houses as well as theatres. They also attracted all kinds of pedlars selling goods such as water-melons and, until the end of the nineteenth century, curios like jade belts and brushes.[2] In fact, like the drama of earlier centuries, the Peking Opera drew much of its importance through its significance as a social phenomenon, and its close connection with society was undoubtedly a major reason for its growth in popularity.

Restrictions on the Drama

I have shown in previous sections that the theatre was loved by all strata of the community. The government, however, was constantly suspicious of it, and considered that the theatre could easily encourage immorality and intrigue. Many restraints and restrictions were placed upon the building of theatres, the kind of person who could frequent them, the content of dramas and the times when performances could take place. In general, however, the government's success in enforcing the restrictions was far from complete.

It was forbidden to build public theatres in the Inner City, and in 1671 an edict was issued to this effect.[3] It appears that the order did not remain effective permanently. Probably the upsurge in the

[1] *MHSP*, p. 8b.
[2] See *P'in-hua pao-chien*, 1 (*hui* 3), 9b–10a. The 'side-businesses' are discussed by Ch'i Ju-shan in *Chang-ku*, pp. 186–90.
[3] *TCHT*, 1039, 14b.

popularity of the drama which followed Wei Ch'ang-sheng's arrival caused some people to disobey the decree. In any case, the government felt called upon to renew the earlier order. A second proclamation banning the building of *hsi-yüan* in the Inner City was issued in 1799, and others followed it in 1802 and 1811.[1]

Although the proscription was obeyed until the middle of the century,[2] it was applied less rigidly in later decades. As noted earlier, there were *tsa-shua kuan* in the Inner City, but the government was uncertain whether to recognize the distinction between a *hsi-yüan* and a *tsa-shua kuan*. In 1870 it decided on the hard line and an order was directed against the two remaining Inner City variety houses, the Ching-t'ai yüan and the T'ai-hua yüan.[3] It cannot have been effective, since both are listed in a Peking guidebook of 1887 and even placed in the category of *hsi-yüan*.[4] After the Boxer Uprising, the law against Inner City theatres lapsed altogether and Chen-chün stated in 1907 that nobody knew about it.[5]

The Inner City was the seat of government and the region where the Imperial Palaces were situated. But it is more important from the point of view of the edicts under discussion that the area was where the Eight Banners (Pa-ch'i) or army of the Manchus was stationed.[6] The authorities were afraid that these men 'might become accustomed to idle pleasures' if *hsi-yüan* were allowed in the Inner City.[7] Moreover, the Manchu emperors' constant suspicion concerning intrigue and rebellion made them anxious to avoid any dissension among the bannermen whose loyalty was of course particularly important to them. The Ch'ing rulers

[1] See Wang Hsiao-ch'uan, *Yüan Ming Ch'ing san-tai chin-hui hsiao-shuo hsi-ch'ü shih-liao*, pp. 51–2, 60.

[2] *MHSP*, p. 4a.

[3] *Ta-Ch'ing Mu-tsung I huang-ti shih-lu*, 286, 11a–b.

[4] *Ch'ao-shih ts'ung-tsai*, 6 *hsi-yüan*, 2b.

[5] *T'ien-chih ou-wen*, 7, 27a.

[6] According to Fang Chaoying, the number of companies in the army stationed in Peking reached its peak in 1735 and remained almost unchanged from then until 1912. He estimates the potential army of the Manchus in Peking in 1690 at 83,294 men. See 'A Technique for Estimating the Numerical Strength of the Early Manchu Military Forces', *Harvard Journal of Asiatic Studies*, xiii (1950), 193–9. It should be pointed out here that there were Chinese and Mongol banners, as well as Manchu, in the army of the Ch'ing emperors. Moreover, not all bannermen were soldiers. (See Spence, *Ts'ao Yin and the K'ang-hsi Emperor*, pp. 2 ff.) However, it seems to have been chiefly the military that the government had in mind in issuing the edicts I have considered here concerning the Pa-ch'i.

[7] *Yen-ching sui-shih chi*, p. 89. See also Bodde, *Annual Customs*, p. 96.

suspected that the *hsi-yüan* were used as meeting-places for secret societies to plot disturbances and rebellion, and a number of edicts were issued forbidding bannermen to visit them. There is a certain irony in this because, as pointed out earlier, the *wa-she* of Hang-chou had been erected specifically to entertain the army.

In 1724 Yung-cheng prohibited the members of the Pa-ch'i from attending the theatres.[1] However, it was later found that the number of *hsi-yüan* in the Outer City had risen dramatically, and many bannermen, even those on duty, were going there to eat and amuse themselves. A further imperial sanction was therefore issued in 1762 forbidding them to go to the theatres; copies of the edict had to be posted up outside all the *hsi-yüan*.[2]

The order was not always observed and was repeated in 1774.[3] In 1776 the punishment for offenders was set at 100 strokes of the rod.[4] Even this measure failed to solve the problem. The proscription of 1799 which forbade the building of theatres in the Inner City drew attention to the fact that there were still bannermen who frequented the theatres and wasted their time there in pleasure and intrigue.[5] Moreover, orders issued on 30 November and 1 December 1806 forbade them not only to attend the drama but even to perform on the stage.[6] This prohibition was inherent in those just mentioned, but the necessity to spell it out clearly suggests that the government's dilemma had grown more serious with time, and no solution was in sight.

Officials, too, were barred by law from the theatre in 1724.[7] A further edict of 1803 orders that if they should disguise themselves and go secretly to the drama or hold banquets without due reason, investigations should be held with the object of preventing a repetition of such behaviour.[8] Eight years later the veto was repeated. This time the reason for it was made clear, namely that the government was increasingly perturbed over the attentions paid by certain officials to young actors, and the consequent decline in morals among administrative personnel.[9] Like the decrees relating to the army and the theatre, these three were

---

[1] *Ta-Ch'ing Shih-tsung Hsien huang-ti shih-lu*, 18, 4a–5a.
[2] *TCHT*, 1039, 14b.   [3] *TCHT*, 1039, 15a.   [4] *TCHT*, 829, 12a.
[5] See Wang Hsiao-ch'uan, *Yüan Ming Ch'ing*, p. 51.
[6] *Ta-Ch'ing Jen-tsung Jui huang-ti shih-lu*, 169, 11a–13a, 16b–18a.
[7] *Ta-Ch'ing Shih-tsung Hsien huang-ti shih-lu*, 18, 4a–5a.
[8] *TCHT*, 1039, 16a.
[9] *Ta-Ch'ing Jen-tsung Jui huang-ti shih-lu*, 244, 26a–b.

frequently flouted. Officials continued to indulge in the pleasures of the theatre and Chang Chi-liang remarks that those of the sixth rank or higher would remove and conceal the hats indicating their status before entering the *hsi-yüan*.[1]

Officials and bannermen were few by comparison with the whole population. A much larger section of the community excluded from the *hsi-yüan* was the women. No direct proclamation appears to have been issued against the attendance of women at the theatre. However, late in the eighteenth century a certain painter called Lang Pao-ch'en (*hao* Su-men, 1763–1839),[2] suggested to the Emperor that the theatres be closed to women and his proposal was accepted. This is implied in the following poem of unknown authorship dating from the last years of the Ch'ien-lung era:

> At noon there were many fragrant chariots at the corners of the
> alleys [i.e. women going to the theatre],
> The pearl curtains hung high as they [i.e. the women] listened
> to the *sheng* and the singing.
> Unexpectedly they came across Lang the Crab,
> Who caused all the female crabs to run away in confusion.

Lang Su-men was called 'the Crab' because he was good at painting crabs. The poet is ridiculing his attitude and refers to the women as female crabs to contrast them with him.[3]

According to Ch'i Ju-shan, Lang's extraordinary proposal remained in force throughout the nineteenth century. Only at certain exclusive family *t'ang-hui*, often put on by female companies, and some rather expensive and infrequent performances at Inner City temples, were women permitted to watch the drama. Sessions of the second kind were attended only by women,[4] yet they still caused concern to the government and were banned by imperial edict in December 1869.[5] It was not until after the 1911 Revolution that women were finally allowed into the theatres. Even then they were at first obliged to sit in a different area from the men.

[1] *CTTLC*, 3, 3a.

[2] The painter's dates, *ming* and *hao* are given in *San-hsü i-nien lu*, 9, 181.

[3] This poem is quoted in Chou I-pai, *Hsi-chü shih*, p. 737, Ch'i Ju-shan, *Pien-ch'ien*, p. 7a and Ch'i Ju-shan, *Kuo-chü man-t'an*, I, 166. Both scholars interpret it as implying a ban on the attendance at the theatre by women.

[4] Ibid., I, 167–8; Ch'i Ju-shan, *Chang-ku*, p. 176.

[5] *Ta-Ch'ing Mu-tsung I huang-ti shih-lu*, 271, 2a–b.

The reasons why Lang Pao-ch'en put forward his suggestion are not recorded. Yet it is well known that the rigid separation of the sexes was a characteristic of the Ch'ing period.[1] Another factor in the prohibition of women in the *hsi-yüan* was the stress laid by the government on maintaining high moral standards in the theatres. I have already remarked in chapter two how Ch'ien-lung set up a commission in 1777 to examine and revise all dramas, and in chapter four described the reaction of the government to Wei Ch'ang-sheng's ribaldry. An edict of 1813 further emphasizes this point. While recognizing that the people were free to establish and attend *hsi-yüan* in the Outer City, it stipulates at the same time that all dramatic pieces must avoid lewd songs and should be conducive to virtue. Officials were ordered to watch over what happened and ensure that no rule of propriety was infringed.[2] The rule which banned such people from the theatre was waived for this purpose.

There were also restrictions on the time when drama could be performed. For the actors the most arduous of these was that which forbade theatrical enjoyment during the mourning period for an emperor, empress, or dowager. For the first 100 days all plays were suspended. After that, singing was allowed but drums and gongs still excluded. Moreover, the *hsi-yüan* remained closed till the full mourning period of 'three years' (actually about twenty-six months) was over. Managers who infringed this regulation were charged as criminals, although among the spectators only those of official rank were ever punished. Usually companies split up and actors found what work they could at *t'ang-hui* and in the various guild-halls. As a result of this they were often out of work, and, even when invited to perform, lacked many of their normal items of equipment.

The period of mourning included also the anniversary day of an emperor's, empress's, or dowager's death.[3] The most famous example of an infringement took place in 1689. The famous drama *Ch'ang-sheng tien* by Hung Sheng (1646?–1704)[4] had been

---

[1] See van Gulik, *Sexual Life in Ancient China*, p. 335, where an explanation of the puritanical outlook of the Manchu emperors in sexual matters is given.

[2] *TCHT*, 1039, 17a.

[3] Ch'i Ju-shan, *Chang-ku*, pp. 49–50.

[4] See Hummel, *Eminent Chinese of the Ch'ing Period*, p. 375. The drama *Ch'ang-sheng tien* has been translated by Yang Hsien-yi and Gladys Yang under the title *The Palace of Eternal Youth*. Reference is made to the incident mentioned here pp. 317–18.

completed in 1688 and won the approval of the Emperor K'ang-hsi. It quickly became very popular in high-ranking circles in Peking. A banquet was organized in the famous Cha-chia lou of Peking to perform it, but the day chosen was the anniversary of an empress's death. Chao Chih-hsin (1662–1744),[1] an official and poet who had helped write the music of *Ch'ang-sheng tien*, happened to be present and was dismissed from office.[2] Hung Sheng was also punished, together with many others, and spent the rest of his life in poverty.

Another period when reverence demanded the cessation of theatrical activities was during the fasting which accompanied prayers for rain. In an agricultural society, such as that of China, the lives of millions of people might depend on good rains at the right time, and a decree of 1807 points out that the Emperor himself practices self-denial when praying for rain. It would therefore be unseemly for the people to enjoy themselves at the theatre at such a time. The language of this edict is very mild and appreciative of the difficulties involved, especially for the actors whose livelihood was dependent on the drama. The Emperor has specifically rejected a suggestion that drama be forbidden not only during the fast, but until rain actually falls. No threat is made of punishment for offenders, and there is little hint of police action.[3] This being the case, it is likely that many people paid no more than lip-service to the proscription.

If many of the edicts mentioned so far were largely disregarded, there was at least one period when custom, not law, ordained that the theatres be closed. This was at the end of each lunar year. In the third quarter of the twelfth month a day was chosen to 'put away the seals' (*feng-yin*), that is to stop all official work until after New Year. Soon after that, the theatres suspended all activities for a short time. On the first of the following month (*yüan-tan*), they reopened and ushered in the new year with 'good luck dramas in which, on the whole, death and killing had no place'.[4]

Drama was suspended not only during certain specified periods

---

[1] See Hummel, *Eminent Chinese*, p. 71.

[2] *Liu-nan sui-pi*, 6, 110–11. See also *Liang-pan Ch'iu-yü an sui-pi*, 3, 102–3 and Aoki Masaru, *Hsi-ch'ü shih*, pp. 381–2.

[3] *TCHT*, 1039, 16a–17a.

[4] Ch'i Ju-shan, *Chang-ku*, p. 97. See also *Yen-ching sui-shih chi*, pp. 88–9, translated in Bodde, *Annual Customs*, p. 95. Ch'i's remark that 'killing had no place' does not of course extend to the death of evil persons or spirits.

but also at certain hours of the day. I mentioned earlier that the main phase of the day's performance normally ended at sunset. This was because of the demands of the law. In 1764 an imperial sanction was issued that 'it should be absolutely forbidden to sing at night in any of the *hsi-yüan* within the walls of the city'.[1]

The attitudes of the Manchu rulers to the popular drama are summed up in a most interesting edict of 1852. It runs in part:

It has never been forbidden to hold banquets. However, for a long time people have been vying with each other to make these occasions more extravagant. Dramas are held at night and people bring women along with them to banquets where they eat and drink. This situation has been worsening daily and is wasteful and improper. Pieces performed should encourage goodness and correct evil, and they should bring out proper feelings in people. But if, [as is the case with dramas performed nowadays,] the music is extravagant and the acting techniques conducive to quarrelsome attitudes and anger, there will be an increase in sexual misdemeanours, robbery will be propagated and evil practices encouraged. There is an even greater relationship between this sort of art and human feelings. For this reason, the head of the military police (*pu-chün t'ung-ling*) and the censors of the *ya-men* and the regions inside the city walls must first put out a proclamation that they are not going to tolerate this behaviour any longer. If the said crimes persist, they should arrest the manager of the *hsi-yüan* or *hsi-chuang* concerned and punish him.[2]

Several points are made clear in this decree. In the first place, it confirms that drama was not allowed at night and that it was considered wrong to take women to the theatre. Secondly, it tells us that both these prohibitions were frequently disobeyed. Thirdly, the proclamation brings out very strongly the idea that drama can and does affect the morals of a society. The ethical aspect of the drama has been mentioned several times in this work, but in few places is it so clearly stated as in this edict. The somewhat puritanical thinking behind this doctrine is very ancient in China and was particularly characteristic of the Manchu rule. It is, indeed, still very much alive in contemporary China.

There is an extremely important implication behind the fact that the range of prohibitions against the theatre was so wide. It is

---

[1] *TCHT*, 1039, 15a. I have considered the restrictions on night drama in greater detail in *The Chinese Theatre*, chapter two.

[2] *TCHT*, 1039, 17a–b.

that the Manchu government recognized the intimate relationship between the drama and society. They were aware that the theatre was more than a place for enjoyment and relaxation; it was also a major social force, the influence of which extended deeply into the lives of the people. From the point of view of the Manchu emperors, it was logical that the authorities should supervise and guide it carefully.

The Social Status of Actors

The restrictions which the Ch'ing government placed on the theatres, coupled with the overt love for the drama of many members of the imperial family, especially Ch'ien-lung and the Empress Dowager Tz'u-hsi, underlines the ambivalent attitude of the Manchus towards the theatre. The acting profession was regarded in a similar way by society—with mixed feelings. On the one hand actors could be very favoured persons. It will already have become clear than many of them were rich and famous, and that the art which they provided was widely appreciated among all strata of society. Moreover, many of their patrons were scholars or other highly placed people. On the other hand, the social status of actors was low. I have already described in chapter two how actors were definitely looked down upon by the community from early times until the Ch'ien-lung period. This had not changed radically by the time of the T'ung-chih Restoration. It remained true that few people would willingly see their sons take up acting. This would involve a considerable loss of face and according to a modern sociologist 'to have a son who was an actor was like having no son at all.'[1] Furthermore, it was regarded as a disgrace to accept an actor as a son-in-law, even if his acting and singing ability were greatly admired.

The failure of society to alter its basic contempt for the acting profession may be explained by four principal factors.

Firstly, atttitudes tend to change slowly, if at all. Chinese society during the period 1770–1870 was certainly in transition, but the thinking of government and most influential circles was still conservative. Consequently the pressure for change in social values was not great.

In the second place, there was still a great deal of evidence to corroborate the ancient cry that actors were immoral. I have

[1] P'an Kuang-tan, *Chung-kuo ling-jen hsüeh-yüan chih yen-chiu*, p. 237.

noted examples among them of gambling (Yü Ssu-sheng) and opium-smoking (Lin Yün-hsiang, Yü Ssu-sheng, even Ch'eng Chang-keng) and mentioned the prevalence of homosexuality.[1] The fact that the blame for this last deviation could hardly be placed on the actors themselves did not alter society's attitude. There were also artists whose married life left much to be desired. Yang Mou-chien writes of one called T'ao Yüeh-hsien who exchanged wives and concubines with certain friends. Many others did not wish to be associated with this and 'did not mix with him, so his disciples could only get into the small companies'. It was only by persistent effort on their part that this situation changed. By 1842 they 'were worming their way into the Ho-ch'un and Sung-chu troupes'.[2]

No doubt all these immoralities existed in other strata of society without serious effects on the respectability of their members. The real key to the low status of actors was that the hallowed halls of the official bureaucracy, entry into which was the chief means of social advancement, was virtually closed to the acting profession. The edicts of 1652 and 1770, which forbade actors, their sons, and their grandsons, to sit for the examinations, remained generally effective until the end of the Manchu dynasty, although it was not completely unknown for the descendants of actors to achieve success in the examinations.[3]

It has been pointed out by the contemporary scholar Ho Ping-ti that money became an increasingly important factor in entering the bureaucracy as the Ch'ing dynasty progressed.[4] Yet although many actors became rich, very few ever became officials. Even the magic of money could not overcome the social stigma attached to them or their lack of family connections with influential people. According to Chang Chi-liang, there was a certain *tan* artist in the

[1] I may add that, in view of the constant references I have found to homosexuality in books on actors, I am slightly suspicious of van Gulik's general conclusions on its extent in China, although admittedly he is explicit in excluding the Ch'ing period from his study. See *Sexual Life*, pp. 48, 163. Some of the scholars mentioned in the present work showed no signs of shame because of their vice (e.g. Pi Yüan, Chu To-shan). On the other hand, homosexuality never seems to have become socially respectable beyond very limited circles. This can be inferred from the fact that the authors of almost all the works on *tan* I have cited wrote under a pen-name. Some, like Chang Chi-liang and Yang Mou-chien, can be identified, but the majority cannot.

[2] *MHSP*, pp. 10a–b.

[3] P'an Kuang-tan, *Chung-kuo ling-jen*, p. 237.

[4] *The Ladder of Success in Imperial China*, pp. 46 ff.

Chia-ch'ing period who became the magistrate of a county,[1] but he was exceptional. Those actors who left their profession sometimes became small merchants. The famous *Ch'in-ch'iang* actor, Wang Kuei-kuan, and Ch'en Feng-lin, well known in the 1830s, are good examples. But positions of higher social standing than this were in general beyond the reach of anybody who had ever acted professionally.

Finally, it was considered that actors normally came from lowly families. There is an interesting story which illustrates this attitude. One of the disciples of T'an T'ien-lu was one day performing in a public theatre. The spectators included an official who thought the actor seemed to come from a much better background than most members of the profession. He summoned the young man to his house and asked who he was and where he came from. It turned out that the official's surmise had been correct. He asked the actor how it was that he had fallen into such bad straits. How could it be that the son of a good family had been reduced to such a state? The other replied that when he was seven or eight years old he had got lost and been bought as a *hsiang-kung*. On hearing this story, the official immediately arranged for the young performer to be released from his bond so that he could return home.[2]

The precise class background of actors who flourished before 1870 is unfortunately rarely given in the sources. However, those actors whose origin is known were mostly the sons of peasants or other poor people (e.g. Shen Hsiang-lin, Chao San-kuan). Furthermore, since so many actors were recruited by being bought from their parents on contract, there can be no doubt that the majority came from poor families. It must have been dire necessity which would drive a father to sell his child.

Yet there were isolated cases of actors who had been born into families with good social position. One was Yü Hung-ts'ui, a member of the Ch'un-t'ai company. He was born in 1820 of an old family, and was the son of an official. He went to Peking in 1830 and there he was taught along with other boys.[3]

It is not surprising that actors who entered their profession voluntarily should in general have come from better backgrounds than those who had been given no choice in their profession.

[1] *CTTLC*, 2, 6a.   [2] *Hsin-jen kuei-chia lu*, p. 20a.
[3] *CAKHC*, pp. 4a–5a.

Among the *p'iao-yu* we find a number from fairly good families, and one writer says of the early amateurs that they were the most respected among actors because 'most of them were scholars'.[1] We saw in chapter six that Chang Erh-k'uei, among the first of the famous *p'iao-yu*, came from a family of officials. According to Chou Chih-fu, the well known *ch'ou* actor Liu Kan-san, who was born in 1817, was the son of a government runner (*i*) in the salt administration in Tientsin.[2] This was hardly an exalted position,[3] but the family had been improving its status, and Kan-san's father had enough social pretensions to order his son to study and become a scholar. Kan-san tried to obey, but found scholarship beyond him. He then turned to amateur acting.[4]

The growth of the *p'iao-yu* system, the rise of the upright *lao-sheng* actors like Ch'eng Chang-keng, and the personal wealth of many actors seem to have effected a slight and gradual improvement in the social standing of many members of the acting profession. The partial rise was accentuated by the fact that a number of actors were educated, and that some mixed among people of good standing. For instance, we saw earlier that the nobles and *literati* of Peking were anxious to make the acquaintance of Wei Ch'ang-sheng. In the middle of the eighteenth century, actors sometimes attended banquets as guests together with scholars,[5] and in the course of time could even be the hosts. It appears, therefore, that there were exceptions to the general rule that actors were beyond the social pale. Gradations existed among them, and the low status of the profession as a whole did not prevent individual actors from becoming partly accepted by men of good family.

In an analysis of the social position of actors completed in 1934 and published in 1941, P'an Kuang-tan investigated the back-

[1] Hsü Chiu-yeh, *Li-yüan i-wen*, p. 2a.

[2] *Ching-hsi chin pai-nien so-chi*, p. 2.

[3] See the detailed discussion of government runners in T'ung-tsu Ch'ü, *Local Government in China under the Ch'ing*, pp. 56–73.

[4] Chang Tz'u-hsi, *Yen-tu ming-ling chuan*, p. 3b. Chang claims that Liu's family had been pharmaceutical dealers for generations, but this does not necessarily conflict with Chou Chih-fu's account.

[5] In Wu Ching-tzu's famous novel *Ju-lin wai-shih* (34, 331) one character asks another, 'When you invite scholars to a meal, sir, would you let an actor sit at the same table?' The reply was, 'That has been done for a long time now'. I have followed the translation of Yang Hsien-yi and Gladys Yang in *The Scholars*, p. 459. In the earlier novel *Chin P'ing Mei*, the actors are always fed separately. See, for instance, *Chin P'ing Mei tz'u-hua*, 43, 6b, and Egerton, *The Golden Lotus*, II, 221.

ground of certain distinguished performers of the late Ch'ing and Republic. He found thirty-four with merchant-dealer and thirty-three with official or aristocratic backgrounds, eleven from peasant and nine from artisan origins, five with medical connections and one who had been a robber.[1] Many of the examples he gives were originally amateurs.[2] One of them, Chin Pan-chü, was even a prince of the Manchu imperial family.[3] Yet, despite these figures, P'an still claims that 'apart from the actors from old theatrical families and those who, as officials or men of high position, had turned to become amateurs, ninety-nine per cent came from desperately poor families.'[4] There is no doubt that even in his time they were not highly regarded by society and the age-old prejudice against them was still very much alive.

Actors as a Professional Body: Guilds

The low position of actors in the community was accompanied by a certain degree of solidarity among them and a definite feeling that they constituted a professional body. The nature of acting demands group co-operation and theatrical companies must act in harmony, at least on the stage, or their standards will fall. But there is also evidence of the existence of a sub-culture among actors which reached out far beyond individual companies and concerned the whole profession.

One expression of this sub-culture was the religious life of actors. They worshipped and sacrificed to a number of gods who were recognized as protectors of their profession.

The main patron god of actors was called Lao-lang shen (or Tsu-shih yeh, i.e. 'the founder of the profession'). The temples built for the use of actors were mostly named after him and dedicated to his honour. Moreover, stage artists usually kept an image of this god in their house and offered sacrifices to him in the hope that he would protect them and send good fortune.

Most actors believed Lao-lang to be a divine manifestation either of Emperor Ming-huang (712–56) of T'ang or Emperor

---

[1] *Chung-kuo ling-jen*, pp. 224–5.

[2] Examples of those amateurs of merchant origin are Sun Chü-hsien, Liu Ching-jan, Kung Yün-fu, Yüan Tzu-ming, and Hsü Yin-t'ang. See ibid., pp. 225–6 and compare the *p'iao-yu* in Ch'i Ju-shan, *Ch'ing-tai p'i-huang ming-chüeh chien-shu*, pp. 134 ff. See also Ch'i Ju-shan, *Chang-ku*, pp. 170–2.

[3] *Chung-kuo ling-jen*, p. 226.

[4] Ibid., p. 231.

Chuang-tsung (923–6) of Later T'ang.[1] These two rulers were well known as patrons of the theatres. Ming-huang was the founder of a drama school in the Pear Garden (*Li-yüan*) in his capital Ch'ang-an,[2] and so famous did the garden become that the term *li-yüan* came to mean simply 'the theatre'; Chuang-tsung was expert in music and the drama and was accounted a good actor.[3]

The worshipper clearly has the right to dictate the identification of his god. Yet it appears that in earlier times actors believed Lao-lang to be a deified manifestation not of any historical personnage but of a star in the I-hsiu, the twenty-seventh of the 'twenty-eight lunar mansions' (*erh-shih-pa hsiu*).[4] As early as the Chin period (265–420 A.D.) the I-hsiu was considered to guide the fortunes of actors.[5] The shrine of the court performers on Ching-shan was specifically dedicated to this lunar mansion[6] and Yang Mou-chien reports that in his time the tablets in actors' houses equated Tsu-shih yeh with a star in I-hsiu.[7] Even in the present century the steles found in the dwellings and temples of theatrical personnel gave the same identification.[8]

The principal feastday of Lao-lang was the 18th of the third lunar month. This was the day from which the theatre calendar was calculated and many actors joined a new company at that time. Celebrations were held to honour Lao-lang. Chang Chi-liang reported in 1829 that on that day 'all the *tan* actors held processions in honour of the god and they were called *hsiang-kung hui*'.[9] A more recent author describes the ceremonies as follows:

At the end of every year, after the closing of the theatres, and on the 18th of the third month, there are always sacrifices to Tsu-shih... If they [the actors] have a public building, then they sacrifice to him [there]. But if they do not ... they must make prior arrangements with a restaurant and come to an agreement on the rules. On the day itself, they carry [the image of Tsu-shih] reverently from the *hsi-yüan* to the restaurant, and people playing musical instruments lead the way ... After arrival at the restaurant, they make offerings and all the members of the company must come forward, burn incense and per-

[1] Ch'i Ju-shan, *Chang-ku*, p. 30.   [2] *Chiu T'ang-shu*, 28, 8b.

[3] *Hsin Wu-tai shih*, 37, 2a.

[4] I-hsiu contained twenty-two stars. It is identified with Western constellations in Joseph Needham and Wang Ling, *Science and Civilisation in China*, III, 237. A chart showing its position is given facing p. 250.

[5] *Chin-shu*, 11, 16a.   [6] *Ch'en-yüan shih-lüeh*, 16, 38b.

[7] *MHSP*, p. 27b.   [8] See Ch'i Ju-shan, *Chang-ku*, pp. 30–1.

[9] *CTTLC*, 3, 6a.

form ceremonial acts. When the ceremony is over, they assemble and eat there. After their meal is finished they leave, being led off by the original musical instruments, and put Tsu-shih back in his original place.[1]

After Lao-lang shen the most important member of the actors' pantheon was Hsi-shen, the God of Joy. In contrast to their main patron, this deity was honoured not only by stage-artists, but also by the people in general, who regarded him as a protector of happy marriages.[2] Actors, however, had their own view of him and believed that the dolls used in operas to represent babies were images of Hsi-shen. While on the stage they could play with the doll as the drama required, but after their exit had to pay it respect. To avoid the necessity of a continuing ritual the face of the image was then turned downwards. It is not clear why actors came to regard the stage-doll as a divine manifestation, and Ch'i Ju-shan has put forward three suggestions, all told to him by old actors.

Firstly, t'ang-hui and dramas associated with them were frequently held to celebrate a birthday or the arrival of a child. This made the reverence of a doll representing a baby extremely appropriate, especially since the god in question was a patron of happy marriages. The second theory concerns a story among actors that one of their trade found great difficulty in learning his art. He dreamed that a child came to teach him and was then able to progress; this led to the worship of the stage-doll as a god. The final explanation of the origin of the cult lies in a legend, popular among actors, that the eldest son of T'ang Ming-huang went to sleep peacefully in a large clothes trunk and never woke up. It was believed that he was canonized as Hsi-shen. For this reason, actors always took care not to sit on the opening of the trunks for their theatrical costumes.[3] The three stories are not particularly informative from a historical point of view, but are interesting for the insight they give into the way legends proliferated so easily among Chinese actors, who, like their counterparts in other countries, tended to be superstitious.

Although the group spirit of the actors is clear from their religion, their organized collective activity is seen best in the guilds (hui-kuan) which they established. It is worth remarking at the outset that there were three different kinds of hui-kuan in

[1] Ch'i Ju-shan, Hsi-pan, p. 28b.
[2] See Doré, Recherches, IIème partie, pp. 1089–90.
[3] Ch'i Ju-shan, Hsi-pan, p. 30a.

Manchu China. The first was rather like an exclusive club. The Wu-hu hui-kuan, which dated from the Yung-lo period of the Ming (1403–25) and was the earliest *hui-kuan* established in Peking, was one example. It was open only to natives of Wu-hu, Anhwei province, who served as officials of the central government. The second type was designed for officials, as well as merchants or candidates for the examinations, from a particular region. By the early Ch'ing, both kinds had to a large extent become hostelries for examination candidates from one part of China.[1] A third kind of *hui-kuan* (which was also called *hang-kuan*) was that composed of members of the same trade, craft or profession. In practice, this type was not always clearly distinct from the one just mentioned since there was a tendency for the members of one trade to come from the same region. Yet in each guild there appears to have been a greater emphasis either on a common profession or place of origin.[2] The *hang-kuan* were social and religious bodies which arranged for banquets or communal sacrifices, but when it was necessary they could act together strongly in defence of their own interests. They could thus fulfil a mercantile and socio-religious role.[3]

The principal guild of the actors was called Li-yüan kuan or Li-yüan hui-kuan and it belonged to the third category. But before considering its functions, let us look briefly at the sources about it, the date of its origin, and some questions about its leadership.

Most of our knowledge of the early history of the actors' guilds is derived from steles. Even these are, unfortunately, somewhat uninformative about the *hui-kuan* themselves and consist largely of lists of companies or actors who contributed money towards a particular venture. The earliest is dated 1732 and refers to the Li-yüan hui-kuan, which must therefore have been functioning more

[1] See Ho Ping-ti, *Chung-kuo hui-kuan shih-lun*, pp. 13–21. The *Ch'ao-shih ts'ung-tsai* of 1887 lists (3 *hui-kuan*, 2a–35b) nearly 400 *hui-kuan*. Each is named after one area of China, and its members were examination candidates from the region in question. For an analysis of these regional guild-halls in Peking, see Ho Ping-ti, *Hui-kuan shih-lun*, pp. 23 ff.

[2] See Sybille van der Sprenkel, *Legal Institutions in Manchu China*, pp. 90–1.

[3] See Katō Shigeshi, *Shina keizai*, II, 557–84; Katō Shigeshi, 'On the Hang or the Associations of Merchants in China', *Memoirs of the Research Department of the Toyo Bunko* 8 (1936), pp. 76–9. Katō believes that only this third type of *hui-kuan* should be translated as 'guild'. The others are, strictly speaking, 'guild halls'. The *Ch'ao-shih ts'ung-tsai*, 3 *hang-kuan*, 1a–b names only eight *hang-kuan*, but the list is not exhaustive.

than forty years before the great era of Peking's drama began with the arrival of Wei Ch'ang-sheng.

The names of some of the leaders (*hui-shou*) of the Li-yüan hui-kuan are preserved on the steles. In 1732 the guild was headed by Tsou Chih-shan, who came from Wan-p'ing county near Peking,[1] and in 1790 by Kuan I-tsung. In 1816 the six chief members were Kao Yüeh-kuan, Hu Ta-ch'eng, P'an Lan-t'ing, Ch'en Shih-yün, Huo Yü-te, and Han Yung-li. By 1827 Han had become the *hui-shou* while the other five most prominent members were Yin Pien-chih, Kao Yüeh-kuan, Ch'en Shih-yün, Ch'ih Pao-ts'ai, and Li San-yüan.[2] This means that three of the leading members in 1816, Kao Yüeh-kuan, Han Yung-li, and Ch'en Shih-yün, were still taking an active interest in the direction of guild affairs eleven years later. We may perhaps infer from this that there was some constancy in the management of the guild.

This was not so of all guilds in Peking. For instance, that of the bankers, Cheng-i tz'u, changed leaders frequently.[3] In most guild-halls of people from the same place of origin, headmen were elected by the members.[4] But when the Li-yüan hui-kuan was overhauled at the time of the T'ung-chih Restoration, its leader, Ch'eng Chang-keng, was appointed by the goverment.[5] It may be that earlier leaders were similarly chosen, which would explain why changes were fairly rare, but there is no evidence in the primary sources on this subject.[6]

The functions of the Li Yüan hui-kuan appear to have been similar to those of other craft or professional guilds. In the first place this was certainly a religious organization. Its headquarters lay in a temple dedicated to Hsi-shen and Lao-lang beside the Ching-chung Temple in the south-east of the Outer City.[7] In

[1] *PCLYCS*, p. 2a.
[2] *PCLYCS*, p. 3b–5b.
[3] Katō Shigeshi, *Shina keizai*, II, 583.
[4] Sybille van der Sprenkel, *Legal Institutions*, p. 93.
[5] Ch'i Ju-shan, *Chang-ku*, p. 155.
[6] J. S. Burgess writes of the leadership of the actors' guild in the late 1920s as follows: 'The Actors report that "there are three heads, two officials in charge of the current year, two officers of the month, four treasurers, four who take charge of general affairs, four directors." These are honorary positions. There is, in addition, "an accountant . . . and a servant who looks after the guild . . ."' See *The Guilds of Peking*, p. 135. Some changes had apparently taken place since the nineteenth century.
[7] *PCLYCS*, p. 2b.

addition to catering for the sacrifices the guild arranged communal social activities. There was a stage in the temple where operas could be performed during festivals or dinners.[1] Such a practice was common not only in the actors' guild but also in many others; quite a few guilds maintained a private stage and sometimes allowed those without to use it.[2]

Whether the Li-yüan hui-kuan was active in the protection and general interests of its members during the late Ch'ing is not at all clear from primary sources. Probably it followed the pattern of other similar guilds in defending its members against people outside the profession. But if an actor needed assistance against a more senior member of his own trade, the *hui-kuan* could hardly be expected to help. The case of Lin Yün-hsiang mentioned in chapter six illustrates this clearly. When he was betrayed by his master Liu Cheng-hsiang, he turned for help not to his guild but to wealthy friends.

Like other craft guilds, that of the actors could punish its members for a breach of the rules of the trade. The eighteenth-century novel *The Scholars* claims that 'if an actor did anything wrong, his whole guild had to go to the [Lao-lang] temple to burn incense, while on their return to the centre the case would be tried by all; and they could beat or punish the offender, who dared not complain.'[3] This can be taken as reflecting reality in most Chinese actors' guilds of the time. One way of punishment in many *hui-kuan* was to make the guilty person pay for a theatrical

[1] *PCLYCS*, p. 5a. See also *Ti-ching sui-shih chi-sheng*, p. 13.
[2] There was a stage in the Cheng-i tz'u (Katō Shigeshi, *Shina keizai*, II, 559) so that the members of the bankers' guild could hold banquets and dramatic performances there. The men of the booksellers' guild (Wen-ch'ang hui-kuan) were permitted to use it and would sometimes eat and watch drama in the Cheng-i tz'u (p. 580). A stele of 1741 also records the building of a stage in the Yen-liao hui-kuan (p. 563). This last guild was for dye merchants from P'ing-yao in Shansi (p. 565) and was one of the most important in Peking. Referring to the larger guild-halls all over China for people from the same area, D. G. MacGowan wrote in 1886: 'all that the arts of gilding and carving, masonry and sculpture, can effect is done to render Guild-halls imposing, the most striking portion being a court for theatrical performances in honour of the gods. At one end is a stage; at the other, shrines; in surrounding balconies the privileged witness plays, while feasting and chatting; the open court being free to the general public.' See 'Chinese Guilds or Chambers of Commerce and Trades Unions', *Journal of the China Branch of the Royal Asiatic Society*, xxi, 3 and 4 (1886), 139.
[3] *Ju-lin wai-shih*, 24. 244. I have used the translation of Yang Hsien-yi and Gladys Yang in *The Scholars*, p. 343.

performance to entertain the members.[1] It is quite likely that such a practice was followed also in the Li-yüan hui-kuan.

Another function of the actors' guild was to organize charitable work, such as giving special dramas to raise funds for the poor or the sick.[2] In fact, in the steles of the guild the subject to which most space is devoted can be put under the heading of 'charity': the cemeteries established for the accommodation of dead members.[3]

The earliest stele, that of 1732, concerns a graveyard arranged by the principal actors' guild in the south-west section of the Outer City. The nineteen companies which contributed towards the cost of the venture are listed, but very little is recorded about the cemetery itself.[4] Another stele, dated 1827, reports that a graveyard called An-ch'ing was built for the acting community in Ssu-yen ching, which lay in the centre of the Outer City's eastern half. Some land beside the Kuan-ti Temple had fallen into ruin and for some time nobody had taken the trouble to look after it. The guild therefore bought the land with some money contributed by eighteen actors and delegated a senior member, Ch'eng Yü-ch'üan, to arrange and supervise its repair. Fifty-five actors of the guild, including Kao Yüeh-kuan, Ch'en K'ung-cheng, Yin Pien-chih, Chou Hsiao-feng, and Tung Hsiu-jung, contributed money for the cost of the labour, and in the winter of 1826 workers were hired to begin it. By the beginning of the following year the land was ready for use as a graveyard and was soon afterwards opened publicly at a ceremony led by Kao Yüeh-kuan, Ch'en K'ung-cheng, and Ch'eng Yü-ch'üan. Unfortunately, it was soon found that local people were interfering with the cemetery by digging the earth there so that the bones of the dead were disturbed and left uncovered. In December 1831 or January 1832, it was announced that measures had been taken to prevent any further occurrences of such behaviour.[5]

---

[1] 'When quarrels arise, umpires intervene or are called in, who condemn the aggressor to go to the expense of a play and a dinner; the feast taking place in a gallery affording a view of the stage and play (the guests being the arbitrators, the two litigants, and select friends), while the court is free to the public'. MacGowan, 'Chinese Guilds', p. 184.

[2] Burgess, *The Guilds of Peking*, p. 171.

[3] In the late 1920s, Burgess found nine guilds which arranged for public cemeteries for members. Other charitable work provided included funeral expenses (nine guilds) and medical help (seven guilds). Poor relief was also given by five guilds for the public. Ibid., p. 173.

[4] *PCLYCS*, pp. 1a–2a.   [5] *PCLYCS*, pp. 5b–7a.

Another function to which much space is given on the steles was the repair of the main actors' temple. The stele of 1785 records that, at the instigation of Peking's Li-yüan hui-kuan, the capital's companies and *hsi-yüan* contributed money towards the restoration of the Hsi-shen Tsu-shih Temple. In the following years, further repairs were made: some of the buildings were repainted and the images of the gods reclothed. The process of maintenance was a constant one. In the second decade of the nineteenth century several halls, including that dedicated especially to Hsi-shen, were refurbished and repainted. But the crowning achievement was probably the overhaul of the temple stage in 1816. The decision to take this action was made by the guild leadership under Kao Yüeh-kuan, and money for it was donated by all the public companies and *hsi-yüan* of the capital, whether large or small.[1]

It is interesting that the theatres should have given money for the upkeep of the actors' temples and its stage. It shows that the managers of the *hsi-yüan* took an interest in the activities of the guild, and implies a close relationship between the managers of the theatres and the leaders of the Li-yüan hui-kuan.

I have so far mentioned only the main actors' *hui-kuan* in Peking, but there were certainly others. The Ch'un-t'ai company, for instance, ran its own. Its members probably belonged also to the main guild and could be active in both at once: Yin Pien-chih is listed not only as a leader of the Li-yüan hui-kuan but also as a member of the Ch'un-t'ai company guild.[2] Other companies no doubt copied this famous troupe too. The novel quoted earlier mentions that there were several actors' guilds in Nanking;[3] this seems to allow the conclusion that a great theatrical city was provided with more than two *hui-kuan* for stage-artists. Yang Mou-chien records that 'in the cities of Kwangtung province the actors' guilds are commonly called Lao-lang Temple',[4] and this implies that *hui-kuan* for performers of the theatre were found in all urban centres, not merely the big and important ones.[5]

[1] *PCLYCS*, pp. 2b–5b.
[2] Many of the members of the Ch'un-t'ai guild are listed *PCLYCS*, pp. 8b–9a.
[3] *Ju-lin wai-shih*, 24, 244; and the translation by Yang Hsien-yi and Gladys Yang, *The Scholars*, p. 343.
[4] *MHSP*, p. 27b.
[5] This was true also of all kinds of *hui-kuan*, including those open to people by region rather than profession or trade. According to Ho Ping-ti (*Hui-kuan shih-lun*, pp. 67 ff.), there was an unusually high concentration of *hui-kuan* in central and upper Yangtze provinces, such as Kiangsi, Hunan, Hupeh, and Szechwan.

But the main conclusion to be drawn from Yang's statement is that the guilds of actors invariably shared with those of other trades and professions a primarily socio-religious bent. These were units which encouraged group spirit among the personnel of the theatre and could give them a certain pride in their professional activities.

The ability of the actors' guild to carry out extensive renovations on the Hsi-shen Tsu-shih Temple and to establish cemeteries shows that it could collect substantial sums of money, and this implies a reasonable degree of cohesion and organization. As a collective social force, actors were by no means inconsiderable. Although they continued to be a generally despised class in society, there was a growing feeling among them that they constituted a profession which the community as a whole could not ignore.

At the same time, the *hsi-yüan* and other theatres came to occupy an increasingly important place in the life of the Peking populace. Although they were not new at the time of Wei Ch'ang-sheng, their number and the size of their audiences grew substantially after that time and they offered the people ideal places to relax and enjoy themselves.

The growth of professionalism among actors and the rise in importance of the theatre as a social phenomenon can be partly explained by the success of the Peking Opera as an art. But this statement can also be reversed. That is to say that the growth in popularity of the Peking Opera was the direct result of the increasing cohesion of the acting profession and the expanding social significance of the theatres. There developed, in fact, a vicious circle. The arrival of Wei Ch'ang-sheng and his followers produced a favourable impact on the popularity of the drama in Peking. This led to the development of certain social tendencies which, in turn, intensified still further the influence on the people of the Peking Opera.

It is ironic that the very inferiority of the social status of actors was a factor in the rise of the Peking Opera. At the time of its growth, the more aristocratic arts, like literature and painting, were becoming increasingly stereotyped; and their decline was accentuated by the conformity demanded in the official examinations. By virtue of their position as social outcasts, the acting profession escaped the deadening effect of such social pressures.

Their menial position thus left them greater freedom, in a negative sense, to develop higher standards of theatrical entertainment. And where standards are high, popularity will grow.

Successive governments recognized that the influence of the drama in Peking was expanding and saw also that this development was of great social significance. The Manchu emperors welcomed the new art which some of them were glad to patronize and enjoy. At the same time, they were concerned that its developing force should be used as a bulwark of the society they ruled, and took measures to ensure that the theatre was not turned against them or the moral standards they upheld.

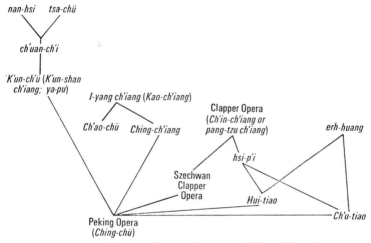

10. Diagram Showing the Development of the Peking Opera

If the social factors mentioned above help account for the rise and development of the Peking Opera, the limited success of the Manchu emperors in enforcing their prohibitions testifies to the extent of its popularity. The great love of the people for the new style of drama was to be the best guarantor of its durability, and it was much less affected than most of the other major regional styles by the civil wars, economic disruption, and general turmoil which was to be China's lot in the century or so which followed the Opium War. Even after Peking was demoted from its position as national capital, it remained the most important centre for the traditional Chinese drama. This was mainly because the social background which encouraged it was stronger in

Peking than elsewhere and consequently more difficult to destroy. It was not until the War against Japan (1937–45) and the triumph of the Communists in 1949 that radical social transformation necessitated a new community basis on which the Peking Opera could flourish.

APPENDIX A
REIGN-TITLES OF THE
CH'ING DYNASTY

Shun-chih	1644
K'ang-hsi	1662
Yung-cheng	1723
Ch'ien-lung	1736
Chia-ch'ing	1796
Tao-kuang	1821
Hsien-feng	1851
T'ung-chih	1862
Kuang-hsü	1875
Hsüan-t'ung	1909

APPENDIX B
NOTES ON SOME COLLECTIONS
ABOUT THE THEATRE

THE PURPOSE of this appendix is to provide some background information about those writers and works in book-collections (*ts'ung-shu*) which have been of the greatest use to me in the preparation of this book. This section is not intended as a general discussion of sources on Chinese drama or on the Peking Opera.[1] It is heavily slanted, in accordance with the subject of the book, towards the social aspects of theatre in the Ch'ing, and towards the rise and development of the Peking Opera during the century 1770 to 1870.

The earliest collection of recent times on the drama is the *Tu-ch'ü ts'ung-k'an* (1917) in which Tung K'ang, a well known bibliophile and official of the Republic, brought together eight works of the Yüan, Ming, and Ch'ing. Four years later the *Ch'ü-yüan* was printed, with fourteen books of the Ming and Ch'ing. In 1925 this collection was reprinted, altered and enlarged, under the title *Ch'ung-ting ch'ü-yüan*, for which Ch'en Nai-ch'ien, one of the foremost scholars of the Chinese drama in his time, assembled twenty books on the theatre. The following decades saw the publication of the *Tseng-pu ch'ü-yüan* and the *Hsin ch'ü-yüan* (1940), which contain respectively twenty-six and thirty-five works, almost all of the Yüan, Ming, Ch'ing, and Republic.

The most recent large collection of works on the Chinese drama is the *Chung-kuo ku-tien hsi-ch'ü lun-chu chi-ch'eng*. It was published in 1959–60 and contains in ten volumes forty-seven works ranging in time of writing from the T'ang to the late Ch'ing. Unlike earlier collections of its kind, it is fully punctuated. Furthermore, it includes comments on existing editions and the author or authors of each work. It is by far the most useful of the six collections.

Most of the books in these *ts'ung-shu* treat the drama from a literary, musical, and historical point of view. Although they have very little to say on Peking Opera itself, there is a wealth of valuable material on the origins of the Peking theatre in the Ming and early Ch'ing. The works included in the collections overlap only to a certain extent. For

[1] For a general bibliography of Chinese drama see Lo Chin-t'ang, *Chung-kuo hsi-ch'ü tsung-mu hui-pien*. A much less general work is Daniel Shih-p'êng Yang, *An Annotated Bibliography of Materials for the Study of the Peking Theatre*. This book concentrates almost entirely on recent studies. It includes brief discussion on the volumes it lists.

example, even though *Chung-kuo ku-tien hsi-ch'ü lun-chu chi-ch'eng* contains forty-seven works as against *Hsin ch'ü-yüan's* thirty-five, few books found in the latter appear in the former.[1] On the other hand, most works in *Ch'ung-ting ch'ü-yüan* are also in *Chung-kuo ku-tien hsi-ch'ü lun-chu chi-ch'eng*.

It is impossible and unnecessary in a short appendix of this sort to treat all the works contained within these collections. I therefore restrict discussion to three of particular relevance to the present study. These are, in chronological order of composition, the *Chü-hua*, the *Chü-shuo*, and the *Hua-pu nung-t'an*.

The author of the *Chü-hua* was the famous Szechwanese scholar and bibliophile Li T'iao-yüan (1734–1803). Li enjoyed a distinguished official career, but his success was interrupted in 1782, when a set of the *Ssu-k'u ch'üan-shu* under his care was damaged by rain.[2] Because of his carelessness, Li was sentenced to exile in I-li, but managed to redeem himself through the payment of a fine. He retired in 1784 to his native town and there resided until his death.[3]

Li T'iao-yüan was an extremely prolific writer. He is known both for his prose and his poetry. His *Yü-ts'un ch'ü-hua* deals with the dramatists of the Yüan, Ming, and early Ch'ing and their works, and is included in the *Ch'ü-yüan*, *Ch'ung-ting ch'ü-yüan*, *Tseng-pu ch'ü-yüan*, and *Chung-kuo ku-tien hsi-ch'ü lun-chu chi-ch'eng*. Like most of Li's writings, it is also found in his great *collectanea*, the *Han-hai*.[4]

Li was unusual among eminent scholars of his time in being keen on the popular drama, which was not then considered a respectable form of art. His interest is evident in his *Chü-hua*, where the *hua-pu* is given ample treatment. This work was written about 1775. It is made up of two *chüan*, the first on the systems and styles of drama, the second on the stories of the pieces.

The earliest edition of the work is in the original edition of the *Han-hai*. In the 1882 version of the collection, the *Chü-hua* is included

---

[1] A full list of the works in the six collections can be found in Lo Chin-t'ang, *Chung-kuo hsi-ch'ü*, pp. 230–5, 238–40.

[2] The *Ssu-k'u ch'üan-shu* had been collected between the years 1773 and 1785 under the editorship of Chi Yün (1724–1805) and others. At first, four essentially identical sets were made, each comprising a total of some 36,000 volumes. The first two were completed in 1782 and the second of them was to be housed in the Wen-su ko at Shen-yang. See Hummel, *Eminent Chinese of the Ch'ing Period*, pp. 120–1. It was this set that Li T'iao-yüan, who had been ordered to take it to Shen-yang, allowed to be damaged.

[3] Li T'iao-yüan's biography can be found in ibid., pp. 486–8.

[4] The *Han-hai* was compiled and printed over the years 1778 to 1784. It was re-edited and republished during the Chia-ch'ing and Tao-kuang periods. In 1882 it was published again with a total of 159 titles, about fifty of them by Li T'iao-yüan himself. Ibid., p. 487; *Chung-kuo ku-tien hsi-ch'ü lun-chu chi-ch'eng* (*CKKT*), VIII, 3–4.

as the nineteenth and twentieth *chüan* of the *T'ung-su pien*. The *Chung-kuo ku-tien hsi-ch'ü lun-chu chi-ch'eng* edition follows the original version of the *Han-hai*, but makes a few emendations.[1]

The *Chü-shuo* and *Hua-pu nung-t'an* were written not long after the *Chü-hua*. Both are by Chiao Hsün (1763–1820), a classical scholar from Yang-chou in Kiangsu who lived in or near that city most of his life. Unlike Li T'iao-yüan, Chiao enjoyed no distinction in the government service having failed in the metropolitan examinations in Peking in 1802. He was, however, a life-long friend of the famous official Juan Yüan (1764–1849), who was a relation of his. Chiao devoted much time to mathematics and wrote also on astronomy and other subjects. In 1809 he was commissioned to compile a gazetteer on his native city, the *Yang-chou fu-chih* (1810 edition).[2]

Chiao Hsün begins his *Chü-shuo* by recording how he came to compile the work. In the winter of 1792, he had found an old collection of extracts on the drama in a bookshop. When he was recuperating from an illness in 1805, he felt he lacked the energy to study the Classics or the Histories and decided to edit and alter the collection. The final work contains quotations from 166 books,[3] many of them very rare, and provides invaluable information about actors, tunes, dramas, and authors from the earliest times to the Ch'ing.

The *Chü-shuo* is included in all the six collections so far named, except the *Hsin ch'ü-yüan*. The edition copied in the earliest, Tung K'ang's *Tu-ch'ü ts'ung-k'an*, is unknown but may have been an early copy of Chiao's 1805 version. There survives also a manuscript of the work in the Peking National Library (Pei-ching t'u-shu kuan). It bears Chiao's seal and is probably his original manuscript, but it is not as complete as the *Tu-ch'ü ts'ung-k'an* edition. The later collections follow Tung K'ang's version,[4] but in the *Chung-kuo ku-tien hsi-ch'ü lun-chu chi-ch'eng* some amendments have been made to conform with the manuscript in the Peking Library.[5]

Like Li T'iao-yüan, Chiao Hsün departed from the norm expected of the scholars in his time in being very fond of the regional *hua-pu* theatre. This is made clear in his *Hua-pu nung-t'an*, prefaced in 1819, which gives stories and sometimes critiques and comments on regional pieces the author had seen in or near Yang-chou. Though short, it contains much unique material on the *hua-pu* drama. Chiao's original manuscript is still extant. There is also an early edition of his work in the *Huai-pin tsa-tsu*, which was compiled by Hsü Nai-ch'ang and is prefaced 1910. The text of the two editions is identical and has been followed in the *Chung-kuo ku-tien hsi-ch'ü lun-chu chi-ch'eng*.[6]

[1] *CKKT*, VIII, 65. [2] Hummel, *Eminent Chinese*, pp. 144–5.
[3] Listed in *CKKT*, VIII, 77–80.
[4] *CKKT*, VIII, 76. [5] *CKKT*, VIII, 217. [6] *CKKT*, VIII, 223.

There is a definite slant in the works contained in the collections mentioned so far. Though valuable for background material, these books are little concerned with the primary subject of this work—that is, the rise and development of the Peking Opera during the century 1770 to 1870. For such a study one needs information on the numerous outstanding actors who performed in Peking at that time, on the types of drama in which they played and on the social aspects of their art. The books discussed of up to this point supply little information on these matters. For material of this kind we must turn to another collection, the *Ch'ing-tai Yen-tu li-yüan shih-liao*, and its supplement, the *Ch'ing-tai Yen-tu li-yüan shih-liao hsü-pien*.

The task of gathering together the books of these two collections was undertaken in the twenties and thirties of the present century by Chang Chiang-ts'ai, normally called by his *hao* Tz'u-hsi. He was assisted by friends, notably Fang Wen-hsi, himself an expert on the music of the drama. Wang Chih-chang writes that 'among all the large and small bookshops in Peiping city, and even the bookstalls spread out on the streets, there was not one they failed to follow up, and there was none that did not know them.'[1] The *Ch'ing-tai Yen-tu li-yüan shih-liao* was originally published in Peiping in 1934 and the *hsü-pien* in 1937. Both were republished in Taipei in 1965, photographed from the earlier edition. This time they formed part of a much larger series, the *Chung-kuo shih-hsüeh ts'ung-shu*, compiled under the direction of Wu Hsiang-hsiang.

Chang's collection opens with several prefaces by distinguished experts on Chinese drama. They include the well known *tan* actor Ch'eng Yen-ch'iu and the scholar Wang Chih-chang, known as the author of a definitive work on the Ch'ing court theatre called *Ch'ing Sheng-p'ing shu chih-lüeh*. Both Ch'eng and Wang applaud the fact that a Chinese has for the first time completed a serious study of the late Ch'ing Peking theatre.

There are thirty-eight works in the *Ch'ing-tai Yen-tu li-yüan shih-liao* and thirteen in its supplement. Many of them were rare at the time of the collections' original publication. Almost all the material concerns the period from 1770 onwards, very little space being devoted to the first century of the Ch'ing. It will be worthwhile to discuss the books which have been of the greatest use in the preparation of the present work.

The first book in the collection is the *Yen-lan hsiao-p'u* in five *chüan*. The author's own introductory remarks (*li-yen*) state that it was begun in the summer of 1783 and finished in the autumn of 1785. Except in the fifth *chüan*, it deals only with actors of the period 1774 to 1785.[2]

---

[1] *Ch'ing-tai Yen-tu li-yüan shih-liao* (*CTYT*), Wang Chih-chang's preface, p. 1b.
[2] See *Yen-lan hsiao-p'u* (*YLHP*), 5, 1a and *pien-yen*, pp. 1a–b.

For each there are short notes stating his place of origin and characteristics, and naming the company of which he was a member. A poem or poems dedicated to the actor follow each biography.

The first *chüan* is devoted to one actor, Wang Kuei-kuan (discussed above in chapter four), and contains many poems in his praise. It is followed by two on the actors of the popular theatre, principally the *Ch'in-ch'iang* style. The fourth *chüan* concerns the actors of the more sophisticated *K'un-ch'ü*. In the final one there are additional articles, not only on actors, but on related subjects as well.

The author of *Yen-lan hsiao-p'u* made a practice of mixing in theatregoing circles. It is clear from his introductory notes (*pien-yen*) that he had seen on the stage most of the actors he describes, and also took the trouble to investigate inscriptions about them in Peking's theatres. He was thus in an excellent position to make judgments about them and also to find out about their lives. In the final *chüan* he has based most of his material on information related to him by friends, and on occasion has simply inserted a passage written by someone else.

The *Yen-lan hsiao-p'u* became a constant stand-by for writers on the Peking theatre early in the nineteenth century, and Chang Chi-liang makes frequent references to it in his *Chin-t'ai ts'an-lei chi*. It was still common in the 1830s, but appears to have become rarer in later decades. When Yeh Te-hui (1864–1927)[1] came to compile his famous collection, *Shuang-mei ching-an ts'ung shu*, he wanted to include the *Yen-lan hsiao-p'u*, but found great difficulty in obtaining a copy. He searched Peking on and off for over twenty years from 1886 on and eventually came across a rather tattered copy with many mistakes and unclear places. He learned from this version of an original block-print edition said to be in the handwriting of Yü Chi (1739–1823) from Jen-ho in Hang-chou,[2] whom he assumed to be the author. However, he failed to find a copy of this better edition and the version he eventually included in his collection is taken from the only copy he possessed.[3]

Yeh's view of the authorship of *Yen-lan hsiao-p'u* was strengthened by a passage in a collection of miscellaneous notes on the history of the Ch'ing, especially the Ch'ien-lung and Chia-ch'ing eras, by the Manchu prince Chao-lien (1780–1833):[4] 'Wang Hsiang-yün [i.e. Wang Kuei-kuan] . . . loved to paint black orchids which he did with great delicacy, so the compiler of the Han-lin Academy (*t'ai-shih*) Yü Chi wrote the *Yen-lan hsiao-p'u* for him.'[5]

---

[1] Hummel, *Eminent Chinese*, p. 184.

[2] See Yü's biography, ibid., p. 939.

[3] See Yeh Te-hui's preface (dated 1911) to *YLHP* in *Shuang-mei ching-an ts'ung shu*. [4] Hummel, *Eminent Chinese*, pp. 78–80.

[5] *Hsiao-t'ing tsa-lu*, 8, 8b–9a. It is true that Chao-lien here uses a different character for *yen* (煙 instead of 燕) from the one in the normal title of *YLHP*.

Later on, Chang Tz'u-hsi and Fang Wen-hsi did in fact find a copy of the original edition which Yeh Te-hui had wanted so much to obtain; it bore on it the seal of Wu T'ai-ch'u[1] who is certainly the author. This is confirmed by Yang Mou-chien,[2] and even the copy Yeh Te-hui had found was signed in the author's preface by 'Tai-ch'u', with no surname given.

T'ai-ch'u was the *tzu* of Wu Ch'ang-yüan from Jen-ho in Hang-chou, who enjoyed a modest official career, and in another of his works, the *Ch'en-yüan shih-lüeh*, he gives his place of origin, *ming* and *tzu* at the beginning of each *chüan*. It is of interest, too, that this latter book is devoted entirely to detailed information about the city of Peking. Moreover, it is prefaced by Yü Chi who begins his remarks by re-cording that Wu Ch'ang-yüan lived in the capital for more than ten years. These matters strengthen the claim to reliability of the *Yen-lan hsiao-p'u*, and they also provide a possible explanation for the confusion over its authorship. Yü Chi and Wu Chang-yüan were friends and came from the same place; Yü could easily have written out Wu's text in his own calligraphy, inadvertently leading some people to the belief that he was actually the author.

Less is known about the background of the second work in Chang's collection, namely the *Jih-hsia k'an-hua chi* in four *chüan*, which is similar to *Yen-lan hsiao-p'u* in containing short sections on actors, each followed by a poem in dedication. Its author wrote under a pen-name, Hsiao T'ieh-ti tao-jen, but it is not possible to identify him. The writer's preface is dated 28 October 1803, but the work was later edited and expanded slightly by other men (also pen-named and impossible to identify). According to the epilogue, it was presented to Ch'en Kuei-lin from An-ch'ing, an actor whom Hsiao T'ieh-ti tao-jen especially admired. The *Jih-hsia k'an-hua chi* was apparently extremely rare before Chang Tz'u-hsi incorporated it into his collection. Aoki Masaru makes no mention of it in his great work on the Chinese theatre, *Shina kinsei gikyoko shi*, published in Kyoto in 1930 and later translated into Chinese under the title *Chung-kuo chin-shih hsi-ch'ü shih*.

Another work of great importance is the *T'ing-ch'un hsin-yung*, written in 1810. It was known to Aoki but he notes that it was rare.[3] The author wrote under the pseudonym Liu-ch'un ko hsiao-shih, but none of his other names is recorded. According to the introductory

___

However, in the table of contents (p. 5b) the character is given correctly and there is no doubt that Chao-lien is referring to the same work, especially in view of his mention of Wang Hsiang-yün.

[1] *CTYT*, Wang Chih-chang's preface, p. 1b.
[2] *Hsin-jen kuei-chia lu (HJKCL)*, p. 2b.
[3] Aoki Masaru, *Chung-kuo chin-shih hsi-ch'ü shih*, pp. 709, 736.

notes of Fang-ts'ao tz'u-jen, the writer lived in Peking for more than ten years and knew personally more than half of those actors he discusses in his book. He was consequently well qualified to write about the Peking theatre and its artists. The form of the book is similar to that of *Yen-lan hsiao-p'u*. None of the poems on the actors is by Liu-ch'un ko hsiao-shih himself, but the poets do include Fang-ts'ao tz'u-jen and Hsiao Nan-yün chu-jen, both of whom contributed introductory notes to the book. The latter also helped edit and correct the text.

There are three main sections in the *T'ing-ch'un hsin-yung*. The first deals with the actors of the Anhwei companies and the second with those of the *Ch'in-ch'iang* troupes. The third is more general and contains notes on actors of all important styles heard in Peking. By and large, the most famous artists are reserved for the last section.

The next significant work in *Ch'ing-tai Yen-tu li-yüan shih-liao* is the *Chin-t'ai ts'an-lei chi* in three *chüan*, which is contained also in the second collection (*chi*) of the *Ch'ing-jen shuo-hui* (1928). The preface of the author, Chang Chi-liang, is dated 12 January 1829.

Chang's *tzu* was Heng-fu and he wrote under the name of Hua-hsü ta-fu. He was born in 1799 in Chien-ning, Fukien province, and in 1824 sat for the local examinations, coming first. The following year he went to Peking, but his prospects for an official career were there ruined by a clash with the salt commissioner (*ts'o-shih*) Tseng Pin-ku. Tseng held a drinking party to honour Chang, who was now famous in Peking as a poet. Everybody flattered the young guest, but he made no attempt to disguise his contempt for this behaviour. Tseng was eating melon-seeds, some of which had attached themselves to his beard. Somebody plucked the seeds off and Chang burst into laughter. He even wrote a note the following day upbraiding Tseng for his bad manners. The official never forgave the young scholar for this insult, and did his best to undermine Chang's reputation with all the important people of the city. He had some success in his attempt and Chang got the reputation for being mad. It was at about this time that he wrote the *Chin-t'ai ts'an-lei chi*. The style of the work was admired in many circles, but owing to the jealousy of some influential people at court, its author remained poor and was not accepted among the literary pundits of the capital, which Chang soon decided to leave. In 1843 he fell ill. At that time he heard that a friend of his, Yao Shih-fu, had spoken in defence of the British, who had recently defeated China in the First Opium War, and been arrested. In order to help him, Chang made another trip to the capital, but on the way he fell sick again and died in Peking on 30 November.[1]

The *Chin-t'ai ts'an-lei chi* is more comprehensive in its scope than the

---

[1] *CTYT, chu-che shih-lüeh*, pp. 1b–2a.

other works from Chang Tz'u-hsi's collection mentioned so far. It gives not only the biographies of twenty-one important actors (first *chüan*), and many poems on stage personnel (second *chüan*), but also other valuable material, especially on the social background of the theatre (third *chüan*). For example, it provides information on the kinds of theatre in nineteenth-century Peking and on the customs which surrounded them. The author's credibility is strengthened by the fact that he was on very intimate terms with some of the actors he describes, and much of his information on other matters is drawn from personal experience.

Possibly the most important author represented in the *Ch'ing-tai Yen-tu li-yüan shih-liao* is Yang Mou-chien, born in about 1805. His *tzu* was Chang-sheng and he wrote under the pseudonym of Jui-chu chiu-shih. He came from Mei-hsien in Kwangtung and may, like most of that county's people, have been a Hakka. He was fairly broad in his interests and studied a variety of subjects, including mathematics and music. In 1831 he passed the *chü-jen* examinations and went the following year to Peking where he took up a post in the Imperial Academy (Kuo-tzu chien). In 1833 he sat for the annual spring examinations for the *chin-shih* degree (*ch'un-wei*) held in Peking. However, the chief examiner Juan Yüan, who had earlier been his teacher, disliked his papers and he failed. Bitterly disappointed, he turned to profligacy and spent more and more of his time in immoral dealings with actors. In October 1837 he was arrested owing to irregularities in the examinations and imprisoned for several months, after which he was exiled to Hunan. He eventually returned to Kwangtung where he lived in semi-retirement, teaching, until his death.[1]

Yang Mou-chien wrote four books on actors: *Hsin-jen kuei-chia lu*, *Ch'ang-an k'an-hua chi*, *Ting-nien yü-sun chih*, and *Ti-ch'eng hua-yang*. The first three of these are included in *Ch'ing-tai Yen-tu li-yüan shih-liao*, but the fourth is lacking there. This work consists of sample biographies included also in the first three books and it adds very little to them. It is contained in the second *chüan* of the fifteenth collection of the *Hsiang-yen ts'ung-shu* (1910).

As its name implies,[2] the *Hsin-jen kuei-chia lu* refers to the years 1831–4 and was begun in those years. The first draft was finished in 1837,[3] but Yang Mou-chien afterwards added to the book and one section is dated 1842.[4] The *Ch'ang-an k'an-hua chi* was also written in stages and in Chang's collection the author's introduction is dated September

---

[1] *CTYT, chu-che shih-lüeh*, pp. 2a–b; see also *HJKCL*, pp. 1a, 2b; *Ting-nien yü-sun chih*, p. 1a, and *Meng-hua so-pu* (*MHSP*), pp. 30b, 32a.

[2] The years *hsin-mao, jen-ch'en, kuei-ssu*, and *chia-wu* correspond to 1831, 1832, 1833, and 1834.

[3] *Ti-ch'eng hua-yang*, p. 2a.   [4] *HJKCL*, p. 8a.

1837, that is, just before his arrest. This work, too, was enlarged and amended later on. The *Ting-nien yü-sun chih* deals mainly with the year 1837, but is prefaced 13 April 1842 by the author, and most of it appears to have been written after Yang's departure from Peking. These three works contain one *chüan* each.

Yang Mou-chien wrote one further work, the *Meng-hua so-pu*, which is dated 4 May 1842 at its conclusion. It also consists of only one *chüan*, but is somewhat longer than the three books just considered and much broader in scope. It contains an enormous amount of information on Peking's theatres, acting companies and artists, and is incomparably the most important work of the period for any study of the social background of the theatre.[1]

Yang Mou-chien's works are written in a discursive and varied style. The author is frequently sentimental, recalling the happy lost days he spent in Peking, but he can also be light-hearted. He repeats anecdotes and rumours freely, though fortunately he usually warns the reader when his information is unreliable. It is clear from the way he writes that he bases his material on personal observations, intimate friendships with actors, and informal chats with long-standing theatre-goers. In particular, he was on very close terms with a man called Ch'en Hsiang-chou, who was an avid enthusiast of the drama. Ch'en was somewhat older than Yang and had lived in Peking for some thirty years at the time of his association with Yang in the 1830s.[2] He was therefore able to tell the younger man a good deal about the theatre of earlier decades.

Yang's four main books are included as separate works in the second collection of the *Ch'ing-jen shuo-hui*, but appear together in an edition of 1886 and in the seventh collection of the *Pi-chi hsiao-shuo ta-kuan* (published under the Republic) as the four chapters of the *Ching-ch'en tsa-lu*. In contrast to the *Ch'ing-tai Yen-tu li-yüan shih-liao* edition, the last mentioned is provided with some punctuation marks.

In a postface included in the 1886 and *Pi-chi hsiao-shuo ta-kuan* editions, a certain Ni Hung from Kuei-lin claims that Yang's four chapters remained in his possession for more than thirty years and were first printed in 1886. The preface of the 1886 edition was written by the manager of the T'ung-wen shu-chü in Shanghai, where the *Ching-ch'en tsa-lu* was published. Yang Mou-chien never saw the four books, and Ni Hung describes him as a 'deceased friend'. However, it appears that the *Ti-ch'eng hua-yang* was published during Yang's life-time.[3]

The works in *Ch'ing-tai Yen-tu li-yüan shih-liao* considered up to this

---

[1] In the *Hsin ch'ü-yüan* there is a work entitled *Ching-ch'en chü-lu*. It begins with one section drawn from *Ch'ang-an k'an-hua chi* and one from *T'ing-nien yü-sun chih*, but is otherwise a heavily abbreviated version of *MHSP*.

[2] *MHSP*, p. 1a.

[3] See *CTYT, chu-che shih-lüeh*, p. 2b.

point all concern *tan* actors. Many of the later works in the collection deal also with the careers of the *lao-sheng* who came increasingly to dominate the Peking stage in the latter half of the nineteenth century. Two of these books are of particular importance for the earliest generation of famous *lao-sheng*: the *Li-yüan chiu-hua* and the *Chiu-chü ts'ung-t'an*, each in one *chüan*.

The first of them is by Wu Tao, who wrote under the pen-name Chüan-yu i-sou. He was born in Yün-nan prefecture (K'un-ming). Early in life he moved to Shantung and in 1870 went to Peking for the examinations. In 1876 he became a *chin-shih* graduate and was given office. He had always been keen on the theatre, but in his early days in the capital had lived in the Inner City under the charge of his tutor, who forbade him such low-brow pleasures. After taking office he happened to hear a performance by Ch'eng Chang-keng and Hsü Hsiao-hsiang. He was deeply impressed and determined to make a thorough study of the theatre. He would go to a performance every second day and shared his enthusiasm and impressions with a fellow official Sun Ch'un-shan,[1] who himself took up acting as an amateur.[2] In his *Li-yüan chiu-hua*, Wu Tao makes critiques of major actors and gives brief biographical notes. In addition, he records many anecdotes about performers and the theatre, sometimes providing some insight into the personality of a particular artist.

The *Chiu-chü ts'ung-t'an* is a similar kind of work. It was written by Ch'en Yen-heng, a Szechwanese who lived much of his life in Peking. Ch'en was an active musician; he learned to sing and was also an exremely good *hu-ch'in* player, having been taught this art by Mei Lan-fang's uncle, Mei Yü-t'ien, who was famous for his ability on the instrument.[3] Ch'en was on good terms with the great *lao-sheng* T'an Hsin-p'ei, whose dramas owed much to his assistance. He was well versed in all aspects of the theatre and is the author of several books about it.[4] His is the only work I have considered here which was written under the Republic.

Three other works in Chang Tz'u-hsi's collection deserve special mention. They are the *Pei-ching li-yüan chang-ku ch'ang-pien*, the *Pei-ching li-yüan chin-shih wen-tzu lu*, and the *Pei-p'ing li-yüan chu-chih tz'u hui-pien*, all three edited by Chang Tz'u-hsi himself. The first consists of passages on the theatre collected from earlier works, many of them very rare. Chang has assembled a number of fascinating stories about the personal lives of actors, especially Ch'en Yin-kuan, government edicts concerning the theatre, some literature relevant to the drama *Ch'ang-sheng tien*, and other material as well. The second contains the

[1] *CTYT, chu-che shih-lüeh*, pp. 4a–b; *Li-yüan chiu-hua*, p. 1a.
[2] See Mei Lan-fang, *Wu-t'ai sheng-huo ssu-shih nien*, I, 99.
[3] Ibid., I, 6–7. [4] *CTYT, chu-che shih-lüeh*, p. 4b.

texts of important theatrical steles which Chang and his friends found in Peking. Wang Chih-chang records that Chang, Fang Wen-hsi, and he himself had spent much time searching in places such as T'ao-jan t'ing and the Ching-chung Temple for inscribed steles about the Ch'ing theatre. They found a good deal of valuable epigraphical material, and this was then printed together in a single work.[1] The third book is actually in the supplement to Chang's collection, *Ch'ing-tai Yen-tu li-yüan shih-liao hsü-pien*. It is made up of extracts on the theatre from lyric poems on Peking, ranging in period of composition from 1809 to Chang's own time.

The books discussed in this appendix are but a portion of those contained in the collections about the theatre I have named. There are also a number of works in them on which I have drawn for my information but not considered here. These include *Yen-t'ai hung-chao chi* and Ch'en Tan-jan's *I-ling chuan* which, for my purposes, have been of only secondary importance. Finally, some of the most valuable sources for the present work, such as Li Tou's *Yang-chou hua-fang lu*, remain outside the scope of this appendix simply because they are not included in collections devoted to the theatre. Yet certain general remarks can be made about the pre-1911 sources I have used, and they would not require radical alteration even had the foregoing treatment been much more complete and less selective.

One particularly important feature of the works I have mentioned is that the majority are primary sources in the strictest sense of the word. Most of the authors were writing about matters of which they had first-hand knowledge. With the major exception of Chiao Hsün in his *Chü-shuo*, they were not discussing events which had taken place centuries before and which they themselves knew only through other books. The authors writing on Peking fall into two categories: those, like Chang Chi-liang and Yang Mou-chien, whose interests lay mainly in actors as people, and those, such as Wu Tao and Ch'en Yen-heng, whose enthusiasm was reserved more for the drama itself than for the persons of its exponents. Yet all are of the highest value in their own way, and even though it is as well to remember their limitations, all drew their comments and information from personal experience.

It is true that not a single one of the authors on Peking was a native of the city; they came from a variety of provinces, Wu Ch'ang-yüan from Chekiang, Chang Chi-liang from Fukien, Yang Mou-chien from Kwangtung, Wu Tao from Yunnan, and Ch'en Yen-heng from Szechwan. Yet all lived in Peking for long periods of time and had a deep feeling for the city. Possibly their observations were more acute in some ways because they were outsiders, since the man born and

---

[1] *CTYT*, Wang Chih-chang's preface, pp. 3a–b.

brought up in a city frequently becomes so used to its customs that he ceases to notice them. Certainly all the authors I have mentioned seem to have been endowed with keen powers of observation, and to have been enthusiastic about recording what they saw and heard.

Few of the writers dealt with above enjoyed successful official careers. Some are known to have failed in the metropolitan examinations and to have seen their prospects in the civil service destroyed as a result. In a way, this helps to guarantee that the sources are reliable, for unlike the successful official, who was under social pressure to eschew the *hua-pu* drama, the failed scholar could establish close contacts with constant theatre-goers, actors, and the ordinary theatres. Furthermore, the unsuccessful scholar would probably have more sympathy for a popular art like Peking Opera. Thus, the incident of the melon-seeds marks Chang Chi-liang out as a rebel against stereotyped conventions, the kind of person who might deliberately develop a love for a form of art which the respectable man professed to despise. On the other hand, there is often something of the dilettante in such people, and some of the sources lack the hallmarks of serious scholarship. For this reason care is required in accepting remarks on highly technical details by people such as Chang and Yang Mou-chien. Fortunately the bitterness often found in the unsuccessful man is not obvious in the works of these two authors, and does not seem to have clouded their judgment, at least where the theatre was concerned.

Finally, as the reader will have noticed, the history of most of the texts can be established with considerable clarity. This is not surprising, since the majority were written less than two centuries ago and Ch'en Yen-heng's as late as the 1930s, but it is nevertheless important that texts should be known to be based on reliable editions.

The primary sources do not enable us to form a complete picture of Peking's theatre between 1770 and the T'ung-chih Restoration. For example, there is little material on the economics or administration of the popular theatre. Yet there is enough to obtain some idea of how the Peking Opera developed, what the theatrical world was like in those days, and how it functioned in society. These are the questions I have tried to answer in the present work.

APPENDIX C
THE DRAMAS

FOR CENTURIES there was a definite prejudice among Chinese scholars against *hua-pu* dramas, which were considered too vulgar to be taken seriously as music or literature. For this reason scholars rarely deigned to compose, let alone publish, texts for the popular theatre. Dramas which flowed from the brushes of educated men were almost exclusively *tsa-chü* or *K'un-ch'ü*.

Actors, too, refrained from publishing the texts of dramatic pieces. Very often a role in a scene became regarded as the special property of one or several actors, and these men guarded the secrets of that part with some jealousy. They were frequently reluctant to show the texts or music of their special roles to any other person. Although actors were usually glad to pass on particular points of acting or dramas of their own to their disciples, instances can be found in which old actors burned the texts and music of their special roles to prevent their being handed down to posterity. In any case actors had no desire to see the secrets of their art made public.[1]

It is therefore not surprising that the surviving body of *hua-pu* dramas written in the Ming or Ch'ing is so very small. The most famous collection of the Ch'ing period to include popular theatrical pieces is the *Chui pai-ch'iu*, prefaced 1770. Of its twelve collections, the sixth and eleventh include a variety of *hua-pu* scenes, some of which are *Kao-ch'iang* or *Ch'in-ch'iang* items.

Early texts of Peking operas are also rare. Indeed, for the period up to the end of the Hsien-feng reign, there are only two known published works which are devoted to the texts of Peking operas. The first of these is the *Chi-lo shih-chieh* by an author pen-named Kuan-chü tao-jen, that is 'the Taoist who Watches Drama'. It is prefaced 1840 by its author and contains the texts of eighty-two scenes. The other is the *Shu-chi t'ang chin-yüeh* by Yü Chih from Wu-hsi in Kiangsu and contains twenty-eight dramatic pieces. The author's preface is dated the first lunar month of 1860. In the history of the Peking Opera this work is not important. It appears that Yü Chih's dramas never became popular and only one of the scenes in the *Shu-chi t'ang chin-yüeh* has held the stage until recent times.[2]

---

[1] See Chou Chih-fu, *Chin pai-nien ti Ching-chü*, p. 48.

[2] This is the *Chu-sha chih* (*The Red Birth-mark*), for the text of which see also Wang Ta-ts'o, *Hsi-k'ao*, I. (In references to this work I have not given page-

It was not until the Republic that an attempt was made to collect the texts of Peking operas into one work. The *Hsi-k'ao*, edited by Wang Ta-ts'o, contains some 500 scenes, both *Ch'in-ch'iang* and *p'i-huang*, and was published in Shanghai in 1918–19. Through this work we can obtain some idea of the tunes and words used in the dramas of earlier times.[1]

Despite the paucity of surviving literature of the *hua-pu* theatre, it is to some extent possible to find out which pieces were performed in Peking after the arrival of Wei Ch'ang-sheng. Works like the *Yen-lan hsiao-p'u*, *Jih-hsia k'an-hua chi*, and *T'ing-ch'un hsin-yung* give the names of a large number of plays and record which actors excelled in performing them. In this regard the *T'ing-ch'un hsin-yung* is especially useful, since its author took considerable care to report the scenes that had made each actor famous. Furthermore, the names of 272 pieces performed by the Ch'ing Sheng-p'ing company survives from 1824, and the various editions of the *Tu-men chi-lüeh* name the roles and scenes in which actors were famous.

Not only is it possible to establish the range of dramas performed in Peking, but in most cases the stories of the pieces are known. There are two main reasons for this. In the first place, most dramas held the stage for a long time and survived down to the present century. Although the texts and music may have undergone some development, it is unlikely that the stories changed significantly. Secondly, apart from small-scale folk dramas, items given in the theatres of Peking were based on earlier *tsa-chü*, *K'un-ch'ü*, or novels. Stories from famous early works like *The Romance of the Three Kingdoms* and *The Water Margin* had for centuries been popular among story-tellers and actors. Most current Peking operas based on these books are essentially the same in their plot as the relevant section of the novel, and it is probable that eighteenth- and nineteenth-century actors also followed the original story rather closely.

My purpose in this appendix is to examine briefly a cross-section of the theatrical pieces mentioned in the present work. My intention is to show the origin of each piece, to record which actors of the period 1770 to 1870 were famous in it and to relate its story. However, I have made no attempt at literary analysis.

(1) *Ch'ing-feng t'ing* (*The Ch'ing-feng Pavilion*): One scene, *Kan-tzu*

---

numbers because the pagination starts afresh at the beginning of each drama.) Details about the *Chu-sha chih*, including the plot, may be found in T'ao Chün-ch'i, *Ching-chü chü-mu ch'u-t'an*, p, 288, and cf. also Cecilia Zung, *Secrets of the Chinese Drama*, p. 253.

[1] Samples of more recent collections can be found in Lo Chin-t'ang, *Chung-kuo hsi-ch'ü tsung-mu hui-pien*, pp. 222–30, Daniel Shih-p'êng Yang, *An Annotated Bibliography of Materials for the Study of the Peking Theatre*, pp. 31–56.

(*Pursuing a Son*), of this piece is contained in the eleventh collection of the *Chui pai-ch'iu*,[1] so that at least part of the drama was popular during the Ch'ien-lung period. The story of the whole piece is summarized by Chiao Hsün in the *Hua-pu nung-t'an*. Since that work refers to the Yang-chou area in the eighteenth and nineteenth centuries, it is clear that *Ch'ing-feng t'ing* was popular in the region of that time. It is not, however, mentioned in early theatrical works relating to Peking in the Tao-kuang or earlier periods.

According to Chiao Hsün, the story is based on the tenth-century work *Pei-meng so-yen*,[2] which is historical. This drama consequently has a foundation in reality. There is a Ming *ch'uan-ch'i* called *Ho-ch'ai chi* (*The Story of the United Clasp*) or *Ch'ing-feng t'ing*, which is prefaced 1602 and was written by Ch'in Ming-lei. Its story is, apart from the end, similar to that described in the *Hua-pu nung-t'an*.[3]

Chiao Hsün writes enthusiastically of the *Ch'ing-feng t'ing*, which, as he knew it, was a *hua-pu* item. He tells us that in his youth he went to see the village drama with his father. It happened that *Ch'ing-feng t'ing* was performed. Only the day before, *K'un-ch'ü* had been given and received with little enthusiasm by the audience. Chiao writes that when the actors came on the stage for *Ch'ing-feng t'ing*, 'Everybody clenched his teeth in anger, but later they were all very happy. When the cymbals and drums stopped, everyone looked at each other quietly . . . When they went home, they talked about it for more than ten days. Somebody said that *hua-pu* was not as good as *K'un-ch'ü*, but that is the view of a low person.'[4]

Chiao Hsün describes the story of *Ch'ing-feng t'ing* as follows. The concubine of a minister bears a son, Jen-kuei, but because of the first wife's jealousy, the child is sent away and brought up by a retired scholar, Chang, and his wife. Being extremely poor, Chang and his wife grind soy-beans for *tou-fu* and weave in order to earn enough money to educate the boy. Meanwhile, Jen-kuei's real mother sinks more and more into misery, and some years later leaves home in search of her son. The two meet and go together to the capital, where Jen-kuei does well in the examinations and is given office.

After her adopted son's departure, Chang's old wife is so upset that she falls ill. Her husband takes her to the Ch'ing-feng Pavilion to await the return of Jen-kuei, although both are about seventy years old. The young man happens to pass by the pavilion on business and rests there. The two old people recognize him, come forward and tell him of their sad state. They ask him to accept them as servants, but he refuses and instead offers them money. The old woman throws it back

---

[1] *Chui pai-ch'iu*, XI, 2, 73–82.   [2] *Hua-pu nung-t'an*, p. 227.
[3] See below, p. 249, note 1.   [4] *Hua-pu nung-t'an*, p. 229.

in his face, dashes herself against the pavilion and dies. Chang, following her example, commits suicide. Suddenly the pavilion is struck by thunder, and the ungrateful son is killed.[1]

The historical facts as recorded in the *Pei-men so-yen* can be stated thus. The high-ranking official Chang Hsi of the T'ang had several sons by his main wife and one, Jen-kuei, by a prostitute. Because of the jealousy of his first wife, Hsi did not dare to accept the child into his own household and sent him to be brought up by a retired scholar, who was also named Chang. The boy grew up and received a good education. Somebody told him that the scholar was not his real father and that the latter held a high rank at court. Jen-kuei stole a letter which his father had written to the scholar and then left for the capital. Hsi, however, was already dead, so Jen-kuei went to find his family. Chang Hsi's first wife acknowledged him as her husband's son and he was accepted into his father's house. He went for the *chin-shih* examinations, passed and was given office. Later, however, he committed suicide under unknown circumstances. The scholar, Chang, bitterly disappointed at Jen-kuei's departure, had meanwhile died.[2]

Dramas Especially Popular with Tan Actors

(2) *Mai yen-chih (Selling Cosmetics)*; This piece is sometimes called simply *Yen-chih* and is contained in the *Chui pai-ch'iu*, where it is shown as a Clapper piece.[3] The story comes from a Yüan *tsa-chü, Liu-hsieh chi (Leaving Shoes).*[4] There is a Ming drama on a similar subject, called *Yen-chih chi,*[5] but it is not mentioned in the *Ch'ü-hai tsung-mu t'i-yao* and cannot have been well known in the 1780s. Cheng San-kuan of the Pao-ho (military) company could perform in *Mai yen-chih* and also other scenes based on the *Liu-hsieh chi.*[6] Actors of the early nineteenth century known to have performed in *Mai yen-chih* include Chang Hsiao-ts'ai-lin of the Ssu-hsi company, Hsü Shuang-pao of the Ta Shun-ning, Ch'ang Hsiu-kuan of the Shuang-ho, and Wu Pien-lin of

[1] Ibid., pp. 227–8. In the *Ho-ch'ai chi* the names of the leading characters have been changed. In the end, Jen-kuei (renamed Wang Pao-erh) is happily reunited with his parents while his father's first wife commits suicide. His adopted parents are richly rewarded. See *Ch'ü-hai tsung-mu t'i-yao,* 9, 426–8.

[2] *Pei-meng so-yen,* 8, 68.   [3] *Chui pai-ch'iu,* VI, 1, 23–9.

[4] On the *Liu-hsieh chi* see Lo Chin-t'ang, *Hsien-ts'un Yüan-jen tsa-chü pen-shih k'ao,* pp. 319–21. There was also a Yüan *nan-hsi* which was similar in content to the *tsa-chü.* It was called *Wang Yüeh-ying yüeh-hsia liu-hsieh (Wang Yüeh-ying leaves Shoes Beneath the Moon),* and is mentioned by Hsü Wei in his *Nan-tz'u hsü-lu* (p. 251). The work is now lost but short extracts have been found by Ch'ien Nan-yang quoted in other sources. See *Sung-Yüan hsi-wen chi-i,* pp. 11–12. For further bibliography on surviving sections of Sung and Yüan *nan-hsi* see Lo Chin-t'ang, *Chung-kuo hsi-ch'ü,* pp. 169–73.

[5] See Aoki Masura, *Chung-kuo chin-shih hsi-ch'ü shih,* pp. 481–2.

[6] *Yen-lan hsiao-p'u* (YLHP), 2, 4a.

the Ta Shun-ning (1810).[1] It was still performed in the Tao-kuang period, for Wang Hsiao-t'ien-hsi of the Ch'un-t'ai company gained his reputation in it[2] and I remarked in chapter seven that Yang Mou-chien attended a performance of the piece in the Kuang-te lou. Li Yü-shou of the Ch'un-t'ai company is reported to have performed the role of Wang Yüeh-ying in this piece during the 1870s.[3]

The story of *Mai yen-chih* goes as follows. The beautiful Wang Yüeh-ying sells cosmetics in Ch'ang-an (Hsi-an). She is thinking of a handsome young scholar from Lo-yang called Kuo Hua who has come into her shop to talk to her on the pretext of buying cosmetics. Her mother has seen the two talking together and reprimanded them. They have, however, fallen in love. Kuo Hua enters and the two make merry for some time.[4] In the original *Liu-hsieh chi* they later marry after many vicissitudes.

(3) *Mai po-po* (*Selling Cakes*): Li Tou considered this little piece to be among the best of the *Ching-ch'iang* dramas.[5] Wang Kuei-kuan of the Ts'ui-ch'ing company is mentioned as acting in the drama,[6] so that it must have been adapted as a *Ch'in-ch'iang* piece by the 1780s. It was later taken over by the Anhwei companies. The young actor Tsung Ch'üan-hsi of the Ho-ch'un company performed in it (1810),[7] and the famous *ch'ou* Liu Kan-san of the Ssu-hsi is reported to have sung the part of Wei Hu in 1864.[8] A work of 1873 lists eight actors who played the role of Wang San-chieh.[9]

Mai po-po is a comic scene in a longer drama *Pao lien-teng* (*The Precious Lotus-Lamp*) which concerns Ch'en-hsiang, born of the union between a scholar and an immortal. Ch'en-hsiang kills the son of his teacher and escapes. His mother is imprisoned beneath the sacred mountain Hua-shan in Shensi for her relations with a mortal, but is eventually saved by Ch'en-hsiang.[10] The earliest known drama on this theme is now lost. It is *Ch'en-hsiang t'ai-tzu p'i Hua-shan* (*Ch'en-hsiang Rends Hua-shan Open*) by Chang Shih-ch'i of the Yüan.[11]

---

[1] *T'ing-ch'un hsin-yung* (*TCHY*), *Hui-pu*, p. 12a; *hsi-pu*, pp. 1a, 5b, 7a.

[2] *Ch'ang-an k'an-hua chi* (*CAKHC*), pp. 20a–b.

[3] *Chü-pu ch'ün-ying* (*CPCY*), p. 21b.

[4] *Chui pai-ch'iu*, VI, 1, 23–9. Cf. Wang Ta-ts'o, *Hsi-k'ao*, XXVIII. The text is given slightly differently in these two works.

[5] *Yang-chou hua-fang lu* (*YCHFL*), 5, 131.

[6] *YLHP*, 2, 2a–b.   [7] *TCHY*, *Hui-pu*, pp. 18b–19a.

[8] See Chou Chih-fu, *Tu-men chi-lüeh chung chih hsi-ch'ü shih-liao*, p. 34.

[9] *CPCY*, pp. 2a, 10b, 13a, 15a, 17a, 26b, 27a.

[10] See the story of the Peking opera *Pao lien-teng* summarized in T'ao Chün-ch'i, *Ching-chü chü-mu*, pp. 295–6. A translation into English of the piece may be found with comments in Arlington and Acton, *Famous Chinese Plays*, pp. 324–32.

[11] This drama is mentioned in *Lu-kuei pu*, I, 113. However it is not listed among the complete surviving *tsa-chü* of the Yüan in Lo Chin-t'ang, *Hsien-ts'un Yüan-jen*. Further bibliography on extant Yüan *tsa-chü* can be found in Lo Chin-t'ang,

After Ch'en-hsiang kills his teacher's son, his tutor Wei Hu is exiled to Kwangtung and is accompanied on the way by a guard. The two rest at the stall of a young woman, Wang San-chieh, who is selling cakes. Wei Hu wants to buy some but has no money. Various buffooneries follow and the guard begins flirting with Wang. Wei Hu, seeing that his attention is thus distracted, flees and cannot be found.[1] This is the scene *Mai po-po*.

(4) *Kun-lou* (*Falling from a Tower*): The story of *Kun-lou*, the *Ch'in-ch'iang* drama which made Wei Ch'ang-sheng's name a household word in Peking, is not precisely known. According to Chou I-pai, it was about Wu Hsin, the son of Wu Tzu-hsü, and Huang Sai-hua of the Ch'un-ch'iu period.[2] (Both characters are fictional, although Wu Tzu-hsü was a historical figure.) Unfortunately, Chou does not state his authority, and he admits elsewhere that he is unsure of the details of the plot of *Kun-lou*. It appears that the drama was also called *Lan-chia chuang* (*The Village of the Lan Family*)[3] and this piece is mentioned as a love-story performed by Fei-lai-feng (surname Tai) of the San-ho company in 1810.[4] Further information on the content of Wei Ch'ang-sheng's *pièce de résistance* is lacking.

The drama *Kun-lou* is given by Li Tou as a *Ching-ch'iang* item.[5] However, it is unlikely to have been performed in that style earlier than 1779. It is so much connected with the name of Wei Ch'ang-sheng that we may assume that it was he who first brought it as a *Ch'in-ch'iang* to Peking and Yang-chou. However, it is striking that none of Wei's most famous disciples in Peking is recorded as having performed it. The drama was the best known of all those played by Wei and one might therefore expect that he would transmit it to his followers. Possibly it was indecent, and *Kun-lou* was the item the authorities had in mind when they banned Wei Ch'ang-sheng from the stage. Alternatively, Wei may have regarded it so much his own that he refused to pass it on in Peking. Perhaps it was never properly revived there and, apart from isolated performances such as those by Tai Fei-lai-feng, died out in the capital.[6] Certainly it is not mentioned in any of the late lists of Peking operas.

Chung-kuo hsi-ch'ü, p. 324. Cf. also Ch'en Wan-nai, *Yüan Ming Ch'ing chü-ch'ü shih*, pp. 248 ff. Other research work confirms that Chang Shih-ch'i's drama is no longer extant.

[1] See T'ao Chün-ch'i, *Ching-chü chü-mu*, p. 296. The text of this drama may be found in Wang Ta-ts'o, *Hsi-k'ao*, X.

[2] Chou I-pai, *Chung-kuo hsi-chü shih chiang-tso*, p. 223.

[3] Chou I-pai, *Chung-kuo hsi-chü shih*, p. 578.

[4] *TCHY, pieh-chi*, pp. 13a–b.   [5] *YCHFL*, 5, 131.

[6] On the subject of the drama *Kun-lou*, Professor Liu Ts'un-yan consulted Chou Chih-fu by letter. These suggestions I owe to his reply, which is dated 22 Sept. 1967.

(5) *Piao ta-sao pei wa-tzu* (*Sister-in-law Carries a Baby on her Back*):
This piece was also called *Pei-wa chin-fu* (*Entering a Mansion Carrying a Baby*), *Pei-wa* or *Ju-fu* and was already popular as a *Ch'in-ch'iang* piece during the 1780s, when Yü San-yüan of the I-ch'ing company performed in it. This actor was noted for his rustic qualities on the stage,[1] a fact which, as we shall see, made him very suitable for the *tan* part in *Pei-wa*. Wei Ch'ang-sheng acted the *tan* role in his old age (see chapter four), and in 1803 Chang Pao-kuan of the En-ch'ing company was seen in *Pei-wa*. One author records that Liu Ch'ing-jui, Wei Ch'ang-sheng's famous disciple, performed in the drama in 1804.[2] It was adopted also by the Anhwei companies. Actors famous for their skill in the piece included Yang T'ien-fu of the Ssu-hsi company (1806), Hsia Shuang-hsi of the Ho-ch'un, and Wu Lien-kuan of the San-ch'ing (1810). *Pei-wa* was still performed as a Clapper opera, however, for Han Ssu-hsi of the Clapper company Ta Shun-ning acted in it in 1810.[3] The 1864 and 1876 versions of the *Tu-men chi-lüeh* record that Liu Kan-san performed the role of Li P'ing-erh[4] and a work of 1873 mentions eleven actors who excelled in the drama.[5] From the above it can be seen that actors of all important Peking styles, except *K'un-ch'ü*, acted in *Pei-wa*. It is included in the *Hsi-k'ao*, which shows it as containing no sung sections.[6] There was probably very little difference between the drama as a *Ch'in-ch'iang* or *p'i-huang* item.

Pei-wa is a light moralistic little piece and appears to be a folk drama in origin. Chang Yüan-hsiu has been living as an inferior on his cousin, Li P'ing-erh, who has devoted himself to agriculture. Yüan-hsiu's father-in-law is angry at his behaviour and frequently insults him. One day, Chang finds a precious cup and promptly presents it to the government. For this action he is forthwith given high rank and also a fine residence. He summons his cousin and the latter's wife. Li's wife, carrying a baby on her back, goes with her husband to Chang's mansion to congratulate him on his success. Yüan-hsiu's father-in-law also comes to wish him well, but Chang thinks him insincere and insults him. However, Li and his wife succeed in placating their cousin, and reconcile him with his father-in-law.[7] *Pei-wa* is really a comedy in praise of the purity and simplicity of Li P'ing-erh and his wife, for the two remain unaffected by Chang's demands on them and by his high position.

(6) *K'ao-huo* (*Stoking a Fire*): This play is also called *Shao-hua shan*

[1] *YLHP*, 2, 6b.   [2] *Jih-hsia k'an-hua chi* (*JHKHC*), 4, 6a, 18a.
[3] *Chung-hsiang kuo*, p. 12a; *TCHY*, *Hui-pu*, p. 20a; *pieh-chi*, pp. 4a, 13a.
[4] See Chou Chih-fu, *Tu-men chi-lüeh*, p. 34.
[5] *CPCY*, pp. 2a, 5a, 11a, 11b, 13b, 15a, 17b, 18a, 26a, 27a.
[6] Wang Ta-ts'o, *Hsi-k'ao*, XVI.
[7] T'ao Chün-ch'i, *Ching-chü chü-mu*, p. 449.

(*Shao-hua Mountain*) and was popular as a *Ch'in-ch'iang* drama. It was, as remarked in chapter four, one of Ch'en Yin-kuan's showpieces in the 1780s. Possibly it was learnt by him from his master Wei Ch'ang-sheng, but in any case appears to have been the creation of the *Ch'in-ch'iang* actors. It was adopted by the Anhwei companies and the actor Hao Kuei-pao of the Ssu-hsi company (1810) performed in it.[1] When *Ching-chü* actors sang it in later times, they used *pang-tzu ch'iang* music,[2] and this had no doubt been the case also early in the nineteenth century.

The girl Yin Pi-lien has been promised in marriage to Ts'ang Jun-ho, the son of a high-ranking official. She does not want to marry him and begs her father to escape with her. They pass by Shao-hua Mountain where they are kidnapped and taken up to a place in the hills. They later become separated and Pi-lien's captor forces her to marry the scholar Ni Chün, but the latter is already engaged, and in the marriage chamber refuses to look at his bride. Instead, he sits up all night stoking a fire. Pi-lien understands his attitude and asks for his help to escape, and this he gladly gives her.[3]

(7) *Hsiao kua-fu shang-fen* (*The Little Widow Goes up to a Grave*): This drama was already known—and banned—in Peking during the Cheng-t'ung period (1436–50) of the Ming.[4] It is first mentioned as a *Ch'in-ch'iang* drama when a friend of Wu Ch'ang-yüan's commented harshly on its performance by Kao Ming-kuan before 1785.[5] By 1810 it had become part of the repertoire of the Anhwei companies, for it is reported that Fan T'ien-hsi of the Ch'un-t'ai company was famous in it in that year.[6] Yang Mou-chien writes also that Wang Hsiao-t'ien-hsi of the same troupe excelled in the drama during the 1830s,[7] and a work of 1873 notes six actors who performed in it at that time.[8] The piece is nowadays called *Hsiao shang-fen* and is accompanied by the *ti-tzu*.[9]

Like *Pei-wa*, this is a simple moralistic item. It draws its story, greatly simplified but essentially little changed, from the Yüan dynasty *nan-hsi*, *Liu Wen-lung ling-hua ching* (*Liu Wen-lung's Ling Flower Mirror*).[10] Liu Lu-ching leaves his wife Hsiao Su-chen to go to the capital for the examinations. He does not return for a long time and Su-chen, thinking him dead, offers sacrifices at his imagined grave.

[1] *TCHY, Hui-pu*, p. 2a.
[2] Chou I-pai, *Hsi-chü shih*, p. 604. See the text of the drama in Wang Ta-ts'o, *Hsi-k'ao*, XII.
[3] See T'ao Chün-ch'i, *Ching-chü chü-mu*, p. 169.
[4] See Wang Hsiao-ch'uan, *Yüan Ming Ch'ing san-tai chin-hui hsiao-shuo hsi-ch'ü shih-liao*, p. 14.
[5] *YLHP*, 5, 5b–6a.   [6] *TCHY, Hui-pu*, p. 9a.   [7] *CAKHC*, pp. 20a–b.
[8] *CPCY*, pp. 3b, 11a, 16b, 17b, 21b, 27a.
[9] See Aoki Masaru, *Hsi-ch'ü shih*, p. 484.
[10] See Ch'ien Nan-yang, *Hsi-wen chi-i*, pp. 214–18.

Liu passes the examinations, is given office as the magistrate of a county and returns home in glory. He passes Su-chen on the way and recognizes her. She, however, refuses to believe her good fortune. By his knowledge of their past together she is eventually persuaded that her husband has really returned to her, and the two are happily reunited.[1]

Religious Dramas

(8) *Mu-lien:* The story of Mu-lien (Ta Mu-ch'ien-lien; Sanskrit, Mahā-Maudgalyāyana), a disciple of the Buddha, who descends to hell to save his mother, is an ancient one in China. It is based on two short Buddhist Sūtras, including the *Avalambana Sūtra,* translated into Chinese under the title *Yü-lan-p'en ching* by the great monk Fa-hu (Dharmarakṣa, *c.* 230–after 308).[2] This scripture tells how Mu-lien descends to one of the Buddhist hells to see his mother, who is undergoing punishment for her wicked life. He gives her food, but she cannot eat it because it is changed into burning coals before entering her mouth. Buddha tells Mu-lien that he can save his mother by making offerings of food and other things on the fifteenth of the seventh month. The remedy was also applied to other persons in Mu-lien's position and in later centuries the day became an important festival in China (*Chung-yüan chieh*).[3]

The story of Mu-lien grew extremely popular and is found in the popular Buddhist tracts (*pien-wen*) of the T'ang and later periods. Through the ages many variations on the legend arose, and the *pien-wen* do not adhere closely to the original Sūtra. The longest known, discovered in Tun-huang in 1900, is called *Ta Mu-ch'ien-lien ming-chien chiu-mu pien-wen* and is dated 921.[4] It bears little relation to the *Avalambana Sūtra,* being based chiefly on what Waley calls 'monkish

[1] T'ao Chün-ch'i, *Ching-chü chü-mu,* p. 453. For the text of the drama see Wang Ta-ts'o, *Hsi-k'ao,* IV.

[2] I have followed Zürcher's dates for Dharmarakṣa. See *The Buddhist Conquest of China,* pp. 65, 67. The biography and works of the monk are discussed pp. 65–70. The *Yü-lan-p'en ching* has been translated into French by Chavannes in *Dix inscriptions chinoises de l'Asie Centrale,* pp. 53–7. The *Yü-lan-p'en ching* was generally held to be the equivalent of the *Ullambana Sūtra* but this is probably a mistake. See also the treatment of Jaworski, 'L'Avalambana Sūtra de la Terre Pure', *Monumenta Serica,* i (1935–6), 82–3. Jaworski gives the Chinese text of a later Sūtra on Mu-lien, pp. 90–3, and translates it into French, pp. 94–9.

[3] The *Ti-ching sui-shih chi-sheng* describes (p. 25) how in eighteenth-century Peking the Avalambana Festival was marked by performances of dramas about Mu-lien on high straw stages set up in the streets and alleys of the city. See also *Yen-ching sui-shih chi,* pp. 71–2, and Bodde, *Annual Customs and Festivals in Peking,* pp. 60–2, for a treatment of the festival in nineteenth-century Peking.

[4] Several *pien-wen* from Tun-huang are contained in Wang Chung-min a.o., *Tun-huang pien-wen chi,* pp. 701 ff. That mentioned above can be found pp. 714–44. Part of it has been translated into English by Waley in *Ballads and Stories from Tun-huang,* pp. 217–34.

folklore'.[1] The Mu-lien story was represented also in the popular literature of the Yüan.[2]

Mu-lien's feat had been dramatized as early as the Northern Sung, when a *tsa-chü* called *Mu-lien chiu-mu* (*Mu-lien Saves his Mother*) was performed in K'ai-feng in the evening of the seven days before and including the Avalambana Festival.[3] One of the earliest of all the *ch'uan-ch'i* was also called *Mu-lien chiu-mu*,[4] but the author of this piece is unknown. The Ming dynasty dramatist Cheng Chih-chen later wrote an opera called *Mu-lien chiu-mu ch'üan-shan chi*, dealing with the same story.[5] We have already seen that dramas about this Buddhist hero were commonly performed everywhere in China among all classes of people in the Ming and Ch'ing. The rich would go to great expense to have a drama about him acted when a relation of the family died.[6] In some villages of Anhwei, festivals were held in the winter every five or ten years, at which three full nights were devoted to a performance of the Mu-lien story.[7]

When K'ang-hsi held a public banquet in 1683 to celebrate his victory over the rebellion of the Three Feudatories, the main drama given was *Mu-lien ch'uan-ch'i*,[8] probably Cheng Chih-chen's version. Later on, Chang Chao (1691–1745) readapted the story for the court drama. His work was called *Ch'üan-shan chin-k'o* and was arranged in ten volumes (*pen*), each divided into two *chüan* and twenty-four scenes (*ch'u*). The music is partly *K'un-ch'ü* and partly *I-yang ch'iang*, the text based on Cheng Chih-chen's *Mu-lien*.[9] Chao-lien records that 'it was performed at the end of the year; various spirits and werewolves would come out to replace the exorcisms of ancient times.'[10] The function of the drama was thus the same at court and among the ordinary people, but it is curious that the imperial family chose the end

[1] Ibid., p. 216. It may be added that the legend was also used, among other places, in the Ming popular novel *Nan-yu chi* where Mu-lien is renamed Hua-kuang. See Liu Ts'un-yan, *Buddhist and Taoist Influences on Chinese Novels*, pp. 165–6, and cf. also Lu Hsün, *Chung-kuo hsiao-shuo shih-lüeh*, pp. 160–2, tr, Gladys Yang and Yang Hsien-yi, *A Brief History of Chinese Fiction*, pp. 199–202.

[2] See Cheng Chen-to, *Chung-kuo su-wen-hsüeh shih*, II, 318–27.

[3] *Yu-lan chü-shih Tung-ching meng-hua lu*, 8, 49.

[4] *Lu-kuei pu hsü-pien*, p. 295.

[5] *Ch'ü-hai tsung-mu t'i-yao*, 35, 1638–42. Cheng Chih-chen's drama is also discussed by Kuraishi Takeshirō in his article, '"Mu-lien chiu-mu hsing-hsiao hsi-wen" yen-chiu', in Cheng Chen-to, ed., *Chung-kuo wen-hsüeh yen-chiu*, pp. 457–66.

[6] See Doré, *Recherches sur les supersitions en Chine, IIème partie, Le panthéon chinois*, p. 162.

[7] See Kuraishi Takeshirō, 'Mu-lien chiu-mu', p. 465.

[8] *Ch'un-hsiang chui-pi*, 3, 19a. See also above, p. 116.

[9] Wang Ku-lu, *Ming-tai Hui-tiao hsi-ch'ü san-ch'u chi-i*, p. 15; *Ch'üan-shan chin-k'o, fan-li*, pp. 1a-b.

[10] *Hsiao-t'ing hsü-lu*, I, 4a.

of the year rather than the Avalambana Festival for the date of performance. The court theatre annals show that *Ch'üan-shan chin-k'o* was given complete for some decades. For instance, from the eleventh to the twentieth days in the twelfth lunar month of the Chia-ch'ing reign's twenty-fourth year (26 January to 4 February 1820) the ten *pen* were acted out in sequence in the Ch'ung-hua kung,[1] which lay in the north-western quarter of the Forbidden City. However, after the Tao-kuang period, the court discontinued the practice of performing it in full and only isolated scenes were played.[2]

The legend of Mu-lien was also absorbed into the Peking Opera under the title *Mu-lien chiu-mu* and its story in that form may be summarized as follows. Liu Ch'ing-t'i of the T'ang is angry because her husband and son, Mu-lien, are firm believers in the Buddha. She expresses her fury by burning and destroying Buddhist Sūtras. After her death she is taken to hell by devils. Mu-lien goes there to look for her, but an official of the underworld prevents the two from seeing each other. Through his piety, Mu-lien eventually succeeds in finding his mother. She repents her stubborn attitude and is saved.[3]

(9) *Hsi Mu-lien (Trying to Seduce Mu-lien):* When the story of Mu-lien was first made into a popular drama in Peking is not exactly known. Early works like the *Yen-lan hsiao-p'u* and *T'ing-ch'un hsin-yung* make no mention of any piece dealing directly with Mu-lien and his mother,[4] nor is its performance recorded by Yang Mou-chien. However, by the T'ung-chih period, *Hsi Mu-lien* has been absorbed into the repertory of the Peking Opera and it is mentioned twice in a work of 1873.[5]

Hsi Mu-lien tells of an incident within the whole story of Mu-lien. Because his mother has gone to hell, he vows to go to the Western Heaven to worship Buddha in order to effect the release of his mother. Kuan-yin changes herself into a beautiful girl with a view to tempting him. Mu-lien remains firm and resists her. He is thus able to achieve his objective.[6]

(10) *Ssu-fan (Longing for the World):* The *Ch'üan-shan chin-k'o* occupies in all 240 scenes and it is therefore not surprising that there should be subsidiary plots in it. The most famous of them is the *K'un-ch'ü* scene *Ssu-fan*. This piece is included in the *Chui pai-ch'iu*, where it

[1] See Chou Chih-fu, *Ch'ing Sheng-p'ing shu ts'un-tang shih-li man-ch'ao*, 6, 1a.

[2] See Wang Chih-chang, *Ch'ing Sheng-p'ing shu chih-lüeh*, p. 81.

[3] T'ao Chün-ch'i, *Ching-chü chü-mu*, p. 185. For the text see Wang Ta-ts'o, *Hsi-k'ao*, II.

[4] According to Chou I-pai (*Hsi-chü shih*, p. 601), the drama *Ma-chi (Cursing a Chicken)*, which is mentioned *YLHP*, 2, 4a, is based on a side-plot in the story of Mu-lien. However, Kuraishi Takeshirō claims that the scene is not found in Cheng Chih-chen's version of *Mu-lien*. See 'Mu-lien chiu-mu', p. 465.

[5] *CPCY*, pp. 12a, 26a.

[6] T'ao Chün-ch'i, *Ching-chü chü-mu*, pp. 185-6.

is said to be part of a drama called *Nieh-hai chi* (*The Records of Sin*).[1]
However, the contemporary scholar Chao Ching-shen doubts the
existence of such a work and believes rather that *Ssu-fan* was adapted
from the *Ch'üan-shan chin-k'o*.[2]

Li Tou records that *Ssu-fan* was performed by a famous member of the
Ch'un-t'ai company in Yang-chou.[3] Many *tan* actors of Peking are
known to have played the part of the young nun in *Ssu-fan*. The
earliest was Chang Hui-lan of the Pao-ho company,[4] the famous
K'un-ch'ü group of the 1780s. The records of the first decade of the
nineteenth century show a number of actors who excelled in the part.
I list them below.

ACTOR	COMPANY	DATE
Ch'en Kuei-lin (from Yang-chou)	San-ch'ing	1803
Han Chi-hsiang	Ni-ts'ui	1803
Liu Feng-lin	Ssu-hsi	1803
K'ung T'ien-hsi	Pao-hua	1803
Ch'en Shou-lin	San-to	1806
Li Lü-lin	Ch'un-t'ai	1806
Chao Hsiao-ch'ing-ling	San-ch'ing	1810
Cheng San-pao	San-ch'ing	1810[5]

The *Chü-pu ch'ün-ying* of 1873 records several actors who were
noted for their performance in *Ssu-fan*[6] and the scene was given at
court as an item separate from the complete *Ch'üan-shan chin-k'o*.[7]

The story concerns the young girl, Miss Chao, who enters a nunnery
as a novice. She grows very tired of the life in the convent and,
yearning for male company, escapes down the mountain.[8] The next

---

[1] *Chui pai-ch'iu*, VI, 2, 72.

[2] *Ming-Ch'ing ch'ü-t'an*, pp. 156 ff. The relevant scene is the ninth of the fifth
volume. See *Ch'üan-shan chin-k'o*, V, 1, 43a ff. A comparison between this scene
and *Ssu-fan* leaves no doubt that there is connection between them. However,
Cheng Chih-chen's version of the Mu-lien drama also includes *Ssu-fan* as the
fourteenth scene of the first *chüan*, though there are wide differences in detail
from the *Chui pai-ch'iu* (see Kuraishi Takeshirō 'Mu-lien chiu-mu', pp. 463–4).

[3] *YCHFL*, 5, 131.

[4] *YLHP*, 5, 2b.

[5] *JHKHC*, 1, 3a; 2, 11b, 12b–13a; 4, 12a; *Chung-hsiang kuo*, pp. 9b, 10b;
TCHY, *Hui-pu*, pp. 1a, 16a.

[6] *CPCY*, pp. 11a, 12a, 13b, 20b, 23b, 26a, 28a.

[7] Wang Chih-chang, *Ch'ing Sheng-p'ing shu*, pp. 100, 117.

[8] See *Chui pai-ch'iu*, VI, 2, 72–6. Cf. Wang Ta-ts'o, *Hsi-k'ao*, XXIV. A translation of *Ssu-fan* with comments can be found in Arlington and Acton, *Famous
Chinese Plays*, pp. 319–23.

two scenes of *Ch'üan-shan chin-k'o* describe how she meets a monk, who has also left his monastery, and continues her escape with him.[1]

(11) *Hsiang-shan:* Another religious drama is *Hsiang-shan*. This piece is based on a Buddhist legend, possibly of Sung origin,[2] about the princess Miao Shan who became Kuan-yin, the Goddess of Mercy. There is a Ming *ch'uan-ch'i* called *Hsiang-shan chi* (*The Story of Hsiang-shan*), which was written by Lo Mou-teng and prefaced 1598 by its author.[3] *Hsiang-shan* is mentioned in 1810 as being performed slightly differently by the Anhwei and *Ch'in-ch'iang* companies. The *tan* actor Li Hsiao-hsi of the Clapper Shuang-ho troupe was famous for his performance in the drama about 1809,[4] and it must therefore have been absorbed into the repertoire of the popular Peking theatre by then.

The story runs as follows. A certain king, Miao Chuang, reigns over a prosperous state, but lacks a son to succeed him, a fact which causes him great sorrow. All his children, of whom he has three, are daughters. The youngest, Miao Shan, has been very pious from her childhood and loves to chant Buddhist Sūtras. Miao Chuang wants her to get married, but Miao Shan is anxious to leave her father's palace and go to the mountains, where it is her hope to practice asceticism. The king is annoyed by her attitude, but Miao Shan refuses to change her mind. In a fury her father strangles her. However, she is miraculously brought back to life and taken to the Pai-ch'üeh Temple on Hsiang-shan. The king finds out what has happened and sends soldiers to burn the temple. Later he falls gravely ill. Miao Shan changes herself into a small boy and leaves Hsiang-shan to see her father. She tells him that he can be cured only through the hands and eyes of a member of his family. The king's relations are reluctant to offer their help, so Miao Shan herself gives her hands and eyes, thereby curing the king. The latter then goes to Hsiang-shan and gives thanks for his recovery. He repents of his crimes and places his confidence in Buddha. Because of her self-sacrifice, Miao Shan becomes the Bodhisattva Kuan-yin.[5]

Dramas Based on Popular Novels

Probably no novel has fired the imagination of the actors and

---

[1] See *Ch'üan-shan chin-k'o*, V, 1, 48a ff.

[2] The popular literature of the Sung may have included this story. See Cheng Chen-to, *Su-wen-hsüeh*, II, 308, and cf. T'ao Chün-ch'i, *Ching-chü chü-mu*, p. 433. But it was probably not known earlier than that. See Doré, *Recherches, IIème partie*, pp. 141–2.

[3] *Ch'ü-hai tsung-mu t'i-yao*, 18, 856.   [4] *TCHY*, *hsi-pu*, pp. 6a–b.

[5] I have given here the story of the recent Peking opera, basing myself on T'ao Chün-ch'i, *Ching-chü chü-mu*, pp. 433. The story of the Ming *ch'uan-ch'i* is similar but not identical to that given above in the text. A detailed account of the Kuan-yin legend can be found in Doré, *Recherches, IIème partie*, pp. 94–138.

audiences of the Peking Opera more than *The Romance of the Three Kingdoms*. This book was written by Lo Kuan-chung[1] of the late Yüan and early Ming, but many editions of it appeared later.[2] During the K'ang-hsi period, Mao Tsung-kang made some changes in the text and revised the novel into 120 *hui*. It is this version which has since become regarded as standard.[3]

Although much of the material of *The Romance of the Three Kingdoms* is fictional, the novel is based on reality and was intended as a historical narrative.[4] It deals with the civil wars of the last years of the Later Han dynasty and the era which followed, a period known as the Three Kingdoms (San-kuo). The fortunes of the states of Shu in the south-west, Wu in the south-east and Wei in the north are described in detail, and the author records the exciting exploits of warriors like Liu Pei of Shu, a scion of the Han imperial family, Ts'ao Ts'ao of Wei, regarded as a traitor because he usurped the power of the Han dynasty,[5] and Kuan Yü, a sworn brother of Liu Pei's.

Stories from the late Han and Three Kingdoms have for centuries been popular among the Chinese. Even before Lo Kuan-chung wrote his famous novel, story-tellers would relate incidents about the heroes of the period. The poet Li Shang-yin refers to this practice in the late T'ang,[6] and in the Sung dynasty Su Shih wrote, 'children in the streets . . . would sit down to listen to old stories, including ones about the Three Kingdoms. When they heard of Liu Pei's defeat, they would fret and even shed tears. When they heard of Ts'ao Ts'ao's defeat, they would brighten up and applaud.'[7]

The heroes of the second- and third-century civil wars were the subject of many dramas throughout later ages. Kuan Han-ch'ing, the famous thirteenth-century dramatist, deals with the period in his *Kuan*

---

[1] Professor Liu Ts'un-yan has completed a comprehensive study, to be published shortly, of Lo Kuan-chung and his works. Its title is 'De l'authenticité des romans historiques de Luo Guanzhong' and it will appear in vol. 2 of *Mélanges de sinologie, offerts à Monsieur Paul Demiéville*.

[2] For a study of some of these editions see Liu Ts'un-yan, *Chinese Popular Fiction in Two London Libraries*, pp. 25–7, 30, 63, 75, 150.

[3] See Lu Hsün, *Chung-kuo hsiao-shuo*, p. 138, tr. *A Brief History*, p. 172. Further detail on the novel is given in *Chung-kuo hsiao-shuo*, pp. 132 ff., tr. *A Brief History*, pp. 163 ff.

[4] See C. T. Hsia, *The Classic Chinese Novel*, p. 34. The author makes a literary analysis, especially of the characterization of the main figures in the novel, pp. 34–74. For more bibliography on the work see pp. 388–92.

[5] But Ts'ao Ts'ao is not always depicted as a villain and Lo Kuan-chung's novel sometimes presents him in a sympathetic light. Ibid., pp. 64–9.

[6] Ibid., pp. 9–10. The relevant poem, entitled 'Chiao-erh shih', is given in *Ch'üan T'ang-shih*, 541, 6244–5.

[7] *Tung-p'o chih-lin*, 1, 5–6. I have used the translation of Gladys Yang and Yang Hsien-yi which can be found in *A Brief History*, pp. 419–20.

Ta-wang chan-tao hui (*Lord Kuan Goes to the Feast*)[1] and elsewhere. The Ming dynasty *ch'uan-ch'i*, *Ku-ch'eng chi* (*The Story of Ku-ch'eng*), concerns mainly Kuan Yü,[2] while other dramas of the period also relate stories about this and other warriors involved in the famous civil wars. In the Ch'ing dynasty, the imperial house took up the stories for the court drama. As noted in chapter five, Yin-lu (1695–1767) was ordered to adapt them into the *Ting-chih ch'un-ch'iu*. This could be played *in toto* or in part during any season of the year. Its last recorded performance at court took place at irregular intervals over the period from 10 October 1847 to 30 April 1849, but the last few sections were never given.[3]

Despite their popularity at court, the stories of the ancient civil wars are not mentioned in the primary sources for the popular Peking theatre during the period of the *Ch'in-ch'iang* actors or the early years of the Anhwei companies. This is because works like the *Jih-hsia k'an-hua chi* deal only with *tan* actors, while the major roles in the Three Kingdoms pieces were all men and called for distinguished *lao-sheng*, *ching*, and *ch'ou* performers. With the coming of the great *lao-sheng* like Ch'eng Chang-keng, dramatic pieces based on *The Romance of the Three Kingdoms* began to take an extremely important place on the Peking stage. In recent times there have been more Peking operas based on this novel than on any other.[4] I shall discuss below four examples of such plays, all of which are set in the period before the final collapse of the Han in 220 A.D.

(12) *Cho-fang Ts'ao* (*Arresting and Releasing Ts'ao Ts'ao*): Early actors famous in this piece include Yü San-sheng, Chang Erh-k'uei, and Hsieh Yin-hsüan, listed in the *Tu-men chi-lüeh* of 1845,[5] and Chou K'ai-yüeh, Ch'ien Wang-san, and T'ung-tzu-hung, given in the 1864 version of the guide-book.[6] All of these except Chou K'ai-yüeh and Ch'ien Wang-san (Ts'ao Ts'ao) excelled in the role of Ch'en Kung. The *Chü-pu ch'ün-ying* records several actors who performed in *Cho-fang Ts'ao* in the 1870s.[7]

The story is taken, without change, from the fourth *hui* of the novel

---

[1] This piece has been translated by Gladys Yang and Yang Hsien-yi in *Selected Plays of Kuan Han-ching*, pp. 178–204. I owe the translation of the title to them.

[2] See *Ch'ü-hai tsung-mu t'i-yao*, 18, 894–6.

[3] See Wang Chih-chang, *Ch'ing Sheng-p'ing shu*, p. 80. The *Ting-chih ch'un-ch'iu* has been reprinted in the *Ku-pen hsi-ch'ü ts'ung-k'an chiu-chi*, no. III. For further material on this drama see Chou Chih-fu, *Chen-liu ta-wen*, pp. 81–6.

[4] In T'ao Chün-ch'i, *Ching-chü chü-mu*, pp. 68–113, are given the stories of 135 Peking operas based on the *San-kuo yen-i*. T'ao presents (pp. 249–65) only some 40 based on the *Shui-hu chuan*.

[5] Chou Chih-fu, *Tu-men chi-lüeh*, pp. 22, 31, 51.

[6] Ibid., pp. 16, 59, 64.

[7] *CPCY*, pp. 2b, 5a, 6b, 7b.

(Mao Tsung-kang's version), which is based partly on the historical facts of 189 A.D.[1] The wicked minister Tung Cho has deposed the reigning emperor and established Hsien-ti on the throne. Ts'ao plans to kill Tung but, thinking that his plot has been discovered, flees without achieving his purpose. Tung Cho realizes that Ts'ao has been trying to take his life and sends out an order for his arrest. Ts'ao Ts'ao escapes to Chung-mou county in Honan and is seized there by an official. The magistrate of the county, Ch'en Kung, respects Ts'ao and secretly releases him. The two then leave together and on the way they meet an old friend of Ts'ao Ts'ao's father, Lü Po-she, who offers them shelter. Ts'ao wrongly suspects the man of criminal intentions towards him and, to prevent his supposed plans, kills Lü and his entire family. Ch'en Kung is repelled by Ts'ao Ts'ao's infamy and leaves him.[2]

(13) *Chan Ch'ang-sha* (*The Battle for Ch'ang-sha*): This drama is included in the list of 1824 which shows the repertory of the Ch'ing Sheng-p'ing company.[3] It was in *Chan Ch'ang-sha* that Mi Hsi-tzu (discussed in chapter five) so stunned his audience with the magnificence of his art in the role of Kuan Yü that nobody played the piece for a long time. Not until the T'ung-chih period, when the San-ch'ing company rearranged the whole of *The Romance of the Three Kingdoms* into an extended drama, was it seen again in Peking. Ch'eng Chang-keng was famous in the role of Kuan Yü when this revival took place.[4]

The story of *Chan Ch'ang-sha* is taken, unchanged, from the fifty-third *hui* of the novel.[5] Kuan Yü of Shu attacks Ch'ang-sha in present-day Hunan. The defending commander, Han Hsüan, sends out his old general Huang Chung to fight the attacker. Huang's horse stumbles, but Kuan Yü declines to take advantage of the accident. The following day the two champions again engage in combat. Huang Chung has been ordered to shoot Kuan Yü. He fires an arrow at his opponent but, in order to repay the latter's generosity of the previous day, aims it deliberately at the base of the plume of Kuan's helmet. Han Hsüan is furious with Huang for having missed the opportunity of winning the contest and wants to behead him. One of Han's subordinates, who had earlier been in the service of Liu Pei, then incites the people of Ch'ang-sha to rise in rebellion against their leader and Han Hsüan is killed. The

---

[1] See *San-kuo yen-i*, 4, 30 ff., translated Brewitt-Taylor, *San-kuo, or Romance of the Three Kingdoms*, I, 39–43. The historical account can be found in *San-kuo chih*, I, 5. A detailed comparison of this story with the historical facts is given by Kung Te-pai in *Hsi-chü yü li-shih*, pp. 129–36.

[2] T'ao Chün-ch'i, *Ching-chü chü-mu*, p. 69. An English translation of *Cho-fang Ts'ao* is given in Arlington and Acton, *Famous Chinese Plays*, pp. 133–50. An early text of the drama may be found in Wang Ta-ts'o, *Hsi-k'ao*, I.

[3] Chou Chih-fu, *Ching-hsi chin pai-nien so-chi*, p. 4.

[4] Ch'i Ju-shan, *Ch'ing-tai p'i-huang ming-chüeh chien-shu*, pp. 1, 4–5.

[5] *San-kuo yen-i*, 53, 433 ff., translated Brewitt-Taylor, *San-kuo*, I, 548 ff.

city surrenders to Liu Pei and Huang Chung is induced to go over to the side of Shu.[1]

This incident is only partly historical. The surrender of Ch'ang-sha and Huang Chung is factual, but the personal combat between Huang and Kuan Yü and the assassination of Han Hsüan are fictional. According to the standard history, Han surrendered to Liu Pei.[2]

(14) *Jang Ch'eng-tu* (*Yielding Ch'eng-tu*): This drama is also called *Ch'ü Ch'eng-tu* (*Taking Ch'eng-tu*) or *Chan Ch'eng-tu* (*The Battle for Ch'eng-tu*). It was one of the pieces of the Ch'ing Sheng-p'ing company in 1824.[3] Famous early exponents of the role of Liu Chang include Ch'eng Chang-keng, Wang Hung-kuei, Hsieh Yin-hsüan, Huang San, and Ch'iang Wu-shih. Yü San-sheng was well known as Ma Ch'ao and Chang Erh-k'uei as Liu Pei.[4]

The story is taken from the sixty-fifth *hui* of the novel,[5] and is in essence an accurate representation of an event which took place in 214 A.D.[6] The general Ma Ch'ao has surrendered to Liu Pei who now wants to take the city of Ch'eng-tu in Szechwan. Ma Ch'ao advances to the attack. Liu Chang, in command of the city, realizes that to save the people from massacre he must surrender to his enemies. Despite the opposition of some of his subordinates, this is the course he adopts, and Liu Pei then enters Ch'eng-tu.[7]

(15) *Ting-chün shan* (*Ting-chün Mountain*): This piece was part of the repertoire of the Ch'ing Sheng-p'ing company in 1824.[8] The most famous early exponent of the role of Huang Chung was Yü San-sheng.[9]

Ting-chün shan is based on the seventieth and seventy-first *hui* of *The Romance of the Three Kingdoms*,[10] but it is slightly simplified and not identical to the novel. The scene describes battles between the states of Shu and Wei and refers to the year 219. Chang Ho of Wei has suffered defeat and, afraid of punishment from his superior, makes an attack on the Chia-meng Pass. The old generals, Huang Chung and Yen Yen of Shu, join forces and drive him off. Taking advantage of their victory,

[1] T'ao Chün-ch'i, *Ching-chü chü-mu*, p. 88. Cf. Wang Ta-ts'o, *Hsi-k'ao*, VI.

[2] *San-kuo chih*, 36, 948; 32, 879. See also Kung Te-pai, *Hsi-chü*, pp. 176–7.

[3] Chou Chih-fu, *So-chi*, p. 4.

[4] Chou Chih-fu, *Tu-men chi-lüeh*, pp. 13, 43, 51, 61, 65; *Li-yüan chiu-hua*, pp. 3a–b.

[5] *San-kuo yen-i*, 65, 540–1, translated Brewitt-Taylor, *San-kuo*, II, 52–4.

[6] *San-kuo chih*, 31, 869; 32, 882; 36, 946. See also Kung Te-pai, *Hsi-chü*, pp. 192–5.

[7] T'ao Chün-ch'i, *Ching-chü chü-mu*, p. 95.

[8] Chou Chih-fu, *So-chi*, p. 4.

[9] See Chou Chih-fu, *Tu-men chi-lüeh*, p. 22.

[10] *San-kuo yen-i*, 70, 580 ff.; 71, 585 ff., translated Brewitt-Taylor, *San-kuo*, II, 108 ff.

they attack T'ien-tang shan in south-western Shensi, where Ts'ao Ts'ao of Wei is keeping his supplies. Huang Chung then leads a force to attack the nearby Ting-chün shan, at the time held by Ts'ao's army. In the first battle Huang Chung is defeated and the garrison commander of Chia-meng Pass captured. In the one that follows, however, Huang Chung succeeds in taking prisoner the nephew of the enemy commander, Hsia-hou Yüan, who proposes an exchange of prisoners. Huang Chung first recovers his captured garrison commander and then shoots Yüan's nephew with an arrow just as the latter is about to go back to his own side. As Huang had planned, the enemy commander is enraged at this action and pursues him to a wild place. There Yüan is killed by Huang Chung, who is then able to take possession of Ting-chün shan for the forces of Shu.[1]

This story greatly embellishes the historical facts. However, the standard history does record the defeat of Chang Ho by the forces of Shu, Huang Chung's victory over Hsia-hou Yüan at Ting-chün shan in 219 A.D. and Yüan's death at the hands of Huang Chung.[2]

Apart from *The Romance of the Three Kingdoms*, by far the most famous source of stories for the Peking Opera is *The Water Margin*. However, the primary sources do not indicate that the early famous *Ching-chü* actors mentioned in the present work paid any attention to this novel, possibly because of its emphasis on rebellion. I have therefore chosen to describe instead one drama based on another, less well known novel, *The Romance of the Yang Family Generals*, which deals with the exploits of the generals of the Yang family at the beginning of the Northern Sung. It is a late Ming work, probably by Hsiung Chung-ku, and contains fifty *hui*.[3]

The main character in the early part of this novel is Yang Yeh, who with his sons renders the imperial Sung house great service in its struggle against the Liao people (Khitan) to the north. Yang Yeh was a historical figure and is given a biography in the standard history of the Sung. In the novel he has eight sons, but only seven of them are mentioned in the Sung history and none but the eldest is accorded a biography there.[4]

Stories about the Yang generals have been popular among the Chinese people since the Yüan dynasty. Several *tsa-chü* of that period are centred on them. Chu K'ai's *Hao-t'ien t'a* (*The Hao-t'ien Pagoda*) is an example. Many *K'un-ch'ü* of the Ming and Ch'ing also use the Yang

---

[1] T'ao Chün-ch'i, *Ching-chü chü-mu*, pp. 98–9. Cf. Wang Ta-ts'o, *Hsi-k'ao*, VI.

[2] *San-kuo chih*, 9, 272; 32, 884; 36, 948. See also Kung Te-pai, *Hsi-chü*, pp. 200–3.

[3] There are in existence a number of versions and editions of popular novels with stories about the Yang family. For a study of some of them see Liu Ts'un-yan, *Chinese Popular Fiction*, pp. 17–18.

[4] *Sung-shih*, 272, 1a ff.

generals as their subject.[1] The most famous of them is the *Chao-tai hsiao-shao*, a court drama, prefaced 1813, by a group of people headed by Chang Sheng-yin.[2] It is reported to have been performed complete in the T'ung-lo yüan of the Old Summer Palace in 1837–8, 1844–5, and 1858–9. From 1898 to 1900 it was given once more, but was never finished and used, instead of *K'un-ch'ü* music, the styles of the Peking Opera, *erh-huang* and *hsi-p'i*.[3]

There is no evidence that dramas about the Yang family heroes were performed at the Ch'ing court before 1813 and the same is true of Peking's popular theatres. The *tan* actors of the *Ch'in-ch'iang* and early Anhwei companies do not appear to have paid any attention to the Yang generals. This is because, like those in *The Romance of the Three Kingdoms*, the main characters in *The Romance of the Yang Family Generals* are mostly men, although they also include the famous heroine, Mu Kuei-ying. It is not until the Tao-kuang period that there is evidence of the great popularity of dramas about the warriors of the Yang family.

(16) *Liang-lang shan* (*Liang-lang Mountain*): One of the best known *hua-pu* pieces about the Yang generals is *Liang-lang shan*. Chiao Hsün devotes some space to describing it[4] so that it must have been popular in the Yang-chou region in his time. It was quickly adapted into a *Ching-chü* and called *Liang-lang shan, Li Ling pei* (*The Stele of Li Ling*), or *P'eng-pei* (*Dashing Against the Stele*). Yü San-sheng and Mei Tung, a *lao-sheng* actor of the Ta Ching-ho company, are noted in the *Tu-men chi-lüeh* of 1845 as exponents of the role of Yang Chi-yeh, and, according to the 1864 and 1876 versions of the guide-book, Ch'iang Wu-shih was known for his performance of the same role.[5]

The story of the recent Peking opera *Liang-lang shan* is taken, essentially unchanged, from the eighteenth and nineteenth *hui* of the novel.[6] It runs as follows. Yang Chi-yeh[7] goes to war against the Liao. He is defeated and captured at Liang-lang shan and sends his seventh son, Yang Yen-ssu, to seek help from the generalissimo P'an Hung.[8]

[1] See a list of Yüan, Ming, and Ch'ing dramas about the Yang generals in Chou I-pai, *Hsi-chü shih*, p. 688.

[2] The *Chao-tai hsiao-shao* has been reprinted in the *Ku-pen hsi-ch'ü ts'ung-k'an chiu-chi*, no. VIII.

[3] See Wang Chih-chang, *Ch'ing Sheng-p'ing shu*, pp. 82–3; Chou Chih-fu, *Ch'ing Sheng-p'ing shu*, 6, 9a–13a.

[4] *Hua-pu nung-t'an*, p. 227.

[5] See Chou Chih-fu, *Tu-men chi-lüeh*, pp. 22, 55–6, 65.

[6] *Yang-chia chiang yen-i*, 18, 45–7; 19, 47.

[7] Yang Chi-yeh is given the same name in the *Chao-tai hsiao-shao* but is called by his historical name, Yang Yeh, in the novel *Yang-chia chiang yen-i*.

[8] In the novel and *Chao-tai hsiao-shao*, the generalissimo is called P'an Jen-mei, but the *ming* of the historical P'an was Mei. His biography can be found in *Sung-shih*, 258, 14a–17a, where there is no mention of the names Jen-mei or Hung.

But because Yen-ssu had earlier killed his son, P'an Hung takes revenge by binding Yang's seventh son and having him shot. When Yen-ssu does not return, Chi-yeh sends his sixth son, Yen-chao, to court. Reinforcements do not turn up and Yang's men and horses suffer acutely from hunger and cold. Yeh thereupon moves forward and comes to a stele in honour of Li Ling, the famous general of the Former Han dynasty who lived for many years among the Hsiung-nu. He dashes himself against the stele and dies.[1]

The plot of this piece is widely different from the historical facts. These are perhaps not quite so easy to dramatize as the version given in the novel. Yet they are recorded in some detail in the Sung history and, since they are both interesting and affecting, it will be worthwhile to repeat them here.

During the Five Dynasties period (907–60), China had lost sixteen of its northern prefectures to the Khitan Liao. The early Sung emperors tried to regain the area and in 986 mounted a full-scale operation to this end. P'an Mei was in charge of it, while Yang Yeh and Wang Shen were among his main deputies. After some initial Sung successes, the Khitan sent out an enormous force to counterattack. Yang Yeh advised caution in accepting the challenge and put forward a plan which involved waiting a while and making strenuous efforts to defend the people of the area from massacre. Wang Shen accused him of cowardice and suggested going immediately on to the offensive against the oncoming Khitan forces. Yang Yeh was galled into accepting the bait to lead his troops into the Ch'en-chia Valley, while P'an and Wang agreed to wait at the entrance with reinforcements in case of emergency.

Once the battle had begun, Wang sent an observer to an overlooking mountain and the intelligence arrived that Yang Yeh was gaining a victory. In the hope of winning a greater share of the credit in the eyes of the emperor, Wang then withdrew from the entrance of Ch'en-chia Valley to attack on another front, despite P'an Mei's attempts to prevent him. Soon afterwards it was learned that Yang had been defeated after all. His son Yen-yü had been killed in action and he himself captured. P'an Mei and Wang Shen responded by taking flight, and Yang Yeh, seeing that his position was hopeless, 'went without food for three days and died'. P'an and Wang were stripped of their ranks.[2] The war with the Khitan dragged on until 1004, when a peace treaty was signed acknowledging the permanent loss by the Sung of its sixteen prefectures.

P'an Mei was certainly not the traitor he is painted in the novel, and belongs among the many colourless figures whose names have been

[1] T'ao Chün-ch'i, *Ching-chü chü-mu*, pp. 213–14. See the text of the drama in Wang Ta-ts'o, *Hsi-k'ao*, II.
[2] *Sung-shih*, 272, 1b–3a. See also Kung Te-pai, *Hsi-chü*, pp. 326–9.

vilified in Chinese fiction.[1] Yet the end result of disaster for the Sung was the same both historically and in the novel. The playwrights and actors no doubt believed that a villain would create a more powerful impact on the audience than a weakling. It was their job to produce good theatre, and a little poetic licence was all part of the game.

The pieces described above are but a small proportion of the total number performed. Nevertheless, they show something of the range of the dramas seen in Peking during the late eighteenth and nineteenth centuries. Some are light entertainment, some point a moral, others recount the deeds of heroes. Most of them were seen in China until quite recently and some have been made especially famous through great actors of the present century. T'an Hsin-p'ei and Yü Shu-yen excelled as Yang Yeh in *Liang-lang shan*, and other examples could be mentioned. Nowadays, however, none of the dramas discussed in this appendix is performed on the Chinese mainland, and only pieces with contemporary revolutionary themes can be seen. The complete suspension of the traditional drama could conceivably be permanent, but it is also possible that future decades will witness a partial revival of the historic items which were once so popular. But to speculate on the future is not the concern of the historian and only time can settle this question.

[1] It may be added that Chu K'ai already painted P'an Mei as a villain in his *Hao-t'ien t'a* and showed Yang Yeh as committing suicide at the Li Ling stele. A scene of this drama is included in the *Chui pai-ch'iu* (II, 3, 175–82). See also Lo Chin-t'ang, *Hsien-ts'un Yüan-jen*, pp. 274–6.

11. China Proper South from Peking (Ching Period)

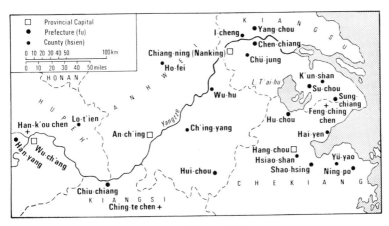

12. Lower Yangtze River

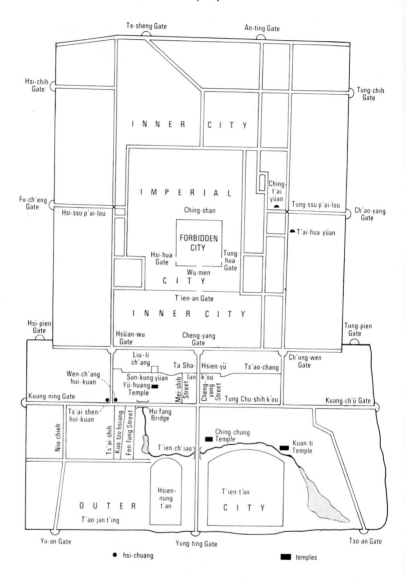

13. This plan of Peking is based on the charts in *Ch'en-yüan shih-lüeh* and a map printed with Hyacinthe Bichurin's *Description de Peking*

LIST OF WORKS CITED

The following does not purport to be a comprehensive list of all books on the rise of the Peking Opera, but of those cited in the present work. The titles of dramas, *ch'uan-ch'i*, *pien-wen*, and Buddhist Sūtras are not included unless a specific place in them has been cited directly in the footnotes. Individual *shih* 詩 are not given here.

The first part of the list (Chinese works before 1912) includes collections *(ts'ung-shu)* published since 1912 if the works contained in them were written earlier than that year. Dates between brackets refer to the author of a work and not to the work itself. Many books given in this section of the list were written by authors known only by pen-name, and others are compilations. I have therefore thought it more convenient to arrange it by titles than by authors. In the footnotes throughout the present work, the author is not normally indicated for Chinese books written before 1912.

The second and third part of the list (Chinese and Japanese works since 1912, and European-language works) are listed according to author. I have given the first edition and that to which references are made in the notes (where the two are different). A number of these works have been reprinted recently: Hummel's, Boulais's and Burgess's, among others, in Taiwan, Brewitt-Taylor's in Tokyo, and so on. However, I have thought it unnecessary to detail all impressions of the books. I have noted the number of volumes where there are more than one, but in the footnotes throughout the book have given volume numbers only when the pagination starts afresh at the beginning of each volume. Post-1911 compilations of extracts from pre-Republican works are given under the editor in the second part of the List of Works Cited unless such compilations exist only as part of a collection. In the section on Western-language works, characters are given for Chinese authors only when they appear on the title-page of the book or article in question.

a. *Chinese Works (before 1912)*

Ch'ang-an k'an-hua chi 長安看花記, by Yang Mou-chien 楊懋建, 1837. In *CTYT*, II.

Ch'ang-t'an ts'ung-lu 常談叢錄, by Li Teng-ch'i 李登齊 (late Ch'ing). Extract quoted in *PCLYCK*, pp. 13a–b.

Chao Kung-i kung tzu-chih kuan-shu 趙恭毅公自治官書, compiled by Chao Shen-ch'iao 趙申喬 a.o., 1724.

Ch'ao-shih ts'ung-tsai 朝市叢載, by Yang Ching-t'ing 楊靜亭 a.o., 1887. (Quoted sections: *hsi-yüan* 戲園, *hui-kuan* 會館 and *hang-kuan* 行館.)

Chen-chou feng-t'u chi 眞州風土記, by Li Hsiu-fang 厲秀芳 (1794–1867). In *HFHC*, VI.

Ch'en-shih tsung-p'u 陳氏宗譜, compiled by Ch'en Ch'uan-sen 陳傳森 a.o., 1909. (Quoted section: *liu-fang nien-kuei chi-ssu* 六房年規祭祀.)

Ch'en-yüan shih-lüeh 宸垣識畧, by Wu Ch'ang-yüan 吳長元, 1788.

Chi-lo shih-chieh 極樂世界, by Kuan-chü tao-jen 觀劇道人, 1840.

Chiao-fang chi 敎坊記, by Ts'ui Ling-ch'in 崔令欽, 762. In *CKKT*, I.

Chin-li Huang-shih chia-p'u 錦里黃氏家譜, compiled by Huang T'ao 黃濤, 1769.

Chin-ling ts'ung-k'e 金陵叢刻, edited by Fu Ch'un-kuan 傅春官, 1897–1905.

Chin P'ing Mei tz'u-hua 金瓶梅詞話, author unknown, late Ming. Tokyo, 1963 (photorep. of 1617 edition).

Chin-shu 晉書, compiled by Ch'en Hao 陳浩 a.o., under T'ang T'ai-tsung (627–50). *Po-na* edition.

Chin-t'ai ts'an-lei chi 金臺殘淚記, by Chang Chi-liang 張際亮, 1829. In *CTYT*, I.

Ch'in-yün hsieh-ying hsiao-p'u 秦雲擷英小譜, by Yen Ch'ang-ming 嚴長明, Ts'ao Jen-hu 曹仁虎, and Ch'ien Tien 錢坫, *c.* 1780. In *Shuang-mei ching-an ts'ung-shu*.

Ching-ch'en chü-lu 京塵劇錄, by Yang Mou-chien 楊懋建, 1842. In *Hsin ch'ü-yüan*.

Ching-ch'en tsa-lu 京塵雜錄, by Yang Mou-chien 楊懋建, 1886.

Ching-shih ou-chi 京師偶記, by Ch'ai Sang 柴桑, 1701. In *HFHC*, VI.

Ch'ing-chia lu 淸嘉錄, by Ku Lu 顧祿, 1830. In *Pi-chi hsiao-shuo ta-kuan*, II.

Ch'ing-jen shuo-hui 淸人說薈, edited by Lei Chin 雷瑨, Shanghai, 1917–28.

Ch'ing-lou chi 青樓集, by Hsia T'ing-chih 夏庭芝, 1355. In *CKKT*, II.

Ch'ing-tai Yen-tu li-yüan shih-liao 淸代燕都梨園史料, edited by Chang Tz'u-hsi 張次溪, Peiping, 1934. Taipei, 1965 (*Chung-kuo shih-hsüeh ts'ung-shu XXIX* 中國史學叢書 29). (Quoted sections include *chu-che shih-lüeh* 著者事畧.)

Ch'ing-tai Yen-tu li-yüan shih-liao hsü-pien 淸代燕都梨園史料續編, edited by Chang Tz'u-hsi 張次溪, Peiping, 1937. Taipei, 1965 (*Chung-kuo shih-hsüeh ts'ung-shu XXIX*).

Ch'ing-yüan meng-han tsa-chu 青源夢厂雜著, by Yü Chiao 俞蛟, n.d. Sections quoted in *PCLYCK*, pp. 8a–9a, 12a–13a.

Chiu T'ang-shu 舊唐書, compiled by Chao Ying 趙瑩 a.o., 945. *Po-na* edition.

Ch'iu-p'ing hsin-yü 秋坪新語, by Fou-ch'a san-jen 浮槎散人, 1792. Two sections quoted in *PCLYCK*, pp. 9a–12a.

Cho-keng lu 輟耕錄, by T'ao Tsung-i 陶宗儀, 1366. *Ts'ung-shu chi-ch'eng* edition.

Chu-chi Chung-shih tsung-p'u 諸暨鍾氏宗譜, compiled by Chung Huan-kuang 鍾煥光 a.o., 1922. (Quoted section: *Shu K'uei-kung ch'eng-hsien ssu-t'ien ch'an-chi* 叔奎公承先祀田產記.)

Chuang-hui t'ang wen-chi 壯悔堂文集, by Hou Fang-yü 侯方域, 1652. *Wan-yu wen-k'u* edition.

Chui pai-ch'iu 綴白裘, edited by Wan-hua chu-jen 玩花主人 and Ch'ien Te-ts'ang 錢德蒼, 1770. Peking, 1955.

Ch'un-hsiang chui-pi 蓴鄉贅筆, by Tung Han 董含, 1705. In *Shuo-ling*.

Chung-hsiang kuo 衆香國, by Chung-hsiang chu-jen 衆香主人, 1807. In *Ch'ing-tai Yen-tu li-yüan shih-liao hsü-pien*.

Chung-kuo ku-tien hsi-ch'ü lun-chu chi-ch'eng 中國古典戲曲論著集成, edited by the Chung-kuo hsi-ch'ü yen-chiu yüan 中國戲曲研究院, Peking, 1959–60.

Ch'ung-ting ch'ü-yüan 重訂曲苑, edited by Ch'en Nai-ch'ien 陳乃乾, 1925.

Chü-hua 劇話, by Li T'iao-yüan 李調元, c. 1775. In *CKKT*, VIII.

Chü-pu ch'ün-ying 菊部羣英, by Han-chiang hsiao-yu hsien-k'e 邗江小游仙客, 1873. In *CKKT*, II.

Chü-shuo 劇說, by Chiao Hsün 焦循, 1805. In *CKKT*, VIII.

Ch'ü-hai tsung-mu t'i-yao 曲海總目提要, by Tung K'ang 董康 a.o. (An attempt to recompile the lost eighteenth-century *Ch'ü-hai* 曲海 from the *Yüeh-fu k'ao-lüeh* 樂府考畧), Shanghai, 1928. Peking, 1959.

Ch'ü-yüan 曲苑, editor unknown, Hai-ning, 1921.

Ch'üan-shan chin-k'o 勸善金科, arranged by Chang Chao 張照 (1691–1745). In *Ku-pen hsi-ch'ü ts'ung-k'an chiu-chi*, V.

Ch'üan T'ang-shih 全唐詩, compiled by P'eng Ting ch'iu 彭定求 a.o., 1707. Peking, 1960.

Fa-ying pi-chi 法嬰祕笈, by Shuang-ying an sheng 雙影盦生, 1855. In *CTYT*, II.

Fu-Yü hsüan-hua lu 撫豫宣化錄, compiled by T'ien Wen-ching 田文鏡, 1727.

Han-hai 函海, by Li T'iao-yüan 李調元, 1881–2. Taipei, 1968 (photorep. of 1881–2 edition).

Han Chung-li tu-t'o Lan Ts'ai-ho 漢鍾離度脫藍采和, author and date unknown. In *Yüan-Ming tsa-chü*.

Hang-su i-feng 杭俗遺風, by Fan Tsu-shu 范祖述 (fl. 1863). In *HFHC*, VI.

Hsi-ching fu 西京賦, by Chang Heng 張衡, c. 126 A.D. In *Wen-hsüan*, 2.

Hsiang-t'an hsien-chih 湘潭縣志, compiled by Ch'en Chia-yü 陳嘉榆, 1889.

Hsiang-yen ts'ung-shu 香豔叢書, compiled by Ch'ung-t'ien-tzu 蟲天子, 1909–11.

Hsiao-fang hu-chai yü-ti ts'ung-ch'ao 小方壺齋輿地叢鈔, edited by Wang Hsi-ch'i 王錫祺, 1891–7.

Hsiao-shan Ch'ang-hsiang Shen-shih hsü-hsiu tsung-p'u 蕭山長巷沈氏續修宗譜, compiled by Shen Ping-hui 沈丙輝 a.o., 1893. (Quoted section: *tsung-yüeh* 宗約.)

Hsiao-t'ing hsü-lu 嘯亭續錄, by Chao-lien 昭槤, 1817–26. In *Hsiao-t'ing tsa-lu.*

Hsiao-t'ing tsa-lu 嘯亭雜錄, by Chao-lien 昭槤, c. 1815. Shanghai, n.d.

Hsiao-ts'ang shan-fang shih-chi 小倉山房詩集, by Yüan Mei 袁枚, 1736–97. In *Sui-yüan san-shih-liu chung.*

Hsiao-ts'ang shan-fang wen-chi 小倉山房文集, by Yüan Mei 袁枚 (1716–98). In *Sui-yüan san-shih-liu chung.*

Hsieh-to 諧鐸, by Shen Ch'i-feng 沈起鳳, 1791. In *Pi-chi hsiao-shuo ta-kuan,* I.

Hsien-ch'ing ou-chi 閒情偶寄, by Li Yü 李漁, 1671. In *CKKT,* VII.

Hsin ch'i-hsieh 新齊諧, by Yüan Mei 袁枚, c. 1781. In *Sui-yüan san-shih-liu chung.*

Hsin ch'ü-yüan 新曲苑, edited by Jen Chung-min 任中敏, Shanghai, 1940.

Hsin-jen kuei-chia lu 辛壬癸甲錄, by Yang Mou-chien 楊懋建, 1842. In *CTYT,* I.

Hsin T'ang-shu 新唐書, compiled by Ou-yang Hsiu 歐陽修 a.o., 1060. *Po-na* edition.

Hsin-ting shih-erh lü Ching-ch'iang p'u 新定十二律京腔譜, compiled by Wang Cheng-hsiang 王正祥, 1684.

Hsin-ting shih-erh lü K'un-ch'iang p'u 新定十二律崑腔譜, compiled by Wang Cheng-hsiang 王正祥, 1676. Shanghai, 1958.

Hsin Wu-tai shih 新五代史, compiled by Ou-yang Hsiu 歐陽修 a.o. (1007–72). *Po-na* edition.

Hsing-an hui-lan 刑案匯覽, compiled by Chi Han 季涵 a.o., 1834.

Hsüeh-cheng ch'üan-shu 學政全書, compiled by Kung-a-la 恭阿拉 a.o., 1812.

Hua-chien hsiao-yü 花間笑語, by Fou-ch'a san-jen 浮槎散人, c. 1805. Section quoted in *PCLYCK,* pp. 7b–8a.

Hua-pu nung-t'an 花部農譚, by Chiao Hsün 焦循, 1819. In *CKKT,* VIII.

Huai-fang chi 懷芳記, by Lo-mo an lao-jen 蘿摩庵老人, 1876. In *CTYT,* II.

Huai-pin tsa-tsu 懷閩雜俎. edited by Hsü Nai-ch'ang 徐乃昌, 1907–10.

Huan-yu chi-wen 宦遊紀聞, by Chang I 張誼 (Ming). In *Su-hsiang shih ts'ung-shu*.

Hung-lou meng 紅樓夢, by Ts'ao Chan 曹霑 and Kao O 高鶚, 1792. Peking, 1957.

I-ling chuan 異伶傳 by Ch'en Tan-jan 陳澹然, *c.* 1910. *CTYT*, III.

I-nien lu wu-chung 疑年錄五種, edited by the Tōa gakujutsu kenkyū kai 東亞學術研究會, Tokyo, 1915.

Jih-hsia k'an-hua chi 日下看花記, by Hsiao T'ieh-ti tao-jen 小鐵篴道人, 1803. In *CTYT*, I.

Ju-lin wai-shih 儒林外史, by Wu Ching-tzu 吳敬梓, *c.* 1750. Peking, 1962.

Jung-mei chi-yu 容美紀遊. by Ku Ts'ai 顧彩, *c.* 1703. In *HFHC*, VI.

K'e-tso chui-yü 客座贅語, by Ku Ch'i-yüan 顧起元, 1617. In *Chin-ling ts'ung-k'e*.

Ku-chü chüeh-se k'ao 古劇脚色考, by Wang Kuo-wei 王國維, 1911. Peking, 1957 (in *Wang Kuo-wei hsi-ch'ü lun-wen chi* 王國維戲曲論文集, pp. 227–46).

Ku-pen hsi-ch'ü ts'ung-k'an chiu-chi 古本戲曲叢刊九集. edited by the Ku-pen hsi-ch'ü ts'ung-k'an pien-chi wei-yüan hui 古本戲曲叢刊編輯委員會, Peking, 1964.

Kuang-yang tsa-chi 廣陽雜記, by Liu Hsien-t'ing 劉獻廷 (1648–95). Peking, 1957 (*Ch'ing-tai shih-liao pi-chi ts'ung-k'an* 清代史料筆記叢刊).

Kuo-ch'ao ch'i-hsien lei-cheng 國朝耆獻類徵, edited by Li Huan 李桓, 1890. Taipei, 1966 (photorep. of original edition).

Lan-feng Wei-shih tsung-p'u 蘭風魏氏宗譜, compiled by Wei Ting-san 魏鼎三 a.o., 1878.

Li-yüan chiu-hua 梨園舊話, by Wu Tao 吳燾 (*chin-shih* 1876). In *CTYT*, III.

Liang-huai yen-fa chih 兩淮鹽法志, compiled by Hsieh K'ai-ch'ung 謝開寵, Chi-shan 佶山 a.o., 1806.

Liang-pan Ch'iu-yü an sui-pi 兩般秋雨盦隨筆, by Liang Shao-jen 梁紹壬, 1837. Hong Kong, 1956.

Liu-nan sui-pi 柳南隨筆, by Wang Ying-k'uei 王應奎, 1740. *Ts'ung-shu chi-ch'eng* edition.

Lu-kuei pu 錄鬼簿, by Chung Ssu-ch'eng 鍾嗣成, 1330. In *CKKT*, II.

Lu-kuei pu hsü-pien 錄鬼簿續編, author unknown, early Ming. In *CKKT*, II.

Lü-yüan ts'ung-hua 履園叢話, by Ch'ien Yung 錢泳, 1825. In *Pi-chi hsiao-shuo ta-kuan*, III.

Meng-hua so-pu 夢華瑣簿, by Yang Mou-chien 楊懋建, 1842. In *CTYT*, II.

Meng-liang lu 夢粱錄, by Wu Tzu-mu 吳自牧, 1274. In *Tung-ching meng-hua lu (wai ssu-chung)*.

Ming-chou Wu-shih chia-chi 茗州吳氏家記, compiled by Wu Jui-ku 吳瑞穀, 1591. Section quoted in Taga Akigorō, *Sōfu no kenkyū*, pp. 684–6.

Ming-shih 明史, compiled by Chang T'ing-yü 張廷玉 a.o., 1739. *Po-na* edition.

Ming-t'ung ho-lu 明僮合錄, by Yü-pu-tiao t'u 餘不釣徒 and Tien-ch'un-sheng 殿春生, 1867. In *CTYT*, II.

Nan-hsün sheng-tien 南巡盛典, compiled by Kao Chin 高晉, 1771. Edition of 1882.

Nan-tz'u hsü-lu 南詞敍錄, by Hsü Wei 徐渭, 1559. In *CKKT*, III.

Ning-po fu-chih 寧波府志, compiled by Chang Shih-ch'e 張時徹, and Chou Hsi-che 周希哲, 1560.

Ou-pei ch'üan-chi 甌北全集, by Chao I 趙翼 (1727–1814), 1877.

Pan-ch'iao tsa-chi 板橋雜記, by Yü Huai 余懷, c. 1650. In *Shuang-mei ching-an ts'ung-shu*.

Pei-ching li-yüan chang-ku ch'ang-pien 北京梨園掌故長編, edited by Chang Tz'u-hsi 張次溪, Peiping, 1934. In *CTYT*, III.

Pei-ching li-yüan chin-shih wen-tzu lu 北京梨園金石文字錄, edited by Chang Tz'u-hsi 張次溪. Peiping, 1934. In *CTYT*, III.

Pei-meng so-yen 北夢瑣言, by Sun Kuang-hsien 孫光憲 (d. 968). *Ts'ung-shu chi-ch'eng* edition.

Pei-p'ing li-yüan chu-chih tz'u hui-pien 北平梨園竹枝詞薈編, edited by Chang Tz'u-hsi 張次溪, Peiping, 1937. In *Ch'ing-tai Yen-tu li-yüan shih-liao hsü-pien*.

P'ei-yüan t'ang ou-ts'un kao 培遠堂偶存稿, by Ch'en Hung-mou 陳宏謀 (1696–1771). Sectons quoted in Tanaka Issei, *Shindai chihō geki shiryō shū*, I, 31–34; II, 3–4, 31–32, 71.

Pi-chi hsiao-shuo ta-kuan 筆記小說大觀, edited by the Chin-pu shu-chü 進步書局, Shanghai, Republic.

P'ien-yü chi 片羽集, by Lai-ch'ing ko chu-jen 來青閣主人, 1805. In *CTYT*, I. (Quoted sections include *t'i-tseng chu-jen* 題贈諸人.)

P'in-hua pao-chien 品花寶鑑, by Ch'en Sen 陳森, 1849. The edition used cannot be identified by place or date, which are not indicated. The sixty *hui* are divided into eight *chüan* and the title of the work is given also as *I-ch'ing i-shih* 怡情佚史.

Po-an hsin-pien 駁案新編 compiled by Ch'üan Shih-ch'ao 全士潮 a.o., 1781. In *Po-an hui-pien*.

Po-an hui-pien 駁案彙編, edited by the T'u-shu chi-ch'eng chü 圖書集成局, 1883.

San-hsü i-nien lu 三續疑年錄, compiled by Lu Hsin-yüan 陸心源, 1880. In *I-nien lu wu-chung*.

San-kuo chih 三國志. by Ch'en Shou 陳壽 (233–97). Peking, 1959.

San-kuo yen-i 三國演義, by Lo Kuan-chung 羅貫中, edited by Mao Tsung-kang 毛宗崗 n.d. Peking, 1953.

Shan-hsi t'ung-chih 山西通志, compiled by Tseng Kuo-ch'üan 曾國荃 a.o., 1887.

Shu-chi t'ang chin-yüeh 庶幾堂今樂, by Yü Chih 余治, 1860.

Shuang-mei ching-an ts'ung-shu 雙楳景闇叢書, edited by Yeh Te-hui 葉德輝 1903–11.

Shui-hu chuan 水滸傳, by Shih Nai-an 施耐菴, and Lo Kuan-chung 羅貫中, edited by Chin Sheng-t'an 金聖歎, n.d. Peking, 1954.

Shuo-ling 說鈴, compiled by Wu Chen-fang 吳震方, 1702–5. Taipei, 1968 (photorep. of 1799 edition).

Su-hsiang shih ts'ung-shu 粟香室叢書, edited by Chin Wu-hsiang 金武祥, 1881–1918.

Ssu-yu chai ts'ung-shuo 四友齋叢說, by Ho Liang-chün 何良俊, 1569. Peking, 1959 (*Yüan-Ming shih-liao pi-chi ts'ung-k'an I* 元明史料筆記叢刊之一).

Sui-yüan san-shih-liu chung 隨園三十六種, by Yüan Mei 袁枚 (1716–98), 1908.

Sui-yüan shih-hua 隨園詩話, by Yüan Mei 袁枚 (1716–98). In *Sui-yüan san-shih-liu chung*.

Sung-shih 宋史, compiled by T'o-t'o 脫脫 a.o., 1346. *Po-na* edition.

Ta-Ch'ing Hsüan-tsung Ch'eng huang-ti shih-lu 大清宣宗成皇帝實錄, compiled by Chia Chen 賈楨 a.o., 1856. In *Ta-Ch'ing li-ch'ao shih-lu*.

Ta-Ch'ing hui-tien shih-li 大清會典事例, compiled by K'un-kang 崑岡 a.o., 1899. Taipei, 1963 (photorep. of 1899 edition).

Ta-Ch'ing Jen-tsung Jui huang-ti shih-lu 大清仁宗睿皇帝實錄, compiled by Ts'ao Chen-yung 曹振鏞 a.o., 1824. In *Ta-Ch'ing li-ch'ao shih-lu*.

Ta-Ch'ing li-ch'ao shih-lu 大清歷朝實錄, Manchuria, Kuo-wu yüan, c. 1937.

Ta-Ch'ing Mu-tsung I huang-ti shih-lu 大清穆宗毅皇帝實錄, compiled by Shen Kuei-fen 沈桂芬 a.o., 1880. In *Ta-Ch'ing li-ch'ao shih-lu*.

Ta-Ch'ing Shih-tsung Hsien huang-ti shih-lu 大清世宗憲皇帝實錄, compiled by Chang T'ing-yü 張廷玉 a.o., 1742. In *Ta-Ch'ing li-ch'ao shih-lu*.

T'ai-ho cheng-yin p'u 太和正音譜, by Chu Ch'üan 朱權, 1398. In *CKKT*, III.

T'an-po 曇波, by Ssu pu t'ou-t'o 四不頭陀, 1852. In *CTYT*, II.

T'ao-an meng-i 陶菴夢憶, by Chang Tai 張岱 (1597–1684?). *Ts'ung-shu chi-ch'eng* edition.

T'eng-yin tsa-chi 藤陰雜記, by Tai Lu 戴璐, 1796. Taipei, 1969 (*Pei-p'ing ti-fang yen-chiu ts'ung-k'an I* 北平地方研究叢刊第一輯, photorep. of 1877 edition).

Ti-ch'eng hua-yang 帝城花樣, by Yang Mou-chien 楊懋建, c. 1837. In *Hsiang-yen ts'ung-shu*, XV, 2.

Ti-ching sui-shih chi-sheng 帝京歲時紀勝, by P'an Jung-pi 潘榮陛, 1758. Peking 1961 (printed together with *Yen-ching sui-shih chi*).

T'ien-chih ou-wen 天咫偶聞, by Chen-chün 震鈞, 1907.

Ting-an hsü-chi 定盦續集, by Kung Tzu-chen 龔自珍 (1792–1841), 1868. *Ssu-pu ts'ung-k'an* edition.

Ting-nien yü-sun chih 丁年玉筍志, by Yang Mou-chien 楊懋建, 1842. In *CTYT*, II.

T'ing-ch'un hsin-yung 聽春新詠, by Liu-ch'un ko hsiao-shih 留春閣小史, 1810. In *CTYT*, I. (Quoted *chüan*: *Hui-pu* 徽部, *hsi-pu* 西部 and *pieh-chi* 別集.)

Ts'e-mao yü-t'an 側帽餘譚, by T'iao-hsi i-lan sheng 苕溪藝蘭生, 1878. In *CTYT*, II.

Tseng-pu ch'ü-yüan 增補曲苑, edited by the Ku-shu liu-t'ung-ch'u 古書流通處 a.o., Shanghai, Republic.

Tu-ch'eng chi-sheng 都城紀勝, by Kuan-pu nai-te weng 灌圃耐得翁, 1235. In *Tung-ching meng-hua lu (wai ssu-chung)*.

Tu-ch'ü ts'ung-k'an 讀曲叢刊, edited by Tung K'ang 董康, 1917.

Tu-Lung chi 度隴記, by Tung Hsün 董恂, c. 1850. In *HFHC*, VI.

Tu-men chi-lüeh 都門紀畧, by Yang Ching-t'ing 楊靜亭 a.o., 1845–1907. Sections quoted in Chou Chih-fu, *Tu-men chi-lüeh chung chih hsi-ch'ü shih-liao*, passim.

Tu-men chu-chih tz'u 都門竹枝詞, author unknown, 1813. Extract quoted in *PPLYCC*, pp. 1b–3a.

Tu-men hui-tsuan 都門彙纂, by Yang Ching-t'ing 楊靜亭, edited and supplemented by Li Ching-shan 李靜山, 1872. (Quoted *chüan*: *tsa-yung* 雜咏, *tsa-chi* 雜記.)

Tung-ching meng-hua lu (wai ssu-chung) 東京夢華錄 (外四種), edited by Chung-hua shu-chü Shang-hai pien-chi so 中華書局上海編輯所, Peking, 1956.

Tung-p'o chih-lin 東坡志林, by Su Shih 蘇軾, 1078–1100. *Ts'ung-shu chi-ch'eng* edition.

T'ung-su pien 通俗編, by Chai Hao 翟灝 (d. 1788). In *Han-hai*, XXVIII.

Wen-hsüan 文選 edited by Hsiao T'ung 蕭統 (501–31). Hong Kong, 1960 (first published 1936).

Wu-ch'ü feng-t'u lu 吳趨風土錄 by Ku Lu 顧祿 (fl. 1830). In *HFHC*, VI.

Wu-lin chiu-shih 武林舊事, by Chou Mi 周密, c. 1290. In *Tung-ching meng-hua lu (wai ssu-chung)*.

Wu-men hua-fang lu 吳門畫舫錄, by Hsi-hsi shan-jen 西溪山人, 1806. In *Shuang-mei ching-an ts'ung-shu*.

Yang-chia chiang yen-i 楊家將演義, by Hsiung Chung-ku 熊鍾谷, late Ming. Hong Kong, *c.* 1960.

Yang-chou fu-chih 揚州府志, compiled by Yang Hsün 楊洵 a.o., 1604.

Yang-chou fu-chih 揚州府志, compiled by Chiao Hsün 焦循 a.o., 1810.

Yang-chou hua-fang lu 揚州畫舫錄, by Li Tou 李斗, 1794. Peking, 1960 *(Ch'ing-tai shih-liao pi-chi ts'ung-k'an)*.

Yang-chou ming-sheng lu 揚州名勝錄, by Li Tou 李斗, 1794. In *Yang-chou ts'ung-k'e*.

Yang-chou ts'ung-k'e 揚州叢刻, edited by Ch'en Heng-ho 陳恒和, Yang-chou, 1930–4.

Yen-ching sui-shih chi 燕京歲時記, by Tun Ch'ung 敦崇 (*hao* Li-ch'en 禮臣), 1900. Peking, 1961 (printed together with *Ti-ching sui-shih chi-sheng*).

Yen-ching tsa-chi 燕京雜記, author and date unknown. In *HFHC*, VI.

Yen-lan hsiao-p'u 燕蘭小譜, by Wu Ch'ang-yüan 吳長元, 1785. In *CTYT*, I.

Yen-p'u tsa-chi 簷曝雜記, by Chao I 趙翼 (1727–1814). In *Ou-pei ch'üan-chi*.

Yen-t'ai chi-yen 燕臺集豔, by Po-hua chü-shih 播花居士, 1823. In *Ch'ing-tai Yen-tu li-yüan shih-liao hsü-pien*.

Yen-t'ai hua-shih lu 燕臺花事錄, by Shu-hsi ch'iao yeh 蜀西樵也, 1876. In *CTYT*, II.

Yen-t'ai hung-chao chi 燕臺鴻爪集, by Su-hai an chü-shih 粟海庵居士, 1832. In *CTYT*, I.

Ying-hua hsiao-p'u 鶯花小譜, by Pan-piao-tzu 半標子, 1819. In *CTYT*, I.

Yu-lan chü-shih Tung-ching meng-hua lu 幽蘭居士東京夢華錄, by Meng Yüan-lao 孟元老, 1147. In *Tung-ching meng-hua lu (wai ssu-chung)*.

Yü-ts'un ch'ü-hua 雨村曲話, by Li T'iao-yüan 李調元, 1784. In *CKKT*, VIII.

Yüan-Ming tsa-chü 元明雜劇, photorep. of twenty-seven *tsa-chü* in the Ting 丁 family library, 1929. Peking, 1958.

Yüan-yüan chuan 圓圓傳, by Lu Tz'u-yün 陸次雲 (fl. late seventeenth century). In *Hsiang-yen ts'ung-shu*, IX, 1.

b. *Chinese and Japanese Works (since 1912)*

Aoki Masaru 青木正兒, tr. Wang Ku-lu 王古魯, *Chung-kuo chin-shih hsi-ch'ü shih* 中國近世戲曲史, Shanghai, 1936. (Original edition: *Shina kinsei gikyoku shi* 支那近世戲曲史, Kyoto, 1930.)

Chang Tz'u-hsi 張次溪, *Yen-tu ming-ling chuan* 燕都名伶傳, in *Ch'ing-tai Yen-tu li-yüan shih-liao hsü-pien*, Peiping, 1937.

Chao Ching-shen 趙景深—*Ming-Ch'ing ch'ü-t'an* 明清曲談, Peking, 1959.

Ch'en Wan-nai 陳萬鼐—*Yüan Ming Ch'ing chü-ch'ü shih* 元明清劇曲史, *Chung-kuo hsüeh-shu chu-tso chiang-chu wei-yüan hui ts'ung-shu XXI* 中國學術著作獎助委員會叢書之廿一, Taipei, 1966.

Ch'en Yen-heng 陳彥衡—*Chiu-chü ts'ung-t'an* 舊劇叢談, in *CTYT*, III, Peiping, 1934.

Cheng Chen-to 鄭振鐸—*Chung-kuo su-wen-hsüeh shih* 中國俗文學史, *Chung-kuo wen-hua shih ts'ung-shu II* 中國文化史叢書第二輯, 2 vols, Ch'ang-sha, 1938.

——ed.—*Chung-kuo wen-hsüeh yen-chiu* 中國文學研究, Shanghai, 1927; Hong Kong, 1963.

Ch'i Ju-shan 齊如山—*Ch'i Ju-shan ch'üan-chi* 齊如山全集, 8 vols, Taipei, 1964.

——*Ching-chü chih pien-ch'ien* 京劇之變遷, *Ch'i Ju-shan chü-hsüeh ts'ung-shu II* 齊如山劇學叢書之二, Peiping, 1935; in *Ch'i Ju-shan ch'üan-chi*, II, Taipei, 1964.

——*Ch'ing-tai p'i-huang ming-chüeh chien-shu* 清代皮簧名脚簡述, in *Ch'i Ju-shan ch'üan-chi*, IV, Taipei, 1964.

——*Hsi-chieh hsiao chang-ku* 戲界小掌故, in *Ch'i Ju-shan ch'üan-chi*, IV, Taipei, 1964.

——*Hsi-pan* 戲班, *Ch'i Ju-shan chü-hsüeh ts'ung-shu VIII*, Peiping, 1935; in *Ch'i Ju-shan ch'üan-chi*, I, Taipei, 1964.

——*Kuo-chü man-t'an* 國劇漫談, 3 chi, in *Ch'i Ju-shan ch'üan-chi*, III, Taipei, 1964.

Ch'ien Nan-yang 錢南揚—*Sung-Yüan hsi-wen chi-i* 宋元戲文輯佚, Shanghai, 1956.

Chou Chih-fu 周志輔—*Chen-liu ta-wen* 枕流答問, Hong Kong, 1955.

——*Chin pai-nien ti Ching-chü* 近百年的京劇, *Chi-li chü hsi-ch'ü ts'ung-shu V* 幾禮居戲曲叢書之五, Hong Kong, 1962.

——*Ching-hsi chin pai-nien so-chi* 京戲近百年瑣記, Hong Kong, 1951. (Original edition of this work: *Tao-Hsien i-lai li-yüan hsi-nien hsiao-lu* 道咸以來梨園繫年小錄, *Chi-li chü hsi-ch'ü ts'ung-shu III*, Shanghai, 1932.)

——ed.—*Ch'ing Sheng-p'ing shu ts'un-tang shih-li man-ch'ao* 清昇平署存檔事例漫抄, *Chi-li chü hsi-ch'ü ts'ung-shu IV*, Peiping, 1933.

——'Tsao-ch'i p'i-huang ming-tan k'ao' 早期皮黃名旦考, *Ta-Hua* 大華 39 (Oct. 1967), pp. 18–21. (The author has written this article under the pseudonym Chen-liu 枕流.)

——ed.—*Tu-men chi-lüeh chung chih hsi-ch'ü shih-liao* 都門紀略中之戲曲史料, *Chi-li chü hsi-ch'ü ts'ung-shu I*, Shanghai, 1932.

Chou I-pai 周貽白—*Chung-kuo chü-ch'ang shih* 中國劇場史, *Hsi-chü hsiao ts'ung-shu* 戲劇小叢書, Shanghai, 1936.

——*Chung-kuo hsi-chü shih* 中國戲劇史, 3 vols, Shanghai, 1953.

——*Chung-kuo hsi-chü shih chiang-tso* 中國戲劇史講座, Peking, 1958.

——*Chung-kuo hsi-ch'ü lun-chi* 中國戲曲論集 Peking, 1960.

Chu Hsiang 朱湘—'Chiang Shih-ch'üan' 蔣士銓, in Cheng Chen-to, ed., *Chung-kuo wen-hsüeh yen-chiu*, pp. 467–88.

Fu Hsi-hua 傅惜華—*Ch'ü-i lun-ts'ung* 曲藝論叢, *Chung-kuo hsi-ch'ü li-lun ts'ung-shu* 中國戲曲理論叢書, Shanghai, 1953.

Fu I-ling 傅衣凌—*Ming-Ch'ing shih-tai shang-jen chi shang-yeh tzu-pen* 明清時代商人及商業資本, Peking, 1956.

Fujii Hiroshi 藤井宏—'Shinan shōnin no kenkyū (1)' 新安商人の研究 (一), *Tōyō gakuhō* 東洋學報 xxxvi, 1 (June 1953), pp. 1–44.

Hatano Kenichi 波多野乾一, tr. Lu-yüan hsüeh-jen 鹿原學人—*Ching-chü erh-pai nien chih li-shih* 京劇二百年之歷史, Shanghai, 1926. (Original edition: *Shina geki to sono meiyū* 支那劇と其名優, Tokyo, 1925.)

Ho Ping-ti 何炳棣—*Chung-kuo hui-kuan shih-lun* 中國會館史論, Taipei, 1966.

Hsi Ming-chen 席明眞—*Ch'uan-chü chien-t'an* 川劇簡談, Chungking, 1955.

Hsia Yeh 夏野—*Hsi-ch'ü yin-yüeh yen-chiu* 戲曲音樂研究, Shanghai, 1959.

Hsieh Kuo-chen 謝國楨—*Ming-Ch'ing pi-chi t'an-ts'ung* 明清筆記談叢, Peking, 1960.

Hsü Chiu-yeh 許九埜—*Li-yüan i-wen* 梨園軼聞, in *CTYT*, III, Peiping, 1934.

Hsü Mu-yün 徐慕雲—*Chung-kuo hsi-chü shih* 中國戲劇史, Shanghai, 1938.

Hua-tung hsi-ch'ü yen-chiu yüan 華東戲曲研究院, ed.—*Hua-tung hsi-ch'ü chü-chung chieh-shao* 華東戲曲劇種介紹 3 vols, Shanghai, 1955.

Inoue Susumu 井上進—*Shina fūzoku* 支那風俗, 3 vols, Shanghai, 1921–2.

Katō Shigeshi 加藤繁—*Shina keizai shi kōshō* 支那經濟史考證, *Tōyō bunko ronsō XXXIV* 東洋文庫論叢第三十四, 2 vols, Tokyo, 1952–3.

Ku Lin-wen 顧麟文, ed.,—*Yang-chou pa-chia shih-liao* 揚州八家史料, Shanghai, 1962.

Kung Te-pai 龔德柏—*Hsi-chü yü li-shih* 戲劇與歷史, Taipei, 1962.

Kuraishi Takeshirō 倉石武四郎 tr. Wang Fu-ch'üan 汪馥泉—'"Mu-lien chiu-mu hsing-hsiao hsi-wen" yen-chiu' 「目蓮救母行孝戲文」研究, in Cheng Chen-to, ed., *Chung-kuo wen-hsüeh yen-chiu*, pp. 457–66.

Lei Hsiao-ts'en 雷嘯岑—'P'i-huang chü chih shih ti chin-chan' 皮黃劇之史的進展, *Wen-hsüeh shih-chieh chi-k'an* 文學世界季刊 20 (1958), pp. 1–9.

Li Hsiao-ts'ang 李嘯倉—'Kan-chü chu-ch'iang ti lai-yüan yü yen-pien' 贛劇諸腔的來源與演變, *Hsi-ch'ü yen-chiu* 戲曲研究 2 (1957), pp. 86–111.

Liu Chi-tien 劉吉典—*Ching-chü yin-yüeh chieh-shao* 京劇音樂介紹, Peking, 1960.

Liu Ching-yüan 劉靜沅—'Hui-hsi ti ch'eng-chang ho hsien-k'uang' 徽戲的成長和現況, in Hua-tung hsi-ch'ü yen-chiu yüan, ed., *Hua-tung hsi-ch'ü chü-chung chieh-shao*, III, 56–78.

Lo Chin-t'ang 羅錦堂—*Chung-kuo hsi-ch'ü tsung-mu hui-pien* 中國戲曲總目彙編, Hong Kong, 1966.

——*Chung-kuo san-ch'ü shih* 中國散曲史 *Hsien-tai kuo-min chi-pen chih-shih ts'ung-shu IV* 現代國民基本知識叢書第四輯, 2 vols, Taipei, 1956.

——*Hsien-ts'un Yüan-jen tsa-chü pen-shih k'ao* 現存元人雜劇本事考, *Ta-hsüeh ts'ung-shu* 大學叢書, Taipei, 1960.

Lu Hsün 魯迅—*Chung-kuo hsiao-shuo shih-lüeh* 中國小說史略, Peking, 1952.

Mei Lan-fang 梅蘭芳, ed. Hsü Chi-ch'uan 許姬傳—*Wu-t'ai sheng-huo ssu-shih nien* 舞臺生活四十年, 2 vols, Shanghai, 1952–4; Peking, 1957.

Meng Yao 孟瑤—*Chung-kuo hsi-ch'ü shih* 中國戲曲史, *Wen-hsing ts'ung-k'an CL* 文星叢刊 150, 4 vols, Taipei, 1965.

Mo I-p'ing 墨遺萍—'Chi chi-ko ku-tai hsiang-ts'un hsi-t'ai' 記幾個古代鄉村戲台, *Hsi-chü lun-ts'ung* 戲劇論叢 2 (1957), pp. 203–6.

Niida Noboru 仁井田陞—*Chūgoku hōsei shi kenkyū* 中國法制史研究, 4 vols, Tokyo, 1959–64.

Ou-yang Yü-ch'ien 歐陽予倩, ed.—*Chung-kuo hsi-ch'ü yen-chiu tzu-liao ch'u-chi* 中國戲曲研究資料初輯, Peking, 1957.

——'Shih-t'an Yüeh-chü' 試談粵劇, in Ou-yang Yü-ch'ien, ed., *Chung-kuo hsi-ch'ü yen-chiu tzu-liao ch'u chi*, pp. 109–57.

——'T'an erh-huang hsi' 談二黃戲, in Cheng Chen-to, ed., *Chung-kuo wen-hsüeh yen-chiu*, pp. 489–502.

P'an Kuang-tan 潘光旦, *Chung-kuo ling-jen hsüeh-yüan chih yen-chiu* 中國伶人血緣之研究, *Chung-shan wen-hua chiao-yü kuan yen-chiu ts'ung-shu* 中山文化教育館研究叢書, Ch'ang-sha, 1941.

Shen P'eng-nien 沈彭年 a.o.,—*Ku-ch'ü yen-chiu* 鼓曲研究, *Ch'ü-i yen-chiu ts'ung-shu* 曲藝研究叢書, Peking, 1959.

Sun Yang-nung 孫養農—*T'an Yü Shu-yen* 談余叔岩, Hong Kong, 1953.

Sung Tz'u 宋詞—'Yang-chü' 揚劇, in Hua-tung hsi-ch'ü yen-chiu yüan, ed., *Hua-tung hsi-ch'ü chü-chung chieh-shao*, I, 32–45.

Taga Akigorō 多賀秋五郎—*Sōfu no kenkyū* 宗譜の研究, *Tōyō bunko ronsō XLV*, Tokyo, 1960.

Tanaka Issei 田仲一成, ed.—*Shindai chihō geki shiryō shū* 清代地方劇
資料集. *Tōyō gaku bunken sentā sōkan II, III* 東洋學文獻センター
叢刊第 2 輯, 第 3 輯, 2 vols, Tokyo, 1968.

——'Shindai shoki no chihō geki ni tsuite' 清代初期の地方劇について,
Nippon-Chūgoku-gakkai-hō 日本中國會報 17 (1965), pp. 143-54.

——'Shindai shoki no sōzoku engeki ni tsuite' 清代初期の宗族演劇
について, *Tōhōgaku* 東方學 32 (June 1966), pp. 102-16.

T'ao Chün-ch'i 陶君起, ed.—*Ching-chü chü-mu ch'u-t'an* 京劇劇目初探,
Shanghai, 1957; Peking, 1963.

Ts'ao Hsin-ch'üan 曹心泉—'Ch'ien-Ch'ing nei-t'ing yen-hsi hui-i lu'
前清內廷演戲回憶錄, *Chü-hsüeh yüeh-k'an* 劇學月刊 ii, 5 (May 1933),
pp. 1-8.

Tsou Wei-teng 鄒葦澄—' "Ssu ta Hui-pan" yü Ching-hsi' 「四大徽
班」與京戲, *Ming-pao yüeh-k'an* 明報月刊 iii, 6 (June 1968), pp.
53-64.

Wang Chih-chang 王芷章—*Ch'iang-tiao k'ao-yüan* 腔調考原, Peiping,
1934.

——*Ch'ing Sheng-p'ing shu chih-lüeh* 清昇平署志略, 2 vols, Peiping,
1937.

Wang Chung-min 王重民 a.o., ed.—*Tun-huang pien-wen chi* 敦煌變
文集, 2 vols, Peking, 1957.

Wang Hsiao-ch'uan 王曉傳, ed.—*Yüan Ming Ch'ing san-tai chin-hui
hsiao-shuo hsi-ch'ü shih-liao* 元明清三代禁毀小說戲曲史料, Peking, 1958.

Wang Ku-lu 王古魯, ed.—*Ming-tai Hui-tiao hsi-ch'ü san-ch'u chi-i* 明代
徽調戲曲散齣輯佚, Shanghai, 1956.

Wang Meng-sheng 王夢生—*Li-yüan chia-hua* 梨園佳話, Shanghai, 1915.

Wang Shu-nu 王書奴—*Chung-kuo ch'ang-chi shih* 中國娼妓史, Shanghai,
1935.

Wang Ta-ts'o 王大錯, ed.—*Hsi-k'ao* 戲考, Shanghai, 1918-19.

Wu Chün-ta 武俊達, ed.—*Yang-chü yin-yüeh* 揚劇音樂, Peking, 1962.

Yang-chou shih wen-lien 揚州市文聯, ed.—*Yang-chou ch'ing-ch'ü hsüan*
揚州清曲選, Nanking, 1957.

c. Works in Western Languages

Arlington, L.C. and Acton, Harold, tr. and ed.—*Famous Chinese Plays*,
Peiping, 1937.

Bichurin, Le Rev. P. Hyacinthe, tr. from Chinese into Russian; French
tr. by Ferry de Pigny—*Description de Peking, avec un plan de cette
capitale*, St Pétersburg, 1829.

Bodde, Derk, tr. and ed.—*Annual Customs and Festivals in Peking as
Recorded in the* Yen-ching Sui-shih-chi *by Tun Li-ch'en, Peiping*, 1936;
Hong Kong, 1965.

Boulais, Le P. Guy, S. J., tr. and ed.—*Manuel du code chinois* 大清律例 便覽, *Variétés sinologiques 55*, 2 vols, Shanghai, 1924.

Brewitt-Taylor, C. H., tr.—*San-kuo, or Romance of the Three Kingdoms*, 2 vols, Shanghai, 1925.

Buck, Pearl, tr.—*All Men are Brothers*, [*Shui Hu Chuan*], 2 vols, London, 1933; London, 1957.

Burgess, John Stewart—*The Guilds of Peking, Studies in History, Economics, and Public Law 308*, New York, 1928.

Carl, Katharine, *With the Empress Dowager of China*, New York, 1905.

Chavannes, Édouard—*Dix inscriptions chinoises de l'Asie Centrale d'après les estampages de M. Ch.-E. Bonin*, Paris, 1902.

Ch'en, Chih-mai—*Chinese Calligraphers and their Art*, Melbourne, 1966.

Ch'ü, T'ung-tsu 瞿同祖—*Law and Society in Traditional China*, *Le monde d'outre-mer passé et présent, Première série, Études IV*, Paris, 1961.

——*Local Government in China under the Ch'ing*, Harvard East Asian Studies 9, Cambridge, Mass., 1962; Stanford, 1969.

Crump, James—*Materials on Yüan Drama, The University of Michigan Center for Chinese Studies Occasional Papers No. 1*, Ann Arbor, 1962.

Doré, Henri, S. J.—*Recherches sur les superstitions en Chine, IIeme partie, Le panthéon chinois, Variétés sinologiques 39, 41, 42, 44, 45, 46, 48*, 7 vols (*Recherches*, VI–XII), Shanghai, 1914-18. (There are in all 18 volumes in Doré's *Recherches*, ranging in year of publication from 1911 to 1938.)

du Halde, Le P. J. B., S. J.—*Description géographique, historique, chronologique, politique, et physique de l'empire de la Chine et de la Tartarie chinoise*, 4 vols, Paris, 1735; La Haye, 1736.

——tr. R. Brookes—*The General History of China, Containing a Geographical, Historical, Chronological, Political and Physical Description of the Empire of China, Chinese-Tartary, Corea and Thibet*, 4 vols, London, 1736; London, 1741.

Eberhard, Wolfram—*Chinese Festivals*, New York, 1952.

Egerton, Clement, tr.—*The Golden Lotus, A Translation from the Chinese original of the novel Chin P'ing Mei*, 4 vols, London, 1939.

Fang, Chaoying 房兆楹—'A Technique for Estimating the Numerical Strength of the Early Manchu Military Forces', *Harvard Journal of Asiatic Studies* xiii (1950), pp. 192–215.

Favier, Mgr Alphonse—*Péking, Histoire et Description*, Peking, 1897; Paris, 1902.

Goodrich, Luther Carrington—*The Literary Inquisition of Chien-lung*, American Council of Learned Societies Studies in Chinese and Related Civilizations I, Baltimore, 1935.

Halson, Elizabeth—*Peking Opera, A Short Guide*, Hong Kong, 1966.

Hedin, Sven, tr. E. G. Nash—*Jehol, City of Emperors*, London, 1932.

Ho, Ping-ti 何炳棣—*The Ladder of Success in Imperial China, Aspects of Social Mobility, 1368–1911, Studies of the East Asian Institute, Columbia University*, New York, 1962.

——'The Salt Merchants of Yang-chou: A Study of Commercial Capitalism in Eighteenth-Century China', *Harvard Journal of Asiatic Studies* xvii (1954), pp. 130–68.

——*Studies on the Population of China, 1368–1953, Harvard East Asian Studies 4*, Cambridge, Mass., 1959.

Hsia, C. T. 夏志清—*The Classic Chinese Novel, A Critical Introduction, Companions to Asian Studies*, New York and London, 1968.

Hung, Josephine Huang—*Ming Drama*, Taipei, 1966.

Hummel, Arthur W., ed.—*Eminent Chinese of the Ch'ing Period (1644–1912)*, 2 vols, Washington, 1943.

Jaworski, Jan—'L'Avalambana Sutra de la terre pure', *Monumenta Serica* i (1935–6), pp. 82–107.

Jenyns, Soame, tr. and ed.—*Selections from the Three Hundred Poems of the T'ang Dynasty, The Wisdom of the East Series*, London, 1940.

Kalvodová, D.—'The Origin and Character of the Szechwan Theatre', *Archiv Orientální* xxxiv (1966), pp. 505–23.

Katō, Shigeshi, 'On the Hang or the Associations of Merchants in China, with Especial Reference to the Institution in the T'ang and Sung Periods', *Memoirs of the Research Department of the Toyo Bunko (The Oriental Library)* 8 (1936), pp. 45–83.

Levy, Howard, S.—*Chinese Footbinding, The History of a Curious Erotic Custom*, New York, 1966.

——tr. and ed.—*A Feast of Mist and Flowers, the Gay Quarters of Nanking at the End of the Ming*, Yokohama, 1966.

Liu, Ts'un-yan 柳存仁—*Buddhist and Taoist Influences on Chinese Novels, volume I, The Authorship of the Feng Shen Yen I*, Wiesbaden, 1962.

——*Chinese Popular Fiction in Two London Libraries*, Hong Kong, 1967. (English and Chinese versions in one volume, Trans.)

——'De l'authenticité des romans historiques de Luo Guanzhong', to appear in vol. 2 of *Mélanges de sinologie, offerts à Monsieur Paul Demiéville*. (Vol. 1 was published in *Bibliothèque de l'Institut des Hautes Études Chinoises XX*, Paris, 1966.)

——*Wu Ch'êng-ên* 吳承恩: *His Life and Career*, Leiden, 1967. (Originally printed in *T'oung Pao* liii (1967), pp. 1–97.)

MacGowan, D. J.—'Chinese Guilds or Chambers of Commerce and Trades Unions', *Journal of the China Branch of the Royal Asiatic Society* xxi, 3 and 4 (Shanghai, 1886), pp. 133–92.

Mackerras, Colin—*The Chinese Theatre in Modern Times (1840–1970)*, forthcoming.

——'The Growth of the Chinese Regional Drama in the Ming and Ch'ing', *Journal of Oriental Studies* ix, 1 (Jan. 1971), pp. 58–91.

——'The Theatre in Yang-chou in the Late Eighteenth Century', *Papers on Far Eastern History* 1 (March 1970), pp. 1–30.

Malone, Carroll Brown—*History of the Peking Summer Palaces Under the Ch'ing Dynasty, Illinois Studies in the Social Sciences* XIX, Illinois, 1934.

Martin, Helmut—*Li Li-weng über das Theater, Eine chinesische Dramaturgie des siebzehnten Jahrhunderts*, Heidelburg, 1966.

Miyakawa, Hisayuki—'The Confucianization of South China', in Arthur F. Wright, ed., *The Confucian Persuasion*, pp. 21–46.

Needham, Joseph (with Wang, Ling)—*Science and Civilisation in China, Volume 3, Mathematics and the Sciences of the Heavens and the Earth*, Cambridge, 1959.

Nivison, David S. and Wright, Arthur F., eds.—*Confucianism in Action*, Stanford, 1959.

Nivison, David S.—'Ho-shen and His Accusers: Ideology and Political Behavior in the Eighteenth Century', in David S. Nivison and Arthur F. Wright, eds., *Confucianism in Action*, pp. 209–43.

Ruhlmann, Robert—'Traditional Heroes in Chinese Popular Fiction', in Arthur F. Wright, ed., *The Confucian Persuasion*, pp. 141–76.

Scott, A. C.—*The Classical Theatre of China*, London, 1957.

——*Mei Lan-fang, Leader of the Pear Garden*, Hong Kong, 1959.

——tr. and ed.—*Traditional Chinese Plays*, 2 vols, Madison, 1967–9.

Sirén, Osvald—*The Imperial Palaces of Peking*, 3 vols, Paris, 1926.

Spence, Jonathan D.—*Ts'ao Yin and the K'ang-hsi Emperor, Bondservant and Master, Yale Historical Publications Miscellany 85*, New Haven, 1966.

Staunton, Sir George—*An Authentic Account of an Embassy from the King of Great Britain to the Emperor of China*, 2 vols, London, 1797.

Twitchett, Denis and Wright, Arthur F., eds.—*Confucian Personalities*, Stanford, 1962.

van der Sprenkel, Otto Berkelbach—'The Geographical Background of the Ming Civil Service', *Journal of Economic and Social History of the Orient* iv, 3 (1961), pp. 302–36.

van der Sprenkel, Sybille—*Legal Institutions in Manchu China, A Sociological Analysis, London School of Economics Monographs on Social Anthropology, No. 24*, London, 1962.

van Gulik, R. H.—*The Lore of the Chinese Lute, An Essay in Ch'in Ideology, Monumenta Nipponica Monographs*, Tokyo, 1940.

——*Sexual Life in Ancient China*, Leiden, 1961.

von Zach, Erwin, tr.—*Die chinesische Anthologie, Übersetzungen aus dem Wen hsüan, Harvard-Yenching Institute Studies XVIII*, 2 vols, Cambridge, Mass., 1958.

Waley, Arthur—*Ballads and Stories from Tun-huang, An Anthology*, London, 1960.

——*The Secret History of the Mongols, and Other Pieces*, London, 1963.

——*Yuan Mei, Eighteenth Century Chinese Poet*, London, 1956.

Wilhelm, Hellmut—'From Myth to Myth: The Case of Yüeh Fei's Biography', in Arthur F. Wright and Denis Twitchett, eds., *Confucian Personalities*, pp. 146–61.

Wright, Arthur F., ed.—*The Confucian Persuasion*, Stanford, 1960.

——See also under Nivison and Twitchett.

Wright, Mary Clabaugh—*The Last Stand of Chinese Conservatism, The T'ung-Chih Restoration, 1862–1874*, Stanford, 1957; New York, 1966.

Yang, C. K.—*Religion in Chinese Society, A Study of Contemporary Social Functions of Religion and Some of Their Historical Factors*, Berkeley and Los Angeles, 1961.

Yang, Daniel Shih-p'êng—*An Annotated Bibliography of Materials for the Study of the Peking Theatre, Wisconsin China Series, No. 2*, Madison, 1967.

Yang, Gladys and Hsien-yi, tr.—*A Brief History of Chinese Fiction*, Lu Hsun, *China Knowledge Series*, Peking, 1959.

——tr.—*The Palace of Eternal Youth*, Peking, 1955.

——tr.—*The Scholars*, Peking, 1957; Peking, 1964.

——tr.—*Selected Plays of Kuan Han-ching*, Shanghai, 1958.

Yang, Lien-sheng—*Money and Credit in China, A Short History, Harvard-Yenching Institute Monograph Series XII*, Cambridge, Mass., 1952.

Yao, Hsin-nung 姚莘農—'The Rise and Fall of the K'un Ch'ü', *T'ien Hsia Monthly* ii, 1 (January 1936), pp. 63–84.

Zung, Cecilia—*Secrets of the Chinese Drama, A Complete Explanatory Guide to Actions and Symbols as Seen in the Performance of Chinese Dramas*, London, 1937.

Zürcher, E.—*The Buddhist Conquest of China, The Spread and Adaptation of Buddhism in Early Medieval China, Sinica Leidensia vol. XI*, 2 vols, Leiden, 1959.

GLOSSARY OF CHARACTERS[1]

Ai-ti 哀帝
An-ch'ing 安慶
An-ch'ing (cemetery) 安慶
An-ch'ing (company) 安慶
An Fu 安福
An-ting (academy) 安定
An-ting (gate) 安定
Cha (-chia) lou 查(家)樓
ch'a-lou 茶樓
Chan Ch'ang-sha 戰長沙
Chan Ch'eng-tu 戰城都
Chang Chao 張照
Chang Chi-liang (*tzu* Heng-fu)
　張際亮 (亨甫)
Chang Chiang-ts'ai (*hao* Tz'u-hsi)
　張江裁 (次溪)
Chang Chin-lin 張金麟
Chang Ch'ing-hsiang 張青薌
Chang Erh-k'uei 張二奎 (or 魁)
Chang Fa-kuan 張發官
Chang Feng-ling 張鳳齡
Chang Ho 張郃
Chang Hsi 張禧
Chang Hsi-lin 覃喜林
Chang Hsiao-ts'ai-lin 張小彩林
Chang Hui-lan 張蕙蘭
Chang Jen-kuei 張仁龜
Chang Kuo-hsiang 張國相
Chang Lien-kuan 張蓮官
Chang Pao-kuan 張寶官
Chang Sheng-yin 張生寅
Chang Shih-ch'i 張時起
Chang Ta-an 張大安

Chang Tai 張岱
Chang Te-lin 張德林
Chang Yü-mei 覃玉美
Chang Yüan-hsiu 張元秀
ch'ang (arena) 場
ch'ang (sing) 唱
Ch'ang-ch'un kung 長春宮
Ch'ang-ch'un yüan 長春園
Ch'ang-hsiang 長巷
Ch'ang Hsiu-kuan 常秀官
Ch'ang-lo 長樂
Ch'ang-sheng tien 長生殿
Ch'ang-yin ko 暢音閣
Chao Chih-hsin 趙執信
Chao-ch'in 招親
Chao Hsiao-ch'ing-ling 趙小慶齡
Chao I 趙翼
Chao-kuan 昭關
Chao San-kuan (*tzu* Nan-ju)
　趙三官 (南如)
Chao-tai hsiao-shao 昭代簫韶
Ch'ao-chou 潮州
Ch'ao-chü 潮劇
Ch'ao-kuan (gate) 鈔關
Ch'ao-yang (gate) 朝陽
Chen-chiang 鎮江
Ch'en Ch'ang-ch'un 陳長春
Ch'en-chia (valley) 陳家
Ch'en Chin-kuan 陳金官
Ch'en Chin-ts'ai 陳金彩
Ch'en Feng-lin (*tzu* Luan-hsien)
　陳鳳林 (鸞仙)
Ch'en-hsiang 沉香

---

[1] This list includes all Chinese proper names and technical terms mentioned in the present work except (i) most of those given in the List of Works Cited; (ii) dynasties and reign-titles; and (iii) very famous geographical names, and a few other extremely common terms like ts'e and chüan.

Ch'en Hsiang-chou 陳湘舟
Ch'en-hsiang t'ai-tzu p'i Hua-shan 沉香太子劈華山
Ch'en Kuei-lin (from An-ch'ing) 陳桂林
Ch'en Kuei-lin (from Yang-chou) 陳桂林
Ch'en Kung 陳宮
Ch'en K'ung-cheng 陳孔蒸
Ch'en Ming-chih 陳明智
Ch'en San-kuan 陳三官
Ch'en Shih-yün 陳士雲
Ch'en Shou-feng 陳壽峯
Ch'en Shou-lin 陳壽林
Ch'en Ssu 陳四
Ch'en Te-lin 陳德林 (or 霖)
Ch'en Tien-chang 陳殿章
Ch'en T'ung-hsiang 陳桐香
Ch'en Yin-kuan (*tzu* Mei-pi) 陳銀官 (渼碧)
Ch'en Yüan-yüan 陳圓圓
cheng 箏
Cheng Chih-chen 鄭之珍
Cheng-i tz'u 正乙祠
Cheng San-kuan 鄭三官
Cheng San-pao 鄭三寶
Cheng-yang (gate) 正陽
Ch'eng-an 成安
Ch'eng Chang-keng (*tzu* Yü-shan) 程長庚 (玉珊)
Ch'eng Chang-pu 程章甫 (or 圃)
Ch'eng Chi-hsien 程繼先
Ch'eng Ch'ien-te 程謙德
Ch'eng-huang (temple, *miao*) 城隍
Ch'eng-huang shen 城隍神
Ch'eng Meng-hsing 程夢星
Ch'eng-p'ai 程派
Ch'eng Shao-t'ang 程少棠
Ch'eng Yen-ch'iu 程硯秋
Ch'eng Yü-ch'üan 程御詮
chi 集
Chi-ch'ing (company) 集慶

Chi-fang (company) 集芳
Chi-hsiang (company) 吉祥
Chi-hsiu (company) 集秀
Chi-shan 稷山
chi-t'ien 祭田
Chi-yü 季玉
Chi Yün 紀昀
Ch'i-hsiu (company) 啓秀
Ch'i-hua (gate) 齊化
Ch'i-kuan 琪官
ch'i-su 耆宿
Chia-meng (pass) 葭萌
Chia Pao-yü 賈寶玉
Chia-ting 嘉定
chia-t'ung 家僮
chia-wu 甲午
Chiang Chen-hung 江振鴻
Chiang Chin-kuan (from An-ch'ing) 江金官
Chiang Chin-kuan (from Su-chou) 蔣金官
Chiang Ch'un (*hao* Ho-t'ing, business-name Kuang-ta) 江春 (鶴亭, 廣達)
Chiang-hsien 絳縣
Chiang Kuo-mao 江國茂
Chiang-ning 江寧
Chiang P'u 蔣溥
Chiang Shih-ch'üan 蔣士銓
Chiang Ssu-erh 蔣四兒
Chiang T'ien-lu 蔣天祿
Chiang T'ing-hsi 蔣廷錫
Chiang-tung (company) 江東
Ch'iang Wu-shih 强五十
'Chiao-erh shih' 驕兒詩
Chiao-fang ssu 教坊司
Chiao-t'ien 叫天
Ch'iao-kuan 巧官
Chien-ning 建寧
Ch'ien-liang ch'u 錢糧處
Ch'ien-men 前門
Ch'ien-shan 潛山

Ch'ien Wang-san 錢王三
Ch'ien Yüan-pao 錢元寶
ch'ih-hsin 池心
Ch'ih Pao-ts'ai 池寶財
ch'ih-tzu 池子
Chin Chin-chung 靳進忠
Chin Feng 金鳳
Chin Kuei-kuan 金桂官
Chin-li 錦里
Chin-ling 金陵
Chin-ling lou 金陵樓
Chin Pan-chü 金伴菊
chin-shih 進士
Chin T'an-erh 金彈兒
Chin-t'ang 金堂
Chin Te-hui 金德輝
Chin-yü (company) 金玉 (or 鈺)
Chin-yüan lou 晉元樓
ch'in (musical instrument) 琴
Ch'in-ch'iang 秦腔
Ch'in-huai (canal) 秦淮
Ch'in Kuei 秦檜
Ch'in Ming-lei 秦鳴雷
ching 淨
Ching-ch'iang 京腔
Ching-chung (temple, *miao*) 精忠
Ching-chü 京劇
Ching-ho (company) 景和
Ching-i t'ang 敬義堂
Ching-shan 景山
Ching-t'ai yüan (or hsüan) 景泰園
(or 軒)
Ching-te chen 景德鎮
ch'ing-ch'ang 清唱
Ch'ing-ch'eng (company) 慶成
Ch'ing-ch'un (company) 慶春
Ch'ing-feng t'ing 清風亭
Ch'ing-feng yüan 慶豐園
Ch'ing-ho yüan 慶和園
ch'ing-hsi 清戲
Ch'ing-lo yüan 慶樂園
Ch'ing-ming 清明

Ch'ing-ming hsi 清明戲
Ch'ing-ning (company) 慶寧
Ch'ing Sheng-p'ing (company)
慶昇平
Ch'ing-shun yüan 慶順園
Ch'ing-yang 青陽
Ch'ing-yang ch'iang 青陽腔
Ch'ing-yüan (company) 慶元
Chiu-ch'eng 舊城
Chiu-chiang 九江
chiu-chuang 酒莊
Cho-fang Ts'ao 捉放曹
cho-tzu 桌子
Chou-chih 盩厔
Chou Hsiao-feng 周小鳳
Chou K'ai-yüeh 周開月
chou-tzu 軸子
Chou Wei-pai 周維柏
Chou Yü 周瑜
ch'ou 丑
Chu-chi 諸暨
Chu Ch'i-lin 朱麒麟
Chu Hsi-tsu 朱希祖
Chu K'ai 朱凱
Chu-ko Liang 諸葛亮
Chu Lao-wu 朱老五
Chu Lien-fen 朱蓮芬
Chu Nien-i 朱念一
Chu San 朱三
Chu-sha chih 硃砂痣
chu-sheng 諸生
Chu To-shan 朱朵山
Chu Wen-yüan 朱文元
Chu Yeh-tung 朱野東
ch'u 齣
Ch'u 楚
ch'u-shih 出師
Ch'u-tiao 楚調
ch'uan-ch'i 傳奇
Ch'uan-ching t'ang 傳經堂
Ch'uan-chü 川劇
Chuang-tsung 莊宗

chuang-yüan 狀元
Ch'uang-shan 闖山
Ch'un-t'ai (company, Peking)
　春臺
Ch'un-t'ai (company, Yang-chou)
　春臺
ch'un-t'ai hsi 春臺戲
ch'un-wei 春闈
chung chou-tzu 中軸子
Chung-ho yüan 中和園
Chung-mou 中牟
Chung-yüan chieh 中元節
Ch'ung-ch'ing (Anhwei company)
　重慶
Ch'ung-ch'ing (*Ching-ch'iang*
　company) 崇慶
Ch'ung-hua kung 重華宮
Ch'ung-ning (temple, *ssu*) 重寧
Ch'ung-wen (gate) 崇文
ch'ü-i 曲藝
chü-jen 舉人
Chü-jung 句容
Ch'ü Ch'eng-tu 取成都
ch'ü-tzu 曲子
Chüan-yu i-sou 倦遊逸叟
Ch'üan-chou 泉州
Ch'üan-fu (company) 全福
chüeh-shih 榷使
Ch'üeh-k'ou (gate) 闕口
Ch'ün-ying hui 羣英會
En-ch'ing (company) 恩慶
erh-fan 二番
erh-huang 二黃
erh-mien 二面
erh-shih-pa hsiu 二十八宿
Fa-hu 法護
Fan Hsiu-lan 范秀蘭
fan-li 凡例
Fan Ta 樊大
Fan T'ien-hsi 范添喜
Fan Yün-kuan 樊雲官
Fang-hu chai 方壺齋

Fang-ts'ao tz'u-jen 芳草詞人
Fang-ts'ao yüan 芳草園
Fang Wen-hsi 方問溪
Fen-fang (street) 粉坊
Feng-ching chen 楓涇鎮
feng-yin 封印
fou 缶
Fu-ch'eng (company) 福成
Fu-ch'eng (gate) 阜成
Fu-ch'eng yüan 阜成園
fu-ching 副淨
Fu-chou (Kiangsi) 撫州
Fu-ho (company) 阜和
Fu-hsi 伏羲
Fu-hua (company) 富華
hai-tzu 孩子
Hai-yen 海鹽
Han Chi-hsiang 韓吉祥
Han-chung 漢中
Han-hsiang (company) 寒香
Han Hsüan 韓玄
Han-lin (academy) 翰林
Han-p'ai 漢派
Han Ssu-hsi 韓四喜
Han Yung-li 韓永立
hang-kuan 行館
Hao Kuei-pao 郝桂寶
Hao P'an-yüeh 郝攀月
Hao T'ien-hsiu 郝天秀
Hao-t'ien t'a 昊天塔
Heng-sheng (company) 恆盛
Ho-ch'ai chi 合釵記
Ho-chien 河間
Ho-ch'un (company) 和春
Ho-fei 合肥
Ho-feng 鶴峯
ho-kun 合滾
Ho Liang-chün (*tzu* Yüan-lang)
　何良俊 (元朗)
Ho-shen 和珅
Ho Sheng-ming 何聲明
Ho Wan-yüeh 何玩月

Hong (merchants) 行
hou-t'ai 後臺
Hou-t'u 后土
Hsi-chih (gate) 西直
Hsi Chu-shih k'ou 西珠市口
hsi-chuang 戲莊
hsi-fang 戲房
Hsi-hua (gate) 西華
Hsi-kuan 喜官
hsi-kuan 戲館
Hsi-lien-ch'eng 喜連成
Hsi-ling-kuan 錫齡官
Hsi-liu 細柳
Hsi-men 西門
Hsi-men Ch'ing 西門慶
Hsi Mu-lien 戲目連
hsi-p'i 西皮
Hsi-pien (gate) 西便
Hsi-shen 喜神
Hsi-shen Tsu-shih (temple, *miao*) 喜神祖師
Hsi-ssu p'ai-lou 西四牌樓
hsi-tiao 西調
hsi-yüan 戲園
hsia-ch'ang men 下場門
Hsia-hou Yüan 夏侯淵
Hsia Shuang-hsi 夏雙喜
Hsiang-chü 湘劇
hsiang-kung (t'ang-tzu) 相公 (堂子)
hsiang-kung hui 相公會
Hsiang-ling 襄陵
Hsiang-shan (chi) 香山 (記)
Hsiang-t'an 湘潭
Hsiang-yang 襄陽
hsiao 簫
hsiao-ch'ang 小唱
Hsiao Ch'in-huai (canal) 小秦淮
hsiao-ch'ü 小曲
Hsiao-fan chü-shih 小樊居士
Hsiao-hui 小惠
Hsiao (kua-fu) shang-fen 小 (寡婦) 上坟 (or 墳)

Hsiao Nan-yün chu-jen 小南雲主人
Hsiao-shan 蕭山
Hsiao-sheng 孝聖
hsiao-sheng 小生
Hsiao Su-chen 蕭素貞
hsiao-tan 小旦
Hsiao-tung (gate) 小東
hsiao-tzu 小字
Hsiao-yü 小玉
Hsiao-yüan 篠園
Hsieh Ssu-erh 薛四兒
hsieh-tzu 楔子
Hsieh Yin-hsüan 薛印軒
Hsieh Yung-sheng 薛溶生
Hsien-nung t'an 先農壇
Hsien-ti 獻帝
Hsien-yang 咸陽
Hsien-yü k'ou 鮮魚口
Hsin-ch'eng 新城
Hsin-ch'ing (company) 新慶
hsin-mao 辛卯
Hsing-hua 興化
hsing-kung 行宮
Hsiung-nu 匈奴
Hsü Hsiao-hsiang 徐小香 (or 湘)
Hsü Kuei-lin 徐桂林
Hsü-ning (gate) 徐寧
Hsü Shang-chih 徐尙志
Hsü Shuang-pao 許雙保
Hsü Shun-lung 許順龍
Hsü Sung-ju 許松如
Hsü T'ien-fu 許天福
Hsü Yin-t'ang 許蔭棠
hsüan 軒
Hsüan-wu (gate) 宣武
hsün-ch'eng yü-shih 巡城御史
hu-ch'in 胡琴
Hu-chou 湖州
Hu-fang (bridge) 虎坊
Hu Hsiao-t'ien-hsi (*tzu* T'ing-hsiang) 扈小天喜 (聽香)

Hu-kuang 湖廣
Hu Lien-hsi 扈連喜
Hu Ta-ch'eng 胡大成
Hu-tan 胡妲
hua 花
Hua-chu ying-en 華祝迎恩
Hua-hsü ta-fu 華胥大夫
hua-ku hsi 花鼓戲
Hua-kuang 華光
Hua-lin (company) 華林
hua-pu 花部
Hua-shan 華山
Huang Chung 黃忠
Huang K'uei-kuan 黃葵官
Huang Sai-hua 黃賽花
Huang San 黃三
Huang San-hsiung 黃三熊
Huang-ts'un 黃村
Huang Yüan-te 黃元德
Hui (rebellion) 回
Hui-chou 徽州
hui-kuan 會館
Hui-lang 惠郎
Hui-p'ai 徽派
Hui-pan 徽班
hui-shou 會首
Hui-tiao 徽調
Hung Chen-yüan 洪箴遠
Hung-ch'iao (garden) 虹橋
Hung Ch'ung-shih 洪充實
Hung-fu (company) 鴻福
Hung Liang-chi 洪亮吉
Hung Sheng 洪昇
Huo Yü-te 霍玉德
i 役
I-cheng 儀徵
I-ch'iang 弋腔
I-ch'ing (company) 宜慶
I-ch'ing t'ang 宜慶堂
I-ho yüan 頤和園
I-hsiu 翼宿
'I-huai' 遺懷

I-huang 宜黃
I-lo tien 頤樂殿
I-yang 弋陽
I-yang ch'iang 弋陽腔
Jang Ch'eng-tu 讓成都
Jehol 熱河
jen-ch'en 壬辰
Jen-ho 仁和
Jen San-tzu 任三子
Jou-shih 肉市
Ju-fu 入府
juan 阮
Juan Ta-ch'eng 阮大鋮
Juan Yüan 阮元
Jui-chu chiu-shih 蘂珠舊史
K'ai-feng 開封
Kan-chü 贛劇
'Kan-hsing' 感興
Kan-su ch'iang 甘肅腔
Kan-tzu 趕子
K'ang-shan (garden) 康山
Kao-ch'iang 高腔
Kao-ch'iao 高橋
Kao Ch'ing-lin (or Shuang-lin) 高慶林 (雙林)
Kao-liang (bridge) 高梁
Kao Lung 高龍
Kao-min (temple, *ssu*) 高旻
Kao Ming 高明
Kao Ming-kuan 高明官
Kao Yüeh-kuan (*tzu* Lang-t'ing) 高月官 (朗亭)
K'ao-huo 烤火
k'o-pan 科班
kou-ch'iang 勾腔
kou-lan 勾欄
Ku A-i 顧阿夷
Ku-ch'eng chi 古城記
ku-ch'ü 鼓曲
Ku Hsi-yü 顧西漁
Ku Mei (Nanking) 顧眉
Ku Mei (Yang-chou) 顧美

Ku Sheng 顧升
Ku T'ien-i 顧天一
Ku Ts'ai 顧彩
kuan (pipe) 管
kuan (temple) 觀
kuan-ch'a 觀察
Kuan Han-ch'ing 關漢卿
Kuan I-tsung 貫義宗
Kuan Ta-wang chan-tao hui 關大王
戰刀會
Kuan-ti (temple, *miao*) 關帝
kuan-tso 官座
Kuan-yin 觀音
Kuan Yü (Kuan-ti or Kuan-kung)
關羽 (關帝, 關公)
Kuang-ch'u (gate) 廣儲
Kuang-ch'ü (gate) 廣渠
Kuang-ho lou 廣和樓
Kuang-hsing yüan 廣興園
Kuang-ning (gate) 廣寧
Kuang-te lou 廣德樓
kuei-ssu 癸巳
K'uei-p'ai 奎派
Kun-lou 滾樓
kun-tiao 滾調
K'un-ch'ü 崑曲
K'un-ming (lake) 昆明
K'un-shan 崑山
K'un-shan ch'iang 崑山腔
Kung (Prince) 恭
Kung Ting-tzu 龔鼎孳
Kung Yün-fu 龔雲甫
K'ung Shang-jen 孔尚任
K'ung T'ien-hsi 孔天喜
Kuo Hua 郭華
Kuo Nai-hsüan 郭耐軒
Kuo-tzu (alley) 果子
Kuo-tzu chien 國子監
lan 蘭
Lan-chia chuang 藍家莊
Lan-chou 蘭州
Lan-feng 蘭風

Lang Pao-ch'en (*hao* Su-men,
P'ang-hsieh) 郎葆辰 (蘇門 螃蟹)
Lao-lang (shrine, *t'ang*) 老郎
Lao-lang (temple, *miao*) 老郎
Lao-lang shen 老郎神
lao-sheng 老生
Li Chieh 李節
Li-ch'üan 醴泉
Li Hsiao-hsi 李小喜
Li Hsiu-kuan 李秀官
Li Kuei-kuan (*tzu* Hsiu-chang)
李桂官 (秀章)
Li Ling 李陵
Li Ling pei 李陵碑
Li Liu 李六
Li Lu-hsi 李祿喜
Li Lü-lin 李綠林
Li Pai 李白
Li P'ing-erh 李瓶兒
Li San-yüan 李三元
Li Shan 李善
Li Shang-yin 李商隱
Li Shih 李十
Li T'iao-yüan 李調元
Li Tsai-yüan 李載園
Li Tzu-ch'eng 李自成
Li Wen-i 李文益
li-yen 例言
Li Yü-shou 李玉壽
li-yüan 梨園
Li-yüan hui-kuan 梨園會館
Liang Ch'en-yü 梁辰魚
Liang-huai 兩淮
Liang Kuei-lin 梁桂林
Liang-lang shan 兩狼山
Liang-shih tien 糧食店
Liang Yu-lan 梁幼蘭
Lin-fen 臨汾
Lin Yün-hsiang 林韻香
ling 令
Liu Chang 劉璋
Liu Cheng-hsiang 劉正祥

Liu Chi 劉基
Liu Ching-jan 劉景然
Liu Ch'ing-jui (*tzu* Lang-yü) 劉慶瑞 (朗玉)
Liu Ch'ing-t'i 劉淸提
Liu Erh 劉二
Liu Erh-kuan (*tzu* Yün-ko) 劉二官 (芸閣)
Liu Feng-kuan (*tzu* T'ung-hua) 劉鳳官 (桐花)
Liu Feng-lin 劉鳳林
Liu-hsieh chi 留鞋記
Liu Kan-san 劉趕三
Liu Kuei-lin-kuan 劉桂林官
Liu-li ch'ang 琉璃廠
Liu Lu-ching 劉祿景
Liu Meng-mei 柳夢梅
Liu Pei 劉備
Liu T'ien-kuei 劉天桂
Liu Tzu-yün 劉子雲
Liu Wen-lung ling-hua ching 劉文龍菱花鏡
Lo (river) 洛
Lo Jung-kuan 羅榮官
Lo Jung-t'ai 羅榮泰
lo-lo ch'iang 羅羅腔
Lo Mou-teng 羅懋登
Lo P'in 羅聘
Lo-t'ien 羅田
lou 樓
Lu Chen-fu 陸眞馥
Lu-ch'eng 鹿城
Lu Tsan-yüan 魯贊元
Lu Tz'u-yün 陸次云
luan-t'an 亂彈
Lung-ho yüan 隆和園
Lung-t'ou 龍頭
Lü Po-she 呂伯奢
Ma Ch'ao 馬超
Ma-chi 罵雞
Ma Chi-mei 馬繼美
Ma Chin (*hao* Hui-hui) 馬錦 (囘囘)

Ma Feng 馬鳳
Ma Wen-kuan 馬文觀
Mai po-po 賣餑餑
Mai yen-chih 賣胭脂
Man-t'un-erh 滿囤兒
Mang-shen 芒神
Mei Ch'iao-ling 梅巧玲
Mei-ho t'ang 梅鶴堂
Mei-hsien 梅縣
Mei Lan-fang 梅蘭芳
Mei-lou 眉樓
Mei-shih (street) 煤市
Mei Tung 梅東
Mei Wen-ting 梅文鼎
Mei Yü-t'ien 梅雨田
Meng Ch'ang-hsi 孟長喜
Mi-fei 宓妃
Mi Hsi (-tzu) 米喜 (子)
miao 廟
Miao (rebellion) 苗
Miao Chuang 妙莊
Miao Shan 妙善
Mien-chou 緜州
Mien-k'ai 綿愷
Ming-chu 明珠
Ming-huang 明皇
mo 末
Mou Ch'i 牟乜
Mu Ch'en-kung 穆辰公
Mu Kuei-ying 穆桂英
Mu-lan 木蘭
Mu-lien 目蓮 (or 連)
Mu-lien chiu-mu 目連救母
Mu-lien chiu-mu ch'üan-shan chi 目蓮救母勸善記
Mu-tan t'ing 牡丹亭
Nan-fu 南府
Nan-ho hsia (street) 南河下
nan-hsi 南戲
Nan-men 南門
Nan-yu chi 南遊記
Nei-ch'eng 內城

nei-hsüeh 內學
Nei-ko 內閣
nei-shen 內神
Ni Chün 倪俊
Ni Hung 倪鴻
Ni-ts'ui (company) 霓翠
Nieh-hai chi 孽海記
Nien (rebellion) 捻
Ning-po 寧波
Ning-shou kung 寧壽宮
Niu (street) 牛
O (surname) 娥
Ou-hsiang t'ang 藕香堂
Pa-ch'i 八旗
pa-chiao-ku 八角鼓
pa-fen 八分
Pa-ta-tzu 八達子
pai 白
Pai-ch'üeh (temple, ssu) 白雀
Pai Erh 白二
Pai Hsiu-ying 白秀英
Pai-lien chiao 白蓮教
pai-mien 白面
P'an Jen-mei (or Hung) 潘仁美 (or 洪)
P'an Lan-t'ing 潘蘭亭
P'an Mei 潘美
pang-ch'iang 幫腔
pang-tzu (ch'iang) 梆子 (腔)
Pao Cheng 包拯
Pao Chih-tao 鮑志道
Pao-feng (temple, tz'u) 報豐
Pao-fu (company) 保符
Pao-ho (company) 保和
Pao-hua (company) 寶華
Pao lien-teng 寶蓮燈
Pao-shan t'ang 寶善堂
pao-t'iao 報條
Pao-ting 保定
pao-t'ou 包頭
Pao Wen-ch'ing 鮑文卿
Pao-ying 寶應

Pei-ching t'u-shu kuan 北京圖書館
Pei Hsiao-shun hu-t'ung 北孝順胡同
Pei-men 北門
Pei-wa 北瓦
Pei-wa (chin-fu) 背娃 (進府)
p'eng 棚
P'eng-pei 碰碑
P'eng Wan-kuan 彭萬官
Pi Yüan 畢沅
p'i 皮
p'i-huang 皮黃
p'i-p'a 琵琶
P'i-p'a chi 琵琶記
Piao ta-sao pei wa-tzu 表大嫂背娃子
p'iao (-yu) 票 (友)
p'iao-fang 票房
p'iao-hao 票號
Pieh-ch'i 別妻
pien-hsiu 編修
Pien-i (gate) 便益
Pien Sai 卞賽
Pien Te-k'uei 邊德奎
pien-wen 變文
pien-yen 弁言
P'ing-lo kuan 平樂館 (or 觀)
P'ing-tse (gate) 平則
P'ing-yao 平遙
'P'o Ch'in-huai' 泊秦淮
pu-chün t'ung-ling 步軍統領
P'u-chou 蒲州
P'u-t'ung 浦侗
San-ch'ing (company) 三慶
San-ch'ing yüan 三慶園
San-ho (company) 三和
san-hsien 三絃
san-shang 散商
San-shou (-kuan) 三壽 (官)
San-to (company) 三多
san-tso 散座
San-yüan (company) 三元
Sha-tzu ch'eng-ch'in 儍子成親

shang-ch'ang men 上場門
Shang Ho-yü 尙和玉
Shao-hsing 紹興
Shao-hua shan 少華山
Shao-yao (alley) 芍藥
She-hsien 歙縣
Shen Chu-p'ing 沈竹坪
Shen Hsiang-lin (hsiao-tzu Kou-erh) 申祥麟 (狗兒)
Shen Ts'ui-hsiang 沈翠香
Shen Wen-cheng 沈文正
sheng (musical instrument) 笙
sheng (type of actor) 生
Sheng Ch'ing-yü 勝慶玉
Sheng-p'ing shu 昇平署
Shih Pao-chu 石寶珠
shih-pu-hsien 十不閒
shou-ling 首領
Shuang-ch'ing (company, Peking) 雙慶
Shuang-ch'ing (company, Yang-chou) 雙淸
Shuang-ho (company) 雙和
Shuang-k'uei (company) 雙奎
Shuang-sai (company) 雙賽
Shuang-ts'ai (company) 雙才
Shun-li (company) 順立
So-erh 瑣兒
ssu 寺
Ssu-fan 思凡
Ssu-hsi (company) 四喜
Ssu-hsien ch'iu 四絃秋
Ssu-k'u ch'üan-shu 四庫全書
Ssu-kuan 四官
ssu-mei 四美
ssu ta Hui-pan 四大徽班
ssu ta ming-pan 四大名班
Ssu-t'u (temple, miao) 司徒
Ssu-yen ching 四眼井
Su-ch'ang (street) 蘇唱
Su-hsiang 素香
Su Hsiao-san 蘇小三

Su Hsien-chih 蘇顯之
Sun Ch'un-shan 孫春山
Sun Chü-hsien 孫菊仙
Sun-kung yüan 孫公園
Sung-chiang 松江
Sung-chu (company) 嵩祝
Sung-shou (company) 松壽
Sung-teng 送燈
Sung Tzu-wen 宋子文
ta-ch'a-wei 打茶圍
Ta-ch'eng (company) 大成
Ta Ching-ho (company) 大景和
ta chou-tzu 大軸子
Ta-ch'un (company) 大春
Ta-hsing 大興
Ta-li 大荔
Ta Mu-ch'ien-lien ming-chien chiu-mu pien-wen 大目乾連冥間救母變文
Ta Sha-lan 大柵欄
Ta Shun-ning (company) 大順寧
Ta-tung (gate) 大東
Ta-t'ung 大同
Tai Fei-lai-feng 戴飛來鳳
T'ai-ho (company) 太和
T'ai-hu 太湖
T'ai-hua yüan (or hsüan) 泰華園 (or 軒)
T'ai-p'ing 太平
T'ai-p'ing-erh 太平兒
t'ai-shih 太史
t'ai-shou 太守
T'ai-yüan 太原
tan 旦
t'an-ch'iang 彈腔
T'an Hsin-p'ei 譚鑫培
T'an-mu 探母
T'an T'ien-lin 譚添淋
T'an T'ien-lu 檀天祿
tang-tzu pan 檔子班
t'ang 堂
T'ang Hsien-tsu 湯顯祖

t'ang-hui 堂會
t'ang-ming 堂名
T'ang Ying 唐英
T'ao-jan t'ing 陶然亭
T'ao Shuang-ch'üan 陶雙全
T'ao Yüeh-hsien 陶月仙
Te-sheng (gate) 德勝
Te-sheng yüan 德勝園
Te-yin (company) 德音
Teng Shih-ju 鄧石如
ti-fang hsi 地方戲
ti-tzu 笛子
tiao-yü t'ai 釣魚臺
t'ieh 貼
T'ieh-kung yüan 鐵弓緣
T'ien-an (gate) 天安
T'ien-ch'iao 天橋
T'ien Hsiang-ling 田祥齡
T'ien Hsüeh-hsin 田學信
T'ien-li chiao 天理教
T'ien-lo yüan 天樂園
T'ien-ning (gate) 天寧
T'ien-ning (temple, *ssu*) 天寧
T'ien-pao-erh 天保兒
T'ien-sheng-hsiu 天生秀
T'ien-t'an 天壇
Ting-chih ch'un-ch'iu 鼎峙春秋
Ting-chün shan 定軍山
Ting Hsiu-jung 丁秀容
Ting Ssu 丁四
T'ing-li kuan 聽鸝館
tou-fu 豆腐
tsa-chü 雜劇
tsa-shua kuan 雜耍館
tsai-hsiang 宰相
ts'ai-ch'iao 踩蹻
Ts'ai San-pao 蔡三寶
Ts'ai-shen (hui-kuan) 財神 (會館)
Ts'ai-shih 菜市
Ts'ang Jun-ho 臧潤和
tsao chou-tzu 早軸子

Ts'ao (river) 草
Ts'ao-ch'ang 草廠
Ts'ao Fu-lin 曹福林
Ts'ao Ts'ao 曹操
Tseng Kuo-fan 曾國藩
Tseng Pin-ku 曾賓谷
Tsinghua (university) 清華
Tso-an (gate) 左安
ts'o-shih 醝使
Tsou Chih-shan 鄒致善
Tsu-shih (temple, *miao*) 祖師
Tsu-shih yeh 祖師爺
Ts'ui-ch'ing (company) 萃慶
Tsung Ch'üan-hsi 宗全喜
Tsung-jen fu 宗人府
tsung-kuan 總管
tsung-shang 總商
ts'ung-shu 叢書
Tu Fu 杜甫
Tu Li-niang 杜麗娘
Tu Mu 杜牧
Tu Tieh-yün 杜蝶雲
tuan-hsiu 斷袖
Tuan-jui (company) 端瑞
Tun-huang 敦煌
Tun Jen 頓仁
Tung-chih (gate) 東直
Tung Cho 董卓
Tung Chu-shih k'ou 東珠市口
tung-hsiao 洞簫
Tung Hsien 董賢
Tung Hsiu-jung 董秀蓉
Tung-hua (gate) 東華
Tung-kuan (gate) 東關
Tung-lin 東林
Tung Pai 董白
Tung-pien (gate) 東便
Tung-ssu p'ai-lou 東四牌樓
Tung-t'ing (lake) 洞庭
Tung Ts'ao-ch'ang 東草廠
T'ung-ch'ing yüan 同慶園
T'ung-chou (near Peking) 通州

T'ung-chou (Shensi) 同州
T'ung-chou ch'iang 同州腔
T'ung-lo yüan (or hsüan) 同樂園 (or 軒)
T'ung-lo yüan (in Yüan-ming yüan) 同樂園
T'ung-tzu-hung 童子紅
T'ung-wen shu-chü 同文書局
tzu 字
tz'u (temple) 祠
Tz'u-an 慈安
Tz'u-hsi 慈禧
wa (-tzu) 瓦 (子)
wa-she 瓦舍
wai 外
Wai-ch'eng 外城
wai-ch'uan 外串
wai-hsüeh 外學
wai-shen 外神
Wan-chia lou 萬家樓
Wan-hsing yüan 萬興園
Wan-p'ing 宛平
Wang Ch'i-yüan 汪啓源
Wang-fu (company) 王府
Wang Hsiao-t'ien-hsi 王小天喜
Wang Hung-kuei 王洪貴
Wang I-hsiang (*ming* Ch'üan-lin) 汪一香 (全林)
Wang Kuei-kuan (*tzu* Hsiang-yün) 王桂官 (湘雲)
Wang Kuei-lin 王桂林
Wang Pao-erh 王寶兒
Wang San-chieh 王三姐
Wang Shen 王俆
Wang Shih-chen (1527–90) 王世貞
Wang Shih-chen (1634–1711) (*hao* Juan-t'ing) 王士禎 (阮亭)
Wang Te-erh 王得兒
Wang Yüeh-ying 王月英
Wang Yüeh-ying yüeh-hsia liu-hsieh 王月英月下留鞋

Wang Yün-hsiang 汪韻香
Wei Ch'ang-sheng (*tzu* Wan-ch'ing, stage-name San or San-erh) 魏長生 (婉卿, 三 or 三兒)
Wei Chung-hsien 魏忠賢
Wei-hsien chü-shih 味閑居士
Wei Hu 魏虎
Wei Liang-fu 魏良輔
Wei-nan 渭南
wen 文
Wen-ch'ang (hui-kuan) 文昌 (會館)
Wen-chou 溫州
Wen-hsi 聞喜
Wen-su ko 文溯閣
wu 武
Wu Ch'ang-yüan (*tzu* T'ai-ch'u) 吳長元 (太初)
Wu Chen-t'ien 吳振田
Wu Ch'eng-en 吳承恩
wu-chi 武技
wu-ching 武淨
wu-ch'ou 武丑
Wu Fu-t'ien (*tzu* Ta-yu) 吳福田 (大有)
wu-hang 武行
Wu-hsi 無錫
Wu Hsiang-hsiang 吳相湘
Wu Hsin 伍辛
Wu-hu 蕪湖
Wu-kung 武功
Wu-la-na 伍拉納
Wu Lien-kuan 吳蓮官
Wu-men 午門
Wu-ming 悟明
Wu Pien-lin 吳采林
Wu San-kuei 吳三桂
wu-sheng 武生
Wu Ta-pao 吳大保
wu-tan 武旦
Wu Tzu-hsü (or Yün) 伍子胥 (or 員)
ya chou-tzu 壓軸子

ya-men 衙門

ya-pu 雅部

Yang Chi-yeh 楊繼業

Yang-chou 揚州

Yang-chou ch'ing-ch'ü 揚州清曲

Yang-chou pa-kuai 揚州八怪

Yang-chü 揚劇

Yang Fa-ling (or Fa-lin) (*tzu* or *hao* Hui-ch'ing, Hsün-ch'ing or Yün-hsiang) 楊法齡 (or 發林) (蕙卿, 薰卿 or 韻香)

Yang Hsiao-lou 楊小樓

Yang Mou-chien (*tzu* Chang-sheng) 楊懋建 (掌生)

Yang Pa-kuan 楊八官

Yang Pao-erh 楊寶兒

Yang Ssu-lang 楊四郎

Yang T'ien-fu 楊天福

Yang Tzu 楊梓

Yang Wu-erh 楊五兒

Yang Yeh 楊業

Yang Yen-chao 楊延昭

Yang Yen-ssu 楊延嗣

Yang Yen-yü 楊延玉

Yang Yüan 楊元

Yang Yüeh-lou 楊月樓

Yao Lan-kuan 姚蘭官

Yao Shih-fu 姚石甫

Yao-wang 藥王

Yen Ch'ang-ming 嚴長明

Yen-chih (chi) 胭脂 (記)

Yen-ch'ing t'ang 衍慶堂

Yen-hsi t'ang 燕喜堂

Yen-liao hui-kuan 顏料會館

Yen Shih-fan (*hao* Tung-lou) 嚴世蕃 (東樓)

Yen Sung 嚴嵩

Yen Yen 嚴顏

Yin-hua 銀花

Yin-lu 胤祿

Yin Pi-lien 殷碧蓮

Yin Pien-chih 殷采芝

Ying-en (brige) 迎恩

Yu-an (gate) 右安

Yung-ch'ing (company) 永慶

Yung-hsing 永瑆

Yung-hsüan 永璇

Yung-ting (gate) 永定

Yü Chi 余集

Yü-ch'ing (Anhwei company) 玉慶

Yü-ch'ing (*Ch'in-ch'iang* company) 餘慶

Yü-hsing yüan 裕興園

Yü-huang (temple, *miao*) 玉皇

Yü Hung-ts'ui 俞鴻翠

Yü-kuan 玉官

Yü-lan-p'en ching 盂蘭盆經

Yü Lao-ssu 余老四

Yü Mei-kuan 余美觀

Yü-ming t'ang 玉茗堂

Yü-p'ai 余派

Yü San-sheng 余三勝 (or 盛)

Yü San-yüan 于三元

Yü Shu-yen 余叔岩

Yü Ssu-sheng 余四勝

Yü-tzu 魚子

Yü Tzu-yün 余紫雲

Yü Wei-ch'en 余維琛

Yü-yao 餘姚

yüan 園

Yüan Mei 袁枚

Yüan-ming yüan 圓明園

yüan-tan 元旦

Yüan Tsu-chih 袁祖志

Yüan Tzu-ming 袁子明

yüeh-ch'in 月琴

Yüeh-chü 粵劇

Yüeh Fei 岳飛

yüeh-hu 樂戶

Yün-ho 運河

yün-shang 運商

INDEX*

* The explanations in parentheses are of three kinds; (i) classifications of the headings, (ii) statements of the place of the drama company, temple, etc., and (iii) a direct translation into English of a Chinese term. Those of the third kind are placed in inverted commas as well as parentheses. The classifications are intended as a guide only and do not give an exhaustive explanation of the headings.